John Henry Overton

Life in the English Church (1660-1714)

John Henry Overton

Life in the English Church (1660-1714)

ISBN/EAN: 9783743336179

Manufactured in Europe, USA, Canada, Australia, Japa

Cover: Foto ©Lupo / pixelio.de

Manufactured and distributed by brebook publishing software (www.brebook.com)

John Henry Overton

Life in the English Church (1660-1714)

CONTENTS.

CHAPTER I.
GENERAL SKETCH.

			PAGES
Introduction			1–2
State of Church during the Rebellion			3–6
,,	,,	Reign of Charles II. . . .	6–10
,,	,,	,, James II. . . .	10–11
,,	,,	,, William and Mary .	11–14
,,	,,	,, Queen Anne . . .	14–15

CHAPTER II.
CLERGY OF THE PERIOD.

THE RESTORATION PERIOD.

Clergy who died just after the Restoration	17
,, a little before the Restoration . .	18–19
Gilbert Sheldon	19–20
Matthew Wren	20
John Pearson	21
John Cosin	21–23
Peter Gunning	23–25
George Morley	25–26
John Earle	26–27
John Hacket	27–29
Seth Ward	29–30
John Fell	30–32

CONTENTS.

	PAGES
John Dolben	33–34
Jeremy Taylor	34–35
Other Prelates of the Caroline Age	35–36
Herbert Thorndike	36–37
Barnabas Oley	37–38
Isaac Barrow	38–39
Robert South	40–41
Richard Busby	41–43
Isaac Basire	43–44
Richard Allestree	44–45
Edmund Pocock	45–46
Thomas Marshall	46–47
Parish Priests of the Period	47–49
The Cambridge Platonists	49–53

REVOLUTION AND QUEEN ANNE PERIODS.

William Sancroft	53–57
John Tillotson	57–60
Thomas Tenison	60–62
John Sharp	62–65
Henry Compton	65–67
Gilbert Burnet	67–70
Thomas Ken	70–74
Edward Stillingfleet	74–76
William Beveridge	76–77
Simon Patrick	77–79
Richard Kidder	79–80
George Hooper	80–81
John Lake	82
Other Prelates of the Period	83–87
Humphrey Prideaux	87–88
Dennis Granville	88–90
Thomas Comber	90
Lancelot Addison; Jonathan Swift	91
George Hickes	92
John Kettlewell	92–94
Samuel Wesley (the Elder)	94–96
Joseph Bingham	96–97
Anthony Horneck	97–99
Thomas Bray	99–100
Isaac Milles	100–101
Other Clergy of the Period	101–105

CHAPTER III.

FAITHFUL LAITY OF THE PERIOD.

(1) MEN.

	PAGES
Peter Barwick	107–108
Sir Richard Browne	108–109
John Evelyn	109–111
Thomas Willis	111–113
Izaak Walton	113
Robert Boyle	113–116
Sir Matthew Hale	116–117
Sir Thomas Brown	117
Sir Edmondsbury Godfrey	117–118
John Kyrle ('The Man of Ross')	118
Edward Hyde, Earl of Clarendon	118–119
Elias Ashmole	119–121
Sir Christopher Wren	121–122
Viscount Weymouth	122–123
Simon and William, Lords Digby	123–124
Heneage Finch, Earl of Nottingham	124–125
Daniel " "	125–126
Henry Hyde, Earl of Clarendon	126–127
Laurence Hyde, Earl of Rochester	127
Robert Nelson	128–129
Henry Dodwell	129–132
Francis Cherry	132–133
Samuel Pepys (as a Diarist)	133
Ralph Thoresby	133–135
James Bonnell	135–136
Other Laymen	136–138

(2) WOMEN.

Dorothy, Lady Pakington	139
Margaret Godolphin	140
Pious Ladies about the Court	140–141
Lady Ranelagh	141–142
Mary, Countess of Warwick	142–144
Lady Margaret Maynard; Lady Frances Digby	144
Lady Elizabeth Hastings	144–146
Rachel, Lady Russell	146–147
Countess of Derby; Lady Conway	147

CONTENTS

	PAGES
Mary Astell	148–149
Susanna Hopton	149–150
Damaris Cudworth	150
Misses Kemeyse—Katherine Philips ('The Matchless Orinda')	151
Mrs. Evelyn	152
Wives of Clergy	153–155
Elizabeth Burnet	155
Susanna Wesley	156–157

CHAPTER IV.

RESTORATION OF ORDER.

Difficulties in the Way	158–159
Fabrics.—Devastation of Cathedrals	159
,, Parish Churches	160
Reparation of Cathedrals	161–162
,, Parish Churches	162–163
Services.—Private Baptisms	163–165
Infrequent Communions	165–168
Paucity of Communicants	168–170
Concessions to Puritan Scruples	170–171
Daily Prayers	172–175
Catechising in Church	175–178
Pulpit Prayers	178–181
Disuse of Chancels	181–182
Irreverent Behaviour in Church	182–183
Instrumental Music in Church	184–185
New and Old Versions of Psalms	185–187
Irregularities in Church Psalmody	187–188
Use of the Surplice	188–189
Church Officers.—Lecturers	190–192
Readers	192–193
Parish Clerks	193–194
Finances.—Briefs	194–196
The Offertory	196
Ritual and Furniture.—Bowing to the East	197–198
Altar Lights	198
Altar Rails	199
Altar-pieces and Paintings	200–201
King's Arms in Churches	201
Pews	202–203
Notices in Church	203–204
Services of Nonjurors	204–206

CHAPTER V.

RELIGIOUS AND PHILANTHROPICAL SOCIETIES.

	PAGES
The Religious Societies	207-213
Societies for the Reformation of Manners	213-216
Society for Promoting Christian Knowledge	216-218
Society for the Propagation of the Gospel in Foreign Parts	218-222
Parochial Libraries	222-224
Charity Schools	224-228
Corporation of the Sons of the Clergy	228
Queen Anne's Bounty	228-230
Hospitals, &c.	230

CHAPTER VI.

PREACHING OF THE PERIOD.

Love of hearing Sermons	231-232
Complaints of the Lack of Sermons	232
Length and Abstruseness of Sermons	233
Quotations from the Learned Languages in Sermons	234
Preaching of Jeremy Taylor	235-237
„ Isaac Barrow	237-238
„ Robert South	238-240
„ Thomas Ken	240-241
„ Edward Stillingfleet	241-242
„ John Dolben	243-245
„ John Tillotson	245-248
„ John Sharp	248
„ Francis Atterbury	248-249
„ William Beveridge	249-250
„ Simon Patrick	250-251
„ Gilbert Burnet	251
„ Anthony Horneck	251-252
„ W. Smythies—S. Wesley	252
„ Richard Lucas	252-253
Other Preachers	253-255
High Standard of Preaching	255-257
Change in the Style and Language of Sermons	257-258
„ Length of Sermons	258-259
Written and Unwritten Sermons	259-260

CHAPTER VII.

DEVOTIONAL AND PRACTICAL WORKS.

	PAGES
'The Whole Duty of Man'	261–264
Other Works by the same (?) Author	264
Jeremy Taylor's Devotional Works	265
Hammond's 'Practical Catechism'	265–266
Ken's 'Practice of Divine Love' (Catechism)	266–267
Other Catechetical Works	267–268
Lake's 'Officium Eucharisticum'	268–269
Patrick's 'Book for Beginners, or Help to Young Communicants'	269
Other Eucharistic Works	270–271
Comber's 'Companion to the Temple'	271–272
Sherlock's 'Discourse of Religious Assemblies' and 'Of Death'	272
Scott's 'Christian Life'	272–273
Rawlet's 'Christian Monitor'	273–274
Beveridge's 'Private Thoughts'	274–275
Patrick's Practical Works	275–276
Reprints of Earlier Devotional and Practical Works	276–278
Lucas's 'Practical Christianity'	278–279
„ 'Enquiry after Happiness'	279–280
Scougal's 'Life of God in the Soul of Man'	280–281
Burnet's 'Address to Posterity,' &c.	281
Worthington's 'Great Duty of Self-Resignation to the Divine Will'	281–282
Devotional Works that were originally Sermons	282
Norris's Devotional Works	282–283
R. Boyle, W. Melmoth, Sir M. Hale	284–285
Steele and Addison as Practical Writers	285
R. Nelson's Practical and Devotional Works	285
Susanna Hopton's „ „	286
Mary Astell's „ „	286–287
Eliz. Burnet's 'Method of Devotion'	287
Lady Masham's 'Discourse concerning the Love of God'	287–288
Devotional Works specially intended for Clergymen	288
Other Devotional Works	288

SACRED POETRY.

Ken's 'Poems, Devotional and Didactic'	289
Norris's Poetry	290
Patrick's „	290

Addison's Poetry	291
S. Wesley's „	292
Comber's „	293
Susanna Hopton's Poetry	294
Other Sacred Poetry	294
Dearth of Sacred Poetry	295

CHAPTER VIII.

THE CHURCH AND SOCIAL LIFE.

Social Status of the Clergy	296
Great Inequalities among them	297
The Supply exceeded the Demand	297–298
Domestic Chaplains	298–300
Distinction of Ranks very Marked	300–301
Clergy travestied in Light Literature	301–302
'Contempt of the Clergy'	302
Poverty of the Clergy	303–305
Supposed Ignorance of the Country Clergy	305–306
Reasons for supposing they were not Ignorant	306–308
Prosperity of some of the Clergy	308–309
Clergy practised Medicine	309–310
Clergy who had seen Military Service	310
„ and the Legal Profession	310–311
Active Part taken by the Clergy in Politics	311
The Church and Amusements	311–312
Part which the Clergy took in Amusements	313
Stillingfleet on Clerical Amusements	313–316
Church Teaching on the Sunday Question	316–317
Recreation on the Lord's Day	317–319
Royal and Parliamentary Utterances about Sunday	320–321
The Church and the Royal Society	321–322
Extent to which the Clergy mixed in Social Life	322–323
The Dress of the Clergy	323–325
Church Discipline	325–330
Money Commutations for Penance	326
Effects of Church Censures	328–329
Casuistry and Casuists	330–334
Family Prayer	334–335
Boldness of the Clergy in rebuking Vice	335–338
Conduct of the Clergy during the Great Plague	339–341
Theology of the Caroline Age too Refined to be Popular	341

CHAPTER IX.

THE CHURCH AND OTHER RELIGIOUS BODIES.

	PAGES
The English Nonconformists	342–348
Reformed Churches abroad	348–351
Romanists	351–353
The Episcopal Church of Scotland	353–354
The Irish Church	354
LIST OF AUTHORITIES	358–368
INDEX	369–376

LIFE IN THE ENGLISH CHURCH.

1660-1714.

CHAPTER I.

GENERAL SKETCH.

INTRODUCTION.

It is a frequent complaint that Church History has been too much confined to a history of disputes between Christians. The complaint is not altogether just. For in any work which professes to be a complete history of the Church in any age, a narrative of controversies must necessarily occupy a very large space. It would, no doubt, be a blessed thing if the Church of Christ could be built, like Solomon's temple, without the noise of axes and hammers; but this is a beautiful dream which has never been realised —not even in the Apostolic age. There is, however, some danger lest the dust raised by the axes and hammers should hide the real progress made by the builders, and the fair proportions of the building. And, so far as the Church of England is concerned, there is no period in her history in which there is more danger of this than the stormy period with which these pages have to deal. In this volume it is proposed, as far as possible, to disentangle the life of the Church from her controversies; to show how her clergy lived and worked;[1] how her faithful laity, both men and

---
[1] Chap. II.

women, were affected by her influence;[1] how her services were conducted;[2] how kindred societies were organised to be her handmaids;[3] what was the special character of her preaching[4] and the books which fed her devotion;[5] what was her relation to the social life of the period,[6] and to other Christian communities, at home and abroad.[7] This, though apparently a less ambitious, is in reality a far more difficult task than to write a history of her controversies. For in the latter case, though it may be hard to give a right judgment on the points at issue, it is not hard to ascertain what those points were, and to narrate faithfully what was said about them. But it is hard to ascertain precisely what were the leading features in the Church life of any period; the inductive faculty must be most judiciously exercised, for there is the greatest danger of drawing general conclusions from insufficient data, of mistaking the exception for the rule. Again, the investigator is embarrassed by the very abundance of his materials; if his work is to be confined within at all reasonable limits, he must ask his reader to trust him to an extent which few other authors have to do. And once more, a writer who desires to present an attractive picture of Church life, is terribly tempted not to give a due prominence to blemishes; the present writer has not, knowingly at least, yielded to this temptation; he knows that 'the spouse of Christ on earth is not like His spouse in Heaven, without spot or wrinkle or any such thing,'[8] but he is strangely mistaken, if a picture of her life during this period drawn impartially will not be worth studying, and will not be found to contain many noble features.

Before entering into details, it is desirable to give a short general sketch of the Church life of the period, and its

[1] Chap. III. [2] Chap. IV. [3] Chap. V.
[4] Chap. VI. [5] Chap. VII. [6] Chap. VIII.
[7] Chap. IX. [8] Dr. Bray.

relation to the different reigning sovereigns. And it is really not going beyond the subject if we begin by casting at least a passing glance upon the position of the Church during the Rebellion; for her after-life was largely moulded, both for good and evil, by the circumstances through which she then passed. All that the State *could* do to crush the life out of her was done; but that all was really nothing at all. Never was her life more vigorous than when she was spoken and thought of as-dead and buried; never was her liturgy more venerated than when it was proscribed; never were her faithful ministers more firmly attached to her principles than when the profession of those principles entailed the ruin of every worldly prospect. The very defacement of her grand old edifices, grievous as the spectacle must have been to every faithful churchman, was in one way turned to her advantage; for it taught churchmen to realise that the Church was not dependent upon bricks and mortar, or any external support, animate or inanimate. The bitter antagonism she encountered was not without its advantages; it forced men to be decided in their principles; the question was not now, as it was a few years later, between 'conforming' and 'non-conforming.' A man who professed himself a churchman had drawn the sword and thrown away the scabbard. In short, the fire of persecution was, like all fire, a purifying as well as a destroying element. Let us see the sort of life churchmen led when their cause seemed for the time being hopelessly lost.

In point of fact, it never *was* lost, and no true churchman ever believed that it was; they all looked forward to better times;[1] and meanwhile no act of parliament, no

---

[1] 'The good doctor [Hacket] advised them better, that the Church of England was still in being and not destroyed, rather refin'd by her sufferings. . . . And in these lowest of times he was full of faith and courage, that he himself should still live to see a better world one day,' &c. (Plume's *Life of Hacket*.) Bishop Brownrigg collated Seth Ward to the Precentorship of Exeter Cathedral, 'in full confidence that the king would be restored and the professor confirmed in his office,' though he was laughed at for

exercise of military power, could prevent them from worshipping God in their own way. The well-known picture in the hall of Christ Church, Oxford, representing Fell, Dolben, and Allestree conducting the forbidden services, is a typical instance. Hacket's house was made a meeting-place of the clergy. Dr. Hewett performed the Church services in S. Gregory's church, near S. Paul's. Jeremy Taylor is found preaching as a churchman to churchmen in 1654, and, after his release from the Tower, ministering in a private house.[1] Peter Gunning ministered in the chapel of Exeter House, Strand, in spite of the Protector's protests. One of the weapons of the Puritans was, in a rather amusing way, turned against themselves. The law against ministrations in churches did not apply to the lecturers, who were originally a sort of free lances, independent of parochial organisation; and therefore Pearson and others were enabled to evade the law by acting as lecturers, 'the door being left so widely ajar that there was room for Rutulian as well as Trojan to enter in.'[2] Cromwell could not even keep his own family from the infection; his two daughters were staunch churchwomen, attending Dr. Hewett's ministry, and being married according to the rites of the Church of England.

doing so. (*Some Particulars of the Life &c. of Seth Ward, Bishop of Sarum.*) Jeremy Taylor looks forward to the time 'when it shall please God, who hath the hearts of princes in His hands, and turneth them as the rivers of waters, when men will consider the invaluable loss that is appendant to the destroying such forms of discipline and devotion in which God was purely worshipped, and the Church was edified, and the people instructed to great degrees of piety, knowledge, and devotion.' (*Apology for Set Forms of Devotion*, 1646.) Bishop Skinner, when he ordained Bull in 1655, would not give him letters of Orders, but 'withal assured him that when the ancient Apostolical government of the Church should be restored, which he did not question but a little time would bring about, they should be sent him,' &c. (Nelson's *Life of Bishop Bull*, p. 40.)

[1] *Life*, by Heber, p. xxxix (3rd ed., 1839).

[2] Bishop Pearson's *Minor Works, with Memoir of Author*, by E. Churton (1844), p. xxxi. Dr. Warmestry was lecturer at S. Margaret's, Westminster, Anthony Faringdon at S. Mary Magdalene, Milk Street.

When we turn from town to country, the undiminished vitality of the Church strikes us even more forcibly. Many of the country clergy still held their livings, though of course on a most precarious tenure. Lewis Atterbury (father of the bishop) remained incumbent of Milton,[1] Pocock, of Childrey,[2] Sanderson, of Boothby Pagnell, Stillingfleet, of Sutton, Bull, of Suddington.[3] Usher preached almost within a stone's throw of Whitehall.[4] Salisbury Cathedral was scrupulously kept in repair by a number of anonymous churchmen, who employed workmen evidently in sympathy with the spirit of the work.[5] Many of the clergy officiated in private houses—Morton, for instance, in the family of Sir C. Yelverton,[6] Juxon at Chastleton House,[7] Barnabas Oley at Exeter House,[8] Hammond at Westwood.[9] Many used the Church prayers without book, and thus seemed to conform to the Directory.[10] Many held firmly to their principles, but contented themselves with quietly pursuing employments not connected with the din of controversy. Such were many of those who formed the germs of the Royal Society, such were several of the Cambridge Platonists, such were Brian Walton and his learned colleagues, who utilised their enforced leisure in raising that great monument of their industry, the Polyglott Bible; such were Beveridge and Cave, who were quietly laying in those stores of knowledge which afterwards took shape in the 'Pandectæ Canonum SS. Apostolorum' and the 'Historia Literaria.' Many again went abroad, Morley to Antwerp, where he

---

[1] *Memoirs &c. of Bishop Atterbury*, by Folkestone Williams, i. 3.
[2] *Life of Edward Pocock* (Twells, 1816), p. 140.
[3] Nelson's *Life*, pp. 41, 76. Stillingfleet was actually appointed to Sutton in 1657, Bull to Suddington in 1658.
[4] Skeat's *History of the Free Churches of England*, p. 61.
[5] See Pope's *Life of Bishop Seth Ward*, pp. 62-3.
[6] Walker's *Sufferings of the Clergy*, p. 50.
[7] *Memoirs of Archbishop Juxon*, by W. H. Marah.
[8] Walker. [9] *Life*, by Bishop Fell.
[10] E.g. Bull and Sanderson. See Nelson's *Life of Bull*, and Walton's of Sanderson.

regularly performed all the services of the Church, Cosin to France, Basire to the furthest regions of the East. Some, like Matthew Wren and Jeremy Taylor, might have been found in prison, still firm to their principles. Many of those who became most famous in after times were ordained by bishops who were not afraid of performing their episcopal functions at the most imminent risk to themselves. Bishop Skinner, sometimes alone, sometimes attended by Dr. Bathurst, held frequent ordinations. Patrick was ordained by Hall, the ejected Bishop of Norwich, Tenison by Bishop Duppa, Stillingfleet by Bishop Brownrigg. In a word, it was found, to use the language of Sancroft, that 'there were caves and dens of the earth, and upper rooms and secret chambers for a church in persecution to flee unto, and there would be her refuge.'[1] Or, at the worst, they could echo the grand apostrophe of Jeremy Taylor—'I shall crave that I may remember Jerusalem, and call to mind the pleasures of the Temple, the order of her services, the beauty of her buildings, the sweetness of her songs, the decency of her ministrations, the assiduity and economy of her priests and Levites, the daily sacrifice, and that eternal fire of devotion that went not out by day nor by night; these were the pleasures of our peace, and there is a remanent felicity in the very memory of those spiritual delights which we then enjoyed, as the antepasts of Heaven, and consignation to an immortality of joys.'[2]

REIGN OF CHARLES II.

If the life of the Church was so vigorous at the time when every outward support was withdrawn, and every effort used to extinguish it, ought not its vigour to have been increased when the restoration of the monarchy gave her once more the upper hand? Ought she not to have

---

[1] D'Oyly's *Life of Sancroft*, i. 41.
[2] *Apology for Authorised and Set Forms of Devotion*.

substituted at once a sober, rational religion for the wild fanaticism and sour Puritanism which had of late prevailed? She *ought* to have done so, and she *would* have done so, if she had had a fair field and no favour; but, as a matter of fact she did not. And since the immorality of the Restoration period has frequently been adduced as a proof that our Church has not the power of leavening the nation for good, it is necessary to put the facts in a right light. It should be remembered, then, that she was embarrassed on all sides. Consider the colossal difficulty of the work to be done. It is putting the case far too mildly to say that the Church had to deal with the reaction against the overstrained severity of Puritanism. A comparison has sometimes been drawn between the license of the Regency period in France, when the death of Louis XIV. had set the Court free from the artificial piety which had marked the later years of the Grand Monarch's reign, and the license of the Restoration period in England. But the cases are not parallel; for in France the reign of strictness had not spread far beyond the pale of the Court; it had pervaded every corner of England. And the Church of England was in a far worse position for stemming the torrent of impiety than the Gallican Church was. For this reason. In France it was the Church itself which had been carried away by the wave of asceticism, and the Church itself which fell back with the ebb-tide. But in England the dissoluteness of the period was combined with a strong, and, in its way, sincere, but at the same time very embarrassing attachment to the Church.[1] Austerity on the part of the clergy seemed like siding with their enemies and against their friends. It is difficult to realise, much more to describe, the utter disgust which the great

[1] 'How is an old Cavalier like me to be known from those cuckoldy Roundheads that do nothing but fast and pray, if we are not to drink and swear according to our degree?' asks Whitaker, Lady Peveril's old steward, in Sir Walter Scott's novel. Sir Walter was always true to the spirit of the times, if not always accurate in details.

majority of the nation had conceived against Puritanism, and the immense sense of relief, when the burden, under which they had long been chafing, was removed. It was like Æolus removing the mountain which shut in the cavern of the winds, and it would hardly have been a more hopeful task to attempt to stay the course of the winds, than to check the torrent of unbridled license which was the inevitable result of the release of the long pent-up elements. And how was the Church prepared to grapple with the evil? Badly in every way. In the first place, her relation to her restored sovereign was most embarrassing. The fact that the fortunes of the Church and the Monarchy seemed to be inseparably bound together; the sad circumstances connected with the death of her last king, who, whatever his faults were, was at least faithful to his Church, and, in fact, died for her;[1] the contrast with the iron rule of military tyranny and the utter disorder into which the nation had fallen, ecclesiastically as well as civilly; all this naturally tended to throw a glamour over royalty and to increase the enthusiasm of churchmen in its behalf. Royalty in the abstract was, to pious churchmen, the very incarnation of a lofty purity of mind and morals, a dignity of character befitting the nursing father of the grandest and oldest of all English institutions; royalty in the concrete was—Charles II![2] It is with reluctance that I even hint at this source of the Church's weakness; for enough, and more than enough, has been written about the bad qualities of this king, while sufficient account has not been taken of the extraordinary temptations of his position, both in exile and on the throne, temptations which were strong enough to ruin a far firmer character than his.

[1] At least, he may be said so far to have died in her defence, inasmuch as if he had consented to give up the Church, his life would undoubtedly have been spared.

[2] 'Bishop Juxon, who had known the piety of Charles I., was so overwhelmed by an interview he had with his son that he is said never to have held up his head again.'—Perry's *History of the Church of England*, ii. 313.

Nor should it be forgotten that English churchmen have reason to regard his memory, at least on two accounts. His Church appointments were almost invariably good,[1] and he was a steady and intelligent patron of literature and the fine arts[2] which have ever been favourable to the prosperity of a Church which is the natural home of cultured men. At the same time it is but bare justice, in estimating the influence which the Church exercised, not to forget the fatal barrier to that influence raised by her connection with such a king. The Church and the Monarch, wrote Stillingfleet, 'like Hippocrates' twins, rise and fall together.' What a twin to be bound to! Besides the indirect injury he did by his libertinism both in deed and in opinion, he was directly her enemy; he notoriously disliked her clergy and set his courtiers against them.[3]

There was yet another obstacle to the Church's influence, which is not so obvious, but which, in point of fact, was perhaps the greatest of all. Much has been written against the severe laws which were passed to force men into conformity; their cruelty and injustice to the conscientious dissenter has been incessantly and very rightly pointed out; but has sufficient notice been taken of their cruelty and

---

[1] It will be remembered that Dr. Johnson called attention to this fact.

[2] Witness his kindness to the learned antiquary, Elias Ashmole (see Ashmole's *Diary* for 1660), his foundation of the Observatory at Greenwich, and his personal interest in scientific observations.

[3] See, *inter alia*, Sir John Reresby's diary:—'I was at the king's couchée. His Majesty was in very good humour and took up some time in displaying to us the fallacy and emptiness of those who pretend to a fuller measure of sanctity than their neighbours, and pronounced them to be, for the most part, abominable hypocrites and the most arrant knaves; as instances of which he mentioned several eminent men of our own times, nor spared to introduce some mitred heads among the rest, whom he pretended to be none of the best, though their devout exterior gave them the character of saints with the crowd.' (*Travels and Memoirs of Sir John Reresby*, p. 238.) Conceive the results of such edifying discourse coming from one who was gifted with extraordinary powers of fascination, who was far above the average in point of intelligence, and who was in the position of a king!

injustice to the Church itself? What policy could be more utterly fatal to the prosperity of any institution than one which was obviously adapted to drive the conscientious men out, and to keep men of easy conscience within its pale? But that was precisely what the penal laws had a direct tendency to do, and, as a matter of fact, did. A large number of the Church's officers were not churchmen at all, but merely 'conformists'[1]—a very different thing. With such a staff how could she do justice to her principles?[2] The marvel is, not that she did so little, but that she did so much for good, under these conditions.

REIGN OF JAMES II.

The influence of the Church had begun to tell largely upon the morals of the nation some years before the death of King Charles; one proof of which is seen in that remarkable outburst of religious fervour which gave rise to the 'Religious Societies' in 1678, of which more will be said presently; and this influence certainly did not decrease during the three years that James II. was upon the throne. Of the many infatuations of that infatuated prince, none was greater than his absurd hope that the Church of England was about to make way for that Church whose cause he espoused with all the fervour of a pervert. Unwittingly, he conferred a very great benefit upon the Church which he

---

[1] Not even 'conformists' in the sense of conforming loyally to the order and discipline of their Church. Archdeacon Basire declares that 'many churches are provided with such as are in effect noe ministers; and are soe far from conforming themselves that they preach against those that are conformed' &c. (Hunter's Collection of MSS., ii. 68.) Dean Granville complains of 'the non-conformity, or rather semi-conformity of the clergy (who did with zeale more than enough and sometimes too bitterly inveigh against non-conformists),' &c. (*Remains*, Surtees Miscellanea, Part I., p. 136). 'Of all nonconformists, I confesse I have most indignation against those that can accept of a fat benefice and preferment, and yet not conform' &c. (*Ib.* Part II. p. 41. Entry December 1697.)

[2] This point is well brought out in the *Church Quarterly Review*, July 1877.

had abandoned, by giving her the opportunity of proving beyond a doubt how utterly irreconcileable her principles were with those of Rome. The people at large were confirmed in the confidence which the well-informed had long held, when they saw her defending her position on true Catholic, as opposed to Roman Catholic, grounds; and the nonconformists themselves joined in her praises. Nineteen-twentieths of the nation were now, nominally at least, within her fold. Her services were more numerous, better attended, and more devoutly joined in than they had ever been since the Reformation. Her popularity was at its height; the memorable episode of the 'Seven Bishops' was not a mere fitful outburst of enthusiasm, but the expression of a feeling which had existed for some years, and which extraordinary circumstances now called forth. Her internal dissensions, which had never been great since the Restoration,[1] were now less marked than ever. And there is an apologetical tone about the writings of the comparatively few who dissented from her, which seems to indicate that, if matters had gone on as they had begun, most of them would have been won over, and we might have seen realised the grand idea of a Church truly coextensive with the nation, and adequately supplying all that nation's spiritual wants. She hardly realised her own strength; she could well have afforded to dispense with those artificial defences which a mistaken zeal had raised about her; in fact she would have been stronger without them. If one had to pick out a period when our Church was at its strongest and its best, it would be hard to select a better than when its temporal defender was one of the bitterest foes it ever had.

REIGN OF WILLIAM AND MARY.

If the progress of Church life was not so much impeded as one might have expected it to be by the stirring events of

---

[1] I am speaking of 'churchmen,' not 'conformists.'

the Revolution era, the reason is that, after all, political changes cannot affect much the work of truly pious men who are guided by definite principles. Otherwise, the violent party-spirit which arose must have been simply ruinous to Church work. The internal dissensions of the Church were immensely aggravated. The deliberate and undisguised endeavours of King James to Romanise the nation had bound together by a sense of one common danger all churchmen. Minor differences were forgotten, and they worked together, shoulder to shoulder, in defence of the institution they all loved. But when the danger was past, and when they had to answer another question, 'Under which king, Bezonian, speak or die!' the spirit of union was at once changed for a spirit of discord. Churchmen were placed in a dilemma. If they threw their vast influence into the scale of the exiled James, they ran the risk of being unfaithful to their country as citizens, if into that of William and Mary, of being unfaithful to their Church, at least as her doctrines had been all but universally understood and explained for the last thirty years. Some shrank from one, some from the other horn of the dilemma, and each tried to impale the other on the horn which he had himself avoided. Some tried to run with the hare and hunt with the hounds; not intentionally perhaps, but, as a matter of fact, their attitude can be only so described; and when compromise once takes the place of principle, the moral effect on the character is inevitably damaging. In estimating the loss which the Established Church sustained from the secession of the nonjurors, numbers are a very imperfect guide. Say that they were but a handful in comparison with the vast majority who took the oaths, yet the loss of a handful of the best and most conscientious men is no slight loss. The most healthy organisation can ill afford to be deprived of some of its best blood. But it was far more than this. Many of those who nominally acquiesced in the new settlement sympathised in their hearts with the nonjurors;[1] or at any rate were far more in sympathy with them than with those whom the king delighted to honour. In fact, there were two hostile camps in the Church, roughly represented by the two Houses of Convocation. On the one side were all, or nearly all, the newly appointed bishops, a small sprinkling of the clergy, and the majority of the middle class among the laity; on the other side, the majority of the clergy, many of the nobility and higher gentry, and the majority among the lower classes.[2] Such a division was obviously most injurious to the growth of Church life. In almost every parish there were High Churchmen and Low Churchmen (it was now that these detestable names first became general) thwarting one another.[3]

It did not mend the matter that the 'Defender of the Faith' was a Dutch Presbyterian who had no sympathy whatever with any of the Church's distinctive principles and practices. The queen, indeed, had been brought up a strict churchwoman,[4] and if left to herself would doubtless have been a true nursing mother; she did what she could during her short life, and a marked alteration for the worse in the relation of royalty to the Church is perceptible after her death; but, at best, she was quite a secondary personage; and her painful position as the supplanter of her own father

[1] Birch says (*Life of Tillotson*, p. 191), 'The majority of the Lower House (of Convocation, 1689) had a reserved kindness for the non-juring bishops and clergy,' and these undoubtedly represented the feelings of their constituents. The same feeling is shown in the petition presented to King William, in which they 'passionately entreated that the Church might not suffer so great a loss as to be deprived of them.'

[2] See Rapin, vol. xii. p. 236. See also Walter Bagehot's interesting essay on 'Bolingbroke as a Statesman.' (*Biographical Studies*, p. 165.)

[3] There is a most interesting letter (not published) in the British Museum, among the MSS. of White Kennet, in which the writer describes the confusion thus introduced into the parish of Shottesbrook. See also a letter from Ken to the Dean of Worcester (Hickes), on the same subject. (Letter X. in Bishop Ken's *Prose Works*, Round's edition.)

[4] At least, so far as the influence of Dr. Ed. Lake, one of her spiritual directors, went; the churchmanship of Dr. Compton, her other director, was of a different type.

did not add to her power. The happiest event for the Church during this reign was the passing of the Toleration Act; for the enforced conformity of unwilling minds, and the odium which attached to those in whose favour persecuting laws were, by a most mistaken policy, enacted, were real drawbacks to her spiritual influence. But on the whole the Church suffered a severe check to the flourishing progress she was making during this crisis.

REIGN OF QUEEN ANNE.

In each of the preceding periods it has been found necessary to notice the difficulties set in the way of Church life by the hostility or indifference of the reigning sovereigns. These difficulties were now removed, for Queen Anne was a thorough churchwoman, according to her lights. But though the Church was now free from one of the embarrassments from which she had suffered ever since the Restoration, there were still great impediments to her spiritual progress. Chief among them was the inextricable confusion which now existed between civil and ecclesiastical affairs. Politics have constantly been the bane of Church life, but never more so than in the reign of Queen Anne. Many of the so-called Church questions which violently agitated men's minds were really far more of a political than of an ecclesiastical character. The fact is, that though it is exceedingly doubtful whether the State was of much use to the Church, there is no doubt that the Church was of very great use to the State; it was a name to conjure with, and it was used accordingly.[1] Nothing marks more strongly the popularity of the Church at this period than the evident fact that no one had the least chance of a hearing unless he professed a friendship for, or at least no

---

[1] Archbishop Sharp, with his wonted plain common sense, pointed this out. See his *Life*, by his son (ed. by Newcome), pp. 256-7.

hostility to her. Those who were her bitterest enemies assumed an apologetical tone.[1] If the Church did not take as much advantage as might have been expected of the splendid opportunity which now seemed to be offered to her, the reason was that she was too much absorbed in the vortex of politics. But this and other points will be brought out more clearly when we pass from a general view to specific details.

[1] See, *inter alia*, Viscount Bolingbroke's *Works*, passim, and all the Deistical literature. Perhaps it is hardly fair to rank Defoe as a bitter enemy, but he was avowedly a dissenter, and his tone is the same.

CHAPTER II.

CLERGY OF THE PERIOD.

The hagiology of the Church of England has yet to be written. Romanists and all classes of dissenters have celebrated their worthies far more fully than we have done; but our silence has not been for lack of material— rather from a superabundance of it.[1] Even in dealing with less than a twentieth part of the period over which the Church of England extends, the difficulty is enormous. And so there is need to apologise both for the length, and also for the brevity, of this chapter and the next. The number of lives sketched is so great that there is a fear of confusing the reader and wearying his patience; and yet the omissions are so many that he may also have reason to complain that some favourite is neglected or too curtly treated. It will add to the clearness of the chapter to subdivide it and treat, first, of the clergy of what may be roughly called the Restoration period, and then, of those of the Revolution period.

[1] Even two hundred years ago, a divine wrote: 'The members of the Church of England have been reputed, of all others, the slackest to celebrate their own worthies, partly, I conceive, from the humility and modesty of their principles and education, partly from the great multitude of incomparable scholars therein to be commemorated, that such labours would be almost infinite.' (Plume's Preface to the *Life of Hacket*.) The labours naturally increase with increasing years. 'A true and wholesome hagiology,' remarks Mr. Mozley very truly (*Reminiscences*, ii. 372), 'may be now impossible; yet may not that be lamented, and may we not dwell on that which might have been?' See also some good remarks on the very period with which we have to do, in *Remains of A. W. Haddan*, 'Review of Debary's History,' &c.

THE RESTORATION PERIOD.

At the Restoration, there was obviously but one man to whom the Primacy, vacant since the execution of Laud sixteen years before, could be offered. If he had any regard for his father's memory, Charles II. could hardly have passed over **William Juxon** (1582-1663). That old and trusted friend, that most faithful and honest adviser, who had been with Charles I. to the very end and received his last commission on the fatal January 30, passed, almost as a matter of course, from Fulham to Lambeth, to the universal satisfaction of the nation.[1] But with the weight of seventy-eight years upon him—and the last twenty of them such years!—the good old man could hardly be expected to take a very prominent part in Church life. He lent to the revived Church the halo of a great name round which clustered many sad and solemn associations, but he had hardly time to do more than sing his 'Nunc dimittis,' and then rejoin his lost master. In 1663 he quietly passed away, beloved and regretted by all.[2]

Many other great men only just lived to see the mighty change they had so long yearned for, and must be regarded rather as survivals of the past, than as actually belonging to the period with which we are concerned. Such were **Accepted Frewen**, who, having been deprived both of his ecclesiastical and his private fortune, died

---

[1] 'This day (September 20, 1660) was a day of rejoicing to all that love order in the Church. For this morning, that Most Reverend Father William (Juxon) was translated from London to Canterbury.' [Then follows much praise]. (*Public Intelligencer*, No. 39).

[2] 'June 4, 1663.—Heard this day the Archbishop of Canterbury, Juxon, a man well-spoken of by all for a good man, is dead' (*Pepys' Diary*). Lord Campbell calls him 'a most kind-hearted, pious man, and so inoffensive that even faction could not find fault with him' (*Lives of Chancellors*, vol. iv. p. 7, n.) Lloyd, 'the delight of the English nation, whose reverence was the only thing that all parties agreed on' (*Memoirs of those that Suffered*). See also Wilson's *Merchant Taylors*, p. 670. Burnet in his *Own Times* depreciates Juxon, for which he is taken to task by Nathaniel Salmon. (*Lives of English Bishops &c.* p. 7.)

Archbishop of York in 1664; and **Brian Walton**, the promoter and sole editor of the Polyglott Bible, who, having been deservedly promoted to the see of Chester, died in 1661;[1] and **Robert Sanderson**, who survived to be placed at the head of that diocese in which he had been suffered to live in a humble cure all through the troubles, and died in 1663; and Archbishop **Bramhall**, the 'Athanasius Hibernicus,' who died in the same year; and **Thomas Fuller**, the quaint chronicler of England's Worthies, and a worthy himself, who died when honours were just beginning to be showered upon him, in 1661; and **Brian Duppa**, who had been the constant attendant upon Charles I. and tutor of Charles II., and who, if he could not influence the conduct of his reckless pupil, at least secured his respect, for Charles kneeled to receive his blessing just before the good Bishop of Winchester's death in 1662; and **John Barwick**, faithfullest of faithful churchmen through the Rebellion, who died Dean of S. Paul's in 1664.

Many great churchmen died, Moses like, while the Church was still in the wilderness, some having received, and some not quite, a Pisgah view of the promised land. Such were **Joseph Hall** (1574–1656), whose beautiful 'Contemplations' are still read and admired, and whose 'Hard Measure,' giving a sufferer's account of his sufferings, is particularly valuable, the ejected clergy not being given to parade their hardships; and **Henry Hammond** (1605–1660), a model parish priest before the troubles began, and during the troubles one of the mainstays of the royalists; and **Archbishop Usher** (1580–1656), most learned and conciliatory of divines, who, though inclined to Puritanism on some points, suffered severely during the Puritan ascendency; and **Thomas Morton** (1563–1659), the venerable Bishop of Durham, whose patriarchal age seemed to be prolonged that he might just see the dawn of better days

---

[1] See Todd's *Memoirs of Walton*. The 'Polyglott' was completed in 1657.

for the Church he had served so long and faithfully; and **Ralph Brownrigg** (1593-1659), the brave bishop who dared to exercise his episcopal functions under interdict. These and many other famous men, if they did not live long enough to see the Church restored, contributed greatly to her reputation. The memory they left behind them, and the immortal works some of them bequeathed to posterity, gave a tone to the Restoration period, and contributed in no slight degree to make the Caroline age what, in one sense it certainly was, the golden age of English theology.

But it is time to pass on to those who took an active part in the Church life of the period; and among them the most influential was beyond all question **Gilbert Sheldon** (1598-1677). He was made Bishop of London; but, owing to the age and infirmities of Juxon, he was virtually primate from the moment of the king's return, and became actually so on that good old man's death. Taking the prominent part he did in politico-ecclesiastical matters, there is no wonder that his character should have been differently described, according to the different views of the describers. The discrepancies between the various estimates of him are almost ludicrous.[1] But, after all, it is not very difficult to reconcile them. On certain points all are agreed. His munificence was unbounded. He gave away, or spent upon public works, from the time when he became Bishop of London, a sum which, according to the lowest estimate, amounted to 62,000*l.*, according to the highest 73,000*l.*, either of them an enormous sum, considering the value of money in those days. He was a man of undaunted

[1] Mr. Bevill Higgon says, Burnet ought not to have 'dared to mention Archbishop Tenison in the same day with so great a man as Sheldon.' (*Remarks on Burnet's Own Times*, 1736, ii. 128.) 'This Sheldon, the most virulent enemy and poisoner of the English Church.' (S. T. Coleridge, *Notes on English Divines*, ii. 22.) Burnet (*Own Times*) says 'he seemed not to have a deep sense of religion, if any at all.' N. Salmon (*Lives of English Bishops*, 1733) calls this statement 'unwarrantable.' 'His piety was undoubted.' (*Carwithen*, iii. 172.)

courage; he stayed manfully at his post at Lambeth all through the Plague; he did not shrink from rebuking his royal master, thereby forfeiting the king's favour, which he never regained. He was a most generous patron of learning; if the prelates of the Restoration period shed a lustre on the Church, as they surely did, Sheldon must be credited with much the largest share in their appointment.[1] He had obviously the gift of attaching his friends most devotedly to him. He was emphatically a strong man, with a firm will of his own, perfectly straightforward and candid, without a particle of cant. A man of whom all this can be said has strong claims upon our regard. But on the other hand we can gather, even from his panegyrists' accounts and from his own recorded acts and words, that he was more of a statesman than a divine, that spiritual mindedness was, to say the least, not a conspicuous trait in his character, that he took a leading part in the persecution of nonconformists, and that his disgust at hypocrisy led him, like many others in the anti-puritanical reaction of the time, far too much in the opposite direction.

There was one other prelate who seemed at the Restoration likely to rival, and more than rival, the influence of Sheldon. That one was the venerable Bishop of Ely, **Matthew Wren** (1585–1667), who was liberated from his eighteen years' captivity in the Tower a little before the king's return. Clarendon, who was of course the most influential of laymen, seems to have regarded him as *the* man to whom the Church had to look for her resettlement.[2] But it was hardly likely that a man in his seventy-fifth

---

[1] 'Archbishop Sheldon had the keys of the Church for a great time in his power, and could admit into it and keep out of it whom he pleased,—I mean disposed of all ecclesiastical preferments.' (Dr. Pope's *Life of Bishop Seth Ward*, 1697, p. 53.) So Pepys, *Diary*, September 3, 1662, 'The Bishop of London (Sheldon) is now one of the most powerful men in England with the king.'

[2] See Clarendon's 'Letter to Dr. Barwick' in Kennet's *Register*. Also Bishop Pearson's *Minor Works*, ed. Churton, ii. 81.

year, and broken by captivity, would be vigorous enough to *begin* to take the helm and steer the ark through such stormy waters. He seems quietly to have subsided into his old position, and is known in his later life chiefly for having brought into notice his nephew, the most original of English architects.

Very much the same may be said of the eminent prelate who preached Wren's funeral sermon, **John Pearson** (1613–1686). The author of the 'Exposition of the Creed' added one more great name to the distinguished roll of Caroline prelates, but that is all. He may have been 'a much better divine than bishop,'[1] or he may have 'filled the bishopric of Chester with great honour and reputation;'[2] but from the general course of Church life he certainly stood apart.

Far different was it with **John Cosin** (1595–1671), Bishop of Durham, of whom his biographer says truly 'that he will be ever remembered among the most eminent prelates of the English Church.'[3] At any rate, he stands among the very first of the clergy of the Restoration period. Others may have had a wider influence; for from his remote northern diocese he could hardly extend his influence to the centre and south of the land. Others may have been more learned, or rather, have given more tangible proofs of their learning; for Cosin was an eminently learned man; but no one left deeper traces of his influence so far as its sphere extended. The diocese of Durham was remarkable for its strong churchmanship, in the spiritual sense of the term, during the whole of our period; and we may very clearly trace, directly or indirectly, the marks of Bishop Cosin's influence. In his own writings, and in the notices that are left to us, the portrait of the man is brought

---

[1] Burnet's *Own Times*.
[2] Laurence Echard. See *Pearson's Minor Works*, ed. Churton, with Memoir of Author, p. xcvii, and *Diary of Dr. Worthington*, ed. J. Cropley, p. 232, *n*. Both editors condemn Burnet and agree with Echard.
[3] *Vita Joannis Cosini*, by Rev. T. Smith.

very vividly before us:—a plain blunt man with a definite end in view, and making straight for that end without turning to the right hand or to the left; firm as a rock in his convictions, but by no means cramped or narrow; though a well-read divine, a man of practice rather than theory; utterly unselfish, and of undaunted courage, he was just the sort of man to play the part he *did* play both in adversity and prosperity. No thought ever entered *his* head of disguising in the very least his principles; and so he was the very first to suffer for them.[1] Driven abroad, he was 'the Atlas of the Protestant religion at one of the chief seats of Romanism.'[2] After the Restoration, while others, as Pepys says, were 'nibbling at the Common Prayer,'[3] he was the very first to use it openly in its entirety. Removed from the deanery of Peterborough to the bishopric of Durham, he at once set about the task of restoring Church order; and during the ten years of his episcopate succeeded in doing so,—at least to a greater extent than any other bishop did. There was no diocese where conformity was so general, and where the plain rules of the Church were more rigorously carried out.[4] Such a man could of course brook no obstacles in his way, and as nonconformity was a very great obstacle, he dealt with

---

[1] See Carwithen's *History of the Church of England*, vol. iii. p. 21, and Perry, ii. 375, and Collier, viii. 360.

[2] See Fuller's *Worthies*.

[3] Diary for November 4, 1660.

[4] See, *inter alia*, *Remains of Denis Granville*, Part II., p. 23. Also *Correspondence of Bishop Cosin*, Part II. *passim*, both published by the Surtees Society, and Basire's Funeral Sermon on Cosin, entitled, *The Dead Man's Speech*. A remarkable instance is given in Mr. Low's *History of the Diocese of Durham* (S.P.C.K.), p. 285, *note* H, quoted from Archdeacon Spark, who wrote in 1746, 'When, everywhere else, the surplice in the pulpit was regarded as a badge of party, here, on the contrary, it was the gown. It is only within the last few years that some zealous clergymen have introduced the gown in churches where it was never seen or heard of before;' and the Archdeacon traces the custom back to Bishop Cosin. The famous Durham cope and other vestments with which the name of Cosin is associated are another case in point.

nonconformists in far too rough a fashion; but at the same time he was a strong advocate of intercommunion with the Reformed Churches abroad. His position at Durham was that of a prince as well as a bishop; and his munificence was princely; the account of what he spent on religious and charitable works almost takes one's breath away.[1] He was a man of some asperity of temper, heightened no doubt by a painful disease from which he long suffered; and he was somewhat of a martinet, though evidently able to secure the respect as well as fear of his fellow-workers. Such was Bishop Cosin, a great prelate, if ever there was one in the English Church.

Peter Gunning (1613–1684) had been as conspicuous as Cosin for his undisguised attachment to the Church during the troubles, and after the Restoration he was deservedly promoted, first to the see of Chichester, then to that of Ely. If not so strong, he was a more loveable man than Cosin. Language hardly seems strong enough to express the admiration his friends felt for him. He is 'that learned and pious man, Dr. Gunning;' 'Dr. Gunning, who can do nothing but what is well;'[2] 'that excellent man, Dr. Gunning;'[3] 'the incomparable Peter Gunning;'[4] 'this apostolical man, Dr. Gunning;'[5] even Pepys, who does not often praise clergymen, was favourably impressed by him.[6]

It was not so much by his preaching or his writings,

---

[1] Basire says, 'he spent above 2,000l. a year in pious uses' (*Dead Man's Speech*; Zouch, that 'it is scarcely possible to enumerate the many acts of public beneficence by which Dr. Cosin distinguished himself during the eleven years he held the see of Durham' (*Life of Sudbury*, p. 84). He was styled 'the benevolent Bishop of Durham.' For a detailed account of some of his princely gifts, see his *Correspondence*, Part II. *passim*, especially pp. 169–171.

[2] Evelyn, *Diary*, March 29, $167\frac{2}{3}$, and February 23, $167\frac{3}{4}$.

[3] Sir John Reresby, *Travels &c.*, p. 239.

[4] Peter Barwick, *Vita Joannis Barwick*, p. 22.

[5] Salmon, *Lives of Bishops*, p. 253. Salmon, of course, belonged to the next, but only the next, generation. His *Lives* were published in 1733.

[6] Diary for January 1, $16\frac{59}{60}$.

(though he was eminent for both) as by his dealing with individual souls that Gunning made the deepest impression. Thus John Barwick sent for him to be with him during the last three days of his life, 'which he gave up entirely to God and the study of private piety,' and received from his hands the last viaticum.¹ Evelyn 'carried his son to be instructed of him before he received the Holy Sacrament, when he gave him most excellent advice.' 'And oh,' he adds, 'that I had been so blessed when first I was admitted to that sacred ordinance!'² That admirable lady, Mrs. Godolphin, received some of her early instruction from Dr. Gunning, 'who thought fit that she should be admitted to the Holy Sacrament when hardly eleven.'³ And there is something really touching in the way in which Denis Granville, when he was quite a middle-aged man and a dignitary of the Church to boot, records, 'I did this evening unburthen my conscience to this good bishop (Gunning), my spiritual guide, and submitted my soul to his test and examination,' &c. Gunning took an active part against the Presbyterians at the Savoy Conference, but his life was so unblamable that they could find no reproach against him.⁴ And his strong churchmanship did not interfere with his Christian charity in his private capacity, as his kindness to his distinguished predecessor at Cambridge, Tuckney, proves.⁵ Like Sheldon and Cosin he was extraordinarily liberal. 'Let the scholars he has supported in the University of Cambridge, his several large endowments and benefactions in that place; let the crowds of poor fed daily at his door, and from his table, the widow, fatherless and stranger, indigent foreigners, distressed travellers, publicly fed, clothed

---

¹ *Vita Joannis Barwick*, p. 237.   ² Diary for March 29, 167$\frac{2}{3}$.
³ Evelyn's *Life of Mrs. Godolphin*.
⁴ See *Athenæ Oxonienses*, iv. 140. Barwick calls him 'Malleus schismaticorum' (*Vita Joannis Barwick*). Neale (*History of the Puritans*, ii. 168-9) and Baxter of course do not speak so well of him in consequence.
⁵ *Athenæ Oxonienses*, *ub. supra*, and Granger's *Biographical History*, iii. 249.

and relieved, or privately supplied by him with a plentiful hand,'[1] bear witness.

Another prelate who took a conspicuous part at the Savoy Conference was **George Morley** (1597–1684), successively Bishop of Worcester and Winchester. The active portion of Morley's life belongs to an earlier period, although he survived the Restoration nearly a quarter of a century. In his later life he is chiefly known as the central figure of an interesting group at Winchester, consisting of the children and grandchildren of Izaak Walton (Morley's benefactor during the Rebellion) and the saintly Ken.[2] His ready wit is still remembered through more than one bon-mot, and his discretion was highly valued by Clarendon. In spite of an idle piece of gossip reported by Pepys,[3] it is clear that Morley was a man of great liberality. When he was translated to the wealthy see of Winchester, it is said that King Charles foretold that he would be none the richer for it.[4] And judging from the long list of his benefactions he could not have been.[5] Morley in theology occupied the odd position of a High Church Calvinist, but he was always a very moderate Calvinist, and rendered still more so by the arguments of his friend Sanderson, and his Calvinism did not prevent him from taking as active a part against the Presbyterians at the Savoy Conference as Sheldon, Cosin, and Gunning did; but his antagonism did not interfere with his showing kindness to some of his antagonists.[6] He was once drawn from the privacy into which he retired, in his extreme old age, by Sancroft, who persuaded him to join in the delicate task of attempting to bring back the Duke of York to the Church of his baptism. Possibly the fact of

[1] Sermon at Ely by Dr. Gower, Master of S. John's, on Gunning, soon after his death.
[2] See Bowles' *Life of Ken*, p. 141.
[3] See Diary for Christmas Day, 1662.
[4] Salmon, *Lives of Bishops*, &c.
[5] For an account of these (which are too numerous to be inserted in the text), see Elwes' *Sir C. Wren and his Times*, p. 300.
[6] See Stoughton's *Church and State Two Hundred Years Ago*, p. 361.

Morley having been spiritual guide to the late Duchess of York may have had something to do with the archbishop's request, but the terms of Sancroft's letter show that Morley's high character was the chief reason.[1]

It is but fair to say that of all the five prelates hitherto noticed the reader would not derive so favourable impression from the accounts of nonconformists[2] as he probably will have done from these pages. Not so of **John Earle** (1601-1665), Bishop of Salisbury, of whom all men spoke well, nonconformists as well as churchmen. Not that Earle was lax in his churchmanship; for the sake of it he had suffered the loss both of his preferments and his private property in the civil wars. He had closely identified himself with the royal cause, having been tutor to Prince Charles, and having attended him abroad as his chaplain. But he had learnt, what it is hoped most men have learnt now, that it is impossible to force a religion upon a man by Act of Parliament; and so he opposed with all his might the Five-mile Act, and treated the nonconformists in his diocese with the utmost courtesy. There is a ring about the chorus of praise which was lavished upon him which proves that it was not conventional, and the tenor of it gives us the secret of his almost universal popularity. 'He had,' writes one, 'this high and rare felicity, by his excellent and spotless conversation, to have lived so many years in the Court of England, so near his Majesty, and yet not given the least offence to any man alive, being honoured and admired by all who have either known, heard or read of him.'[3] 'Of Dr. Earle,' writes a contemporary, 'I may justly say (and let it not offend him, because it is a truth

---

[1] See *Correspondence of Henry Hyde, Earl of Clarendon, and of his Brother*, &c., pp. 465-7.

[2] Such as Baxter, e.g.—It is most unfortunate that the only full contemporary account we have of the Savoy Conference is from the pen of one who would naturally take as unfavourable a view as possible of the Church party, of which the five prelates noticed above were the most distinguished representatives.

[3] White Kennet, *Register*.

which ought not to be concealed from posterity, or those that now live and yet know him not), that, since Mr. Hooker died, none have lived whom God hath blessed with more innocent wisdom, more sanctified learning, or a more pious, peaceable, primitive temper, so that this excellent person seems to be only like himself, or our venerable Richard Hooker'[1] 'This Dr. Earle,' writes another, a few years after Earle's death, 'was a person certainly of the sweetest, most obliging nature that lived in our age.'[2] And to turn to a different class of testimony, Pierce, the friend of nonconformists, declares that 'Dr. Earle was a person who could do good against evil, forgive much, and of a charitable heart.'[3] And Baxter writes to him that 'he had frequently heard that in charity and gentleness and peaceableness of mind, he was very eminent,'[4] and notes on Earle's reply, 'Oh that they were all such!' What makes this praise the more striking is that it was written to and of a man who had the knack of writing in a satirical vein, than which nothing is more apt to make enemies.[5] In reading it all we can hardly help thinking of the warning to those of whom all men speak well, and so it is almost with a sense of relief that we read that he died 'to the no great sorrow of those who reckoned his death was just for labouring against the Five-mile Act.'[6] He was a most intimate friend of Bishop Morley.

Another prelate who was universally esteemed was John **Hacket** (1592–1670), Bishop of Lichfield and Coventry, who is justly described by the latest editor of his life, as 'one of the most illustrious prelates of the great Caroline age.'[7] His energy, consistency, and courage during the

[1] Walton, *Life of Hooker.*
[2] H. Cressy to a 'Person of Quality' (Lord Clarendon), written in 1674.
[3] *Conformists' Plea for Nonconformity* (1681).
[4] Letter to Earle, 1662.   [5] See his *Microcosmography,* passim.
[6] *Conformists' Plea,* p. 35.
[7] The Rev. Mackenzie E. Walcott, who, among the many services he has rendered to the historian of the Church of England, has republished in our

Rebellion have been referred to. After the Restoration he refused the bishopric of Gloucester,[1] but subsequently accepted that of Lichfield and Coventry, chiefly, it would seem, because there was an inordinate amount of work to be done there. No prelate in his prime could have worked harder than this grand old man. How he restored his ruined cathedral by 'barefaced begging,'[2] setting a noble example of liberality himself, how he stirred up his clergy to work by going incessantly among them, and preaching in every part of his diocese, how loyally he defended them in the ecclesiastical courts, how lavishly he gave of his substance, being 'resolved to dispense his own in his lifetime and not be like the whale that affords no oil till she die and must disgorge it,' how, in spite of his strong aversion to nonconformity, he would help nonconformists and 'persons with whom he had no Christian communion but in this one thing of giving,' how he died in harness, his last work being the hanging of a great bell in his cathedral, which, as he himself predicted, first tolled for his own death, all this will be found recorded in the lively pages of Dr. Plume, his friend and biographer.[3] But, lest the testimony of an admiring biographer should be suspected of partiality, it may be added that the energy and high reputation of the good bishop are equally admitted by less suspicious witnesses. In 1666 the Corporation of Lichfield, in a letter to Elias Ashmole, speak of 'our ruined cathedral, which by the unwearied labour, prudence, and piety of our good bishop, a second Cedda, and the charity of yourself and others happily deposited in his hands, is (almost to a miracle) so well and so soon

---

day (1865), Dr. T. Plume's *Life and Death of John Hacket*, &c., prefixed to his *Century of Sermons*.

[1] His answer to the King and the Chancellor (Hyde) was epigrammatic; 'he had rather,' he said, 'future times should ask why Dr. Hacket had not a bishopric, than why he had one.'

[2] Roger North, *Lives of the Norths*.

[3] See also Browne Willis' *Cathedrals*, p. 378.

restored again.'[1] Roger North bears an amusing testimony to the importunity of the bishop in behalf of his cathedral, and the admirable order of the services in it, when it was restored.[2] Perhaps the secret of Hacket's wonderful energy to the very last may be found in his favourite motto, 'Serve God and be cheerful;'[3] the same motto was a favourite with Sheldon; no doubt it found special favour in days when the reaction against Puritanism was so strong. It certainly might have been adopted by the next eminent prelate who comes before us.

Seth Ward (1618-1689), successively Bishop of Exeter and Salisbury, was more fortunate than most of his brethren during the troubles; for, though ejected from Cambridge for refusing to take the Covenant, he found a home at Oxford as Savilian Professor of Astronomy, not, however, without taking the oath of allegiance to the existing Government. In some respects he resembled Sheldon; both owed their advancement not altogether to their theological attainments; both were eminent for their social qualities; both are reported to have been very harsh in their treatment of nonconformists, Ward to the extent of injuring the trade of Salisbury by driving people away to Holland,[4] though it is only fair to add that there is said to be no evidence of this, either in the episcopal documents or those of the city of Salisbury, and that the report rests simply on the authority of some anonymous chroniclers.[5] The extraordinary story of his promotion to the see of Exeter through the influence of his lay friends,[6] his hospitable entertainment of all the hunting field when the hunt was

---

[1] See *Memoirs of the Life of that Learned Antiquary, Elias Ashmole, drawn up by himself by way of Diary* (1717).
[2] *Lives of the Norths*, i. 144.
[3] This maxim was appropriately engraven on his tomb.
[4] *Diocesan History of Salisbury*, by Rev. W. H. Jones (S.P.C.K.)
[5] Hatcher's *History of Salisbury*, quoted in *Some Particulars of the Life, Habits and Pursuits of Seth Ward*, 1879.
[6] The story is too long to be inserted, but it will be found in Aubrey's

in his neighbourhood, his own fondness for this and other athletic sports, his freedom and affability 'to his meanest curates,'[1] the evidently jovial character of his admirer, biographer, and avowed imitator, Dr. Pope,[2] all tell the same tale, the tale of a manly, free-handed, light-hearted prelate, rather too much of the secular type, but most acceptable, if for no other reason, as affording an agreeable relief to the reign of saints. But there *were* other reasons. His munificence was splendid; he was largely instrumental in restoring the cathedral at Exeter, and (so far as it was required) at Salisbury, where he also founded a 'College of Matrons' for the widows of clergymen; he had a high reputation as a preacher; his scientific attainments were undeniable, and in a famous lament over the great dead, which is attributed to Ken, his name is coupled with the honoured names of Hall, Usher, Hammond, and Sanderson, and he is thus apostrophised, 'Where is thy unaffected modesty, fixed integrity, immoveable fidelity, unerring capacity, and extensive charity, O bounteous Ward!'[3]

The last three prelates were all remarkably popular. Let us turn, by way of contrast, to one who is now chiefly known as a proverbial instance of unaccountable unpopularity.

'I do not like thee, Doctor Fell,
The reason why I cannot tell,
But this I know full well,
I do not like thee, Doctor Fell.'

Everybody knows these lines, but everybody may not know that the person here gibbeted was Dean of Christ Church,

Letters, iii. 574-5, and quoted in Worthington's *Diary*, vol. xiii. of Chetham Society, p. 302 note.

[1] 'The meanest curates were welcome to his table, and he never failed to drink to them, and treat them with all affability and kindness imaginable.' (*Life of Seth Ward*, &c., by Dr. Walter Pope, 1697.)

[2] Dr. Pope's *Life*, though most graphic and amusing, is by no means trustworthy in all points,—notably in all that concerns Isaac Barrow.

[3] *Expostulatoria, or Complaint of the Church of England*, printed 1711. The evidence of its being Ken's is not conclusive.

distinguished even among the distinguished roll of men who have filled that great post, and Bishop of Oxford. **John Fell** (1625-1686) was son of that Samuel Fell, also Dean of Christ Church, who together with his wife stood out so boldly and suffered so much during the civil wars.[1] He had therefore an hereditary right on both sides to be a staunch churchman, and so he was. Next to Dr. Busby, he had perhaps more to do with the training of rising churchmen than any man living. Christ Church, in his time, rose to the zenith of its fame and prosperity, and the Dean was the heart and soul of Christ Church. It is unfortunate for the reputation of Dr. Fell that his name is inseparably connected with the expulsion of the greatest man that even Christ Church could boast, John Locke. But are he and the canons quite justly blamed for this sad fiasco? They were but carrying out the king's mandate, which if they had not carried out, they would assuredly have been expelled themselves. At any rate Fell was a most successful ruler of the 'House.' A successful, but not a popular one. 'The cause of Fell's well-known unpopularity,' it has been said, 'remains a mystery to the present time.'[2] But surely the cause is not far to seek. The Dean set himself resolutely to curb within due bounds the wild license of the young 'bloods' of the Restoration. It would have been more of a 'mystery' if he had won popularity in the execution of such a task. And the explanation is not a mere conjecture. It is implied by a contemporary. 'He had much zeal,' writes Burnet, 'for reforming abuses; and managed it perhaps with too much heat, and in too peremptory a way. But we have so little of that among us, that no wonder if such men are censured by those who love not such patterns nor such severe taskmasters.'[3] A member of Christ Church to whom

[1] See Walker's *Sufferings of the Clergy*, and Neal's *History of the Puritans*.
[2] *Diocesan History of Oxford*, E. Marshall (S.P.C.K.), p. 150.
[3] *Own Times*, book iv., under 1686.

the Dean was most kind, intimates that he did not brook opposition.[1] The well-known story of his summoning the undergraduates to take up arms for the Crown in the Monmouth rebellion, when Christ Church alone furnished near a hundred pikemen and musketeers,[2] is another instance of his promptitude and resoluteness. But perhaps it would have been a still more pleasing sight to see him kneeling by the bedside of that poor penitent libertine, the Earl of Rochester, whom he helped to snatch as a brand from the burning.[3] When he was made Bishop of Oxford in 1675, 'he had liberty to hold the Deanery *in commendam*, that so excellent a governor should not be lost to the college;' and as he appears to have performed his duty energetically in both offices, we are not surprised to learn that he was said to have been 'worn out with pains and care employed for the public.'[4] Like so many other prelates we have noticed, he was most liberal, almost lavish, in his benefactions,[5] and the terms of enthusiastic regard in which he is spoken of by contemporary, and almost contemporary writers, prove that there were many whose good opinion was worth having, who *did* like thee, Dr. Fell.[6]

---

[1] See the most interesting *Autobiography &c. of William Taswell*, edited by G. P. Elliott. 'The Dean, hearing of my father's ill-treatment of me, frequently made me a present of 2*l*., telling me it was designed as a reward of merit, but I afterwards offended him by voting against his candidate for Public Orator.'

[2] See Macaulay's *History of England*, chap. v., p. 290.

[3] See *Life of John (Wilmot), Earl of Rochester*, by Bishop Burnet, p. 315.

[4] Nathaniel Salmon's *Lives of the English Bishops from the Restauration to the Revolution* (published 1733), p. 316.

[5] The biographer of Prideaux says that 'for his buildings and other benefactions he might be esteemed a second founder of Christ Church.' He 'took upon him the whole charge of the impression of Bull's *Defensio Fidei Nicanæ* (Nelson), p. 164, and helped Anthony Wood to bring out his *Historia et Antiquitates Universitatis Oxoniensis*. (*Life of Prideaux*, p. 95. He rebuilt the Palace at Cuddesdon (Salmon).

[6] 'That great promoter of learning and piety, Bishop Fell.' (R. Nelson, *Life of Bishop Bull*, p. 164.) 'In all respects a most exemplary man.' (Burnet, *Own Times*, book iv. of 1686.) 'Deserving a character too great to be attempted here.' (Salmon, *Lives of Bishops* &c., 316.) 'An eminent

John Dolben (1624–1686), is a name inseparably associated with that of John Fell, his fellow-helper in the Church services at Oxford during the Rebellion. Dolben had a wide and varied experience of life. He had fought with distinction in the royal army, had been an ensign at Marston Moor, was grievously wounded in the siege of York, and was advanced to the rank of major;[1] after the surrender of Oxford he returned to Christ Church and received Holy Orders. After the Restoration his advance was rapid. He was made successively Canon of Christ Church, Archdeacon of London, Dean of Westminster, and Bishop of Rochester, and finally Archbishop of York. Perhaps the fact of his having married Sheldon's niece was no hindrance to his promotion, but he deserved it by his merits. He was a man of great benevolence, generosity, and candour,[2] noted both at Westminster and York as an excellent preacher, ' very conversible and popular, and such every way as gave him a mighty advantage of doing much good.'[3] When Laurence Hyde, Earl of Rochester, was advanced to the post of High Treasurer, Dolben wrote to him, ' I can say no fine things, and I will say no false ones;'[4] and this exactly represented the character of the frank soldier prelate. Taswell gives a curious proof of the retention of his military instincts, telling us how as Dean of Westminster he marched out the Westminster scholars (Taswell himself being one)

---

encourager of learning, excellent governor of his college, and of exemplary conduct in his episcopal character.' (Birch, *Life of Tillotson*, p. 95.) ' Good Bishop Fell was for his piety, learning and wisdom esteemed one of the most eminent prelates of his time.' (*Life of Dean Humphrey Prideaux*, published 1748, p. 19.)

[1] J. Le Neve's *Lives &c. of Bishops*, &c.; see also *Life of Barwick*, with notes, by Hilkiah Bedford.

[2] See *Athenæ Oxonienses*, iv. 188.

[3] Hickes to Comber, on Dolben's appointment to the archbishopric. (*Memoirs of Comber*, p. 189.) Comber himself speaks most highly of him as a ' prelate of great presence, ready parts, grateful conversation, and wondrous generosity.' (*Ibid.* p. 212.)

[4] *Correspondence of Laurence Hyde*, i. 124.

during 'the Great Fire,' and did yeoman's service in stifling the conflagration.[1] He died of smallpox, after having held the archbishopric only three years, but Comber thinks his death was hastened by his grief at the sad prospect for the Church under the Romanising efforts of James II.[2]

There yet remains to be noticed one, who was in many respects the greatest of all the prelates of the Restoration period, **Jeremy Taylor** (1613–1667), Bishop of Down and Connor, and afterwards of Dromore. Strictly speaking, he scarcely comes within our range, for at the Restoration he was at once removed to the sister Church of Ireland. Why the Church of England did not keep one of the greatest of her sons at home is not clear. The fact that he married Joanna Bridges, who was possibly, but by no means certainly, the natural sister of Charles II.,[3] seems a very inadequate reason for his banishment; if the report be true that Sheldon was not his friend, that would be a far more likely cause; but wherever the fault lay, it was surely a grievous mistake to send beyond the sea one who is truly said to have had 'devotion enough for a cloister, learning enough for an university, and wit enough for a college of virtuosi.'[4] What makes it all the more provoking is that the people in his remote Irish diocese do not seem to have appreciated as they ought to have done the treasure that was thrown away among them, and one can quite understand how his sensitive and refined spirit would recoil from the coarseness of the Cameronian Presbyterians by whom he was surrounded. Of course one with whom 'duty was a delight and piety a passion,'[5] would find work to do for God

---

[1] *Autobiography of Dr. Taswell.*
[2] *Memoirs of Dean Comber*, by his great-grandson, p. 212.
[3] The relationship is said to rest on the sole authority of the MS. of Mr. Jones, a descendant of Taylor's. (See *Quarterly Review* for July 1871, art. 'Jeremy Taylor.') Mr. Jones's paper fell into the hands of Heber, Taylor's biographer.
[4] Rust's Funeral Sermon on Taylor.
[5] Heber's *Life*, prefixed to his edition of Taylor's *Works*, p. cxxvi

wherever he went. He undertook at his own expense the rebuilding of Dromore Cathedral,[1] or at least the choir of it; he spent almost all his income on alms and public works; but for one 'who liked not to be pushed at by herds and flocks of people that follow anybody that whistles to them or drives them to pasture,' an Irish bishopric must have been a sadly uncongenial sphere. He will come before us again as a preacher, a casuist, and a devotional writer.

One hardly knows where to draw the line in selecting typical specimens of the great prelates of the Caroline age. There is Bishop Wilkins, who, though he certainly cannot be reckoned among the consistent and heroic type of churchmen, was eminent in many ways:—for his great scientific attainments, for his tolerance in an intolerant age, for his liberality, for his general kindliness, and especially for his kindness to royalists and churchmen in perilous times, though he did not cast in his lot with them.[2] There is Bishop Skinner, conspicuous for his courage in conferring Holy Orders during the Rebellion,[3] who said with truth that he had sent more labourers into the Master's vineyard than any other bishop. There is Bishop Henchman, who held the important see of London for eleven years (1664-1675), and of whom nothing but good is recorded. There is Archbishop Sterne, whom Swift calls 'a sour, ill-tempered man,' but Walker 'a man of eminent worth,'[4] and whom Lord

---

[1] Heber, p. cxxviii.

[2] See Life of Dr. John Wilkins, prefixed to his works (1708) *passim*. It was through his exertions that Barrow was chosen Gresham Professor of Geometry. (See *Quarterly Review* for July 1869.) Newcome (Diary for November 22, 1672) calls him the learned, worthy, pious and peaceable Bishop of Chester; Bull, 'our excellent Bishop Wilkins.' (*Charge to the Clergy of S. Davids*, 1708.) Seth Ward is said to have been 'attracted to Wadham by the fame of the Warden, Dr. Wilkins, a great favourite with royalist gentlemen' (in the Rebellion). (*Some Particulars of the Life &c. of Bishop Seth Ward*.)

[3] See Nelson's *Life of Bishop Bull*, p. 59; *Life of Robert Frampton, Bishop of Gloucester*, p. 11; Walker's *Sufferings of the Clergy*, p. 55.

[4] *Sufferings &c.*, p. 196.

Dartmouth indignantly vindicates from Swift's aspersions. There is Bishop Isaac Barrow, whose fame is eclipsed by that of his more illustrious namesake and nephew, but who has left more than one monument of his liberality,[2] and who, it must be remembered, was for a long time 'the guide, philosopher, and friend' of the great Isaac. There is Bishop Nicolson of Gloucester, *laudatus a laudato viro*, for Bishop Bull 'was always a singular admirer of that condescension and familiarity, of that truly paternal care, which he found in this good bishop, who by his learned writings had defended and maintained the Church of England against her adversaries, when she was under a cloud; and after she had rode out the storm, did not omit to do all that became an excellent prelate for supporting the Catholic faith and discipline professed in her communion.' He died (1672) with the reputation of a truly primitive bishop.[3]

But it is high time to remember that there were other clergy who never rose to the episcopal dignity—some to no dignity at all—but yet added lustre to the Restoration period.

A native of Louth, Lincolnshire, may be pardoned for giving the first place among them to one who was born in a neighbouring village (Scamblesby). Apart from local prejudice, it would be hard to find one more distinguished for learning and piety than **Herbert Thorndike** (d. 1672). Peter Barwick mentions him among his three palmary instances of men 'who with incomparable sanctity of life have adorned the worst age, altogether worthy of a better.'[4] He was a fellow of Trinity College, Cambridge, but was deprived at the Rebellion. At the Restoration he recovered his fellowship and was also made Prebendary of Westminster. Between Cambridge and Westminster he passed the re-

---

[1] Lord Dartmouth's notes on Burnet's *Own Times*.
[2] He improved the Cathedral and Palace at S. Asaph, built almshouses, &c.
[3] Nelson's *Life of Bull*, p. 135.
[4] *Vita Joannis Barwick*, p. 235.

mainder of his days, living in blameless retirement, but still doing good service to the Church with his pen. Next to Walton he had the largest hand in producing the Polyglott Bible. He was a stiff churchman, but extorted by the guileless simplicity of his character the respect of his opponents.[1] He will come before us again as a writer, though many of his works, being of a controversial nature, do not come within our scope.

Another name mentioned by Barwick as a typical instance of 'the best clergy' is that of **Barnabas Oley** (d. 1666), who rose to the dignity of President of Clare Hall, Cambridge, before the Rebellion, but, being a most unflinching churchman, of course lost his preferment by that event. After the Restoration he held the living of Great Gransden and a prebend at Worcester Cathedral; he was also for a short time Archdeacon [of Ely?] but soon gave it up, finding the work incompatible with his other duties. We have an interesting instance of the respect and affection with which he was regarded by the parishioners of Great Gransden, in the letters of one of them to the Bishop of Ely (Turner). The bishop had requested a Mr. Cesar to inquire into the state of affairs in the church of the neighbouring parish of Little Gransden, which was unsatisfactory, and the writer replies that he could not attend the church personally because 'good Mr. Oley hath taught us in Great Gransden that it is our duty to keep our own parish church.' A little later he writes again, 'Since the death of our late reverend vicar we are very sensible of that great and inestimable loss of Mr. Barnabas Oley.'[2] This testimony is borne out by a letter from a Mr. R. Burton to Dean Granville. 'I'm told,'

---

[1] See Dr. Stoughton's *Church of the Restoration*, i. 35. May I take this opportunity of thanking one who differs most widely from my views, for the fairness which he has always studied to show to churchmen? See also Professor Brewer's edition of Thorndike's *Discourse of the Right of the Church in a Christian Commonwealth*.

[2] Quoted in Miss Strickland's *Lives of the Seven Bishops*, &c., pp. 180 and 184.

he writes, 'that this day your friend Mr. Barnabas Oley is to be bury'd. His parishioners are already extreme sensible of their loss of that reverend and eminently worthy, good man.'[1] Oley seems to have been as active at Worcester as at Gransden; the weekly celebration of the Holy Communion at the Cathedral was brought about by his means. He gives us an interesting insight into his own character in the preface to his third edition of George Herbert's 'Country Parson,' the first edition of which he had the courage to put forth in 1652, when such a work would be anything but acceptable. Altogether, though now little known, Barnabas Oley was a striking figure among the clergy of his day, and Mr. Shorthouse has nowhere shown better his remarkable knowledge of the Church life of the period than when he introduces him upon the scene in his famous romance.[2]

If the clergy of the period were ranged according to their intellectual eminence, the very first place,—above archbishops and bishops,—would have to be given to **Isaac Barrow** (1630–1677), who in his comparatively short life won distinction in various departments, any one of which would have been sufficient to render a man famous. A Cambridge man, like the two last we have noticed, he did not, like them, suffer from the Rebellion. Being only an undergraduate when it broke out, he was allowed to remain at the University though he made no secret of his royalist opinions; and so from his boyhood to his death he made Cambridge his home, and rose to the highest position which that University affords—the Mastership of Trinity. His scholarship caused him to be made Professor of Greek, his mathematical knowledge to be the first Lucasian Professor of Mathematics, and his general scientific attainments to be Professor of Geometry at Gresham College, London. But all his other acquirements were subservient to the study of divinity, to which he

---

[1] *Remains of Dean Granville* (Surtees Miscellanea), Part I. p. 212.
[2] See *John Inglesant*, last chapter.

devoted the whole of the later part of his life, resigning his professorships one by one for this purpose. His mathematical professorship at Cambridge he resigned in favour of his still more distinguished pupil, Isaac Newton; and among his many merits, not the least is, that he was the first to recognise and train the extraordinary powers of that great man, and—hardest task of all,—to own gracefully his superiority to himself. As a writer of controversial divinity Barrow ranks in the highest order, and as a preacher, if possible, higher still. Personally he was the most loveable of men, modest, retiring, and full of guileless simplicity, qualities which are not rare in men of the highest intellectual attainments. Scholar-like, he was very absent-minded, and careless about his personal appearance; many ludicrous stories, more or less true, but not worth repeating here, are told about these points. To complete the account of this prodigy, it may be added that his physical strength was almost equal to his intellectual, and his courage equal to his strength. Short-lived as he was, he was, oddly enough, a connecting link between two generations, and two utterly different types of men; for he was mainly supported in his youth at college by Henry Hammond, and he lived to be the friend of John Tillotson, who edited his works. His wide culture and sympathies, and his amiable temper, enabled him to live in perfect amity with both; he took an independent and perfectly definite line of his own, so that it is difficult to label him as belonging to any particular Church party; all that one can say is, that he was from first to last a loyal English churchman, and one of whom the English Church may well be proud.[1]

[1] It would far transcend the limits of this work to enter into any details of the life and writings of this remarkable man. May I therefore venture to refer the reader to my article on 'Isaac Barrow' in the *Dictionary of National Biography*? It will be seen from that, that I do not agree with those who make it a reproach to the Church of the Caroline age, that Barrow was neglected in the distribution of preferment; and a far greater authority, Dr. Whewell, takes the same view. By far the best edition of

From the great Cambridge preacher we naturally turn to the great Oxford one, **Robert** South (1633–1716), whose death broke the last link between the Church of the Caroline and the Church of the Georgian era. It may seem at the first glance out of place to notice here rather than in our next section one who actually outlived the whole period over which this sketch extends. But the reason is, that South came into public notice early in life, and retired early into comparative obscurity. It was during the reign of Charles II. far more than during the next three reigns that he was a prominent figure in Church life. His preaching will of course come before us again, but the man as well as the preacher deserves notice. He was the most unselfish and liberal of men. His wit and eloquence were never used by him as stepping-stones to preferment. 'Twice at least, and probably more than twice, he refused a mitre;'[1] and when he was rector of Islip he did not spend one farthing of the income upon himself. The living was worth 200*l.* a year; of this he gave 100*l.* a year to his curate, (more than three times the amount of the ordinary stipend,) and the rest he spent entirely upon Islip, clothing and apprenticing the poorer children of the place, restoring the chancel of the church,

---

Barrow's *Works* is that put forth for the syndics of the University Press (Cambridge) by the Rev. A. Napier in 1859; and by far the best account of Barrow himself (as regards his Cambridge life) is Dr. Whewell's 'Notice of Barrow's Life and Academical Times,' which will be found in the ninth volume of Mr. Napier's edition; and by far the best bibliography of Barrow's theological works is contained in Mr. Napier's scholarly Preface to Volume I. A short life was published in the form of a letter to Tillotson by Abraham Hill in 1683, prefixed to Tillotson's edition of Barrow's *Works*. The Rev. T. S. Hughes gave an account of his life in 1830, and some exceedingly interesting notices of Barrow and his family may be found in the 'Davy MSS.' in the British Museum (unpublished), to which my attention was kindly directed by the Rev. A. B. Grosart, D.D. See also *The S. James' Lectures on the Classic Preachers of the English Church*, 1877.

[1] An Irish bishopric, the bishopric of Rochester and deanery of Westminster (see *Life*, prefixed to Volume VII. of South's *Sermons*, published 1717), and perhaps the bishopric of Oxford. (See Sancroft's Letter to King James, 1686; D'Oyly's *Life of Sancroft*, i. 235.)

building a new rectory house, and 'building and endowing a school for ever.'¹ It is also said that he resolved to 'lay out what he had received from his canonry at Christ Church on poor vicaridges.'² The details of his career were as follows. He was one of the many eminent churchmen who were educated at Westminster under Dr. Busby, and at Christ Church under Dr. Fell (father and son). To a studentship at the latter place he was elected at the same time as John Locke. He was one of the many who were ordained before the Restoration by a deprived bishop (1659); and after that event he was appointed Public Orator at Oxford. He next became domestic chaplain to Lord Chancellor Clarendon, 'whereby he was on the road to church preferments.'³ In 1663 he was 'installed Prebendary of S. Peter's, Westminster,' and soon after made rector of Islip. In 1670 he became Canon of Christ Church, and there his advancement ended. Upon the Revolution, after long hesitation he took the oaths, but refused to accept any post vacated by a nonjuror, declaring that he would not 'build his Rise upon the Ruines of any one Father of the Church, who for piety, good morals, and strictness of life which every one of the deprived Bishops were famed for, might be said not to have left their equal.'⁴

From the pupil let us turn to the master. **Richard Busby** (1606–1695) is now thought of as the most successful and severest of pedagogues. Of his success at Westminster, where he was head-master all through the Rebellion, there is no doubt; but the tradition of his severity rests upon very slender foundations. That he was a most pious and liberal Christian of the old-fashioned Church of England type is most certain. He 'built in his lifetime a handsome

---

¹ *Life, ut supra.* Hearne says that 'Dr. South told Dr. Hudson that he was resolved never to pocket a farthing of the income of the parsonage of Islip,' and then goes on to narrate what has been mentioned in the text. (See *Reliquiæ Hearnianæ*, vol. i., entry for November 28, 1705. Also the entry for July 12, 1716.)

² Hearne, *ut supra*.   ³ *Life*, prefixed to *Works*.   ⁴ *Life*, p. 115.

church at Willan and a library within the church, and gave books to the value of 150*l.* for the vicar and neighbouring ministers,'[1] and his other gifts and bequests shew that he not only loved the Church, but that he had deeply considered her spiritual needs.[2] Dr. Prideaux might well lament that Busby's offer to found lectures at both Universities to instruct undergraduates in the rudiments of religion was declined;[3] they would not be useless even now. Dr. Busby was quite as anxious to promote the moral and spiritual as the classical training of the young. He employed his leisure in preparing expurgated editions of the classics, 'that his pupils might become acquainted with the beauties of the ancient writers without being tainted by their immorality,'—another work by no means superfluous at the present day. Busby's letters to his friend Basire breathe a spirit of the most ardent piety, without the slightest cant.[4] Peter Barwick seems to have found in him a substitute for his brother John, as a spiritual counsellor.[5] From all we can learn, Wood was quite justified in describing Dr. Busby as 'a person eminent and exemplary for piety and justice,' as well as 'an encourager of vertuous and forward youth; of great learning and hospitality, and the chief person that educated more youth that were afterwards eminent in Church and State than any master of his time.'[6] If any man ever deserved well of the Church, surely Dr. Busby did; and it is therefore a

---

[1] See *Case of Impropriations and Augmentation of Vicarages &c.*, published anonymously by Dr. White Kennet, 1704, where a long list will be found of Dr. Busby's benefactions, both in his lifetime and by his will. This list fully disproves Pepys' assertion of Dr. Busby's well-known covetousness. (*Memoirs*, iii. 211.) Besides, on Pepys' own showing, the Doctor's covetousness was for Westminster, not for himself.

[2] See *White Kennet*, ut supra.

[3] *Life of Dr. Humphrey Prideaux*, p. 92.

[4] See *Correspondence of Isaac Basire &c.* Edited by Rev. W. N. Darnell, 1831, *passim.*

[5] See *Life of Dr. Barwick*, with notes by Hilkiah Bedford.

[6] *Athenæ Oxonienses*, iv. 417.

satisfaction to learn that after the Restoration he was made Prebendary of Westminster, and subsequently Treasurer and Canon Residentiary of Wells.

Busby's friend **Isaac Basire** (1607–1677) was one whose experience during the Rebellion was unique. He was, as his name implies, a Frenchman by birth,[1] but came over to England and was naturalised here before he reached middle age. He flourished in his adopted country before the civil war, under the patronage of Bishop Morton, who made him his chaplain, gave him the rich livings of S. Conless and Egglescliff, and collated him to the seventh stall in Durham Cathedral.[2] On the breaking out of the war he set forth on his travels, and spent fifteen years in various countries of the East, ever keeping in view one object—viz. the dissemination of the Anglo-Catholic faith.

There is something grand in the idea of one solitary missionary making his way boldly into lands into which few Englishmen had penetrated, and trying to win over converts to his Church whithersoever he went. And it was no mere Quixotic attempt, bred of a delusion or an overweening estimate of his own powers; the spiritual knight-errant was so convinced of the strength of his cause, that he felt it had only to be fairly presented to reasonable minds to win them over. And the result proved that he had not miscalculated its strength. He *did* produce a very appreciable impression; he became, in fact, the pioneer of that remarkable attempt at union with the Greek Church which was made, mainly by the nonjurors, in the next generation.[3] Evelyn calls him 'that great traveller, or rather, French Apostle, who had been planting the Church

---

[1] According to some authorities, a native of Jersey. (See *Low's Diocesan History of Durham*, S.P.C.K., p. 285.) But Mr. Darnell distinctly states that he was born at Rouen, and gives the full details of his early life.

[2] But this was in 1643, when it was but a barren honour.

[3] See Mr. Abbey's paper on Robert Nelson and his Friends in *The English Church in the Eighteenth Century*, vol. i. pp. 157–161.

of England in divers parts of the Levant and Asia.'[1] The result of his travels was to confirm him in his churchmanship; 'I have,' he writes a short time before his death, 'surveyed most Churches, Eastern and Western, in fifteen years' ecclesiastical pilgrimage (during my voluntary banishment for my religion and loyalty), and I dare pronounce the Church of England, what David said of Goliath's sword, "There is none like it," both for Primitive Doctrine, worship, discipline, and government.'[2] After the Restoration he was reinstated in his preferments, and also made Archdeacon of Northumberland. In this capacity he exerted himself to carry out all the vigorous reforms of Bishop Cosin, whose funeral sermon he preached, and of whose life he wrote a 'Brief,' which is a model for modern biographers, condensing, as it does, within a hundred racily written pages, all that was really necessary to be said. Not being in advance of his age, Basire was too ready to call in the secular arm to enforce conformity; 'I find,' he writes to his son, 'by sad experience that the Staffe of Beauty (Zech. xi. 7) will not do the work without the Staffe of Bands;' but his correspondence and the whole tenor of his life shew that he was a spiritually-minded man, who valued the 'Staffe of Beauty' most.[3]

Richard Allestree (1619–1680) was a pupil of Dr. Busby, not at Westminster, but at Christ Church, of which he was made a student by Dr. Samuel Fell, the dean. He fought courageously for the king, and no less manfully assisted his friends John Fell and Dolben in performing the proscribed services of the Church. On the king's return he was made Canon of Christ Church, and undertook gratuitously one of the city lectureships. He was made king's chaplain, Regius Professor of Divinity, and ultimately Provost of Eton. The vicarage of Ewelme was attached to the Regius

---

[1] Diary, July 10, 1661.   [2] *The Dead Man's real Speech &c.*, p. 47.
[3] For a fuller account of Basire, may I venture to refer the reader to my article on him in the *Dictionary of National Biography* ?

Professorship, but Allestree 'would not receive a penny of the income, but left it to a friend whose circumstances required such an accession.'[1] His biographer gives other instances of his unselfish liberality, quite sufficient to account for his having died a poor man in spite of his preferments. As Busby at Westminster, so Allestree at Eton, did immense good by inculcating, by precept and example, lessons of piety as well as learning upon the rising churchmen of the day. For a full account of this great and good man the reader may be referred to the lively and easily accessible pages of Bishop Fell.

A still more eminent Christ Church man was **Edmund Pocock** (1604–1691), the great Orientalist and first Laudian Professor of Arabic. He was originally a scholar of Corpus Christi College; after having taken his degree he travelled extensively in Eastern countries, and then settled down in the college living of Childrey, which he was allowed to retain all through the Rebellion. But not without difficulty. The man whose European reputation for learning was perhaps greater than that of any living Englishman was all but turned out of his living for 'ignorance and insufficiency,' on the evidence of the farmers and labourers of Childrey![2] Though they did not succeed in ousting him, his parishioners made themselves so unpleasant that the good man often wished himself back at Aleppo or Constantinople. However, at the Restoration he was transplanted to the more congenial soil of Christ Church, Oxford, where he was better appreciated than by the rustics of Childrey. He was so liberal that Dr. Fell used to complain that he drew

---

[1] Fell's *Life of Allestree*.
[2] 'Sure,' writes his biographer quaintly, 'there was something odd and whimsical in the circumstances and situation of the good man, to be one day caressed by the greatest scholars in Europe, and set up an oracle for resolving difficulties in the abstrusest parts of learning, and the next perhaps, convened to answer the articles exhibited against him by his illiterate parishioners.' (*Life of Pocock*, p. 185). Not perhaps so very odd after all. Drs. Seth Ward, Wilkins, Wallis and Owen had the credit of preventing their University from disgracing itself by his removal.

all the poor of Oxford to Christ Church. Like many great scholars he was almost morbidly meek and modest. His death drew forth the most enthusiastic praise from men who knew him in his later years at Christ Church, notably from Dr. Marsh, the Primate of Ireland, and from John Locke. 'His life,' writes the latter, 'appeared to me one constant calm. I can say of him what few men can say of any friend of theirs, nor I of any other of my acquaintance, that I do not remember I ever saw in him any one action that I did, or could in my own mind, blame, or thought amiss in him.'[1]

Before quitting Oxford we must pass from Christ Church to the humbler region of Lincoln College, whose rector, **Thomas Marshall** (1621-1685), though now forgotten, was evidently a prominent figure in the Church life of his day. He had borne arms for the king at Oxford, and at Oxford he spent the greater part of his ministerial life. Probably with the desire of having some clerical work, he held with the rectorship the living of Combe, a living of very small value, in the gift of the college. Here he visited constantly the penitent Earl of Rochester.[2] The bishop of the diocese thought so highly of his clerical character that he desired him to draw up notes of a catechism to be used by the ministers of the diocese;[3] and Robert Boyle felt that his name would carry so much weight that he persuaded him to write a preface to the Malayan copy of the Gospels and Acts which that good man was at the expense of printing.[4] All the writers who mention Dr. Marshall mention him in terms of praise. He is 'the learned and worthy Rector of Lincoln,'[5] a 'painful preacher, a good man and governor,

---

[1] See *Life of Dr. Edward Pocock*, republished in 1816, *passim*.
[2] See Burnet's *Life of John, Earl of Rochester*, p. 261.
[3] *Athenæ Oxonienses*, iv. 170.
[4] Birch's *Life of the Hon. Robert Boyle*, p. 230. See also Anderson's *History of the Colonial Church*, ii. 474, where it is said that Boyle consulted Marshall before publishing the translation.
[5] Burnet's *Life of Rochester*, p. 261.

and one every way worthy of his station in the Church;'[1]
'a truly reverend and learned man, who seemed to have no
other object besides the promotion of piety and literature.'[2]
He was ultimately promoted to the deanery of Wells, but it
is as Rector of Lincoln that we hear most about him.

Archbishops and bishops, deans and archdeacons, canons
and professors, naturally come forward more prominently in
connection with church life, than plain parish priests. But
there is abundant evidence that there was no lack of excellent specimens of the latter during the Caroline age. Many
who will appear as dignitaries in our next period were
now most usefully engaged in parish work. Beveridge was,
during a great part of the period, labouring heartily and
most successfully at S. Peter's, Cornhill; Sharp, during
sixteen years of the time, at S. Giles' in the Fields;
Patrick was at S. Paul's, Covent Garden, refusing other
preferment because his work in that place was so encouraging. Ken was occupied with parish work, first at
S. John's Soke, Winchester, where it was literally a
labour of love, for he had no stipend; then at Brightstone,
then at Woodhay; Hooper, subsequently his successor at
Bath and Wells, was also his successor, and a most
worthy one, at Woodhay; Bull was still at Suddington,
allowing his energies and tastes the free play which was
denied to them during the Rebellion; Lancelot Addison
was at Milston, taking, as his practical works show, a high
and sound standard of clerical work; Lloyd (afterwards
bishop) was working the large parish of S. Martin's in the
Fields with great vigour. These all attained to dignities
in the Church; but there were other estimable and diligent
men who lived and died simple parish priests. Such was
Isaac Milles, the very model of a country parson, whose life
extended into the Georgian era, but who, all through the
Caroline era, was working, first as curate at Barley, then

[1] Wood, *Athenæ Oxonienses*.
[2] Noble's *Biographical History of England*, i. 93.

as vicar at Chipping Wycombe, as conscientiously as he afterwards did at High Clere;[1] such was his less known, but equally worthy, elder brother, Samuel, vicar of Royston, who 'succeeded during his residence there, beyond all his predecessors and those who came after him, in bringing over nonconformists to the Church.'[2] Such was Richard Sherlock, the uncle and the trainer of the saintly Thomas Wilson, who wrote his life. Winwick, where he lived as rector for thirty years, and 'was scarce so many weeks absent from his flock,' was so well worked by its active rector with his three curates that 'it became a very desirable place for young divines to improve themselves in the work of the ministry.'[3] Horneck, first at All Saints', Oxford, then at the Savoy; Rawlett at Newcastle; Kettlewell at Coleshill — were all diligent parish priests during the later part of our era, though their lives more properly belong to the next period; and we have many incidental notices of good, hard-working clergymen, who in this, as in every age, lived and died in obscurity. Timothy Borage, e.g., 'quitted the retirement of a scholastic life in Cambridge from the conviction of the duty incumbent on him of exercising in the world the powers committed to him by his ordination,' and was 'an excellent working clergyman at Great Marlow;'[4] while at the neighbouring town of Amersham was a rector who is described by the same authority as 'in all respects a pious, learned, and excellent man.' Sancroft's successor in the rectory of Houghton-le-Spring, Mr. Davenport, is described as 'a man of most blameless and apostolic life, and of munificence which is even yet remembered;'[5] and, to pass from the north to the south, Dr. Granville 'was much satisfied to find Moreclack [Mortlake] supplied by a worthy

---

[1] See the *Life of the Rev. I. Milles*, republished in 1812.
[2] *Ibid.* p. 15.
[3] See *Life of Richard Sherlock*, D.D., *Rector of Winwick*, by Bishop Wilson, prefixed to Sherlock's *Practical Catechism*.
[4] See *Life of Isaac Milles*, p. 47.
[5] See *Surtees Miscellanea*, where there is much more praise of him.

person, one Mr. Jones.'[1] But it is obviously impossible to specify all the worthy parish priests, who were scattered, in no small proportion, throughout the country. Neither must we dwell upon the work of the clergy in another field, that of sacred literature. It was in the period with which we are now dealing that Stillingfleet published his 'Origines Sacræ' and many other works;[2] Timothy Puller his well-known treatise 'On the Moderation of the Church of England;'[3] Fullwood his 'Roma ruit'—'one of the most important theological productions of the time;' Towerson his standard work on the Church Catechism, which will be noticed presently; Comber the first part of his 'Companion to the Temple;' Simon Lowth his admirable 'Catechetical Questions;' Beveridge many of his voluminous and very popular works; Patrick some of his earlier treatises; Edmund Castel his grand 'Lexicon Heptaglotton'—most of these were composed in the retirement of country livings. The list might be swelled almost indefinitely; but enough has been said to show that the clergy of the Caroline era were not slack in contributing to what has always been the glory of the Church of England—its sacred literature.

THE CAMBRIDGE PLATONISTS.

Before turning to the clergy of the next period it is necessary to say a few words about a set of men (all clergymen), whose lives, no less than their writings, form a remarkable episode in the Church life of the seventeenth century. If this were a history of religious thought, a considerable space would have to be devoted to the Cambridge Platonists; but their lives, blameless and beautiful as they were, stood so far apart from the general life of the Church and nation that a very short notice will suffice. And first, a caution

[1] *Remains of Dean Granville*, Part I. (Surtees Miscellanea), p. 174.
[2] See *Life and Character of Bishop Edward Stillingfleet*, published 1710.
[3] An excellent edition of this has been republished by the Rev. R. Eden, in our own day.

E.

must be given against being misled by names. The Platonists were called 'Latitudinarians' and 'Rationalists,' and not inappropriately; but they must not be confounded with others to whom the same titles were given. Their 'latitude' was not as against the creed of the Church of England, but as against the Calvinism and general narrowness of the Puritans of the Commonwealth;[1] and their 'rationalism' was rather a levelling up than a levelling down; for by 'reason' they understood not merely the ratiocinative faculty but 'the breath of a higher, diviner reason,'[2] 'the first participation from God,'[3] 'the sacerdotal breastplate of the λόγιον or rationale,'[4] 'the candle of the Lord,' 'a beam of divine light.'[5] Most of them sprang, during the Commonwealth, from the Puritan college, Emmanuel, and they evidently caused a sensation quite out of proportion to their numbers or to their activity, for they do not seem to have been at all inclined to proselytise. An Oxford correspondent writes to a Cambridge friend, in 1662, that 'he can come into no company but he finds the chief discourse to be about a new sect of men, called Latitude-men,' and he begs his friend, S. P. (probably Simon Patrick), to tell him all about them. S. P. explains that they were called Latitude-men 'in opposition to that hide-bound, strait-laced spirit that did prevail' before the Restoration; 'that they are so far from being dangerous to the Church that they seem to be the very chariot and horsemen thereof,' and that they desired to benefit the Church by

---

[1] S. T. Coleridge, who had many points in common with the Platonists, clearly distinguishes the latitudinarianism of More, Cudworth, &c., from the disposition to explain away the articles of the Church on the pretext of their inconsistency with right reason. (*Notes on English Divines*, p. 119.) Burnet gives a most confused and inadequate account of them, mixing them up with men of his own way of thinking, from which they were quite alien. (*History of My Own Times*, book ii. under year 1661.)

[2] Tulloch's *Rational Theology* &c., ii. 135.

[3] Whichcote, Aphorism 459. 'The spirit in man is the candle of the Lord, lighted by God, and lighting man to God,' &c. (Sermon).

[4] Henry More. [5] John Smith's *Select Discourses*, p. 399.

'letting her old loving nurse, the Platonick Philosophy, be admitted again into her family in place of Aristotle and the school-men.'[1] But their attachment to the Church of England was of rather a peculiar character. It was based partly on æsthetic grounds. They admired her decent grandeur and splendour, and thought 'it would be a sorry exchange to accept of Presbytery instead;'[2] and they also valued her creeds and formularies as among the greatest bulwarks against Hobbism, the tendency of which they perceived earlier than most persons.[3] The lives of the Platonists are well worth studying. A more elevating study than the life, say, of Henry More, or of that wonderful young man, John Smith, 'whom it pleased the only wise God, in whose hands our breath is, to call home to the spirits of just men made perfect, after He had lent him to this unworthy world for about thirty-five years,'[4] or, in fact, of almost any of the band, it would be difficult to conceive; and materials for the task are so abundant, that we can gain almost as vivid a conception of their life and character as of that of any of our contemporaries. But the temptation to pursue the subject further must be resisted; for to yield to it would be to transgress our rule, viz. to select only *typical* instances of Church life; for the lives of the Cambridge Platonists were wholly exceptional. It

[1] *A Brief Account of the New Sect of Latitudinarians, together with some Reflections upon the New Philosophy, by S. P., of Cambridge, in answer to a Friend at Oxford.* The whole tract is thoroughly well worth reading. See also *Cambridge Characteristics in the Seventeenth Century,* by J. B. Mullinger, of S. John's (the Le Bas Prize), 1867, and *Rational Theology and Christian Philosophy in England in the Seventeenth Century,* by J. Tulloch, D.D., 1862. But after all, the most vivid picture of the Platonists is drawn in their own writings, which are very accessible and most fascinating reading.

[2] These were the words of Dr. Henry More, but they express the views of all the Platonists.

[3] By far the most powerful treatise that ever was written against Hobbism was by a Platonist, Cudworth's *Intellectual System.*

[4] These are the beautiful words of another Platonist, John Worthington, in his 'Address to the Reader,' prefixed to his edition of his friend John Smith's magnificent Discourses.

is, however, but just to add one remark. The purity and saintliness of the Platonists' lives must in fairness be regarded as the logical outcome of their system. It would be doing them a grievous injustice to look upon them as a set of harmless dreamers whose airy speculations had little or nothing to do with practical holiness. They taught that purity of heart and life was the only true way to knowledge,[1] a theory which they worked out with exquisite taste and beauty, and which they certainly endeavoured to carry into practice. But their ideas were too refined for general, working purposes; they flew above the heads of the commonplace world. Their admirers became absorbed in other parties. Patrick, their early defender and disciple, identified himself with the High Church party; so did the excellent John Scott, so did George Rust, the 'fidus Achates,' panegyrist, and ultimately successor of Jeremy Taylor, though none of the three ever lost entirely the Platonic tincture; Edmund Fowler, afterwards Bishop of Gloucester, a friend of the Platonists and a defender of them with his pen[2] though he never thoroughly entered into their spirit, became a low churchman of the most commonplace type; Howe, one of the best of the nonconformists, who was deeply tinged with Platonism, and was an intimate friend and ardent admirer of some of the most eminent Platonists, was quite content to cast in his lot with the dissenters:[3] while More's 'heroine pupil,' Lady Conway,

[1] See the whole of Discourse I. of John Smith's *Select Discourses*, which insists upon this point with a beauty of language and thought to which there are few parallels in the English tongue. Cf. also the well-known saying of Henry More, ' The Oracle of God is not to be heard but in His holy temple—that is to say, in a good and holy man,' &c. (See his Preface to his *General Collection of Philosophical Writings*, p. 6.)

[2] See his *Free Discourse on the Platonists*. Fowler was much more like Burnet than like the Platonists. I am surprised that so generally accurate a writer as Von Ranke should assert that ' Burnet allied himself to the Cambridge Platonists.' (*History of England*, book vi.) Surely he had hardly any point in common with them.

[3] See *Life and Character of John Howe*, by Henry Rogers, pp. 21, 22.

joined the Quakers, in spite of her tutor's remonstrances; as also did a Mr. Archdale, in consequence of reading More's works.[1]

But if the peculiar tenets of the Platonists proved a rope of sand which could not bind any considerable body of Englishmen in one coherent system, it was not because they were wanting in definiteness, but rather because the English mind refused to assimilate such ethereal food. It may be said of the Platonist that 'his soul was like a star, and dwelt apart;' but it was a peculiarly bright star, and added lustre to the firmament of the English Church, to which, in its own peculiar way, it essentially belonged.

CLERGY OF THE REVOLUTION PERIOD AND IN THE REIGN OF QUEEN ANNE.

First in point of dignity and date among the notable clergy of the Revolution period is **William Sancroft** (1617–1693). He had been of course a prominent man, almost from the time of the Restoration; but as his name is most conspicuous in connection with the Revolution, it is, on the whole, more suitable to group him among the clergy of that era, though he had passed the allotted span of life when the Revolution took place. He was elected fellow of Emmanuel, Cambridge, before the Rebellion, but lost his fellowship for refusing to take either the Covenant or the Engagement. He went forth into voluntary exile, and by his energy was able not only to support himself, but also to help his friend Dr. Cosin, who, when he became Bishop of Durham, lost no time in showing his gratitude; for he immediately gave Sancroft the rich living of Houghton-le-Spring and a canonry at Durham; and he was anxious to procure for him the still greater benefit of a good wife, but could not persuade Sancroft to take advantage of his kindness in this last point. For a short time Sancroft was

---

[1] See *Life of Isaac Milles*, p. 152.

Master of his old College. He was next made Dean, first of York, then of Canterbury, and then of S. Paul's, where he fully kept up the high standard raised by his predecessors, Barwick and Sudbury. On the death of Sheldon, Sancroft was advanced at a bound to the primacy, to the surprise of all, and the disgust of some over whose heads he had been raised.[1] The contrast between Sancroft and Sheldon was most striking; both were staunch churchmen, but Sancroft had imbibed far more thoroughly the true spirit of Church principles than Sheldon ever did; one natural and happy consequence of which was a marked improvement in the treatment of nonconformists.[2] Sancroft knew that spiritual not carnal weapons were the Church's true defences; he had far too much faith in the vitality of the Church to be over-eager in calling in the aid of the secular arm; and he was most sincerely anxious to devise some scheme for comprehending nonconformists within her pale without compromising any principle. He was a modest, retiring, contemplative man,[3] with little of the *bonhomie* and none of the statesmanlike qualities of his predecessor. His mode of life was most simple and frugal, and the violent contrast which it presented in this respect to that of Sheldon naturally caused him to be charged with

[1] 'December 30, 1677.—This day, Dr. W. Sandcroft [sic], Dean of S. Paul's, was declared Archbishop of Canterbury, contrary to the expectation of all the Court, and to the dissatisfaction of many bishops who resented his leap from the deanery of Paul's over their heads unto the primacy. It could not be imagin'd at Court what or who urg'd the king to promote him, unless (as 'twas most generally suppos'd) a particular esteem and kindness His Majesty always had for him,' &c. (*Diary of Dr. Edward Lake*, republished for the Camden Society, 1846.) White Kennet says, 'The king was under some difficulty to find a proper person, but at last, by the recommendation of his brother, the Duke of York, he resolved upon Sancroft, as a person of great prudence and moderation.' (*History of England*, vol. iii. p. 361.)

[2] See Wilkins' *Concilia*, vol. iv., where the original circular letters of the archbishops show a marked difference of tone on this point, as soon as Sheldon is succeeded by Sancroft.

[3] See 'Remarks on his Life,' prefixed to his *Occasional Sermons* (1694), p. xvi.

avarice. But the charge was most unjust;[1] for his liberality was as conspicuous as Sheldon's, which is saying a great deal;[2] but he was not the man of business that Sheldon was, and hence though his simple habits must have entailed upon him far less personal expenses than Sheldon in his sumptuousness incurred, he left Lambeth a poor man, while his predecessor died a rich one. He was in no sense a showy man; he was greedy after all kinds of knowledge, and is said to have left behind him more MSS. than almost any man of his time,[3] but he shrank from appearing in print. Perhaps this is not to be regretted, for he had not the art of setting off his wares to the best advantage. It was evidently an effort to him, as it is to most bookish men, to emerge from obscurity; and this seems to be the true explanation of one or two passages in his life which have been construed as proofs of timidity. It certainly would have been well if in 1686 he had either joined the Ecclesiastical Commission or distinctly refused to do so, and not merely excused himself for non-attendance; and if in 1689 he had appeared in the House of Lords and boldly advocated a Regency, and if he had either joined in consecrating Burnet to a bishopric, or declined to have anything to do with the matter, instead of appointing a commission for the purpose. But over and over again he showed that he could be bold as a lion, and active far beyond

---

[1] 'False as Hell,' wrote Swift in language more forcible that polite, in a note upon Burnet's accusation of Sancroft as avaricious. (See Lord Dartmouth's *Notes on Burnet*, iii. 102.) Another writer, commenting on the same charge, writes, ' Viri hujusce sanctissimi vitam recolens, non sine aliquâ indignatione miror, ab historico scriptore, et quidem Episcopo, virtutes ejus adeò non celebrari, ut parsimoniæ et avaritiæ infamia ipsius memoriæ inurere videatur.' (Bishop Godwin, *De Præsulibus Angliæ*.)

[2] See Bishop Godwin, *ut supra*; D'Oyly's *Life of Sancroft*, i. 146, 149; and Miss Strickland's *Lives of the Seven Bishops*, pp. 45-50.

[3] See *Collectanea Curiosa*, from the MSS. of Archbishop Sancroft, given to the Bodleian by Bishop Tanner, 1781, Preface, p. xxxiii. On his reluctance to appear in print, see the 'Remarks on his Life,' prefixed to his *Occasional Sermons* (1694), p. ix.

what his predecessor had ever been. He was the only prominent clergyman in the seventeenth century who twice in his life ' was deprived of all that he could not keep with a good conscience.'[1] The young man who went forth from Cambridge because he could not break his oath of allegiance to the father, and the old man who went forth from Lambeth because he could not break his oath of allegiance to the son, were one and the same from first to last. He had no hesitation about taking the unusual step of suspending a bishop who was unworthy of his high office.[2] He boldly withstood the second personage of the realm and strove to bring him back to his mother church; and he was the life and soul of that brave band of seven who stood in the gap when the same man, now the first personage of the realm, strove to Romanise the country; and he boldly protested against the same king keeping the see of York vacant, truly remarking that he was the only clergyman in the realm who could do so without being suspected of interested motives. Surely all this does not argue timidity; and so far from his being inactive, it seems to me that the extraordinary activity of the bishops and pastors of the Church during the eleven years of his primacy, when churches were better attended and services more frequent than they had perhaps ever been since the Reformation, was in no slight degree the result of the activity of the Primate. His episcopal brethren clearly looked up to him as personally no less than officially their natural leader.[3] And he had evidently the confidence of

---

[1] Nelson's *Life of Bull*, p. 189.   [2] Bishop Wood, of Lichfield.

[3] For proofs of this, see, *inter alia*, the Bishop of Ely's (Turner) letter to him in January 1689. 'Without compliment, your grace is better versed than all of us together,' &c. (See the letter quoted in *Correspondence of Henry Hyde, Earl of Clarendon*, &c., ii. 507.) Bishop Lake of Chichester 'always valued as the principal honour and felicity of his life, his friendship with Archbishop Sancroft.' (See *Defence of the Profession of the Bishop of Chichester*, 1690, p. 8.) Bishop Nicolson thinks that 'the main objection' to the Revolution Government is 'Sancroft's declining to pay allegiance to it,' and 'confesses that his example ought to carry a great deal of authority

the nation. Churchmen of the spiritual, not political, type we might expect to find, as of course we do, among his admirers. But men like Swift, who was a statesman at least as much as a churchman, is equally enthusiastic in his praise;[1] Dryden, the hater of priests of all religions, makes an exception in favour of 'Zadok,' the priestliest of priests.[2] The Princess of Orange writes to him in 1687, 'Though I have not the advantage to know you, my Lord of Canterbury, yet the reputation you have makes me resolve not to lose this opportunity of making myself more known to you,'[3]—a remarkable testimony from the wife of William of Orange. Wake, a bishop of quite a different type, refers to Sancroft as 'that great and wise prelate.' In short, with the single exception of Burnet, it is not easy to find one contemporary or nearly contemporary churchman, who does not speak with tender respect of Sancroft's character; and justly. If he had his foibles, he might have said of all his conduct, what he did say of one memorable incident of his life, 'What I have done, I have done in the integrity of my heart.'

If Sancroft was the antipodes of Sheldon, Sancroft's successor was as unlike the one as he was the other. **John Tillotson (1630–1694)** was the son of a Calvinist clothier at Sowerby near Halifax; he received the rudiments of his education from his grandfather, Mr. Dod, a strict Puritan. At Clare Hall, Cambridge, his tutor, Mr. Clarkson, who had great influence over him, was also a strict Puritan. He was elected fellow of Clare in 1651, of course under Puritan auspices, and was appointed tutor to a son of Mr. Prideaux, Oliver Cromwell's attorney-general. At the Restoration he lost his fellowship as a nonconformist, but he

with it' (Nicolson's *Correspondence*, i. 11), though he himself took a different view.

[1] Swift's *Ode to his Memory* is valuable, if not from a poetical, from an evidential point of view.

[2] See his *Absalom and Achitophel*.

[3] See letter in the *Clarendon Correspondence*, ii. 484.

conformed after the Act of 1662. He married a niece of Oliver Cromwell, and step-daughter of Dr. Wilkins. Among his intimate friends were Thomas Firmin, a very benevolent Socinian, Dr. Bates, the Presbyterian vicar of S. Dunstan's in the West, Mr. Gouge, a liberal dissenter, whose funeral sermon he preached, the excellent nonconformist John Howe, to whom he was wont to send a copy of every sermon he published, William Penn, the Quaker, and finally William, Prince of Orange. With such antecedents and such friends, it would have been strange indeed if he had caught the spirit of the English Church. It is true that he also numbered among his friends some of her truest sons, such as John Sharp, Robert Nelson, Thomas Comber, and Isaac Barrow; and the fact that he could attract to him men of such very different sentiments, is a strong proof of his amiability, no less than of his wide sympathies. It is not necessary to dwell on the facts of his life, and tell how he held for a short time the little living of Keddington, where the villagers were dissatisfied because he did not preach the gospel; how he then became preacher at Lincoln's Inn, and Tuesday lecturer at S. Lawrence Jewry, and not only satisfied but delighted, and attracted from all parts of the metropolis, the most critical congregations; how he was made Dean, first of Canterbury, and then, on the accession of his friend King William, of S. Paul's. Higher than this he never desired to rise; there is evidently sincerity and deep earnestness in his letter to the Earl of Portland, desiring him 'to defend him from a bishopric'; and the reason he gives is a most cogent one.[1] It would have

---

[1] 'I earnestly beg of your Lordship to defend me from a bishopric. Few can believe me in this, but I hope your Lordship does. . . . I do not love either the ceremony or trouble of a great place. When men are children again, it is not fit they should appear in public, but go back into the nursery. I desire to be as useful as I can; but I do not affect to be famous. . . . That little good which I have been able to do has been in the City of London, which I foresee will be stript of its ablest men; and if I can be serviceable anywhere, it is there. . . . I think it may be somewhat for the honour of our religion, and the advantage of the Government, to have one so hearty

been well for him if his desire had been attended to, but in an evil hour for his happiness, he was persuaded by his beloved and loving master to accept the primacy on the deprivation of Sancroft. It was not without many misgivings, and much consultation with his friends,[1] that he at last consented to fill the invidious position. Under any circumstances, considering his antecedents, he would hardly have been the man for the place; but of all times, the time when he undertook it was the most unfortunate. An angel could hardly have given satisfaction. Sancroft most assuredly carried away with him to Fressingfield the sympathies of the vast majority of the clergy; many of those who had no scruple about taking the oaths, had insuperable scruples about accepting sees of which the bishops had been deprived by the civil power; among others, John Sharp, Tillotson's best friend, and Beveridge, two of the most respected clergy of the day. A torrent of invectives in the shape of pamphlets, sermons,[2] and even coarser attacks[3] was poured upon the new Primate's head. And unfortunately neither his temperament nor his training fitted him for bearing such attacks. He was a man of a singularly sweet, gentle, and sensitive nature: he never treated unkindly any living creature, and he felt most keenly any unkind treatment of himself. The career of a popular preacher is the worst conceivable career for training a man to bear heavy blows. Accustomed to see himself surrounded by a crowd of admiring auditors who hung breathless upon his words, he felt the rude shock of assault all the more keenly from the contrast. To his credit be it said, that he was never intoxicated with the

for both without any expectation or desire of preferment by it.' (Quoted in Birch's *Life of Tillotson*, pp. 140-2.)

[1] Among others, oddly enough, Lady Rachel Russell. See Account of her Life, p. 97.

[2] See Birch, pp. 292, 351.

[3] See the story of a mask being sent to him in Macaulay's *History of England*, chapter xvii.

incense which was offered to him as a preacher, and never tempted to retaliation by any of the abuse with which he was pelted as a prelate. But there is little doubt that the latter tended to shorten his life. There is something very touching in the resolution, recorded in his commonplace book, and not found till after his death, 'not to be angry with anybody upon any occasion;' and something more than touching in the story of a packet of papers being also found after his death, with this endorsement: 'These are libels; I pray God forgive the authors, as I do.' He did forgive, but he could not forget; the mere fact of his having kept them so carefully shows what an impression they made upon him. He only held the primacy for three short years, dying a few weeks before the young queen, whom he had loved so well and served so faithfully. Waving the question of his fitness for the archbishopric, and postponing to a future chapter any remarks upon his preaching, we may note that his personal character was most estimable; unselfish, exceedingly charitable, both in the popular and in the higher sense of the term, and containing a happy mixture of qualities not often found in combination; for he was warm-hearted without being in the least warm-tempered; a most ardent friend, without being at all a bitter foe. In fact, there was so much to admire in him that one can only be sorry that he was ever placed in a position in which his gentle nature could not fail to be continually wounded.

Tillotson's successor was **Thomas Tenison** (1634–1715), a man who for thirty years after the Restoration had been engaged most energetically and most successfully as a parish priest, first at S. Andrew's, Cambridge, where he gained deserved credit by staying manfully at his post and ministering to his distressed parishioners during the Plague, and then in London, as rector of the large and very important parish of S. Martin's in the Fields, which he managed admirably. He was known and admired as a preacher, but still more as a parish-worker. Evelyn is afraid 'the paines he takes, and the care of his parish, will weare him out, which would be an inexpressible loss.'[1] In the brave resistance made by the clergy, especially in London, against the efforts of King James to Romanise his subjects, the rector of S. Martin's took a prominent part; it was largely through his efforts that Sharp's suspension for preaching against Popery was removed;[2] and it was through his desire to counteract Romanism that he became one of the originators of one of the most useful and prosperous works of the period, the charity schools, of which more will be said presently. He was appointed to S. Martin's on the recommendation of Patrick, who 'blesses God for having placed so good a man in the post.'[3] The testimony of so near a neighbour and so good a worker himself, is more than sufficient to counterbalance Lord Dartmouth's depreciatory account of his promotion.[4] But in point of fact there is a pretty general unanimity, even among his detractors, about his excellence as a parish priest, and perhaps he would have been thought more highly of if he had lived and died in that capacity. But in 1691 he was most reluctantly removed to preside over the unwieldy diocese of Lincoln, which, according to Kennet, he restored to some kind of discipline and order, and after three years he was removed to Canterbury. Here all unanimity of opinion as to his merits ceases. Whigs like Burnet and Kennet praise the appointment, and the latter boldly declares it was universally approved of.[5] This most assuredly was not the case. Apart from his opinions, which were supposed to be those of Tillotson, and were most unacceptable to the majority of the clergy, he was not considered strong enough for the place, and this feeling was emphasised by the fact

---

[1] *Diary* for March 21, 168¾.
[2] See John Le Neve's *Lives &c. of the Bishops*, &c., p. 239.
[3] *Autobiography of Simon Patrick*, p. 84.
[4] See Lord Dartmouth's *Notes on Burnet*, iv. 238.
[5] *History of England*, vol. iii. 682.

that the man who was generally pointed out as the proper person to fill it was the strongest living clergyman, Bishop Stillingfleet.¹ It would probably have been well for the peace of the Church if Stillingfleet had been appointed, even though his bodily infirmities might have impeded his activity. For in those turbulent times, a prelate with a great name, a name that would inspire awe, was above all things required at the helm. Stillingfleet's was such a name, Tenison's was not. His friends called him firm and steady, 'an old rock,' his enemies, dull and heavy; but neither called him great. In one respect, however, he was certainly more fitted for the post than Tillotson, for he was not in the least sensitive. Abuse, which was showered upon him as plentifully as it had been upon his predecessor, did not trouble him at all. He lived to the age of eighty-one, and left behind him the reputation of an honest and sensible, a solid and stolid, but by no means brilliant man.

It is a pleasant relief to turn from prelates about whom there has certainly been a great diversity of opinion to one about whom there was no diversity at all. **John Sharp**, (1644-1714) is a striking instance of what a plain, straightforward, guileless man, with definite principles, but without very shining abilities, or profound learning, or peculiar attractiveness of manner, or extraordinary enthusiasm, may effect. As rector of S. Giles' in the Fields for sixteen years, as Dean, first of Norwich, then of Canterbury, and above all as Archbishop of York for twenty years, he was respected and beloved in a very remarkable degree. And the fact that he was so is really very creditable to his contemporaries, for from first to last he never once went out of his way to court the popular applause. In one of his sermons ² he has unwittingly given us an exact portrait of

---

¹ The queen was most anxious for Stillingfleet's appointment; Tillotson had strongly recommended him for the primacy, on the deprivation of Sancroft.

² That on 'The Upright Man,' from Psalm cxii. ver. 4.

himself. 'He lives as he believes, is ready to endure anything for religious principles, is honest God-ward, an Israelite indeed, in whom there is no guile; and with respect to men, is just in all his dealings, never takes advantage of credulity, nor abuses confidence reposed in him, hates all mean compliance and dares to speak his mind, is a man of great simplicity and plainness, open and free. You may always know where to have him, for his words and thoughts always go together;—above all things hates a trick; so free is both his heart and actions from all imposture, that he cares not if all the world were privy to them. With the wisdom of the serpent he joins the innocency and simplicity of the dove; he is not steered by the wind of popular applause, but the sense of duty; therefore he is of great courage and resolution; nothing can frighten him from his duty, for he fears none but God. He does not resolve hastily, but after mature deliberation; he always considers more *what* is said, than who says it. You may as soon draw the sun from his line, as him from the steady and strict paths of righteousness.' And so forth. If anyone had been preaching Archbishop Sharp's funeral sermon, giving, after the fashion of the times, a full description of the man, he could hardly have done better than have taken this sermon verbatim. Being a staunch and uncompromising, though not extreme, churchman, Sharp was of course often brought into collision with others, but he always came out of the struggle with general approval. His famous sermon in 1686 against Romanism, just after he had been appointed chaplain to a Romanist king, was manifestly called for,[1] and though it enraged his royal master, was approved of by the vast majority of the nation. And his declining to accept any see vacated by a deprived bishop, though it gave dis-

---

[1] He had been applied to anonymously by a parishioner to give some safeguard against Romanism, and as the danger of Romanism was then most imminent, he could not, without gross neglect of duty, have failed to preach on the subject.

pleasure to King William, was not displeasing to the mass of his fellow-churchmen. Though, like his friend Tillotson, he was on terms of intimacy with nonconformists, such as Baxter, Firmin, and Thoresby, no one ever accused *him* of truckling to dissenters, or being half-one himself, for he made it perfectly clear that it was their persons not their principles that he esteemed. Burnet, as a rule, never praises anyone who differed from himself, but though Sharp differed widely from him, he makes an exception in *his* favour. William Whiston differed from him still more widely, and yet it is William Whiston who calls him ' that very good, that very honest man, Archbishop Sharp.' The nonjurors were not inclined to regard with a favourable eye those clergy who took the oaths, but they, too, bear their testimony to the merits of Sharp. He had the invidious privilege of dispensing a vast amount of ecclesiastical patronage, first through his friend and patron, the Earl of Nottingham, who consulted him about all the preferments he had to bestow as Lord Chancellor, and then through Queen Anne, who took him for her adviser and spiritual director; and yet he never raised against himself any envy, nor ever caused any dissatisfaction, except in one noticeable case where he was clearly in the right [1] He opposed, or at any rate regarded with some suspicion, the Societies for the Reformation of Manners; but no one ever dreamed of suspecting him of being indifferent to the cause which these Societies had at heart, for he made it clearly understood that he thought that cause would be better helped by clergymen adhering to their proper clerical work, and carrying out more fully the plain rules of their Church. No one ever told a sovereign more unreservedly of her faults than

---

[1] When he prevented the author of *The Tale of a Tub* from being made a bishop. Swift, in consequence, gibbeted him in the line:

A crazy prelate, and a r—l prude.

The latter refers to the queen, who in this as in all spiritual matters took Sharp's advice not to elevate Swift to the mitre.

he told Queen Anne, and yet he never offended her. The only blot in his career is an occasional narrowness. Judged by the standard of the nineteenth century, he certainly shewed bitterness in his opposition to Dissenters' Seminaries, but he must be judged by the standard of the times in which he lived; it was on Tillotson's advice that he refused to license a Dissenters' Academy, and no one accused Tillotson of being narrow-minded according to the standard of his day. In one sense he was certainly not a narrow man; he had tastes quite apart from his clerical functions; he was a great reader and admirer of Shakespeare, an extensive collector of coins, and a good numismatist. These, however, were strictly bye-works; his whole heart was in his proper work; and a more beautiful picture of active piety has been seldom drawn than that which his son has left us in the interesting but by no means highly coloured portrait of his father. Everything that the biographer tells us is borne out by what we hear from less interested sources. We may meet with greater men in the course of this chapter, but with none more universally and deservedly esteemed.

We next come to a somewhat different type of prelate from any that have yet been noticed. **Henry Compton** (1633–1713)[1] was the youngest son of Spencer, Earl of Northampton. His father and all his five elder brothers had served the king with conspicuous courage;[2] nor was the future prelate a stranger to military service. Indeed, he is said to have been 'in the field at Edge Hill fight in his cradle, and to have trailed a pike in Flanders under the Duke of York.'[3] At the Restoration he was promoted in rather a different way from those other clergy with whom

---

[1] The short *Life of Henry, late Bishop of London*, gives 1711 as the date of his death, but it is quite clear that John Robinson succeeded him as Bishop of London in 1713, and Compton died in the see.

[2] His father was slain at the battle of Hopton Heath.

[3] *Account of My Own Life*, by Edmund Calamy, ii. 40. As the battle of Edge Hill was fought in 1642, he was rather a large baby for a cradle.

he was afterwards brought into contact; he was made for his services a cornet of the Royal Horse Guards.[1] But soon afterwards he went to Cambridge, and became an officer in another sort of army, that of the Church Militant. Then his promotion was rapid; he was made Canon of Christ Church, then rector of Cottenham, then Master of S. Cross, then Bishop of Oxford, and finally Bishop of London, over which see he presided between thirty and forty years. He was also tutor to the two Princesses, Mary and Anne, both of whom he confirmed and married. Compton was called emphatically the Protestant Bishop. Not that any of the prelates, noticed or to be noticed, were one whit less hostile to the cause of Rome than he was; but Protestantism was his speciality. He was a great patron of converts from Popery and a generous friend to the French Protestant refugees. He manfully resisted the king's mandate to suspend Sharp for preaching against Romanism in 1686, and was consequently himself inhibited from exercising his episcopal functions by the new Ecclesiastical Commission,[2] and he lay under the sentence of suspension until the Revolution. This increased his popularity immensely; 'he was the darling,' writes a contemporary, 'of the city and parliament because of his great zeal in the discouragement of Papists and Popery.'[3] But his Protestantism, combined with the old leaven of his military training, led him into courses quite unbefitting his character.[4] A prelate fully armed, commanding a troop of soldiers and escorting a daughter in her de-

[1] Birch's *Life of Tillotson*, p. 185.
[2] *Memoirs of the Most Material Transactions in England for the last Hundred Years preceding the Revolution*, by James Welwood, p. 175.
[3] See the *Diary of Dr. Edward Lake*, 1677-8. In the next generation, Welwood (*ut supra*) declares that 'this noble prelate by a conduct worthy of his birth and station in the Church acquired the love and esteem of all the Protestant Churches at home and abroad.' (See also Sir John Reresby's *Diary*, p. 321.)
[4] He signed an invitation to the Prince of Orange, and then denied it in the presence of King James. (*Lathbury*, p. 17.)

sertion of a father is not an edifying spectacle; nor was it becoming his sacred character to appear in arms at Nottingham, and declare his readiness to fight for the Prince of Orange. He was much better employed in the proper work of his diocese, in which he appears to have been exceptionally active. One part of his system may be commended (if it be not impertinent in a simple priest to do so) to the imitation of prelates in our own day. He had a method of passing every summer in some new part of his diocese, riding out every day to visit in person the churches and parsonage-houses.[1] Thus seeing with his own eyes the poverty of many of the clergy, he naturally took a great interest in the attempt to better the condition of the smaller cures. He also upheld the Religious Societies, and his support of them greatly conduced to their success.[2] His 'Episcopalia,' six excellent Letters written to the Clergy of London in 1680-6, give one the impression of a man who was personally well-versed in practical work, and also of a man of firmness and independent judgment.[3] In fact he was a good working bishop, not perhaps strong enough to be advanced to the primacy, though he is said to have been twice disappointed at being passed over, but a more than respectable Bishop of London.

It really requires some little effort in one who desires to bring out the good points of the clergy of our period to do justice to the undoubted merits of one, who above all others is responsible for the evil reputation in which they are sometimes held. **Gilbert Burnet** (1643-1715) has shewn so extraordinary a propensity to depreciate the clergy in his 'History

---

[1] Nathaniel Salmon's *Lives of the English Bishops from the Restauration to the Revolution :—Compton.*

[2] See Secretan's *Life of Robert Nelson.*

[3] And certainly not 'weak, wilful, much in the power of others and strangely wedded to a party,' as Birch (*Life of Tillotson*, p. 185), copying Burnet (*Own Times*, iv. 388), and adding a little of his own, describes him. The *Episcopalia, or Letters of Henry, Bishop of London, to the Clergy of his Diocese,* are well worth reading.

of his Own Times,' that it is not surprising that a host of writers have entered their indignant protest against his misrepresentations. Lord Dartmouth,[1] Bevill Higgons,[2] Nathaniel Salmon,[3] Dean Swift,[4] Bishop Atterbury,[5] Roger North,[6] in the last century; Mr. Von Ranke,[7] Mr. Carwithen,[8] Mr. Debary,[9] Mr. Palin,[10] and many others in our own, have sufficiently exposed this great delinquency—a delinquency which is all the more provoking because it has naturally given a handle to adversaries to cast in the teeth of churchmen the evil report of the clergy which 'even one of their own order' has given.[11] Even Lord Macaulay, Burnet's admirer, admits that he possessed qualities which are fatal to accurate writing. A man who is 'boastful, vain, prone to blunder, provokingly indiscreet, often misled by prejudice and passion,'[12] 'utterly destitute of delicacy and tact,' 'viewing every act and every character through a medium distorted and coloured by party spirit,'[13] may have many good points, as Burnet unquestionably had, but surely he mistakes his vocation when he essays to write history; and, of all histories, a history of his own times, where these qualities are of course brought into most vigorous play. But our indignation at the historian must not blind us to the merits

---

[1] *Notes on Burnet's Own Times*, republished at Oxford in 1823.

[2] 'Remarks on Burnet's History of his own Times,' in Volume II. of Higgon's *Historical Works*, 1736.

[3] *An impartial Examination of Bishop Burnet's History*, &c., 1724; and *Lives of the English Bishops*, &c., passim, 1733.

[4] See Lord Dartmouth's work, *ut supra*.

[5] *Works*, passim.   [6] See *Examen*, passim.

[7] *History of England, principally in the seventeenth Century*, passim.

[8] *History of the Church of England*.

[9] *History of Church of England from the Accession of James I. to* 1717.

[10] *Church of England*, 1688–1717.

[11] See, *inter alia*, Edmund Calamy's *Account of My Own Life*, i. 457, and *passim*; *William Carstares, a Character and Career of the Revolutionary Epoch*, by R. H. Story, p. 23 &c.; *History of England* in the *Cabinet Cyclopædia*, a work full of abuse of the Church and clergy, *passim*; and Skeat's *History of the Free Churches*, p. 97.

[12] Macaulay's *History of England*, i. 413.   [13] *Id.* i. 593.

of the man. Burnet's greatest detractors have not denied that he was a most energetic worker, both as a parish priest and as a bishop. No diocese was more carefully attended to by its bishop than that of Salisbury during the twenty-six years when Burnet presided over it. When he reluctantly consented to become tutor to the Duke of Gloucester, it was on the express condition that he should reside at Windsor, which was then within the diocese of Salisbury, and be allowed ten weeks every summer for the purpose of visiting his people:[1] with his usual energy he made the very most of these ten weeks, so that there was hardly a corner of the diocese which was not well acquainted with the burly form and loud voice of its bustling bishop.[2] Nor was his energy confined to his own local work. He thought nothing of going frequently from London to Woodstock to visit the poor penitent Earl of Rochester, of whose conversion he was to a great extent the human instrument.[3] He found time to write letters of good advice to Lady Russell;[4] and if he was not the sole originator of that excellent work Queen Anne's Bounty, as he characteristically claims to have been, there is no doubt that he deserves a great share in the credit of it. Though a self-conscious, he was certainly not a selfish man; he refused many preferments and was liberal with his money, as many, both clergy and laity, to whom he was a kind friend, could have testified.[5] His 'Pastoral Care,' 'Discourses to his Clergy,' 'Conclusion to his History,' and 'Lives of Bishop Bedell, Sir Matthew Hale, and John, Earl of Rochester,' all breathe the spirit of sincere piety, though even some of these are provokingly interspersed with his favourite depreciation of the clergy.

---

[1] *Life of Burnet*, by his son Thomas, p. lvii.   [2] *Id.* p. xliii.

[3] If this depended solely upon Burnet's own testimony we should have to take it *cum grano*; but Mr. Parsons, in his funeral sermon on Rochester, admits the Earl's obligation to Burnet.

[4] *Some Account of Rachel Wriothesley, Lady Russell*, p. 54.

[5] *Life*, p. lxii.

He frequently hurt delicate spirits by his utter want of tact,[1] and his officiousness sometimes led him to interfere in matters which he had much better have left alone; but in most cases one can see that the offence arose from a sort of blundering impulsiveness which really meant well, though it took an odd way of shewing it. He lived in turbulent times, and he was the very last man to pour oil on the troubled waters; he filled a very prominent place in the Church, while both by training and temperament he was not calculated to sympathise with its principles. There is therefore not the slightest difficulty in accounting for his unpopularity among the clergy, without having recourse to the utterly gratuitous explanation attributed to Lord Halifax, that 'his parts were a shame and his life a scandal to them.'[2]

If contrasts be effective, we could not find a more perfect one than by turning from Salisbury to the neighbouring diocese of Bath and Wells. **Thomas Ken** (1637-1711) is one about whose career and character there is a charm which strikes the imagination and kindles the enthusiasm of churchmen of every shade. So happy a blending of humility and gentleness with undaunted courage, of firm and uncompromising principles with large-hearted charity to others, of homely simplicity with delicate refinement, has rarely been found in any age. All the details of his life are interesting, but for these the reader must be referred to his

[1] E.g. Norris of Bemerton, Kettlewell, Dodwell, Ken, Ralph Thoresby.

[2] With these words Thomas Burnet, in the life of his father, concludes a long quotation of abuse of the clergy and praise of Gilbert Burnet, supposed to have been written by Lord Halifax, but of which Thomas had 'mislaid the original.' Lord Dartmouth boldly declares that Lord Halifax could never have said or written anything of the sort, because he had often heard him express anything but a favourable opinion of Bishop Burnet; 'therefore,' he says, 'I believe Tom must have been mistaken, and that it will appear, if ever he finds the original, to be in his father's, not in the marquis's, own handwriting.' Be this as it may, it was surely most injudicious in the son (who appears to have been a fac-simile of his father) to insert so sweeping and slanderous an accusation of all prelates except Bishop Burnet, unless he could produce far better authority than he does.

biographers.[1] It must here suffice to say that he was born at Berkhampstead, and educated at Winchester. Having lost his parents in early life, he was brought up as a kind of adopted son by his eldest sister, the wife of Izaac Walton, with whom he lived in retirement until the Restoration. One can hardly help wishing that the ages of the two brothers-in-law had been reversed, for what a fine subject Ken would have made for one of Walton's 'Lives'! Ken was ordained in 1660, and was soon afterwards presented by his friend Lord Maynard to the small living of Easton in Essex. He did not stay there long, for Bishop Morley gathered round him in the Close at Winchester those true friends of his adversity, the whole family of the Waltons, and among them, Ken, whom he made his chaplain and to whom he gave the living of Brighstone. He next became vicar of East Woodhay, and, contrary to the evil custom of the time, gave up Brighstone on the day of his appointment. He was next made Prebendary of Winchester, and then chaplain to the Princess of Orange in Holland; his influence over the Princess was very great, too great to please her husband, who had no desire that his wife's principles should be moulded by so staunch a churchman, though Ken's Protestantism was as strong as that of the 'Protestant hero' himself. We next find Ken accompanying Lord Dartmouth, as his chaplain, to Tangier. On his return to Winchester he showed his courage by refusing to receive the king's

---

[1] The best known are:—*A Short Account of Bishop Ken's Life*, by W. Hawkins, Esq., his executor and connection, prefixed to Ken's *Prose Works*. This was the earliest life; it was republished (with the *Prose Works*) by J. T. Round in 1838. *Life of Bishop Ken*, by Canon Bowles (1830), whose poetical temperament brought him into harmony with Ken's own. *Life of Thomas Ken, Bishop of Bath and Wells*, by a Layman (1851), which is, perhaps, the best life of all. A brief but well-written memoir by 'G. M.' (George Moberley) prefixed to the Oxford edition (1840) of Ken's *Manual of Prayers for the Winchester Scholars*, and another by J. H. Markland, prefixed to his edition of Ken's *Prayers for the Visitors at Bath* (1849), and a good sketch in Miss Strickland's *Lives of the Seven Bishops*; and we are now promised another biography by the Dean of Wells.

mistress into his lodgings; and this proved unexpectedly a stepping-stone to his advancement; for King Charles, who knew what was right though he did not practise it, determined that 'the good little black man who refused a lodging to poor Nell' should have the next bishopric. He was accordingly made Bishop of Bath and Wells (1684); and his sweet simplicity of character, his earnest desire to do good, his courage to resist evil, and his large-hearted charity were as conspicuous in this new station as when he was in a humbler one. He interested himself in the poor at Wells, who were, he thought, oppressed by their employers, and vainly tried to improve their condition; he shewed an equal concern for the rich but frivolous company who frequented 'the Bath,' and wrote some prayers for their use. He was wont to question beggars on their knowledge of religion, and found them so hopelessly ignorant that he thought the only chance of improvement was in raising up a new generation who should be better taught; so he furnished his clergy with books for the use of children, and became one of the first pioneers of those charity schools which afterwards became so prominent a feature in Church life. He boldly interfered in behalf of the unhappy sufferers in the Monmouth Rebellion, though the damage they had done to his beloved Cathedral must have wounded him in a tender point. He attended his royal patron's death-bed, where even Burnet owns he 'spoke like one inspired.' And as he had boldly rebuked the licentiousness of one brother, he reproved no less boldly the bigotry of another, as his famous sermon at Whitehall, and his courageous reply to King James's remonstrance on the subject testify. Strong churchman though he was, he would take no part in the persecution of dissenters, saying that the Church itself taught him charity towards those who differed from him. His munificence to the French Protestant refugees stands out prominently even among the munificence with which they were everywhere treated. In fact his liberality generally was so great, that after the Revolution he retired under protest from his see, a poorer man than when he accepted it; but he found a supply for his simple wants in the house of his friend Lord Weymouth at Longleat, where he passed the remainder of his blameless life; when Longleat was full of company, he fled to Naish House, the quiet retreat of two pious ladies, the Misses Kemeyse, which he speaks of as 'his retirement into the desert from the noise and hurry of the world.' Like Archbishop Sharp, he had the happy knack of contriving to be friendly with nonconformists without in the least compromising, or being even suspected of compromising, his own Church principles. Among his most frequent visitors at Longleat was a nonconformist gentleman, Mr. Walter Singer, father of Mrs. Elizabeth Rowe, the poetess. In his retirement he composed his immortal morning, evening, and midnight hymns; and in doing so, the old man's memory had wandered back to the scenes of his boyhood; for they were composed, together with the exquisite prayers with which they were originally bound up, for the use of the Winchester scholars, who are recommended to sing the evening hymn every night before they went to bed. His death was of a piece with his life; he awaited it calmly, travelling about with his shroud in his portmanteau; and that the poetical charm which invests his whole life might not be wanting from the last scene of all, an almost dramatic incident occurred at his funeral. He was buried under the chancel window at Frome, the children from the village school which he had established and taught followed him to the grave; the funeral, as was usual in those days, took place before daybreak; but just as the last spadeful of earth was cast upon the grave, the sun rose, and the children sang with their clear young voices,

> Awake, my soul, and with the sun, &c.

The name of Ken has been universally reverenced. Not only has he been an object of hero-worship among High

Churchmen, but men who had little sympathy with his views have sung his praises. Dryden probably took him as the living model of his 'Good Parson'; the most licentious of kings never ceased to value more highly than any other clergyman this most severely virtuous of prelates; Lord Macaulay, whose way of thinking was certainly very different from Ken's, declares that 'his character approaches as near as human infirmity permits to the ideal perfection of Christian virtue.'[1] The admiring biographer of Archbishop Tenison, who had naturally no fellow-feeling with nonjurors as such, yet owns Ken's 'sanctity of life and most approved character in everything else but his want of submission to the prince whom God had set over him!' If it were the wont of the Church of England to canonise, Saint Thomas of Bath and Wells would find a place among the first in her calendar.

If Ken was the saintliest, by far the strongest prelate of the day was universally thought to be **Edward** Stillingfleet (1635–1699). He was educated at S. John's, Cambridge, of which college he was elected fellow in 1653. Having been privately ordained by Bishop Brownrigg, he was presented by Sir R. Burgoin, in whose family he had been tutor, to the country living of Sutton in 1657. Here he wrote his 'Irenicon' and 'Origines Sacræ.' In 1665 he was appointed by the Earl of Southampton to the important living of S. Andrew's, Holborn. In 1670 he was made Canon, and in 1678 Dean, of S. Paul's; in 1689, Bishop of Worcester, in which see he died. The precocity of Stillingfleet's genius was the wonder of his contemporaries. According to Pepys he was recommended for S. Andrew's by 'the Bishops of Canterbury [sic], London, and another because they believed him to be the ablest young man to preach the Gospel since the Apostles.' Pepys himself was much impressed with 'the great Stillingfleet,' 'the famous young Stillingfleet.'[2] When Stillingfleet

---

[1] *History of England*, i. 311.   [2] See *Diary* for April 1665.

attended Bishop Sanderson's Visitation in 1662, the bishop could hardly believe that the young man before him was really the famous Stillingfleet whom he knew only by his works. And he was not one of those precocious geniuses whose later performances disappoint their early promise. He sustained his reputation well to the end. Burnet described him in 1688 as 'the learnedest man of the age in all respects.'[1] One of the reasons given why he was not advanced to the primacy after the death of Tillotson was 'because his great abilities had raised some envy of him.'[2] As a controversial writer against Romanists, Nonconformists, and Socinians, Stillingfleet was regarded by churchmen as their strongest champion; and it is a striking testimony to his high character that among all the opponents whom his controversial works raised against him, not one hinted a doubt of his piety and purity of motive.

Posterity has perhaps hardly endorsed the extraordinary reputation for mental power which Stillingfleet unquestionably had among his contemporaries. Perhaps one reason may be that circumstances have brought into the greatest prominence the two works, (oddly enough, the first and the last he ever wrote,) in which he appears at the least advantage. The 'Irenicon' was written when he was a mere boy; and it is obviously unjust to tie a man down all his life to the opinions he expressed at two-and-twenty. Most men's effusions at that early age have died still-born; and Stillingfleet has to pay the penalty for being too precocious, by laying himself open to the charge of inconsistency.[3] The 'Irenicon' has acquired adventitious celebrity owing to the effect which it produced upon the mind of John Wesley; and churchmen owe a grudge to the

[1] See the letter of Dr. Burnet to the Prince of Orange, in the *Hon. H. Sidney's Diary*, &c.
[2] White Kennet's *History of England*, iii. 682.
[3] Howe unquestionably made a point when he said 'the rector of Sutton was a very different person from the Dean of S. Paul's;' but it should be added that the rector was at the time too young to be even a curate.

juvenile author for having helped to bring about the greatest
secession from the Church that has ever occurred. The
last work in which Stillingfleet employed his pen was
against John Locke; and in this again the great prelate
does not appear at his best. But to appreciate Stillingfleet's
immense reputation among his contemporaries, we must
not look at these works, nor yet at his chefs-d'œuvre, the
'Origines Sacræ,' and 'Origines Britannicæ,' which were
and are more admired than read by any but specialists.
We must look at his letters, his addresses to his clergy, and
his sermons. He had a lawyer-like mind, and a good
knowledge of law, which served him in good stead at a
time when such legal knowledge was of the utmost service
to a clergyman. He also expressed himself in a clear,
nervous style, and was altogether a formidable adversary to
the enemies of the Church and a tower of strength to her
friends.

For plain, homely piety, and practical usefulness in his
generation, no name stands higher on the roll of English
churchmen than that of **William Beveridge** (1638–1707).
He was born at Barrow in Leicestershire, and was educated,
like Stillingfleet, at S. John's College, Cambridge. He was
like Stillingfleet, too, in shewing extraordinary precocity.
At the early age of twenty he published a learned treatise
on the Oriental tongues, which is said to have been held in
great esteem. And he was only twenty-three when he published the work by which he is now perhaps best known, his
'Private Thoughts on Religion.' In 1661 Sheldon gave
him the living of Ealing; and in 1662 he was appointed
by the Lord Mayor and Aldermen of London to the living
of S. Peter's, Cornhill. This was the scene of his successful labours for many years. He was a model parish
priest, and was called 'the great reviver and restorer of
primitive piety.' His influence over young men, who
abounded in that busy centre of trade, was very great.
They thronged to his weekly Communion and formed

religious societies under his direction. Denis Granville (who had been ordained at the same time with him by the great Bishop Sanderson) 'laboured to imitate the pietic and indefatigable diligence of the renowned Dr. Beveridge,'[1] and told his friend Comber, that 'the devout practice and order in his (Beveridge's) church doth exceedingly edifie the city, and his congregation encreases every week.'[2] Beveridge was a retiring, modest man, and 'all the preferment he was ambitious of was to go from his flock in Cornhill unto the shepherd and bishop of souls.'[3] But a clergyman who was eminently successful in so prominent a sphere could hardly be overlooked. He was made successively Archdeacon of Colchester, Prebendary of Canterbury, and finally Bishop of S. Asaph, having refused to take any see vacated by a nonjuror. In all these spheres Beveridge shewed the same activity which had marked his long incumbency of S. Peter's, Cornhill, and when he was dying, 'one of the chief of his order' said of him, 'There goes one of the greatest and one of the best men that ever England bred.'[4] It depends upon what we mean by 'greatest,' as to whether the first epithet can be accepted, but few will deny him the title to be one of the best. His voluminous writings will be noticed in a future chapter.

Much resembling the career of Beveridge was that of **Simon Patrick** (1626-1707). He was born at Gainsborough and educated at Queen's College, Cambridge, where, as we have seen, he was deeply influenced by the Platonists. Traces of his Platonic training he certainly retained to the end, but busy parochial and episcopal work is not conducive to the Platonic frame of mind, and these traces are only observable by those who can read between the lines. After having been chaplain for a while in the house of Sir Walter

---

[1] *Remains*, Part I., p. 236.   [2] *Life of Dean Comber*, p. 179.
[3] *Life and Errors of John Dunton*, p. 363.
[4] *Life of Bishop Beveridge*, prefixed to *Private Thoughts* (edition 1825).

St. John, an estimable gentleman with Puritan leanings, he became vicar of Battersea in 1658, and of S. Paul's, Covent Garden, in 1662. What Beveridge was at S. Peter's, that Patrick was at S. Paul's, one of the most energetic and successful parish priests of his day. In his 'Autobiography' he says nothing about his success; *that* we learn from other sources; but he *does* tell us how kind his parishioners were to him, and how this kindness was increased after he had stayed to minister to the many sufferers in his parish during the Great Plague. Four services were held every day in his church, and the offertories were enormous. In 1669, the Bishop of Lincoln (Fuller) in vain tempted him with the offer of the Archdeaconry of Huntingdon, 'which,' he says, 'I declined, thinking myself unfit.' Neither could he be lured away by the Lord Chancellor's offer of 'the best living in England,' S. Martin's in the Fields. In 1672 he received, 'unsought,' a prebend at Westminster, and in 1679 the deanery of Peterborough. Burnet, who could hardly have agreed with all his opinions, nevertheless recommended him to King William as 'a man of an eminently shining life, who will be a great ornament to the Episcopal order,'[1] and accordingly he was made Bishop of Chichester in 1689, and of Ely in 1691. His long experience in parochial work stood him in good stead as a bishop; he could speak with authority on what had been done in London, and encourage his clergy to go and do likewise.[2] He was an uncompromising churchman, and, like many of his day, was too ready to call in the aid of the secular arm,[3] at least in his earlier ministerial life. His 'Autobiography' is rather a disappointing

---

[1] Letter quoted in *Sidney's Diary*.

[2] See his address to the clergy *On the Work of the Ministry*, 1697, and other Charges, &c.

[3] See his *Friendly Debate between a Conformist and Nonconformist*, which, he tells us, he was 'provoked to write by the insolence of many dissenters.' It is said, however, that in his old age he regretted having written this, and had the candour publicly to acknowledge his error. See Williams' *Life of Sir Matthew Hale*, p. 218, *note*.

book, inasmuch as it does not give us so vivid a picture either of the man or the times as one hopes to find in such a work; but it is negatively valuable as an index of the writer's character; we must go elsewhere, and we do not go in vain, to find a true estimate of his diligence and other virtues, for he does not utter, directly or indirectly, a word of self-praise.

Our admiration of Bishop Ken must not prevent us from doing justice to the merits of his unwelcome successor, **Richard Kidder** (d. 1703). His 'Autobiography' gives one the impression of an earnest, worthy man, and everything that we hear of him from other sources confirms the impression, while we may be sure that if there had been anything to be said to the contrary, his unpopularity in his bishopric would have caused it to be made the most of. But he was clearly a 'conformist' rather than a churchman by conviction. He held the living of Stanground during the Rebellion, and was ejected from it as a non-conformist under the Bartholomew Act; 'but his good sense overcame his prejudices, and he finally adopted the National Church.'[1] This is not exactly the sort of stuff out of which a bishop should be made, least of all a bishop to succeed Ken; and one can hardly be surprised at the indignation of the latter at the intrusion of the 'Latitudinarian traditor' into his beloved see. To do justice to Kidder, it must be said that he shewed the most unfeigned reluctance to accept the bishopric, and when, in an evil hour for his own happiness, he *did* accept it, he strove his very utmost to do good in his diocese.[2] But his position was most unfortunate. Ken was of course a man to leave his mark upon his clergy; was it likely that they would welcome a bishop of the principles of Kidder? His charges are evidently the productions of a man who is thoroughly

[1] Noble's *Biographical History of England,* ii. 101.
[2] 'No man,' he says plaintively, 'could come into a place with a more hearty desire to do good, than I did.'

in earnest; and the anecdote of his boldly refusing to vote in accordance with the expressed wishes of King William's ministry, shews that he was no time-server.[1] Robert Nelson had so high an opinion of his worth that he procured for him the important living of Barnes; and he is said to have been most kind to his ejected predecessor at Bath. In short, as in the case of Tillotson, one cannot help feeling pity for a good man forced into an unsuitable post, and that pity is heightened by his tragical end. He was slain with his wife, in bed, by the fall of a stack of chimneys in the Great Storm of 1703.

It was an intense relief to Bishop Ken,—as perhaps it will also be to the reader,—to turn from the contemplation of poor Bishop Kidder to the happy choice which was made in selecting the next occupant of his see. The relations between Thomas Ken and **George Hooper** (1637-1727) had been peculiarly close. They had been chaplains together to Bishop Morley; they had been chaplains successively to the Princess of Orange at the Hague, where both had incurred the displeasure of the lady's husband by presenting to her too strong a type of English churchmanship; they had been successively incumbents of East Woodhay. Ken therefore had had abundant opportunities of knowing Hooper's worth, and was more than willing to resign his claims to his beloved see in favour of 'the excellent person whom all mankind except these Jacobites have a high esteem of; one most able and willing to preserve the depositum.'[2] The good old man was not wrong

---

[1] 'The Bishop once received a message from the Minister of William III., conveyed by a pert gentleman, requiring him to attend the House of Peers to vote for a measure the Court wished to pass. "You must vote," said the messenger. "Must vote!" replied the bishop. "Yes, must vote; consider whose bread you eat." "I eat no man's bread but poor Dr. Ken's, and if he will take the oaths he shall have it again. I did not think of going to the Parliament, but now I shall undoubtedly go, and vote *contrary* to your commands.'—*Noble*.

[2] Ken to the Bishop of Norwich, March 7, 170¾. See Bishop Ken's *Prose Works* (ed. Hawkins, p. 69).

in his estimate. Hooper's career before he was made
bishop had been a singularly promising one. He was one
of the many great churchmen who had been educated
under Dr. Busby, who said that 'Dr. Hooper was the best
scholar, the finest gentleman, and would make the com-
pleatest bishop that ever was educated at Westminster,'[1]—
an almost unrivalled compliment, considering it came from
one through whose hands the very flower of English
churchmen had passed. When he was at Woodhay, his
neighbour Isaac Milles 'had for this excellent person the
greatest respect and honour, as every one had that ever
was acquainted with his rare endowments. He frequently
mentioned him as the one, of all the clergymen whom he
had ever known, in whom the three characters of perfect
gentleman, thorough scholar, and venerable divine met in
the most complete concordance. He used to say 'that he
was a public blessing to that country, whose affection and
esteem he amply repaid by the invaluable example he set
them.'[2] From Woodhay Hooper was appointed Dean of
Canterbury; and after the accession of Queen Anne was
made Bishop of S. Asaph,[3] and, a few months later, of Bath
and Wells. He was a most successful bishop; beloved in
his diocese, and so happy there that he refused, first the
bishopric of London, and then the archbishopric of York.[4]
He died at Wells at the patriarchal age of ninety, leaving
behind him a high reputation for learning and sanctity,
which his printed works fully bear out.[5]

The history of the immortal seven who stood in the gap
when King James strove to force his religion upon an un-

[1] See *A Short Character of Bishop Hooper*, from Mr. Mist's *Journal* of October 1727, annexed to vol. i. of Dr. Coney's *Sermons*.

[2] *Life of Isaac Milles*, p. 88.

[3] The Prince of Orange was so annoyed at his bold attempts to keep the Princess firm to her Church principles, that he said that if he ever had anything to do with England, Dr. Hooper should continue Dr. Hooper still.

[4] MS. *Life of Hooper*, by Mrs. Prowse.

[5] See the *Works of Bishop Hooper*, 2 vols. 8vo., reprinted at Oxford in 1855.

willing country is so familiar, that a few words will suffice for the five out of the seven who have not been already noticed.

John Lake (1628–1690), like many others, had fought in the royal army before he received Holy Orders. He was conspicuous for his courage in the defence of Basing House and Wallingford Castle, and the same courage, shewn in a different sphere, was a conspicuous feature in his character in after-life. Having been episcopally ordained during the Commonwealth, he became vicar of Leeds at the Restoration, and was shortly after removed by Sheldon to the rectory of S. Botolph's, Bishopsgate. He was next appointed to a canonry at York, and a characteristic anecdote is told of his courage while residentiary there. An evil custom prevailed of lounging about the nave of the Minster while divine service was being performed in the choir. One Shrove Tuesday the bold Canon walked from his seat in the choir, pulled off the hats of the people who were walking and talking in the nave, and, in spite of alarming symptoms of a riot, insisted upon their either coming to worship God, or leaving the church. He was made successively Bishop of Man, of Bristol, and of Chichester. In the latter place it is said that he was so popular with the gentlemen of Sussex that 'his coming to them after his release from his trial was like the return from banishment of S. Athanasius or S. Chrysostom.'[1] At Chichester he established a weekly Communion, revived the good old custom of preaching in the nave, and won over many dissenters to the Church. Though he boldly resisted King James's illegal acts, he never doubted to whom his allegiance was due; in the exciting autumn of 1688 he bravely went about his diocese, exhorting his clergy to obey God and the king, and when the oaths to King William were required he at once threw up his preferment, 'considering that the day of death and of judgment

---

[1] See Prebendary Stephens' *Diocesan History of Selsey—Chichester* (S.P.C.K.), p. 237.

were as certain as August 1 and February 1.'[1] He died the next year, making just before his death a remarkable 'profession,' so outspoken and so earnest that we cannot wonder at its contributing much to settle wavering non-jurors.[2]

Francis Turner (1636-1700) was the friend and contemporary of Ken at Winchester; he succeeded Bishop Gunning at Ely in 1685, and fully maintained the high standard of efficiency in the diocese which had been bequeathed to him by his vigorous predecessor. His Letter to the Clergy in 1686 gives one the idea of a man whose whole soul is in his spiritual work, a man of deeply earnest piety, and of ripe experience in clerical duties; and such, if we may trust Lady Rachel Russell, was the opinion generally held of him.[3] It is therefore a sad pity that the troubled circumstances of the times should have diverted him from spiritual to political affairs. It is quite beside the purpose of the present work to discuss his supposed share in the Fenwick plot, but whatever we may think of his conduct after the Revolution, justice should be done to his previous merits as a clergyman and a prelate, and sympathy must be felt with a man who voluntarily left the affluence of Ely for the life of destitution in which he died. **Thomas White** (1630-1698), was a popular preacher while rector at All Hallows' Barking; he was afterwards domestic chaplain to the Princess Anne, whose Church principles he had no small share in forming. He was made Bishop of Peterborough in 1685, and then set himself to remedy the abuse of pluralities. **William Lloyd** (b. 1627), Bishop of S. Asaph, and afterwards of Worcester, had a high reputation for piety

---

[1] See *A Defence of the Profession of Bishop Lake on his Death-bed*, &c., February 1690.

[2] See *Defence* &c. *ut supra*, and *Rapin's History of England*, vol. xii. 274, *note*.

[3] She writes to Dr. Fitzwilliam, 'Lord Bedford expresses himself hugely obliged to the Bishop of Ely [Turner], your friend, to whom you justly give the title of good, if the character he has very generally, belong to him.' (*Letters of Lady R. Russell*, p. 308.)

and learning;[1] he was a friend of Mr. Dodwell, who was wont to accompany him in his episcopal visitations; but his conduct to the nonjurors after the Revolution was not commendable.[2]

The last of the redoubtable seven, **Sir Jonathan Trelawney** (1650–1721), successively Bishop of Bristol, Exeter, and Winchester, is now known chiefly as the subject of a verse too familiar to need quoting, and as the friend and patron of Atterbury, who has immortalised his name in the preface to his well-known sermons. According to Atterbury, Trelawney was an excellent bishop; but it must in fairness be added that in some of the letters in the 'Trelawney Papers' he does not appear in a very favourable light.[3]

There were several other eminent prelates, some of them more eminent in their way than those already mentioned, who for various reasons only require a passing notice in a work like the present. There are few names, for instance, which stand higher in the scroll of Church worthies than that of **George Bull**, who was allowed to continue in the obscurity of a country living during the greater part of the time with which this sketch is concerned, and was only promoted to the distant see of S. David's in his declining years. But it will suffice to refer the reader to Mr. Nelson's biography of this great man, which has been republished in our own day in a very cheap form, and is thus accessible to all.[4] For the same reason it is unnecessary to dwell on the life of that most estimable of men and bishops, and most moderate of nonjurors, **Robert Frampton**, Bishop of Gloucester, whose life by a contemporary has lately been given to the world.[5] Again, during the later part of our period

---

[1] See Granger's *Biographical History of England*, vol. iii. p. 288, and Lord Macaulay's *History of England*, vol. i. p. 560.

[2] See Brokesby's *Life of Dodwell*, p. 39.

[3] The *Trelawney Papers* were edited by W. D. Cooper for the Camden Society in 1853. See vol. ii. of the *Camden Miscellany*.

[4] Nelson's *Life of Bull*, price 3s. 6d., published by J. H. Parker, Oxford, 1845.

[5] Price 2s., by the Rev. T. S. Evans.

no man took a more conspicuous part in Church questions
than **Francis Atterbury**, Bishop of Rochester, who did very
great service to the Church in a direction where it was
much needed, by vindicating her independence as a spiritual
power; but he can only be noticed in passing, partly because
he will come before us again as a preacher, and partly
because he was too much mixed up with politics to come
within the proper sphere of this chapter.[1] And there is
George Smalridge, Atterbury's successor in one preferment
after another, the 'Favonius' of the 'Tatler,'[2] the friend of
Bishop Bull, and 'the great favourite,' says Bishop Bull's
biographer, 'of all learned and good men throughout the
realm;'[3] but the period of Smalridge's greatest fame was
the Georgian era. Another friend and patron of Bull
was Bishop, or to give him his latest title Archbishop,
Nicolson, who is also praised highly by Nelson.[4] Regarded
on his merits, both moral and intellectual, there is not one
single prelate who more deserves an extended notice than
Bishop **Cumberland**, the most Platonic of those who were
not actually identified with the Cambridge Platonists, who
combined with the rarest intellectual gifts, which he used
diligently for the enrichment of the worlds of science and
theology, the utmost modesty and unselfishness, and also the
utmost energy in the practical work of his calling. But he
was too much 'sui generis' to be noticed at length as a
typical specimen of his order. Bishop **White Kennet's** is a
name which ought not, in common gratitude, to be entirely
omitted in a work like the present, for he is by far the
most voluminous of all contemporary writers respecting
the period with which we are dealing; Bishop **Stratford** of
Chester, too, should be mentioned as one who in a quiet,

---

[1] Another reason why I have not dwelt longer on the lives of Atterbury and Bull is because the lives of both these great men have been written by me for the *Dictionary of National Biography*.
[2] Nos. 72 and 114.   [3] *Life of Bull*, p. 224.
[4] *Ibid.* p. 135. See also Archbishop Nicolson's *Correspondence*, published 1809, *passim*.

unpretending way, did much good in his diocese,[1] and whose name is little known for this very reason, because he was content to stay at home and attend to his proper work, mixing very little in the general life of the Church outside. **Bishop Wake**, again, was regarded by his contemporaries in his early ministerial life as a youthful prodigy of learning and piety,[2] and in his later advancement (which did not reach its climax until a later period than this work embraces) justified the high expectations he had raised.[3] And **Bishop Fowler**, Frampton's successor at Gloucester, deserves mention, who had the honour of being the first to declare his refusal to read King James's illegal declaration; and **Bishop Offspring Blackall** of Exeter, of whom a brother prelate says that 'he never met with a more perfect pattern of a true Christian life in all its parts,' and the utterer of these words himself, **Sir W. Dawes**, Archbishop of York, who will come before us again as a preacher; and the saintly **Thomas Wilson**, Bishop of Sodor and Man, whose episcopate extended so far into the Georgian era[4] that it is difficult to realise that he was actually bishop during the whole of Queen Anne's reign and a great portion of her predecessor's; and **Bishop Lloyd** of Norwich, 'in whose wisdom and integrity Sancroft placed the greatest confidence,' and 'in whom,' writes one who knew the circum-

---

[1] He was a zealous supporter of the Societies for the Reformation of Manners in Cheshire (see Churton's *Life of Bishop Pearson*, prefixed to Pearson's *Minor Theological Works*, p. xcv.), and contributed largely both with his purse and personal efforts towards the repairing of Chester Cathedral. (Archbishop Nicolson's *Correspondence*, pp. 175-6.)

[2] Burnet calls him 'the wonderfullest young man in the world, and the most popular divine now in England' (*Letter to the Prince of Orange*, 1688); and Evelyn (*Diary*, i. 638), speaks of 'dining at Dr. Tenison's with Bishop Ken, and that young, most learned, pious and excellent preacher, Mr. Wake.'

[3] Canon Perry calls him 'a most able and excellent prelate, a good scholar and divine, and a more distinct and decided churchman than his predecessor,' i.e., Dr. Tenison, whom he succeeded as Archbishop of Canterbury. (*History of Church of England*, iii. 278.)

[4] Forty-one years.

stances well, 'the diocese was deprived (when he became a nonjuror) of a very able and worthy pastor, an excellent preacher, a man of great integrity and piety, who thoroughly understood all the parts and duties of his function, and had a mind fully bent to put them all in execution for the honour of God and good of the Church on all occasions;'[1] and **Bishop Thomas** of Worcester, whom Dr. Hickes, the dean, terms 'that excellent bishop worthy of everlasting memory.'[2] And least of all ought we to forget his successor **Bishop Hough**, whose firmness did so much to save the Church of England at a most perilous crisis;[3] and whose extreme gentleness and amiability in later years won the admiration of very different types of men.[4] But if all these were noticed at length this work would swell to the dimensions of a biographical dictionary. We must pass on to notice some of the many worthy clergymen who never attained the mitre.

Next to bishops come deans; and among those who attained to the latter dignity one of the best known is **Humphrey Prideaux** (1648–1724). He was one of the many eminent men educated under Busby at Westminster and Fell at Christ Church. His life was mainly spent in country cures,—Bladon, Saham, and Trowse, until his appointment to the deanery of Norwich in 1702. He

---

[1] *Life of Dr. Prideaux, Dean of Norwich*, published 1748, p. 73.

[2] Preface to the *Collection of Dean Hickes' Letters*, vol. i.

[3] When he successfully resisted King James's attempt to thrust a Romanist president upon Magdalen College. 'I see,' he said, 'it is resolved that the Papists must have our college; and I think all we have to do is to let the world see that they take it from us, and that we do not give it up;' and he acted up to his words. (See *Life of Bishop Hough*, by J. Wilmot, Esq., 1812, p. 30 &c.)

[4] It was long after our period that Pope, speaking of the

        Trophies which deck the truly good and brave,

says,

        Such as on Hough's unsullied mitre shine,

and that Lord Lyttelton (his neighbour when he was at Worcester), in his *Persian Letters*, praised him as worthy to convert a Mahometan.

might probably have risen higher, but he was no preferment-hunter. Both his own writings and all that we are told of him give us the impression of a plain, sensible, clear-headed man, of solid rather than brilliant talents, which he devoted with thorough earnestness to the interests of religion. As a successful pioneer in the great work of Foreign Missions,[1] as a would-be reformer of our Universities at home, as a diligent pastor, archdeacon, and dean, and as a writer whose works are still valued, he passed a life which was most useful, but would not be very interesting to the reader if described in detail.[2]

It will be more lively if not more edifying to pass on to Dean **Dennis Granville**, who was a sort of clerical Pepys, his 'Remains' giving us almost as racy and naïve an account of ecclesiastical as the immortal 'Diary' does of civil life. Granville began his clerical career rather too prosperously. As a son-in-law of Bishop Cosin, and a son of the Earl of Bath, he was loaded with preferments. In the very year after his ordination he received a stall in Durham and the archdeaconry of Durham with the rich living of Easington annexed, and six years later he was promoted to a golden stall and the rich living of Sedgfield. The consequence was, 'Jeshurun waxed fat and kicked.' The rich young pluralist, instead of staying at one at least of his cures, was constantly careering about at Oxford and in London, to which latter place he was attracted by having had the questionable advantage of being made chaplain to Charles II. This of course disgusted so strict a disciplinarian as Bishop Cosin, who complains of his son-in-law's non-residence, and still more of the reason he gave for it, which was in truth the strangest ever given for absenteeism, 'because his wife had taken physic.'[3] In 1674 the future

---

[1] Mr. Anderson, in his *History of the Colonial Church* (ii. 471, &c. &c.), does full justice to his efforts in this direction.

[2] It will be found fully described in his *Life*, published 1718.

[3] *Correspondence of Bishop Cosin* (Surtees Society), Part II. p. 262.

dean received a wholesome check. He was arrested for
debt; and henceforth his life was a much more edifying
one. Indeed, all through, there were the germs of better
things in him. We must not judge of his pluralities and
non-residence by the standard of the present day. Granville was really a conscientious man, but, ' more temporum,'
his conscience was quite easy so long as he took care to
provide proper substitutes, and he *did* take care to do this.
His instructions to his curates at Sedgfield and Easington
are most strict in the enforcement of duty, and, it may be
added, most amusing. The curates are to carry out to the
very letter all the rubrics of the Church, and he bitterly complains when they will not do so. He set himself to establish
weekly Communions in all the Cathedrals in the land, and
daily prayers in all the considerable country parishes in
his archdeaconry. ' Through this work,' he writes, ' will I
go, or I will make a filthy bustle before I dye among the
clergy of the nation, contemptible mushrump and silly
ignoramus as some do make me.' And really he seems to
have had extraordinary success in both attempts. He also
waged internecine war against ' Pulpit Prayers,' and was
considered generally, as he tells us, ' the most exact observer
of rubricks and stickler for conformity.' His directions for
the government of his own household are strict to the verge
of asceticism, and so are the rules he lays down for his
own personal conduct. Hammond among the dead and
Beveridge among the living were the two whom he took for
his models; Gunning was his spiritual father, and Barnabas
Oley the object of his utmost admiration. The standard he
set before him was thus a high one, and to judge by the
testimony of his contemporaries, he did not fall far behind
it. ' You had an uncle,' wrote Lord Lansdowne to Mr.
Bevill Granville on his taking Holy Orders, ' whose memory
I shall ever revere; make him your example. Sanctity
sat so easy, so unaffected and so graceful upon him, that
in him we beheld the very beauty of holiness. He was as

cheerful, as familiar and condescending in his conversation, as he was strict, regular, and exemplary in his piety; as well-bred and accomplished as a courtier, as reverend and venerable as an apostle.' Sir G. Wheler bears witness to his 'pious and devout temper,' and B. Oley, we are told, always spoke of him as 'that truly pious and devout good man, Dr. Granville.' It is necessary to give prominence to such testimony as this because there is a slightly ludicrous flavour about Granville's 'Remains' which might prevent us from doing justice to the serious side of his character. It is hardly necessary to say that the dean refused the oaths and was much annoyed with his friends who took them. It was a grievous blow to him when his ideal clergyman, Beveridge, submitted to the new régime; but his cup of indignation was full when another old friend, Thomas Comber, took, not only the oaths, but also the deanery from which he himself was ejected. With a grim sort of humour he addressed Comber as his steward, and directed him how he might safely send sums of money due from the 'intruder into the deanery' to himself the true dean. It made no difference to Granville's conduct, that on going to St. Germain's he was slighted by the master for whom, as he tells us, he gave up 'the best deanery, the best archdeaconry, and one of the best livings in England,' for it was for a principle, not for a person, that he was contending.

His successor (if, *pace* Dr. Granville, we may venture to call him so) is now better known for his writings than for his life. But **Thomas Comber** (1644-1699) was an excellent man, deservedly held in the highest reputation by his contemporaries, and by none more so than by Dean Granville before that unpardonable offence of the deanery. The early part of his ministerial life he passed in a country cure (East Newton), where he daily used the common prayer, and commenced the work on which his fame chiefly rests, 'The Companion to the Temple.' Of the four years which he spent as precentor at York, and the ten during which he was Dean of Durham, little need be said, except that he quietly did his duty as a sound, moderate English churchman. Like Archbishop Sharp he had the happy knack of gaining not only the esteem but the friendship of men of the most widely different views, without in the least compromising any of his own principles; he numbered among his most intimate friends, Tillotson, Hickes, Sharp, Dolben, and Hilkiah Bedford.[1]

Lancelot Addison (1642-1703), Dean of Lichfield, deserves a passing notice, if not for his own sake, at least for his son's, who has left us a graceful tribute to his merits as a father;[2] but he will come before us again in connection with the devotional works of the period.

The name of Addison naturally suggests another and still greater name, that of **Jonathan Swift** (1667-1742). It would of course be absurd to hold up Swift as a model of Christian piety, but it is equally absurd to represent him as a hypocrite without virtue or religion. That he really believed, and, in his own queer way, strove to practise the religion he preached, becomes the more apparent the more his life becomes known; and in more ways than one the Church owes him a debt of gratitude which she has been somewhat slow to pay. No clergyman ever strove more consistently to benefit his order. Though he plunged deeply into the vortex of politics, he never forgot that he was a clergyman, and he did more, perhaps, than any man of his time to raise the social position and improve the straitened circumstances of his less distinguished brethren, and the great effort to provide for the spiritual wants of London in Queen Anne's time was largely due to his powerful pen.

Another dean to whose merits scant justice has been done, while his weak points have been ruthlessly exposed,

---

[1] See the *Memoirs of Dean Comber*, by his great-grandson.

[2] See *The Tatler*, No. 235, said by some to have been written by Steele, but more probably by Addison.

is **George Hickes** (1642-1715). He may have been betrayed into intemperate language[1] under grievous provocation, and he may have contended intemperately for politico-ecclesiastical doctrines which at one time even Tillotson and Burnet held as well as himself; but there are few men in whose writings can be found a more full and lucid explanation of the position of the Church of England in relation both to the Romanists and the Nonconformists; and for his principles he was ready to sacrifice everything. His many firm friendships show that he was not only a loveable man, but also no mere bigot. For not only did he maintain the closest intimacy with the saintly Kettlewell and Robert Nelson—in itself a strong presumption in favour of his piety—but he did not break off his friendship with Dean Comber after the latter took the oaths;[2] he was on terms of visiting with Ralph Thoresby, and lived with White Kennet at Amersden 'as intimate friend,' after the two had taken violently opposite sides at the Revolution settlement,[3] and the fact of his old pupil, Sir George Wheler, taking preferment in the Established Church did not in the least interfere with the mutual respect and affection they entertained for one another.[3] His immense learning, as displayed both in his works on the Northern languages and in all his controversial treatises, does not come within our scope, but the points mentioned above are worth noting as a proof that even the extremest advocacy of nonjuring principles did not cut off the holder from sympathy with those who, after all, belonged to the same branch of the Church Catholic, though they were divided by accidental circumstances.

John Kettlewell (1653-1695) has been mentioned as a most intimate friend of Hickes. A short sketch of his character will shew how much this speaks for the merits of

---

[1] See *Life of Comber*, p. 360.

[2] See *Short Life of Bishop W. Kennet*, published 1730, and Granger's *Biographical History of England*, p. 120.

[3] See the *Memoirs of Sir George Wheler, Prebendary of Durham*, passim.

the latter. What Ken was among bishops, Kettlewell was among priests, the saintliest and most fascinating character which a Church and age rich in such characters produced. Nature had moulded him in a form which was eminently susceptible of Christian impressions. 'He was from a child of a most devout temper, and would frequently retire to pray by himself and would try to make his schoolfellows pray. He was blessed with a happy constitution, and the grace of God begat in him betimes a hatred of sin and the very appearance of evil.'[1] He went to Oxford, taking his degree at S. Edmund's Hall, and then being elected fellow of Lincoln College, mainly through the influence of his friend Hickes, who was a member of that society. He was then appointed (1682) vicar of Coleshill, by the excellent Lord Digby, who first offered the living to Mr. Rawlett of Newcastle; but the Newcastle people persuaded their vicar not to leave them, and then Lord Digby asked him to recommend 'some one like himself; one who had at heart the salvation of souls, and to whom with safety to his own, he might commit that cure.'[2] Rawlett recommended Kettlewell, with the happiest results. For seven years Kettlewell lived at Coleshill, the very model of a country parson, on the most intimate terms with his patron, and endeavouring to present to his parishioners the full system of the Church, and recommending it to them by his own

---

[1] *Life of Kettlewell* (1719) p. 7. It seems rather base to quote and derive information from a work, and then abuse it, but really this *Life* is most disappointing. In the first place it is buried alive, being only published (so far as I know), together with Kettlewell's works in two huge folio volumes, which is provoking, because Kettlewell the man is more interesting than Kettlewell the writer; but in itself it is not a finished performance. If one might venture to use a homely adage on such a subject, one would be inclined to say 'Too many cooks spoil the broth.' It was 'compiled from the collections of Hickes and Nelson' by Francis Lee; a short sketch by any one of the three (they were all competent men), would have been more acceptable. What an admirable companion to his monograph on Bishop Bull, Nelson might have made!

[2] *A Brief Account of the Life of Rev. Mr. John Rawlet* (published anonymously, but known to have been written by Dr. Bray).

saintly life. His work was most unfortunately interrupted by the Revolution, for he could not conscientiously take the oaths, and therefore lost his living. The rest of his short life was spent in London, where he helped the Church in the only way left to him—by his pen; but he was called to his rest before he quite reached his prime. To praise or quote praise of Kettlewell would be indeed 'to paint the lily, gild refined gold.' 'Such,' says his friend Nelson, 'was the lustre of his eminent sanctity that all parties paid a due veneration to his character;'[1] and the remark appears to have been literally true. From the hagiologist's point of view he holds the very highest place of all among the clergy of his day.[2]

Kettlewell's life was so calm and uniform, that it will be perhaps a relief to turn, by way of contrast, to a more chequered career. Let us take that of **Samuel Wesley** (1662-1735), a remarkable man himself, and the father of a still more remarkable family. He began life as a dissenter, but no one can accuse him of conforming for the sake of gain, for his conformity alienated all his relations from him and rendered him absolutely penniless. He managed, however, to struggle through his Oxford career as a 'poor scholar' or servitor at Exeter College, and, having received Holy Orders, took a London curacy of 28*l.* a year. He was next made chaplain to the Marquis of Normanby, and in 1691[3] rector of South Ormsby in Lincolnshire. Thence he was transferred, through the influence of Queen Mary, to the rectory of Epworth, and here he spent the remainder of his life, nearly forty years. Owing to the extraordinary celebrity of his sons, we are admitted to a close insight into this clerical household, and the first thing that strikes

---

[1] See Nelson's preface to Kettlewell's *Five Discourses on so many very important points of Practical Religion.*

[2] Higher, I think, even than Ken. There is a little asperity (not unprovoked) in some of Ken's later letters, and he did not do justice to the merits of his unfortunate successor, Bishop Kidder. Not a trace of such a spirit can be found either in the writings or the life of Kettlewell.

[3] Not 1693, as Dr. Adam Clarke states.

us is the ardent spirit of piety which evidently pervaded it. Samuel Wesley's sons gratefully own the spiritual advantages they derived from their training in the Lincolnshire rectory. 'Such a family,' writes Dr. Adam Clarke, 'I have never heard of, read of, or known.'[1] Another point is the intellectual activity which was a characteristic of the whole household. Both father and mother and all the numerous family at Epworth were most highly cultured. And a third point, alas! is the pecuniary difficulties in which the household was perpetually involved. These were perhaps inevitable when the rector had no private means, not a large preferment, but a very large family; whether or not they were further increased by his propensity to rush into print may be doubtful. He began to publish at eighteen, and was henceforth incessantly enriching the world with some fresh lucubration in prose or verse. His poverty did not cripple his energy. We hear of him frequently in London, now attending the meetings of Convocation as proctor of the diocese, now preaching most energetically in behalf of the Societies for the Reformation of Manners, now (according to his son John) composing the famous speech which Dr. Sacheverell delivered at his trial before the House of Lords. Poverty was not his only trouble. He was too conscientious to wink at vice in his parishioners, whatever their rank might be. At Ormsby he came into collision with the great man at the Hall,[2] who was living in open sin. At Epworth his troubles thickened; his parishioners appear to have been a more turbulent set than those among whom his successor is now ministering; they were strongly suspected of having set fire to his house, and when he voted according to his conscience at a county

---

[1] *Memoirs of the Wesley Family*; a dull but useful book. A good account of Wesley at Epworth will also be found in *The Mother of the Wesleys*, by the Rev. John Kirk, 4th edition, 1866, and in Tyerman's *Life of Samuel Wesley*.

[2] That is, not, as has been erroneously stated, the Marquis of Normanby, but the Earl of Castleton, the then tenant.

election, they all but made the place too hot to hold him.[1] They did succeed in getting him arrested for debt and sent to Lincoln gaol. In all his troubles he had one firm friend who helped him continually with counsel and money, and the mere fact that Archbishop Sharp, who never countenanced the unworthy, was faithful to him from first to last, is a proof, if proof were needed, of Wesley's worth. He was an excellent parish priest, and his efforts gradually told upon the religious and moral state of his parish. His son Samuel took him as the model for the portrait of his

> Parish priest, not of the pilgrim kind,
> But fixed and faithful to the post assigned,
> Through various scenes with equal virtue trod,
> True to his oath, his order, and his God.

His literary performances, good, bad, and indifferent (for he has left us specimens of all three), do not come within the scope of this chapter.

Neither the piety, nor the intellectuality, nor the poverty of Epworth rectory was exceptional. Another instance of all these will be found in the life of **Joseph Bingham** (1668–1723). Like Wesley he was a man of great literary activity, but, unlike Wesley, he wisely and with eminent success concentrated his attention mainly on one great department of Christian literature.[2] The story of his life is a sad one. It is sad to hear of a good and able man struggling with an infirm and sickly constitution, in want of many necessary books, which he had no opportunity to see and no ability to purchase, copying with his own hand pages of 'Pearson on the Creed' 'to supply the deficiencies of a mutilated book, because he could not afford to spend a few shillings on a

---

[1] His vote at this election gave offence to his eccentric brother-in-law, John Dunton, who complains that 'Sam left the Whigs that gave him his bread to herd with the high-flyers.' (*Life and Errors of John Dunton*.) He had previously declared 'I bid him farewell till we meet in Heaven, and there I hope we shall renew our friendship, for, human frailties excepted, I believe Sam Wesley a pious man.'

[2] *The Antiquities of the Christian Church.*

new copy,' and losing at one blow in the South Sea Bubble all the small and hard-earned profits of his literary work; saddest of all, perhaps, to think that the University of which he was an ornament blighted his career at the outset by affixing on him a most undeserved stigma of heresy on the subject of the Trinity. When he was obliged to resign his fellowship at University College in consequence, the famous Dr. Radcliffe had the honour of presenting him to the small living of Headbourne Worthy without solicitation. Here he lived for fifteen years, when Sir J. Trelawney, Bishop of Winchester, conferred on him the better living of Havant. He deserved a better fate, for, besides being one of the first theological writers of the day, he was a man of blameless life and a good parish priest; but the early part of the eighteenth century is not the only time when a modest, retiring man, with little worldly wisdom, has been allowed to live and die neglected.[1]

Passing from the calm of a country village to the centre of busy London, we find another clergyman in whom were combined straitened circumstances with the very highest reputation and worth. **Anthony Horneck** (1641-1697), a German by birth, was educated at Queen's College, Oxford, and was for two years vicar of All Saints in that city, where he gave promise of his subsequent fame as a preacher and parish priest. We next find him in the family of Lord Torrington, and then incumbent of a country living in Devonshire. But he did not find his proper sphere of work until he was appointed in 1671 preacher at the Savoy Church.[2] For twenty-six years he retained this post, doing

[1] See the *Life of Joseph Bingham*, by Richard Bingham, his lineal descendant, prefixed to the first volume of his works in nine vols.

[2] That is, the chapel attached to the Savoy Palace in the Strand. The parishioners of S. Mary-le-Strand, whose church had been pulled down in Edward VI.'s reign to help to build Somerset House, were attached to this Savoy chapel, and Dr. Horneck regarded them as his parishioners. Hence, by an odd mistake, when S. Mary's church was rebuilt it was popularly called the Savoy Church (see Paterson's *Pietas Londinensis*, Byrom's *Journal*, &c.), which of course it was not and never had been.

incalculable good throughout the whole neighbourhood, for which he received a very scanty pittance, derived mainly from the offerings of his congregation. His income was still further reduced at the Revolution, many of his supporters being offended because he took the oaths. But he struggled on manfully, and ultimately received a little addition to his income by being appointed Prebendary of Westminster, and subsequently of Wells. As a hard worker Dr. Horneck would bear comparison with the most active clergyman of our own active day. His biographer [1] tells us that 'the Doctor had so much business he had hardly time to eat his meat;' and we can well believe it, for the demands upon his time must have been incessant. Besides the ordinary duties of a town clergyman, of which he took a high standard and fulfilled most assiduously, he was one of the originators and principal directors of the Religious Societies, was constantly resorted to in cases of conscience, and was a zealous writer in opposition to Romanism. He died in harness, his end, no doubt, being hastened by overwork. His reputation was undoubtedly very high. Evelyn,[2] the second Lord Clarendon,[3] Burnet,[4] John Dunton,[5] Noble,[6] and many others, bear witness to his sanctity and energy. And yet he was clearly not altogether a popular man. When there was some talk of his being removed to S. Paul's, Covent Garden, the parishioners expressed so strong a repugnance that the appointment

---

[1] Dr. Kidder, Bishop of Bath and Wells.

[2] 'A most pathetic preacher, a person of a saintlike life.' (*Diary* for March 5, 168$\frac{2}{3}$.)

[3] 'I would be very glad to have Dr. Horneck here (in Ireland). I know his piety and course of life, &c.' (*Correspondence of Henry Hyde, Earl of Clarendon*, &c., i. 264.

[4] 'A very good and pious preacher, and a very popular man.' (*Letter to the Prince of Orange*, 1688.)

[5] 'A man of that great usefulness that none ever yet saw him without reverence, or heard him without wonder. A long fixed star in the firmament of the Church.' (*Life and Errors* &c., p. 163.)

[6] 'Endeavoured to reform himself and his flock according to the purest and best model of Christianity. (*Biographical History of England*, i. 102.)

could not even be thought of.¹ He was the only one of those recommended by Burnet to King William who never attained to any high place in the Church; and his name was connected more than that of any other man with the odium which most cruelly attached to the Religious Societies. Lord Clarendon's respect for him only led to his being asked now and then to sup with his lordship. Perhaps, being a foreigner, he did not quite understand English ways, or perhaps he offended people by what White Kennet calls his zealous flights and raptures. At any rate there was some bar to his preferment; his history leaves upon one the sad impression of a good man worked to death, without having received on this side the grave, any adequate recognition of his services.

The name of **Thomas Bray** (1656–1730) will come prominently before us in another connection, but it would be a grievous omission not also to notice his holy, active, and self-denying life in a sketch of the clerical worthies of the period. He was born at Marton in Shropshire. His first clerical work was in a curacy near Bridgnorth; he was then chaplain in the family of Sir T. Price at Park Hall in Warwickshire, who gave him the donative of Long Marsin. His exemplary conduct there attracted the notice of a neighbour of kindred spirit, John Kettlewell, and also of Kettlewell's patron, Lord Digby, who presented him first to the living of Overwhitacre (endowing it with the great tithes), and then to that of Sheldon. But Bray was not destined to live and die in the obscurity of a country parsonage. In 1696 he was sent by the Bishop of London, as his commissary, to Maryland, 'to model that infant church.'² And here commenced that noble work in connection with the Societies,³ to which he devoted not only

---

¹ See Tillotson's letter to Rachel, Lady Russell, in her *Life and Correspondence*.
² *Public Spirit Illustrated in the Life and Designs of Dr. Bray* (published 1746).   ³ See *infra*, chapter v.

his time and energy, but all his little private fortune. In 1706 he was appointed to the living of S. Botolph-without-Aldgate, and was as diligent and successful there as he had been in his other and better known work.[1] It is pleasing to know that the virtual founder of our two oldest Church Societies left behind him a name which was respected by all parties.

If the lives of all the good clergy who were no further distinguished than by quietly doing their duty in their own little corner of their Lord's vineyard were even sketched, 'the world could not contain the books that should be written.' Even of those who lived during the short period which this work embraces, the list has already swelled to a portentous size, and it must suffice to touch very cursorily upon some who have not yet been noticed. A typical instance of the good country parson pure and simple, who was neither a writer, nor a dignitary, nor in any way connected with the general course of Church life, may be found in the interesting biography of **Isaac Milles** (1638-1720).[2] He was a sort of George Herbert without his poetry, and passed all his clerical life in country cures, being for nine years curate at Barley near Royston, six years vicar of Chipping Wycombe, and nearly forty years rector of Highclere near Newbury. In every one of these charges he worked with exemplary zeal and success, winning over nonconformists to the Church, and gaining the respect of all his parishioners, rich and poor. Such lives are not much noticed on earth, but they are not lived to *be* noticed on earth; they *have* their reward where it is sought. And we gather from his biography that

---

[1] See Paterson's *Pietas Londinensis*, sub finem, and Ralph Thoresby's *Diary* for May 15, 1723: 'Walked to the pious and charitable Dr. Bray's, at Aldgate; was extremely pleased with his many pious, charitable, and useful objects;' and on May 21, 1723, 'At Dr. Bray's church the charity children were catechised. Prodigious pains so aged a person takes; he is very mortified to the world; takes abundant pains to have a new church, though he would lose 100*l.* per annum.'

[2] *Life of the Rev. Isaac Milles, once Rector of Highclere.* It was republished at Oxford in 1842.

Isaac had about him clerical neighbours equally obscure and equally exemplary. Some of these have been noticed in the previous section.

Dr. Marsh, vicar of Newcastle-on-Tyne, is said to have been 'a person of great worth and excellency,' and so famous a casuist that he was resorted to as 'a common oracle' by all the neighbourhood.[1] **Mr. Cock,** vicar of S. Oswald's, Durham, was 'unwearied in his labours as a parish priest;' a short life of him was written by Dean Hickes.[2] **Dr. R. Lucas,** Prebendary of Westminster, 'was one on whose character,' writes the editor of his Sermons (to be noticed presently), 'it is needless to enlarge, for the world has done him justice;'[3] but alas! the world has a short memory and has quite forgotten him. **Mr. Plaxton,** the eccentric but worthy vicar of Woodside near Leeds, 'was,' according to Ralph Thoresby,[4] 'very commendably serious and industrious in his cure and brought his parish into an excellent order;' and, according to the same authority, an equally high character belonged to two successive vicars of Leeds, the 'learned and pious **Mr. Milner,**' who became a nonjuror, and 'the excellent **Mr. Killingbeck,** a public blessing to this parish, whose preaching was very affecting and his life answerable to his preaching, truly excellent.'[5] **William Burkitt,** who is now known, where he is known at all, either as a devotional writer or as a man who was before his time in the deep interest which he took in Foreign Missions,[6] was also conspicuous for his blameless life and his self-denying and successful work as vicar of Dedham in Essex.[7] **Charles Leslie** is known for his powerful reasoning on every

---

[1] See *Life of Ambrose Barnes,* p. 412.

[2] See *Remains of Granville,* Part II. p. 169, and Low's *Diocesan History of Durham* (S.P.C.K.).

[3] *Sermons on Several Occasions and Subjects,* in three volumes, 2nd edition, 1722.

[4] Diary for April 3, 1714.   [5] *Diary* for 1690.

[6] See Anderson's *History of the Colonial Church.*

[7] See the *Life of the Rev. Mr. William Burkitt, Vicar and Lecturer of Dedham in Essex,* by N. Parkhurst, 1704. There is a touching story of his

controversial topic, theological and political, of the day, but almost every page of his writings shews also the intense earnestness of his Christian convictions, and we are not surprised to learn from his friend the second Earl of Clarendon, that he was 'a man of incomparable life, who would well do his duty in whatever he undertook.'[1] Further information about this very able and good man will be found in the welcome biography which has been published since the above was written by his relation, the Rev. R. J. Leslie. **Mr. Smythies**, who shares with Dr. Horneck the chief credit of originating the Religious Societies, and who worked contentedly and most successfully for nearly thirty years in a London curacy, is said (and we can well believe it), to have been 'a most humble and hearty Christian, of great patience and resignation to the will of God, and a most mortified man to the world.'[2] **Jeremy Collier**, whose gallant crusade against the most popular amusement of the day raised against him many enemies who jealously watched his conduct, but could find no flaw in it, was 'in the full sense of the word a good man.'[3] **John Johnson**, of Cranbrook, who is now chiefly known as an able exponent of the sacrificial character of the Holy Eucharist,[4] was known also in his own day as an excellent parish priest, equally successful in a town and a country cure.[5] The name of **John Fitzwilliam**, the worthy successor of Ken at Brighstone,[6] and afterwards Canon of Windsor and rector of Cottenham, is pre-

death. 'There were several persons by his dying bed, who, having declared that under God he had been the instrument of their conversion, put him into an extasie of joy.'

[1] Letter from the Earl of Clarendon to the Bishop of Down and Connor, May 25, 1686, in his *Correspondence*, i. 405. See also the testimony of Leslie's friend, Dr. Hickes, in the prefaces to *Several Letters which passed between Dr. G. Hickes and a Popish Priest*, &c., 1705.

[2] *Life and Errors of John Dunton*, p. 369.

[3] Lord Macaulay's *History of England*, ii. 106.

[4] Johnson's *Unbloody Sacrifice*; highly valued by Robert Nelson.

[5] See the *Life of the Rev. John Johnson, Vicar of Cranbrook*, by the Rev. T. Brett, LL.D., published 1748.

[6] See *A Layman's Life of Ken*, pp. 73 and 536.

served from oblivion in the correspondence of Rachel, Lady Russell, where many letters between the two may be found equally creditable to both. Lady Russell, who had known him from her childhood as the honoured chaplain of her father, the Earl of Southampton, consulted him in her sad widowhood on all matters connected with religion, used the prayers he composed for her benefit, and described his life as a 'continual doing good to souls;' the fact that the Doctor became a nonjuror, while the lady of course supported the Revolution settlement, did not in the least affect the confidence between the two.[1] **Thomas Baker** was another estimable nonjuror, who succeeded in securing the good word of men who had no sympathy whatever with such views.[2] And last but not least, the saintly **Nathaniel Spinkes** was a man of whose piety, unselfishness, and culture his brother nonjurors might well be proud, as they obviously were (see 'Life' prefixed to his 'Devotions'); but he will come before us again in connection with the devotional works of the period.

Space forbids us to linger on names which are connected with the Church literature rather than the Church life of the time, though there is no reason to think that their lives were unworthy of their writings. Among such were William Wotton, the great linguist, rector of Middleton Keynes; William Wall, author of the standard work on

---

[1] See *Some Account of the Life of Rachel Wriothesley, Lady Russell*, by the editor of Madame du Deffand's *Letters*, 3rd edition, 1820, p. 45, &c. Also the *Letters of Lady Rachel Russell*, 3rd edition, 1792, *passim*.

[2] Bishop Burnet wrote to him (1714), 'I have so great a regard both to yourself and your friends that I am extremely sorry the Church hath so long lost the service of so worthy men.' (Quoted in the *Memoirs of the Life and Writings of Rev. T. Baker, B.D.*, of S. John's College, Cambridge, from the papers of Dr. Zachary Grey, 1784, p. 32.) He is termed by William Whiston, 'a worthy and learned man,' and by Lord Macaulay, 'the upright and learned Thomas Baker.' (*History of England*, i. 694.) It is curious that both should (quite correctly) apply to him the epithet 'learned,' as the work by which he is best known (*Reflections upon Learning*) was written for the express purpose of showing the insufficiency of human learning.

Infant Baptism, vicar of Shoreham; Dr. Grabe, 'the greatest man,' wrote his friend Hickes, 'in divine literature, as well as the greatest example of Christian piety of this age. I wish I may be worthy to sit under his feet in Heaven;'[1] Henry Wharton, Sancroft's chaplain, and a writer of considerable repute;[2] John Strype, that useful but rather heavy chronicler, who lived in a country vicarage for sixty-eight years; Dr. Towerson, rector of Welwyn, whom we shall meet again as a devotional writer, and whom Dr. Stanhope calls 'a man remarkable for a modest, gentle, affable temper which gave a lustre to his accomplishments;' Dr. Stanhope himself, to whom his contemporaries were indebted for reintroducing them to Bishop Andrewes' 'Devotions,' and whose character seems to have somewhat resembled that of Lancelot Andrewes; Josiah Woodward, minister of Poplar, the historian of the Religious Societies; Edward Wells, Rector of Cottesbach, and author of numerous works, one of which has been revived by 'J. H. N[ewman]' in our own day; T. Fulwood, Archdeacon of Totnes, the opponent of Hickeringill; Thomas Brett, rector of Betteshanger, and a keen controversial writer on the nonjuring side; and, above all, William Cave, a really classical divine, whose 'Primitive Christianity' and 'Historia Literaria' ought to live as long as the English language lives.

There were many other clergymen who were eminent men in their way, but for one reason or another hardly fall within the purview of this chapter; such e.g. as William Sherlock, Dean of S. Paul's and Master of the Temple;

---

[1] Letter from Dean Hickes to Dr. Charlett, Master of University College, Oxford, November 20, 1711. Hearne does not think so highly of him (see *Reliquiæ Hearnianæ* (Bliss), pp. 280-2), but then there were not many of whom Hearne did think highly. Robert Nelson praises him greatly. (See *Life of Bishop Bull*, pp. 219, 221.)

[2] See *Excerpta ex Vitâ MS. Henrici Whartoni a seipso scripta*. Also Wharton's very able and bold *Defence of Pluralities as now practised in the Church of England*, 2nd edition, 1703.

Joseph Glanville, rector of Bath, who has been termed 'the most original thinker of his age;'[1] Ralph Bathurst, Dean of Wells and President of Trinity College, Oxford, and a most successful ruler in the latter capacity;[2] Dr. Aldrich, Dean of Christ Church, whose 'Logic' has tortured many of our older readers, and who has the rare honour of being unreservedly and enthusiastically praised in Hearne's diary;[3] and Dr. John North, Prebendary of Westminster.[4] These and others may have been more notable men of their kind than some who have been noticed, but they can hardly be regarded as typical specimens of *Church* life. But enough, it is hoped, has been said to shew that if any one were disposed to write a hagiology of the English clergy, abundant materials might be found between 1660 and 1714, to furnish a perfectly truthful and thoroughly edifying narrative.

[1] See *Cambridge Characteristics in the Seventeenth Century*, by J. B. Mullinger (the Le Bas Prize), 1867.

[2] See *Life and Literary Remains*, &c., by T. Wharton.

[3] See *Reliquiæ Hearnianæ*. Diary for December 16, 1710, and for April 24, 1717.

[4] See *Lives of the Norths*, by Hon. Roger North, vol. iii.

CHAPTER III.

FAITHFUL LAITY OF THE PERIOD.

(1) *MEN*.

THE trials through which the Church passed during the Rebellion naturally gave a peculiar tone to the Christian character of her laity as well as of her clergy. There was even about the Court itself, and still more through the country at large, an increasing body of faithful lay church-people who by their examples were a living protest against the prevailing profligacy and infidelity; and these were bound together to a greater extent than has perhaps ever been the case before or since by a common bond of churchmanship which had not yet begun to be separated into 'High and Low.'[1] It is purposed to deal with the laity as with the

---

[1] That is, the names had not yet arisen. Of course the sentiments expressed by each existed long before; but after the Restoration the common attachment to the ancient Church of England caused the holders of them to put their differences in the background. As to the names, it is rather difficult to learn when they first became general. Roger North protests against White Kennet for antedating them (*History of England*, vol. iii. 381) in terms more vigorous than polite: 'How in the D—l's name he comes to antedate the distinctions of High and Low Church, I cannot imagine. There was not any dream then [at the Restoration] of a distinction in the Church, but all were Conformists or Nonconformists, Churchmen or Dissenters, Loyal or Fanatic.' (*Examen*, &c., p. 344.) In 1705, Bishop Hooper protests against 'the invidious distinction' (see Tindal's *Continuation of Rapin*, vol. xvii. pp. 208-9); and in 1707 Bishop Fowler of Gloucester does the same from an opposite point of view (*Visitation Charge*). Swift declares in 1703 that 'the very ladies are divided into High Church and Low.' See also South and Burnet on the subject. At the Revolution the titles had become common.

clergy, that is, not to *conceal* their defects, but still to bring into greater prominence the evidences which they gave of a true spirit of piety.

Mention has been made of the interesting biography of John Barwick, written by his brother. That brother might have written an equally edifying Autobiography, for John and Peter were 'par nobile fratrum.' **Peter Barwick** (1619–1705), like his brother John, was a fellow of S. John's College, Cambridge, but was ejected for refusing to take the Covenant. He was faithful to the Church all through the troubles, and at the Restoration was made one of the king's physicians in ordinary. He took a house near S. Paul's for the convenience of attending daily upon God's service in the Cathedral.[1] During the Plague, so far from shrinking from this duty, he seems to have kept the officiating clergy up to their work,[2] and his medical experience seems to have been useful to them in recommending the proper recipients of charity.[3] But though the brave Doctor could not be driven out by the Plague, he was forced out by the Fire which burnt his house down the next year. He then took up his residence, as the next best locality, in the neighbourhood of Westminster Abbey. There he lived for nearly forty years, 'and constantly frequented the six o'clock Prayers, consecrating the beginning of every day to God, as he always dedicated the next part to the poor; not only prescribing to them gratis, but furnishing them with medicines at his own expense, and charitably relieving their

---

[1] See the preface to the *Life of John Barwick*, ed. 1721, translated by Hilkiah Bedford.

[2] See Ellis's *Original Letters*, 2nd series, vol. iv., Letter 310, Rev. S. Bing to Dr. Sancroft, Dean of S. Paul's, August 3, 1665. 'Our prayers are continued three times a day, but not our attendance, for now there are but three petty canons left; the rest are out of town. . . . Dr. Barwick asked me, as all others, if I heard anything concerning the monthly Communion, the which I could say little to.' (See also August 10, 1665.)

[3] *Ellis*, iv. p. 30, J. Tillison [sic] to Dr. Sancroft, August 15, 1665. 'I have acquainted Mr. Bing with your intentions of charity towards the poor, and shall take Dr. Barwick's advice before it be disposed of.'

other wants.¹ Here he drew up the life of his brother; and in this useful combination of literary and practical work he passed his blameless life until 1694, when his eyesight entirely failed him. He was of course obliged then to 'give up his practice, and gave himself to contemplation and the conversation of a few friends, particularly his neighbour Dr. Busby,'² until at the great age of eighty-six, he 'passed from darkness unto light.'

Another fine old veteran who, like Barwick, was staunch to his Church all through the Rebellion, was **Sir Richard Browne**, the father-in-law of John Evelyn. For nineteen years he was the ambassador of the phantom English Court at Paris, and there kept up the Anglican services, 'which were attended by crowds of exiles every Festival and Lord's Day.'³ The same informant calls him 'a man never sufficiently to be praised,' and attributes it to his opening the doors of the embassy chapel to such men as Bramhall, Cosin, and Earle, that very few of the exiles, and those of a vacillating and weak mind, went over to the Papists.⁴ Among those who comforted themselves by attending devoutly to the liturgy of the persecuted Church of England in Sir R. Browne's chapel, were the two princes, the Dukes of York and Gloucester, the former actually forfeiting his mother's favour by preventing his younger brother from turning Romanist!⁵ In fact, so nobly did Sir R. Browne

---

¹ Hilkiah Bedford's Preface, *ut supra*.   ² *Ibid.*

³ ' Hoc sacellum ' (Sir R. Browne's) ' exules singulis Festis ac Dominicis diebus frequentes adierunt.' (*Vita Joannis Cosini*, T. Smith, published 1707.)

⁴ ' Ecclesia Anglicana, licèt domi miserrimum in modum oppressa et sub jugo ingemiscens, foris in exteris plagis, et præsertim in Galliâ sub D. Ricardi Bruni, equitis aurati, viri nunquam satis laudandi, qui per novemdecim annos usque ad restauratam monarchiam istâ Legatione ibi summâ cum laude functus est, auspiciis et tutelâ, quasi triumphos agebat ; et perpauci, vacillantis et infirmæ mentis, ad Pontificios, illâ relictâ, deficiebant.' (*Ibid.*)

⁵ See Miss Strickland's *Lives of the Queens of England: Henrietta Maria*, vol. iv. pp. 306 and 308.

uphold the Anglican Church that its divines 'in their disputes with the Papists (then triumphing over it as utterly lost) used to argue for its visibility and existence from Sir Richard Browne's chapel and assembly there.'[1] It is pleasant to know that one who so bravely supported the Church in her adversity lived long enough to enjoy more than twenty years of her prosperity, for he did not die until the spring of 168⅔.

From the father-in-law we naturally turn to the son-in-law, **John Evelyn** (1620-1706). It has been insinuated that as Evelyn managed to secure, more or less, the favour of all parties during the many changes of his long life, he must have trimmed his sails to meet the popular gale, but there really is no ground for the insinuation. He was from first to last true to his principles as a churchman, but he was so thoroughly amiable, pious, and peaceable a man that he conciliated, without any unworthy compromise, all parties. He certainly had the courage of his opinions or he would never have published his bold 'Apology for the King,' at a time when it was a capital offence to write or speak in favour of the exiled monarch; and his 'Account of England,' written in the person of a foreigner who is disgusted with what he sees of the state of our country in 1659, though published anonymously (as the nature of the work required) must have run the risk of having its true authorship easily traced. At any rate, a churchman should be the last person to complain of Evelyn's favour with the usurping powers, for he invariably used the opportunities which that favour gave him to help distressed churchmen, of whom he has been deservedly termed, 'the Mecænas or the Gaius.'[2] He had the honour of befriending Jeremy Taylor in more ways than one; he cheered him with his company, relieved his poverty, and when that great divine was cast into the Tower used all his influence to procure his release. He continued to worship according to the rites of the Church when such

---

[1] Evelyn's *Diary* for February 12, 168⅔.
[2] *Quarterly Review* for July 1871, 'Jeremy Taylor.'

worship was strictly prohibited, and on one occasion at least, did so with imminent danger to his life.[1] But he held no preferment of which he could be deprived; he was a gentleman of private means, and his marriage added to those means; in right of his wife he became possessor of Sayes Court, near Deptford, the place which he has immortalised in his Diary. He passed the period of his enforced, but very acceptable, retirement during the Rebellion after the fashion of many private gentlemen, partly abroad and partly at home, enriching his mind with varied knowledge. The author of the 'Silva' is best known for his skill in horticulture, but he also took a lively interest in natural philosophy, and was one of the earliest members of the Royal Society. He also studied the fine arts, and wrote with intelligence on sculpture, architecture, and medals. In fact, it was because loyal gentlemen like Evelyn were thrown upon their own resources, and took refuge from the storm of politics and theology in purely intellectual pursuits, that the Restoration period was so remarkable for its intellectuality. On the return of the king it was a sense of public duty rather than inclination, that drew him from his privacy. As a Commissioner for the Sick and Wounded in the southern ports during the Dutch war, he had boundless scope for the exercise of his Christian charity;[2] as a Commissioner for the Rebuilding of S. Paul's he had opportunities of helping that Church, which he calls the most primitive, apostolical, and excellent on earth;[3] and as Commissioner of Trade and Plantations he had the opportunity of securing the ministrations of that Church for the colonies.[4] His duties often required him to be *in* the Court, but he was never *of* the Court. After having witnessed splendid vice flaunting itself there, 'I went home,' he writes, 'contented, to my

---

[1] See Walker's *Sufferings of the Clergy*, pp. 304-5.

[2] See, *inter alia*, Pepys' *Diary*, describing Evelyn's scheme for an Infirmary.

[3] *Diary* for October 2, 1685.

[4] See Anderson's *History of the Colonial Church*, iii. p. 45.

poor but quiet villa. What contentment can there be in the riches and splendour of this world purchased with vice and dishonour?'¹ He found, indeed, even at the Court, patterns of piety and virtue;² but under none of the monarchs with whom he was connected did he find any encouragement of the type of religion which he loved. When the immorality of Charles was exchanged for the bigotry of James he alludes feelingly to the danger which beset the Church from the side of Rome,³ and when this again was exchanged for the Presbyterianism of William he refers with evident regret to 'the new oath that was fabricating for the clergy, driven on by the Presbyterians, our new governors.'⁴ One can well understand with what satisfaction such a man would turn from all these (to him) unsatisfactory phases of Church life to his own private life. The entries which contain his pious meditations on his birthday (October 31), year by year, and on the days when he received the Holy Communion,⁵ and on the religious training of his children, are most touching. Well may his Diary be termed 'one of the finest pictures of the mind of a virtuous, honest man, a true patriot, and a pure Christian, that ever was penned,'⁶ and well may his life be called 'an episode in five reigns, during which he was known by all parties, and beloved by whomsoever known.'⁷ On the death of his elder brother he succeeded to the family estate, retired to Wotton, and threw himself with ardour into the schemes of Christian benevolence which characterised the early years of the eighteenth century.⁸

Thomas Willis (1621–1675) is said to have been 'one of

---

¹ *Diary* for October 4, 1683.
² See his *Life of Mrs. Godolphin*, passim.
³ See *Diary* for October 2, 1685.   ⁴ *Diary* for April 26, 1689.
⁵ See *Diary* for Easter Day, 1673, 1679; Ash Wednesday, 1682; May 6, 1694, &c.
⁶ Elmes's *Sir C. Wren and his Times*, p. 371.
⁷ Willmott's *Life of Bishop Jeremy Taylor*, p. 205.
⁸ See *Diary* for May 3, 1702, &c.

the most famous physicians of his time,'[1] and he was at least as conspicuous for his piety and moral courage. After having taken his degree at Oxford, he took up arms for the king in 1642, but it was on other scenes than the battle-field that his courage was displayed. In 1646 he took a medical degree, and began to practise at Oxford, living in a house opposite to Merton College. This house has become historical; for in it he opened a room for divine worship, where Fell, Dolben, and Allestree 'did constantly exercise as they had partly before done in Canterbury Quadrangle, the Liturgy and Sacraments according to the Church of England, to which most of the loyalists in Oxon, especially scholars that had been ejected in 1648, did daily resort.'[2] The courage requisite to do this, especially after the Ordinance of 1655, is obvious. Willis was, no doubt, well supported by his wife, who was the daughter of Samuel, and sister of John Fell, and to whom he was most tenderly attached. He was one of that philosophical coterie at Oxford which formed the nucleus of the Royal Society, and was one of the earliest elected fellows of that great Society. At the Restoration he was made Sedleian Professor of Natural Philosophy; and in 1666, at the solicitation of Archbishop Sheldon, he removed to London, and was made physician in ordinary to the king. Both at Oxford and in London he made a point of attending daily an early church service before visiting his patients;[3] and when he lived in S. Martin's Lane he 'procured a service to be performed early in the neighbouring church.' And being desirous that other busy people like himself should have similar privileges, 'some years before his death he settled a salary for a reader to read prayers in S. Martin's Church in the Fields early and late every day to such servants and people of that parish who could not, through

---

[1] Wood's *Athenæ Oxonienses*, ii. 402.
[2] Fell's *Life of Henry Hammond*.
[3] See *Autobiography of Simon Patrick*, p. 51 (Oxford edition, 1839).

the multiplicity of business, attend the ordinary service daily there performed.'[1] And he left in his will 20*l*. a year for the continuance of these services. He always devoted his Sunday fees to charitable purposes, and he 'left behind him the character of an orthodox, pious, and charitable physician.'[2]

Izaac Walton (1593-1683), like Dr. Willis, had been most faithful to the Church through her troubles, during which he rendered difficult and sometimes dangerous service to the royal cause and succoured to the best of his ability distressed churchmen; in Walton's home on the beautiful banks of the Dove, Dr. Morley and other loyal gentlemen found a shelter; there too he maintained a close friendship with Dr. Sanderson and Dr. King (afterwards Bishop of Chichester), and there he helped to form the sweet character of Ken, whose eldest sister became his second wife in 1647, and whose youth was spent under his eye. Elias Ashmole, speaking of his services during the Commonwealth, says that he was 'well known and as well loved as known by all good men.' After the Restoration, Dr. Morley, now Bishop of Winchester, repaid his kindness by giving him a home in the Cathedral Close; and there he passed the last twenty-three years of his quiet and blameless life, writing those immortal 'Lives' which have perhaps done as much as any single publication to embalm the memory of the Church's worthies.[3]

Christian characters may be of very different types, and except in their agreement on the one essential point, it would be difficult to find a greater contrast than between Walton and our next subject. **Robert Boyle** (162⁶⁄₇-1691), son of the Earl of Cork, is said to have received his first serious impressions during a terrible thunderstorm in Swit-

---

[1] Fell's *Life of Hammond*.   [2] *Ibid.*
[3] See *Life of Izaac Walton*, by Thomas Zouch, Prebendary of Durham, 1825, and Teale's *Lives of English Laymen* (vol. xxii. of *Englishman's Library*).

zerland; but as he was piously brought up, and as his sister, who was many years older than himself, and to whom he was always most devotedly attached, had been eminent for her piety long before, it is more likely that the incident of the storm only served to ripen the good seed which had been sown at an earlier date. At any rate, from first to last he led a consistently Christian life, his devotion to natural philosophy only tending to enlarge and deepen his religious principles, as it did in many other instances during our period. Wherever there was any good Christian work to be done, there was Robert Boyle ever ready to speed it on with his purse and his brain and all the social influence which his name and position commanded. Of his earlier life he has written an Autobiography in the third person under the name of 'Philaretus,' but as it ends in 1641, it does not carry us very far. His life, however, was constantly before the public, so there is no difficulty in tracing its course. It was a singularly active life, both in the intellectual and the practical spheres; in the intellectual sphere he divided his studies between theology and natural philosophy; or rather, with him the two went hand in hand, for the chief charm to him of his scientific investigations was that they gave him larger and nobler ideas of the Creator.[1] His friends thinking that a clerical life would be most congenial to so deeply religious a man, urged him after the Restoration to seek Holy Orders, but this he declined to do, partly because he did not feel that he had any vocation for the office, and partly because he thought that his writings in defence of Christianity would have more effect as coming from a layman than from a clergyman. He was not an ambitious man; he declined the presidency of the Royal Society, and, more than once, a peerage. His aim was to be useful, and he thoroughly succeeded; few men of his day did more useful work in the departments both of science and religion. His Christian

[1] See his *Christian Virtuoso*, passim.

efforts, though variously directed, all centred in one great object, the spread of the gospel in all lands. He used his influence as a director of the East India Company to induce that society to promote Christianity in the East. The revival of the Society for Propagating the Gospel in New England, after the Restoration, was chiefly due to his efforts; and both with his purse and his brain he contributed towards the translating of the Holy Scriptures and other good books into many languages.[1] In all his pious labours he was warmly supported by his sister, Lady Ranelagh, with whom he lived in London after he had left Oxford, that is, for nearly thirty years. He was a regular worshipper at S. Martin's in the Fields, under Tenison, and held we are told much holy converse with the rector, who ministered to him in his last sickness. His reputation among his contemporaries was extraordinarily high. Addison calls him 'an honour to his country,'[2] his biographer, 'a man superior to titles, and almost to praise,'[3] Edmund Calamy, 'one of the two great ornaments of Charles II.'s reign,'[4] but Samuel Wesley the elder reaches the climax when he compares him to Elijah.[5] Exaggeration apart, he was an excellent man, and his works do follow him; witness the 'Boyle Lectures,' the object and success of which are too well known to need description. As, however, it is desired above all things to be perfectly fair, it must be added that though Boyle was a regular worshipper at his

[1] E.g., hearing that the learned Pocock was prevented by financial difficulties from publishing his Arabic version of Grotius' *De Veritate &c.*, he undertook the whole expense of the publication. (See Anderson's *Colonial Church*, ii. 127.) At his own expense he had the Gospels and the Acts of the Apostles translated into the Malay tongue; and he also offered to publish at his own expense a Turkish version of the New Testament, but the East India Company very properly insisted upon relieving him of a portion of the cost. He contributed largely towards the publication of a Welsh and Irish Bible, and corresponded with Eliot, 'the apostle of the Indians,' respecting a translation of the Holy Scriptures into the Indian tongue.

[2] *Spectator*, No. 531.

[3] Quoted in *Diary &c. of Dr. J. Worthington*, p. 123, *note*.

[4] *Account of My Own Life*, i. 227.   [5] *The Athenian Oracle*, i. 65.

parish church and no other place, a friend of the clergy, and in no way out of accord with the Church's doctrine and discipline, still his Christian character was not so obviously and distinctively the product of the Church's system as were those of the laymen noticed above.

The same may be said of the other pious and distinguished layman whom Calamy couples with Boyle as a great ornament of Charles II.'s reign. **Sir Matthew Hale** (1609–1676) may fairly be reckoned among the great lay churchmen of the Restoration period, inasmuch as 'he always declared himself of the Church of England, and said those of the separation were good men, but they had narrow souls, who would break the peace of the Church about such inconsiderable matters as the points in difference were;'[1] but the last clause seems rightly to describe the extent and character of his churchmanship; that is, it was the breadth rather than the distinctive doctrines and practices of the Church that kept him within her pale. Still, it is clear that his pious instincts found sufficient scope in the Church of his baptism. He was a regular worshipper at her altars and a devout communicant, and observed with particular devotion her festivals. The story of his last Communion is very touching. 'Not long before his death the minister told him there was to be a Sacrament next Sunday at church, but he believed he could not come and partake with the rest; therefore he would give it him in his own house. But he answered, "No; his Heavenly Father had prepared a feast for him, and he would go to his Father's house to partake of it." So he made himself be carried thither in his chair, where he received the sacrament on his knees with great devotion, which it may be supposed was the greater because he apprehended it was to be his last,

---

[1] Bishop Burnet's *Life of Sir Matthew Hale*, p. 49. To the same effect his other biographer, Sir J. Williams, says 'he believed that the calamity of the Church and withering of religion hath come from proud and busy men's additions,' &c.

and so took it as his viaticum and provision for his journey.'[1] In his religious, as in his judicial life one would have liked to see him a little less timid, but still churchmen may gladly welcome in their ranks one who had deservedly so high a reputation for integrity and piety.

May they also welcome another distinguished layman, **Sir Thomas Browne** (1605-1682)? Surely, if his own words are to be believed, they may. The author of the 'Religio Medici' was called by some a Romanist, by others a Quaker, by others an Atheist, but this is what he says of himself: 'To difference myself nearer, and draw into a lesser circle; there is no church whose every point so squares unto my conscience, whose articles, constitutions, and customs seem so consonant unto reason, and, as it were, framed to my particular devotions, as this whereof I hold my belief, the Church of England. Where Scripture is silent, the Church is my text, where that speaks 'tis but my comment.'[2] Dr. Johnson, to whose interesting biography of Sir T. Browne the reader must be referred, strongly contends that he was a Christian and a churchman.

A sad mystery, which has never been cleared up, has drawn attention to another worthy layman, who but for his melancholy end would have long ago passed into oblivion. But every one has heard of the mysterious death of **Sir Edmondsbury Godfrey**, though every one may not be aware that he was an excellent churchman, and so firm and conscientious in the discharge of his duties as a magistrate, that Charles II. (who could appreciate virtues in others which he did not practise himself) used to call him the best justice of peace in the kingdom. During the Great Plague of London, while others fled, he remained manfully at his post, tending the sufferers with his own hand, and feeding the starving and deserted poor. Is it not possible that the immense concourse of clergy at his funeral, over which

---

[1] Burnet's *Life*, p. 74.
[2] *Works of Sir T. Browne*, vol. ii.; *Religio Medici*, § 5, p. 323.

Roger North makes merry, may have been due, not only to the panic which turned the funeral into a Protestant demonstration, but also to the respect which was felt for the memory of a faithful lay churchman?

There is another estimable layman who has been rescued from oblivion by one single incident,—**John Kyrle** (1637–1714),[1] immortalised by Pope as the 'Man of Ross.'

> Who taught that heaven-directed spire to rise?
> 'The Man of Ross!' each lisping babe replies.

But perhaps not only the 'lisping babe,' but many well-informed adults might not be able to reply that it was under the shadow of that heaven-directed spire that the Man of Ross was taught to live the life he so nobly devoted to works of charity and attempts to brighten a little the dreary existence of the country poor. Such, however, was the case. When the church bell rang, every day, week-day and Sunday, he laid all his occupations aside, 'washed his hands for seemliness, and went to pray.' The clergyman of the parish, Dr. Whiting, whose name deserves to be held in memory, was his dearest friend and spiritual adviser; the two went hand in hand in every work of piety and benevolence, and when John Kyrle died, he was buried, by his own special desire, at the foot of him at whose feet he had sat so long during his lifetime.

Hitherto, in these sketches of lay churchmen, we have been able to keep clear of the tangled web of politics; the subjects of them either stood aloof from politics altogether, or it has been perfectly easy to disengage their religious from their political characters. But there is one great layman of the Restoration period, a churchman of churchmen, in whom the religious and political elements were so inextricably mixed up that it is impossible to separate them. That one is Edward **Hyde**, Earl of Clarendon (1608–1674). Historians whose political bias was the very opposite of

[1] According to another authority his date is 1631–1724.

Clarendon's have admitted that he was a man of deep earnestness and sincerity in his religious views; and on the other hand, those whose bias is in the same direction as Clarendon's will hardly contend that his Church policy, which resulted in what has been termed the 'Clarendonian Code,'[1] was altogether a wise or a just one. But it is utterly unfair to judge either him or it by the standard of the nineteenth century, and equally unfair to ignore the fact that he was urged on from below to greater severity against nonconformists than his own judgment approved of. His personal character is not here held up as that of a model Christian. But, after making all deductions for his haughtiness and irritability, his intolerance and his love of amassing and spending money, there yet remains much in him to admire. His strong sense of religion, his devotion to the Church, his integrity and untainted morals, his discountenance of the immorality prevailing at Court, are surely features in his character worthy of admiration. At least a share of the unpopularity which led to his downfall must be attributed to the tacit reproach which his strict life conveyed to the laxity of his surroundings. And moreover, 'the fierce light which beats upon a throne, and blackens every blot,' beats yet more fiercely upon one who, to the disgust of multitudes of far higher social standing, came as near to a throne as a subject, not of the blood royal, nor indeed of gentle blood at all, could well do. An angel in such a position would find many detractors. Lord Clarendon was no angel, but he was a man whose defects were to a great extent the defects of his age, and of the trying circumstances in which he was placed, while his virtues were his own.

Of the many churchmen who utilised their enforced leisure during the Rebellion for the purposes of mental cultivation and learned research, few improved the time more diligently than **Elias Ashmole** (1617–1692), whose

[1] See Lord Campbell's *Lives of the Lord Chancellors*, vol. iv. pp. 19-97, where a full account of the 'Code' will be found.

name is still connected with one of Oxford's most useful buildings. On June 16, 1647, he records, 'One Hor. post merid. it pleased God to put me in mind that I was now placed in the condition I always desired, which was, that I might be enabled to live to myself and my studies; and seeing I am thus retired, according to my heart's desire, I beseech God to bless me in my retirement and to prosper my studies that I may faithfully and diligently serve Him, and in all things submit to His will; and for the peace and happiness I enjoy (in the midst of bad times) to render Him all humble thanks, and for what I attain to, in the course of my studies, to give Him glory.'[1] His prayer was granted, for his whole life was spent in accordance with the spirit of the above entry. After the Restoration he was patronised by the king,[2] but not in the least corrupted nor drawn away from his favourite pursuits. He lived in honourable retirement at Lambeth, and was on visiting terms with his neighbour Archbishop Sancroft.[3] But he did not forget his native place, Lichfield, and its beautiful little cathedral. The Corporation of Lichfield write to thank him for 'the receipt of a silver bowl,—very flowery.' 'Nor,' they add, 'have you only given us this great cratera, but you have largely offered to the repair of his church, our ruin'd Cathedral . . . and you have annually and liberally refreshed Christ in his members the poor of this city.'[4] Twenty-two years later we have a letter from 'the Chapter of the

---

[1] *Memoirs of the Life of that learned Antiquary, Elias Ashmole, Esq., drawn up by himself by way of Diary*, published 1717.

[2] '1660 - Kissed the king's hand.' (Note by editor: 'The king took great notice of him as a scientific man; he had never been noticed by any authorities during the Rebellion.') 'July 19, 1660—Mr. Secretary Morris told me the king had a great kindness for me.' '22nd Ditto.—The king appointed me to make a description of his medals.' See also the entry for January 6, 1675, &c.

[3] 'August 15, 1679.—My Lord's Grace of Canterbury came to visit me at my house, and spent a great part of the day with me in my study.' 'July 26, 1680.—The Archbishop's sister and niece came to visit my wife.'

[4] Letter, dated 'January 16, 1666.' (See *Memoirs*, &c.)

Church of Lichfield,' who speak 'of the honour Lichfield felt in being his birthplace and the place of his education,' and 'of his liberal charity to the city,' and ask him to help them in 'finishing the ring of ten bells,' adding, 'if you help it will add to your reputation for piety and munificence already renowned.' Ashmole cannot be regarded as a *prominent* churchman of the period, but he deserves notice as one out of many instances of the power which the Church had to attract and keep within her pale, men of varied culture and accomplishments.

If this were a history of all the great and good men who lived during the Restoration period, mention would have to be made of the religious and liberal-minded Wriothesley, Earl of Southampton, of that staunch and stainless royalist, James Butler, Duke of Ormond, and of that honourable statesman, Sir William Coventry. But these, and men like them, though certainly not hostile to the Church, can hardly be regarded as typical lay-churchmen. We may therefore pass on to those who, though most of them alive during the Restoration period, came into prominence during the later era which this work embraces. As a sort of connecting link between the two eras let us first take **Sir Christopher Wren** (1632-1723). He is now known only as the most original of English architects, but he had achieved distinction in other fields before he even began to turn his attention to architecture. In very early years he had shewn a precocious genius for science, and when he was scarcely twenty-five years of age he was appointed Savilian Professor of Astronomy at Gresham College. About six years later he took up architecture as a profession, and we all know with what success. All through, he was the pious humble Christian. The son of a dean and the nephew of a bishop could hardly fail to be a churchman, but his churchmanship was not merely hereditary, it was the result of deliberate conviction. His one defect, so far as his worldly interest and perhaps also his usefulness were concerned, really adds to the beauty of his Christian character. He suffered from an almost morbid modesty, and on that account is made to point a moral, under the title of 'Nestor,' by the writers of the 'Tatler' (No. 52). His latest biographer has remarked with perfect truth that 'in a corrupt age all testimony leaves Wren spotless. In a position of great trust and still greater difficulty, his integrity was but the more clearly shown by the attacks made against him. Among the foremost philosophers of his age, he was a striking example that "every good gift and every perfect gift is from above;" no child could hold the truths of Christianity with a more undoubting faith than did Sir Christopher Wren.'[1]

Another eminent layman who is a link between our two periods was **Thomas Thynne, Viscount Weymouth.** He had the inestimable advantage of being directed in his youthful studies by the great Hammond, at Westwood the abode of Thynne's aunt, Lady Pakington, and at college he was the friend and companion of the saintly Ken.[2] Brought up amid such surroundings it is no wonder that he was a staunch and benevolent churchman. In the many pious and charitable schemes of the later part of the seventeenth and the earlier part of the eighteenth century, the name of Lord Weymouth is always prominent. He helped Dr. Bray liberally in his attempt to found parochial libraries, contributed 300*l.* towards his expenses in Maryland, sent forth 'an itinerant missionary' thither at his own cost, largely and frequently aided the Christian Knowledge Society in its home work (judiciously choosing Robert Nelson as his almoner), and was the supporter of every good work set on foot in the neighbourhood of his own home at Longleat. He gave the shelter of his roof to his

---

[1] See *Christopher Wren, his Family and his Times*, by Lucy Phillimore, p. 225. See also, *Sir Christopher Wren and his Times*, by James Elmes, and Wren's *Parentalia*.

[2] See *Life of Ken*, by a Layman, p. 619.

old friend Ken, and supplemented the scanty resources of the deprived bishop. Nor was Ken the only nonjuror who experienced the effects of his bounty. Dr. Smith[1] speaks of 'the prodigious bounty of Lord and Lady Weymouth bestowed on persons in need of such supports,' and Lord Dartmouth owns that 'he was very liberal to nonjurors' and that 'his house was constantly full of people of that sort.' It is fair to add that Lord Dartmouth also says 'he was a weak, proud man' and that 'he was extremely pleased to be cried up by the nonjurors for a very religious man, having affected to be thought so all his life, which the companions of his youth would by no means allow.'[2] Lord Dartmouth gives no proof of all this, while there are strong presumptions to the contrary. Ken distinctly declares that 'the good lord really does conduct his life by the divine maxims recorded by S. Paul.'[3] A fellow of the Royal Society and one 'who was reckoned a very good judge of men'[4] could hardly be without brains; and a nobleman who corresponded with and visited a worthy nonconformist who was socially very much his inferior could not be altogether proud.

The name of **Simon, Lord Digby**, is constantly found associated with that of Lord Weymouth in all schemes of religion and philanthropy. One is apt to look with a little suspicion upon protégés' panegyrics of their patrons, but when those protégés are John Kettlewell and Thomas Bray, we may safely take their testimony without even the proverbial grain of salt. Both these saintly clergymen of course knew Lord Digby intimately, and language seems hardly strong enough to express the admiration they both felt for his character. 'That most dear and exemplary saint;' 'a bright example and a public good;' 'as for

---

[1] A learned nonjuror, author of *Vitæ quorundam Eruditissimorum et Illustrium Virorum* (Usher, Cosin, &c.), *Account of the Greek Church*, &c.
[2] See *Life of Ken*, by a Layman, ii. 619. [3] *Ibid.*
[4] *Life of Mrs. Elizabeth Rowe*, daughter of Mr. Walter Singer, the worthy nonconformist referred to in the text.

religion, that was the height of all his aims and the most open of all his professions;' 'a sincere and zealous son of the Church of England, in whose communion he lived and died;' such is the testimony of Kettlewell.[1] 'That excellent lord, a Luminous Star no doubt now in Heaven, for few had his equals for good sense and solid piety whilst on earth,' such is the testimony of Bray.[2] The known facts of Lord Digby's life fully bear out this testimony. He died at a comparatively early age, and on his death-bed recommended to his brother and successor, **William, Lord Digby**, the carrying out of the good works which he had begun. The exhortation was not given in vain. William proved a worthy successor to Simon. It may be added that the two brothers married two sisters who were both worthy of such husbands.

Among the eminent laymen of our period none held higher positions than the two Earls of Nottingham, father and son. The former, strictly speaking, belongs to the Restoration period, but as the two bore a striking resemblance to one another, and were linked together as churchmen by their connection with one spiritual adviser, it will be convenient to take them together. **Heneage Finch** (1621–1682) passed from one legal honour to another until he became Lord Chancellor. He won the very highest reputation as a lawyer and an orator,[3] but he was equally dis-

---

[1] See Kettlewell's *Life*, passim. [2] See Bray's *Life of Pawlet.*
[3] He was the 'Omri' of Dryden's *Absalom and Achitophel*, and is thus described:

> Sincere was Omri, and not only knew,
> But Israel's sanctions into practice drew;
> Our laws that did a boundless ocean seem,
> Were coasted all, and fathom'd all by him.
> No Rabbin speaks like him their mystic sense,
> So just, and with such charms of eloquence;
> To whom the double blessing does belong,
> With Moses' inspiration, Aaron's tongue.

Lord Campbell says, 'All juridical writers worship him as the first of

tinguished as a staunch and conscientious churchman, whose spotless morals and unimpeached integrity shed a lustre upon the Church which he loved so well and served so faithfully. In the distribution of Church patronage his services were very great. With a lawyer's discernment of character he perceived the peculiar fitness of his chaplain (then comparatively unknown), for advising him upon such matters, and therefore 'he charged it upon his conscience to recommend him' the best man for each post as it became vacant. This was a serious responsibility for a young man, but when it is added that the young man was John Sharp, afterwards Archbishop of York, it will cause no wonder that the result was eminently satisfactory. Among others whom he drew from obscurity was George Bull, whose biographer, Robert Nelson, pays a graceful and well-deserved tribute both to the Chancellor and his chaplain.[1] He also strove, but in vain, to draw into public life the saintly Henry More.[2] He wisely made residence on their benefices a condition of every preferment.[3] In 1681 he was created Earl of Nottingham, and in the following year he died, to the great loss of the Church, but happily

> Uno avulso, non deficit alter
> Aureus.

Daniel Finch, the second earl, was as staunch a churchman and lived as blameless a life as his father, whose spiritual adviser, John Sharp, he wisely adopted as his own. Both father and son were remarkable for a gravity of demeanour which provoked the anger and ridicule of the wild wits about Court among whom they were thrown. The son especially was so austere, that though he was a

---

lawyers,' and quotes many proofs of this. (*Lives of the Lord Chancellors*, iv. p. 309, &c.)

[1] See *Life of Bull*, pp. 155-8.

[2] 'A noble person' (Nottingham) said to More, 'Pray be not so morose or humoursome as to refuse all things you have not known as long as Christ's College.' (Ward's *Life of More*, published 1710, p. 58.)

[3] Carwithen's *History of the Church of England*, iii. p. 160.

High Churchman both in the political and the spiritual sense, he reminded the royalists of the hated puritans. But even those who affected to laugh at his preciseness could not help respecting the spotless integrity of his character. His influence was enormous; he is said to have done more to reconcile churchmen to the Revolution than any other man;[1] and yet, after all, he only half threw the weight of his vast influence into the scale of the new dynasty, for he could only be brought to acknowledge William as king 'de facto.' He professed his readiness to serve his majesty faithfully,—and whatever Nottingham professed he always meant,—but he would never call him the 'rightful and lawful king.' His position of course brought him into close contact with the political side of Church history, and here some of his acts were very questionable, but in judging him we must again beware of the fallacy of judging men of the seventeenth by the standard of the nineteenth century. He refused the high office which his father had held, but his influence was at least as powerful and extensive as that of the great Chancellor. It was not until after the period which this work embraces that his love of the Church led him to enter into the lists as its defender in the Trinitarian controversy,—much to the dismay of Dr. Waterland, who of course understood the whole subject thoroughly, and could by no means join in the gratitude with which his University (Cambridge) welcomed this august champion of the faith.[2]

As we are in high company it will be as well, before we descend to the commonalty, to notice two more noblemen who were noted churchmen in their way, the two brothers Hyde,—Henry, the elder, Earl of Clarendon, and Laurence, the younger, Earl of Rochester. The second Earl of Clarendon was not equal to his father, the famous Chan-

---

[1] See Leopold von Ranke's *History of England, principally in the Seventeenth Century*, iv. p. 566, and v. p. 342.

[2] See Waterland's *Works*, i. pp. 71, 235, &c., and ii. pp. 379-80, &c.

cellor, but he was an able man. With his public life we are not concerned except so far as his very conscientious distribution of patronage, when he was Viceroy of Ireland, was of great service to the Church in that island. With regard to his private life, he was evidently a man with a strong sense of religion. His diary proves that. He cultivated the friendship of pious people like Dr. Horneck, Mr. Charles Leslie (who delighted, his biographer tells us, in Lord Clarendon's society, and acted as his chaplain),[1] Bishop Moore of Norwich, and Lady Ranelagh; he was a regular attendant at public worship, and if he cannot be held as a saint, at any rate he had a very humble opinion of his own spiritual state.

The younger brother, Laurence, Earl of Rochester, was a more famous, and perhaps an abler man. A random expression of Roger North to the effect that 'he swore like a sutler and indulged in drinking, but was the head of the Church party,' has been accepted far too implicitly. North had a personal animosity against him, and one would have liked to see the description confirmed by less prejudiced testimony.[2] Certainly his own diary and correspondence convey a very different impression. There are few things more touching than his reflections on the death of his daughter, in which he frankly confesses his own shortcomings, but in the spirit of one who is really desirous of leading a better life. Of his sincere attachment to the Church there can be no doubt; for her sake he sacrificed all his ambitious hopes, and his consistent regard for her interests should at least cause his memory to be tenderly dealt with by churchmen.[3]

[1] See *Life of Charles Leslie*, by Rev. R. J. Leslie.

[2] Barillon's testimony is still less trustworthy, seeing that the Earl of Rochester was one of the chief hindrances towards his carrying out his plans with Rochester's royal kinsman, for which every Englishman, and especially every English churchman, should be grateful to the earl.

[3] See the *Correspondence of Henry Hyde, Earl of Clarendon, and of his brother, Laurence Hyde, Earl of Rochester, with the Diaries of both*, edited by W. E. Singer, 1828.

Robert Nelson (1656-171⅗) has been so frequently and so lately portrayed,[1] that there is no need to record how, as the son of a rich merchant he was brought up in affluence, how he received his training in church principles from Mr. Bull, how he married the Lady Theophila Lucy, who, to his great grief, became a Romanist, how he took part in every good scheme, originating many and suggesting more, how stirringly he appealed to the gentry to help in works of piety and charity,[2] how he became a nonjuror, and how he returned to the National Church. His character was admired by men of all shades of opinion. We are of course not surprised to hear of Kettlewell's admiration,[3] nor of Hickes 'esteeming the honour of his friendship one of the providential blessings of his life,' nor of Francis Lee describing him as 'a gentleman of that distinguished merit, as it may well be doubted whether he has left his fellow behind him in this great island.' But Tillotson also retained his friendship to the very last, and actually died in his arms; Tenison spoke of him as 'a good and holy man now with God,'[4] Swift, who writes with the bitterest contempt of the nonjurors as a body,[5] calls him 'a very pious, learned, and worthy gentleman;' Hearne, though he was deeply indignant at his return to the National Church, yet, in the very same breath in which he expresses his indignation, calls him 'a pious, good man,'[6] and on the occasion of his death, 'a very learned, religious, and pious gentleman,'[7] and many others might be quoted.[8]

[1] See Secretan's most interesting *Life of Robert Nelson*; Teale's *Lives of British Laymen*; and Mr. Abbey's chapter on 'Robert Nelson and his Friends,' in *The English Church in the Eighteenth Century*.
[2] See *Ways and Means of Doing Good; an Address to Persons of Quality*, &c.
[3] See *Life of Kettlewell*.
[4] See *Life of T. Tenison, Archbishop of Canterbury*.
[5] See *Sentiments of a Church of England Man*, p. 275.
[6] *Diary*, iii. 116. [7] *Diary* for January 23, 171⅗.
[8] Dr. Wells (*Rich Man's Duty*, &c.) says: 'A bishop wrote to me, Mr. Nelson's death is a loss, to everyone who had the happiness to know him,

Is it attributing too much weight to what some may think a matter of secondary importance, to suggest that one reason why Nelson was so universally esteemed was that he was a thorough gentleman, not only in the conventional, but in the highest sense of the term? Some verses attached to his portrait, though not remarkable for poetical merit, bring out this point so truly and clearly that they are worth quoting:

> Such were the lines; such majesty and grace
> Chose to erect their throne in Nelson's face.
> Where'er that pleasing form did once appear
> The world confess'd—The Christian hero's here.
> . . . .
> To others mild, as to himself severe;
> Polish'd though learn'd; obliging, yet sincere;
> Justly with admiration seen and read;
> For all must own the Christian was well bred, &c., &c.[1]

Dr. Johnson affirms that Richardson took Nelson as the model for his Sir Charles Grandison; if this were so, all one can say is that the real man was a higher type of gentleman than the fancy portrait. Nor must we omit another trait in Nelson's character, which, no doubt, also contributed to his universal popularity. He possessed in an eminent degree, that very rare quality, common sense. In this respect Nelson was, among laymen, what Archbishop Sharp was among clergymen; and in this respect he presents a striking contrast to another good layman whose name is, for many reasons, naturally associated with his, **Henry Dodwell (1641-1711)**. Both these good men held, broadly speaking,

---

irreparable; and to the Church of God such an one as I doubt will be sensibly felt, unless God in his great goodness shall be pleased to raise up some person of the like heroical piety in his room; but such a blessing I cannot flatter myself with the hopes of living to see in my days.' See also Noble's *Biographical History of England* (Continuation of Granger), i. p. 262, Birch's *Life of Tillotson*, &c.

[1] The verses are attached to the 3rd edition (1716) of Nelson's *Practice of True Devotion*, and signed 'T. W.' Query: Is not this a misprint for 'S. W.,' that is, Samuel Wesley?

the same opinions on religion and politics; they had many friends in common, and they frequently met in the same house; both became nonjurors, and both returned to the National Church on the same day; both were men of unblemished moral character, of great Christian earnestness, and of staunch Church principles. But the points of contrast between them were more marked than those of resemblance. Dodwell was incomparably the more learned man of the two; he had also more originality, not only of genius but of character; we can picture to ourselves the man Dodwell more completely than the man Nelson. On the other hand, that good sense and that good judgment which were so eminently characteristic of Nelson, were conspicuous by their absence in Dodwell, who was at least as embarrassing to his friends as to his foes; in spite of the vast learning which he brought to support their cause, they must always have trembled to think what Dodwell might write or say next; whereas Nelson's support, if less striking, was sure to be unobjectionable. To complete the contrast, the outward appearance of the two men differed as widely as their minds. Nelson, to judge from his portrait, was made in a large mould, scrupulously neat in his dress, courtly and dignified in his manner, the very pink of propriety;—in short a Sir Charles Grandison in real life. Dodwell was of small stature, very negligent about his dress, eccentric both in thought and expression, and utterly regardless of appearances. He was born at Dublin and educated at Trinity College, of which he was elected fellow. But he soon resigned his fellowship, either because he succeeded to a property, and thought that he ought to make room for a poorer man, or because he was unwilling to take Holy Orders, partly as deeming himself unworthy, and partly as thinking he would be a more disinterested champion of the Christian religion and of the Christian priesthood as a layman.[1] He settled in England, living sometimes in

[1] See Brokesby's *Life of Dodwell*, pp. 21-5, and *Reliquiæ Hearnianæ*, vol. i. p. 235.

London and sometimes at Oxford. In 1688 he was elected Camden Professor of History at Oxford, but was forced to resign his professorship because he would not take the oaths. Henceforth he lived in studious retirement in Berkshire, first at Cookham and then at Shottesbrooke, being attracted to the latter place by the fact that his friend Mr. Cherry lived there. The group at Shottesbrooke has a peculiar interest for the student of Church life at this period. It included, besides Dodwell, Francis Cherry, Francis Brokesby, Thomas Hearne, and White Kennet, all of whom have been, or will be noticed. Of course with White Kennet (the complying rector) Dodwell was not on the best of terms,[1] but by the rest of the Shottesbrooke party he was most highly valued. Cherry calls him 'his best and dearest friend,'[2] Brokesby can hardly find strong enough language to express his admiration of his vast and varied learning, his humility, charity, and self-denial,[3] and Hearne declares that though he was the greatest scholar in Europe, he was humble and modest to a fault, and frequently refers to him as 'that great and good man.'[4] In fact, with all the nonjurors, Dodwell, owing to his vast learning and high personal character, was a great authority. The contemporary author of Bishop Frampton's Life calls him 'that great lay dictator,'[5] and Edmund Calamy who, in spite of their very different opinions, was intimate with him at Oxford, complains that 'he would not brook contradiction;'[6] but Hearne's and Brokesby's testimony show that he left a different impression upon those who knew him best.

---

[1] There is an interesting letter among the Kennet MSS. in the British Museum (to which my attention was kindly directed by Dr. Garnett, the head-librarian), in which Dr. Kennet complains of Dodwell's preventing people from attending the parish church.

[2] See *Letters from the Bodleian*, ed. by Bliss. Letter to Hearne, April 28, 1713.

[3] See Brokesby's *Life*, passim.

[4] See *Life of Mr. Thomas Hearne, from his own MS.* (1772), passim, and *Reliquiæ Hearnianæ*.

[5] P. 203. [6] Calamy's *Account of My Own Life*, i. 282.

Dodwell always had clerical tastes; he loved to accompany Bishop Lloyd on his visitation tours;[1] and when he lived at Shottesbrooke, he regularly attended the clerical meetings at Marlow, where the clergy much enjoyed his learned conversation, though they were often startled by his eccentricities.

His friend Francis Cherry (1668-1715) was an admirable specimen of a class which has, happily, always flourished in England, the class of pious, cultivated country gentlemen. Hearne calls him 'a very learned man, and, which is much more, a very pious, religious, modest, and humble man.' But we are not to gather from this that he was 'learned' in the same sense that Dodwell was. He was simply an intelligent, well-educated gentleman; a first-rate horseman and devotedly attached to hunting, but not a mere Nimrod; he took a great interest in books and the conversation of learned men, and was himself something of a virtuoso. He was a staunch churchman, and a most liberal friend to churchmen in distress. Shottesbrooke Park, his residence, was a perfect harbour of refuge for the nonjurors. But though he was a nonjuror himself, he deeply deplored the schism, and it was a real satisfaction to him when he could return conscientiously to his parish church. He has left us one of the clearest and most satisfactory accounts which we possess of the reasons which led men like Nelson, Dodwell, and himself to stand aloof from the National Church until the canonical rights of the deprived bishops had lapsed. It is a credit to the taste of the county that he was so popular in it as to be called 'the idol of Berkshire.' His love of sport brought him frequently into contact with royalty, and several anecdotes are told of him in this connection which are very characteristic of the man, but hardly belong to the subject of 'Church life.' Among other acts of kindness, Mr. Cherry entirely educated Thomas Hearne, to whose Diary we are most deeply indebted for information

[1] Brokesby's *Life*, p. 39.

about the Church life of the period, though his own life scarcely comes within the range of our subject.

The same may be said of another, and by far the most interesting and vivid of all the diarists of the period, **Samuel Pepys.** As a picture of the times from a certain point of view, Pepys' Diary is unique. But it is far too often forgotten what that point of view was. It was that of quite a young man who set down all his private thoughts, prepossessions, and prejudices, without the least idea that they would ever be published. The Diary is not even a fair and adequate representation of Pepys' own character, for there is little doubt that he changed greatly for the better in his later years, perhaps under the influence of his brother diarist, Evelyn, whom he highly respected. Still less can the immortal Diary be regarded as an adequate authority on other matters, and especially on the matter of Church life. Pepys makes no secret of his dislike of the clergy, and it is simply absurd to repeat gravely as undoubted facts little scandals about them which really rest upon his authority alone. Take the Diary for what it is, that is, as the hastily jotted down impressions of a rather lax young man, and it is delightful and invaluable; but take it as a grave historical authority, and it is, on the face of it, most misleading. It is an admirable picture of Pepys between the ages of twenty-seven and thirty-seven, but Pepys between the ages of twenty-seven and thirty-seven can hardly pose as a pious lay churchman; therefore nothing more need be said about him, except that the writer of such a book as the present owes him both a debt and also a grudge.

The name of Pepys naturally suggests that of another diarist, **Ralph Thoresby.** Thoresby's Diary cannot of course compare for a moment with that of Pepys in point of naturalness, vividness, and general interest, but, from the point of view of this work, it has a peculiar value as shewing the process by which a strictly conscientious nonconformist became a strictly conscientious churchman.

Thoresby's nonconformity was hereditary, his father, for whom he entertained a great respect, having been a Presbyterian. The Thoresbys were a very good old family, and are said to have been able to trace back their pedigree to Canute. The Diary commences in 1677 and ends in 1724, and thus deals with a later period than Pepys'. All through the period Thoresby seems to have attended the church services at Leeds, as well as at his own place. In 1685, when the fear of Romanism was reaching its height, he was drawn more closely to the Church as the strongest bulwark against Popery.[1] The very high regard in which he held the private and the public characters of two successive vicars of Leeds, Dr. Milner and Mr. Killingbeck, still further attached him to our communion.[2] A lay churchman, Mr. Thornton, who was his personal friend, helped on the work. And finally, in 1697, a visit to Leeds of Archbishop Sharp, whose character and preaching he had already learned to admire enthusiastically,[3] completed it. He refers with delight to the Archbishop's 'incomparable sermon' and the crowded congregation; and the next day when ' his Grace was pleased to honour me with a visit, attended by my dear friend Mr. Thornton, and most of the clergy,' the deed was done.[4] The not unnatural remonstrances of his old nonconforming minister were all unavailing. Henceforth he was a most consistent and staunch churchman; he made the acquaintance of such men as Dr. Hickes, Mr. Nelson, Mr. Hearne, and Mr. Wanley, and, in fact, went rather too

[1] 'I joined more constantly in the public prayers and worship, as judging the Church of England the strongest bulwark against Popery.' (*Diary*, i. p. 182.)

[2] See *Diary*, i. p. 191.

[3] 'July 4, 1692.—Had a sight of the best of bishops that ever honoured this town with their presence in my time, Archbishop Sharp, a most excellent preacher, universally beloved.' (*Diary*, i. p. 224.) 'August 1, 1695.—At Bishop Thorp; cannot but admire the learning, piety, moderation, and ingenuity of the Archbishop, and his chaplain, Mr. Pearson.' (*Id.* 309.

[4] *Diary*, i. p. 313.

far to meet the approbation of the Low Churchmen.[1] His life was so blameless that we can well understand the pleasure with which he was welcomed by churchmen. His friend the Archbishop suggested that he should seek Holy Orders, but he preferred working for the Church, to which he henceforth devoted most of his time, as a faithful layman.

Another excellent layman who, like Thoresby, was invited to seek Holy Orders, was **James Bonnell** (1653–1699). But, unlike Thoresby, he was from first to last a staunch churchman. Having taken his degree at S. Catherine's Hall, Cambridge, he became tutor in the family of a Mr. Freeman, who offered to purchase him a living if he would take Orders, as he desired to do. But the offer deterred rather than quickened his ardour to become a clergyman, for 'he reckoned it a great unhappiness to the Church that interest had any share in the disposal of spiritual things.'[2] He spent the last fifteen years of his short life at Dublin in the responsible office of 'Accomptant-General of Ireland,' which his father held before him, living as a most exemplary and energetic lay churchman, taking the deepest interest in the Religious Societies and other good works which then flourished at Dublin. 'Would we,' writes his biographer,[3] 'behold a Church of England man who has all the accomplishments she can give him; who has fully imbib'd her doctrine, and gives himself up to the conduct of her laws, who joyns daily in her devotions, who partakes of her extensive charity and is acted by her primitive spirit; who honours her laws, and lives up to her precepts? Consider Mr. Bonnell well, and it is he.' Funeral sermons are not as a rule to be taken quite literally, but there is a ring about the praise of the Bishop of Killmore and Ardagh, who

---

[1] Bishop Burnet severely rebuked him for becoming 'a rank Tory.' (*Diary*, ii. 235.)

[2] *Life and Character of James Bonnell, Esq.*, by W. Hamilton, Archdeacon of Armagh.

[3] *Id.* p. 244.

preached Bonnell's funeral sermon, which sounds genuine, and he wisely fortifies his statements by quoting several unimpeachable testimonies to Bonnell's excellence. 'I sincerely profess,' he writes, 'I know not where, in the present age, to meet with, every way, the like man. In a word, a person so accomplisht for the public employments he sustained, yet no less accurate in his duties to God, his neighbour, and himself, I fear scarce any age can shew.'

There were many other laymen of whom the Church of our period may well be proud, but who, for one reason or another, can only be touched upon very briefly. There is **Joseph Addison**, the 'parson in the tye-wig.' The greatest literary man of his day was, both by training and conviction, a staunch adherent of the Church of England. There is **Sir Richard Blackmore**, who from a literary point of view stands at the opposite pole from Addison; but in the language of his great biographer,[1] 'as the poet sinks the man rises.' Kettlewell's biographer describes him as 'a gentleman who in his zeal for the service of Religion and for Reformation of manners and principles hath not been surpassed by any of his profession.'[2] In fact, the rhyming physician wrote his numerous and portentous epics expressly in the service of religion. Whether they did her much service is another question; but his piety, if not his poetry, is a credit to that Church of which, from first to last, he was a staunch member. There is **Lord Maynard**, Ken's earliest patron, 'a most exemplary nobleman, who, with his admirable wife, Lady Margaret, lived on most intimate terms of friendship with Ken, and seconded all his endeavours for the good of his flock during his two happy years at Easton.'[3] There is **Sir Edward Atkins**, the friend and neighbour of Humphrey Prideaux at Saham, 'a man

---

[1] Dr. Johnson. See *Lives of Poets*.

[2] *Life of Kettlewell*, compiled from the collections of Hickes and Nelson, p. 11.

[3] Miss Strickland's *Lives of the Seven Bishops*, &c., p. 240.

of great piety, probity, and goodness.' In the reign of James II. he was Lord Chief Baron of the Exchequer, and 'acquitted himself in that post with great justice and integrity, especially towards the clergy, whom he would never suffer to be oppressed, and of whose rights he was remarkably careful whilst he presided in that Court. Refusing the oaths, he was excluded from all place, and retired to Pickenham, and there lived quietly, greatly respected by all his neighbours, to whom he was very useful in reconciling their differences. As his fame spread all over the country, people came from great distances to lay their causes before him.'[1] He had the honour of being the early patron and occasional benefactor of that model country parson, Isaac Milles.[2] There is **Sir Walter St. John**, of whom Bishop Patrick speaks most highly both in his 'Autobiography' and his 'Mensa Mystica.' There is **William Melmoth** (1666–1743), the first joint-treasurer of the S.P.G., an eminent barrister, author of a once very popular devotional work,[3] one of the good men who protested against the licentiousness of the stage, a man whom Mr. Anderson estimates so highly as to term him 'only second to Robert Nelson in the ranks of the lay-members of our Church at this period.'[4] There is **Edward Colston** (1636–1721), the merchant prince, whose memory is still celebrated annually at Bristol, and whose splendid charities shew that he was not only a most benevolent man, but also that he deeply valued the system of that Church of which he was a sincere and worthy member.[5] There is **Walter Chetwynd**, who at the

---

[1] *Life of Dean Prideaux* (published 1748), p. 75.

[2] See *Life of Rev. Isaac Milles*, pp. 45, 46, 70.

[3] *The Great Importance of a Religious Life*. It was republished in 1849, with an interesting memoir of the author.

[4] *History of the Church of England in the Colonies*, &c., by the Rev. J. S. M. Anderson, ii. 559.

[5] In 1696 he built a schoolmaster's house for forty-four boys, who were to be clothed and instructed in reading, writing, arithmetic, *and the Church Catechism*. He gave 6l. a year to the minister of All Saints', Bristol, for reading prayers every Monday and Tuesday morning through the year, in-

consecration of the new church at Ingestre, of which he was 'the pious and generous founder,' in 1677 'offered upon the altar the tythes of Hopton, a village hard by, to the value of 50*l.* per annum, as an addition to the rectory for ever.'[1] There is **Mr. Seymour**, a rich goldsmith and banker of Lombard Street, and most actively zealous in encouraging every good work, among other good works building a church in Spital Fields.[2]

It will be observed that all the laymen who have been noticed belonged to the upper or upper-middle class. It is much to be regretted that no account has been preserved of any pious laymen of the humbler ranks; but perhaps such oblivion was inevitable. 'The life,' writes Dr. Johnson, 'that passes in penury, must necessarily pass in obscurity.'[3] Just as in the epic, 'the brave Gyas and the brave Cloanthus' are names and nothing more, though they may have been as gallant heroes as the Trojan leader himself, so it is in the battle of the faith. The piety of the masses can only be gathered from the accounts of crowded services and well-attended Communions, of which something will be said in the next chapter.

(2) *CHURCHWOMEN OF THE PERIOD.*

The tendencies of the period embraced within the compass of this work were not favourable to the development of women's work in the Church. It was not the fashion of the day for women to occupy a prominent position in any sphere. Though two out of the five sovereigns who reigned in England were women, it is curious to observe how small a part women play in the life of the nation at large. In

---

stituted Lent lectures, gave 6,000*l.* for the augmentation of sixty small livings, gave liberally to the repair of the Cathedral, and towards seating and beautifying All Saints' Church. (See *Edward Colston the Philanthropist, his Life and Times*, by T. Garrard, 1852.)

[1] White Kennet's *Case of Impropriations*, &c., p. 308.
[2] See *Memoir of Sir George Wheler.*   [3] *Lives of the Poets*, ii. 228.

none of the Societies formed at this period for missionary, devotional, or philanthropic objects, does any woman occupy a leading share. The only attempt to form anything like an organisation of women was, as we shall see, promptly nipped in the bud. Readers of the 'Spectator' will remember how the two great essayists, the one chivalrously, the other rather contemptuously, strive to raise the status of women, both agreeing that it was not a high one. The low estimation in which the intellectual powers of the sex were held is strikingly brought before us in connection with the first pious churchwoman who demands our notice.[1]

Dorothy, Lady Pakington (d. 1679), enjoyed exceptional advantages all her life long, both for the improvement of her mind and for her advancement in the spiritual life. She belonged to a family equally noted for its moral and its intellectual eminence, being the daughter of Sir Thomas Coventry; and she was educated under the direction of a very learned man, Sir Norton Knatchbull. Her marriage with Sir John Pakington made Westwood House her home; and Westwood House during the Rebellion was to distressed royalists and churchmen, what Shottesbrooke House after the Revolution was to distressed nonjurors. At Westwood, Henry Hammond found a permanent, and George Morley a temporary home. The mistress was a friend of Fell, Gunning, Henchman, Pearson, Thomas, Dolben, Allestree, —in fact of the most famous churchmen of the period. Hickes knew her well in his early years, and affirms that some of the great men mentioned above considered her knowledge of sacred literature and ethics of all kinds equal to their own.[2] And yet her sex was considered by many an insurmountable *à priori* objection to Lady Pakington's authorship of the 'Whole Duty of Man.'

---

[1] 'In the female world,' writes Dr. Johnson in his *Life of Addison*, 'any acquaintance with books was distinguished only to be censured.'

[2] See Hickes' preface to his *Anglo-Saxon and Mæso-Gothic Grammar*, inscribed to Sir John Pakington, grandson of Dorothy, Lady Pakington.

The Court of Charles II. is not exactly the place where one would expect to find the brightest examples of female piety; and yet on that most uncongenial soil blossomed one of the fairest flowers that ever grew in Christ's garden on earth. **Margaret Godolphin,** *née* Blagge (1652-1678), was before her marriage a maid of honour to the ill-used Queen Catherine. Her short but lovely life has been sketched by the sympathising pen of her devoted friend, John Evelyn; and it would be almost like sacrilege to describe it in other than the simple but most touching language of her biographer; but as his little work is easily accessible and ought to be well known to every true churchman, it is unnecessary to quote it.[1] Suffice it to say, in the language of the accomplished editor, 'she was a true daughter of the Church of England; Puritanism did not contract her soul into moroseness, nor did she go to Rome to learn the habits of devotion.'[2] She observed most strictly all the fasts and festivals of the Church, and in fact formed her whole life, which was a blameless and Christ-like life, on the lines which our Church lays down. Nor was Mrs. Godolphin's life the only instance.

Lady Sylvius, (*née* Howard) was a maid of honour in the Court of Charles II.; and Evelyn writes to her, 'When she (Mrs. Godolphin) left Court, to your ladyship and your sister she left her pretty Oratorye, soe often consecrated with her prayers and devotions, as to the only successors of her virtues and piety; and as I am persuaded the Court was every day less sensible of its losse whilst you both continued in it, because you trode in this religious lady's stepps, so the piety it anywhere still retaines is accountable to your rare example.'[3] But Mrs. Evelyn took a more hopeful view than her husband. 'My wife,' writes the latter, 'would

---

[1] See *Life of Mrs. Godolphin*, by John Evelyn, of Wotton, Esq., now first published, and edited by the Bishop of Oxford (Wilberforce), Pickering, 1847.

[2] Bishop Wilberforce's Introduction to the above, p. xvii.

[3] *Life of Mrs. Godolphin*, p. 60.

often reprove the diffidence I was wont to express when they would sometimes discourse of piety and religion, eminent among the Court ladyes. You (Lady Sylvius) had indeed a sister there, whose perfections would no longer suffer me to continue altogether in this false persuasion, but to believe there were many saints in that country I was not much inclined to.'[1] Other contemporary evidence bears out Mrs. Evelyn's view. Roger North tells us that when his kinsman Dr. John North resided at King Charles' Court, as clerk of the closet, ' divers persons,' especially ladies, took him for their spiritual adviser. And he adds, 'I have heard him say that for the number of persons that resided in the Court, a place reputed a centre of all vice and irreligion, there were as many truly pious and strictly religious as could be found in any other resort whatsoever. And he never saw so much fervent devotion, and such frequent acts of piety and charity, as his station gave him occasion to observe there.'[2] Possibly this may be rather highly coloured; Dr. North's position would naturally make him think the best he could of his surroundings. But at any rate there were many ladies of as high rank as those about the Court, whose piety was as conspicuous as their good breeding. Such were the two sisters, Lady Ranelagh, and Mary, Countess of Warwick, daughters of the Earl of Cork, and sisters of the famous Robert Boyle, already noticed.

Lady Ranelagh, the elder sister (1614-1691), held a prominent position before the world for more than fifty years; and during the whole of that time ' we never see her name but as a living principle of good, diffusing blessings and averting harms.'[3] She went hand in hand in all his good works with her brother, who lived with her nearly forty-seven years.

---

[1] *Id.* p. 28.

[2] 'Life of the Hon. and Rev. Dr. John North,' in the *Lives of the Norths,* by Hon. Roger North, vol. iii. p. 324.

[3] 'Diary and Correspondence of Dr. J. Worthington,' from the *Baker MSS.,* edited by J. Crossley, vol. xiii. of the publications of the Chetham Society, vol. i. p. 165, *note.*

The second Earl of Clarendon often visited her, especially on Sunday afternoons, for the purpose of religious counsel.[1] Indeed she seems to have been a spiritual counsellor to many, preserving all the while the utmost humility and feminine softness.[2] Burnet affirms without exaggeration that 'she employed the whole of her time, interest, and estate in doing good,' and that 'she had with a vast reach both of knowledge and apprehension, an universal affability and easiness of access,'—with much more to the same effect.[3]

The younger sister, **Mary, Countess of Warwick** (1625-1678), was as eminent for her piety as her brother and sister were; but it took a somewhat different shape, owing to her marriage, at the early age of fifteen, with the Earl of Warwick. This nobleman had a strong leaning towards Puritanism, and was a great patron of Puritan divines, whose portentously long sermons he was not content with listening to, but would have repeated at home. The young Countess quite entered into the spirit of her new home. 'God was pleased,' she writes, 'to bring me by my marriage into a noble, and, which is more, a religious family; where religion was both practised and encouraged, and where there were daily many eminent and excellent divines, who preached in the chapel most edifyingly and awakeningly to us.'[4] There was 'a famous household chaplain,' Dr. Walker, 'by whose ministry,' she writes, 'it pleased God to work exceedingly upon me.'[5] She does not, however, forget to own her previous obligations to 'my dear sister Ranelagh, who did constantly before call upon me to turn to God,' and now encouraged her in her new course of life. There was no actual tinge of Puritanism either in Lady

---

[1] See Henry, Earl of Clarendon's *Diary*, ii. 173, and *passim*.
[2] See Worthington's *Diary*, ut supra.
[3] See Burnet's *Funeral Sermon on Hon. Robert Boyle*, appended to Birch's *Life*.
[4] *Autobiography of Mary, Countess of Warwick*, ed. by T. Crofton Croker (Percy Society), p. 15.
[5] *Id.* p. 20.

Ranelagh or her brother Robert, though there would be no violent antagonism to it in either of them; and moreover, the Countess of Warwick always professed herself a churchwoman. As her nonconforming biographer [1] honestly owns, 'she very inoffensively, regularly, and devoutly observed the orders of the Church of England in its liturgy and public service, which she failed not to attend twice a day with exemplary reverence.' She attended the services of the old Church, Chelsea, and often heard Morley preach there. Her Christian character showed itself, among other ways, in unbounded liberality. When the Earl died and bequeathed to her his property, it was said (as anticipating how she would employ it), that he had left his estate to charitable uses.[2] 'Such,' we are told, 'was the fame of her charity and hospitality, that it advanced the rent of houses in her neighbourhood, where she was the common arbitress of controversies, which she decided with great sagacity and judgment, and prevented many lawsuits.'[3] Her diary, which in MS. is of enormous length,[4] and of which the published part is but a fraction, is simply a record of her religious experience, the only facts which she notices besides this, being the names of the preachers she heard; but it may fairly be called (as it has has been), her 'Autobiography,' for religious exercises really made to a great extent the life of this good woman. It would be wearisome and unnecessary to quote the many testimonies to her excel-

---

[1] S. Clarke, a nonconformist who lost his benefice (S. Bennet Fink), in 1662, but it would be most incorrect to call him a dissenter. He expressly tells us himself, 'After the Black Act, &c., I durst not separate from the Church of England, nor was satisfied about gathering a private Church out of a true Church, as I judge the Church of England to be.' (*Autobiography* attached to *Lives of Sundry Eminent Persons in this Latter Age*, by S. Clarke.) There will, of course, be nothing strange in this to the well-informed; but, in spite of every evidence to the contrary, popular accounts persist in confounding nonconformists with dissenters.

[2] See *Life of Bishop Ken*, by a Layman, i. 70.
[3] Granger's *Biographical History of England*.
[4] The manuscript is in the British Museum.

lence which are still extant.¹ Let us pass on to another occasional worshipper at the old church, Chelsea, under Bishop Morley.

Lady Margaret Maynard has been rescued from oblivion chiefly through her connection with Ken, whose pious efforts at Little Easton she heartily supported. Like Lady Warwick she has left us a journal which breathes a like spirit of piety, but is that of a more distinctive churchwoman than the former, as might be expected from one who had sat at the feet of Ken, and been deeply impressed by his preaching.² Ken, in preaching her funeral sermon, drew a picture of a most devoted churchwoman.

Lady Frances Digby stood somewhat in the same relation to Kettlewell at Coleshill as Lady Maynard did to Ken at Easton. She died however in her twenty-third year, 'but,' says Kettlewell in her funeral sermon, 'in her green years she had attained a maturity in goodness.' Kettlewell was not the man to say conventional nothings, even in a funeral sermon; we may therefore fully believe all that he says in her praise. 'I freely confess to your lordship,' he says in his dedication of the sermon to the bereaved husband, 'that my aim has been to speak too little for fear of saying too much. They who knew her best will say that this is not only a true, but a modest character.'³

The last two ladies are known rather as worthy helpmates to pious husbands than as having struck out an independent line of their own. The same cannot be said of **Lady Elizabeth Hastings**, daughter of the Earl of

---

¹ See, *inter alia*, the *Funeral Sermon* by Dr. Walker. Aubrey's *Letters*, ii. 255, S. Clarke (*ut supra*), &c.

² She writes, for instance, after having heard Ken preach on the Holy Communion; 'When the sermon was done, I found my heart exceedingly to long after this blessed feast; and when I remembered the sufferings of our Saviour, I did weep bitterly, and with great earnestness begged of God to give me Christ. My heart was much carried out to bless God, and I had then such sweet communion with Him, that I could say it was good for me to be there.'

³ See *Life of Kettlewell*, p. 704 &c.

Huntingdon, who long survived the period with which this work deals, but who was well known for her many excellences during the latter part of our period. She succeeded in winning the deep respect and admiration of men who were by no means inclined themselves to follow the strictness of her life. Congreve has immortalised her, in rather bombastic and conventional language, in the 42nd number of the 'Tatler,' under the singularly inappropriate title of the 'Divine Aspasia,' and Steele took up the same subject in the 49th number, in a far more touching and genuine strain; but both agree in lavishing upon her the most enthusiastic praise. But it was not among men like Congreve and Steele that Lady Betty Hastings (as she was generally called) sought and found her friends. Being early left a widow, she settled at Ledsham or Ledstow Hall in Yorkshire, and, though still young and beautiful, retired entirely from what is called 'society,' and devoted herself to works of piety and charity. There she enjoyed the conversation of pious churchmen, such as Archbishop Sharp, Richard Lucas, and Robert Nelson. The latter applied to her the text, 'Many daughters have done virtuously, but thou excellest them all;' and Nelson,[1] like Kettlewell, was a man who never flattered or exaggerated. Ralph Thoresby describes with delight a visit he paid to Ledsham Hall, when he was 'extremely pleased with the most agreeable conversation of the pious and excellent Lady E. Hastings.'[2] She not only spent her time and money most lavishly in all sorts of good works in her own neighbourhood, but was ever ready to lend a helping hand to schemes of piety and benevolence in all parts of the world. Bishop Wilson found her a most generous supporter in his various good works in the Isle of Man;[3] she contributed nobly to poor Dean Berkeley's Bermuda mission scheme,[4] and not only helped

---

[1] See Nelson's *Address to Persons of Quality.*   [2] *Diary,* ii. 82.
[3] See Stowell's *Life of Wilson,* p. 281, and Cruttwell's *Life,* p. 18.
[4] 500*l*. See Anderson's *History of the Colonial Church,* iii. 350.

Mrs. Astell most liberally in her design for a 'Protestant Nunnery,' but had the moral courage to support that good lady when she was suffering from most unmerited obloquy.[1]

Rachel Wriothesley, Lady Russell (1636-1713), was, like Lady E. Hastings, for many years a widow of blameless life, and to her widowhood a peculiarly melancholy interest is attached, owing to the sad circumstances of her husband's death. She was the daughter of the pious and high-minded Earl of Southampton, and married first Lord Vaughan; after his death she married Mr., afterwards Lord William Russell, whose tragic end everybody knows. As wife, widow, and mother, Lady Russell was a pattern. Read in the light of after-events, few compositions are more touching than her letters to her second husband, breathing, as they do, a spirit of the most tender affection and ardent piety,[2] and presenting a perfect picture of domestic happiness. How that happiness was rudely shattered by the execution of Lord William, how nobly Lady Russell behaved at and after the trial, assisting her husband as amanuensis, and, after the sentence throwing herself at the king's feet to plead for him whom she loved next to God, need not here be told. When she was left a second time a widow,

---

[1] See *infra*, pp. 148-9, and Ballard's *British Ladies*, p. 317. There is a very poor account, without anything definite or interesting in it, of the good lady, entitled *An Historical Character relating to the holy and exemplary Life of Lady E. Hastings*, by Thomas Barnard, Master of the Free School in Leeds, pub. 1742.

[2] The following is a specimen. 'God knows best when we have had enough here; what I most earnestly beg from His mercy is, that we both live so as, whichever goes first, the other may not sorrow as for one of whom they have no hope. Then let us cheerfully expect to be together to a good old age; if not, let us not doubt but He will support us under what trial he will inflict. These are necessary meditations sometimes, that we may not be surprised above our strength by a sudden accident, being unprepared.' (See *Letters from Lady Russell to her husband, from 1672 to 1682*, attached to *Some Account of the Life of Rachael Wriothesley, Lady Russell*, by the Editor of Madame du Deffand's Letters. A fuller collection of the *Letters of Lady R. Russell* has also been published, 3rd edition, 1792.)

she devoted herself to the education of her children, but did not shut herself entirely out from the world. As to her religious sentiments, the influence of her father, her second husband, and her uncle, a French refugee named Ruvigny, all inclined her to greater liberality towards nonconformists than was usual among church-people of that day; both Tillotson and Burnet (the best side of whose character comes out in his relation to this noble lady) were also her friends, and would of course influence her in the same direction. But personally she was a staunch adherent to the Church of England; her spiritual director was Dr. Fitzwilliam, a nonjuror who had been chaplain to the Earl of Southampton, and retained through life the closest intimacy with his children, especially Lady Russell. His letters to her are written in a tone of authority mingled with deep affection, and her replies clearly imply that she desired to be guided by his counsel. During the minority of her son, who had succeeded to the Earldom of Bedford, great public responsibilities of course devolved upon her, among other ways, in the distribution of church patronage, and she discharged them as she did every duty of her life, with admirable conscientiousness and judiciousness.

Before we descend to the commonalty, two more ladies of rank deserve a passing notice. **The Countess of Derby**, whose memory is embalmed in a prayer written by the saintly Bishop Wilson,[1] and whose assistance is said to have been most valuable to him in his attempts, as chaplain, to reform the household of his generous but rather reckless patron; and **Lady Conway**, sister of the pious and able Heneage Finch, Earl of Nottingham. To the latter, Dr. Henry More's heroine pupil, a prominent place would have to be

[1] 'Grant that we may all follow her steps in the way which leads to eternal life. Let her zeal and sincerity encourage the good to persevere, and her piety provoke the wicked to amend their ways, that at last we may all meet, and become again one family, in the eternal mansions which Thou hast prepared for all that love and fear Thy Name.' (See Stowell's *Life of Bishop Wilson*, p. 28.)

given, if this were a record of all the remarkable women of the period who showed an interest in religion, but as it is simply a sketch of pious *churchwomen*, no more need be said about one who turned Quakeress.[1]

Mention has already been made of **Mary Astell** (1668–1731), a lady of very remarkable intelligence, and no less remarkable piety. She was the daughter of a merchant at Newcastle, but was educated by her uncle, a clergyman, who, observing her intellectual aptitude, devoted himself personally to the cultivation of her mind. Her devotional works will be noticed presently, but one of her writings must be mentioned here in connection with her life. Seeing and lamenting the imperfect education, and the frivolous, aimless lives of many of her sex, she published 'A Serious Proposal to Ladies, &c.' The proposal was that a sort of 'Protestant Nunnery,' or, 'lest the word nunnery should frighten people, a Christian Retirement should be formed, to which ladies who nauseated the world might retire,' to improve their minds and cultivate the spiritual life. The college was to be conducted on strictly Church principles, and its inmates were to enjoy all Church privileges in their fulness, but there was not the slightest foundation for the suspicion, which wrecked it at the outset, that it had a Romanising tendency.[2] A 'great lady,' supposed by some to be the Princess of Denmark, afterwards Queen Anne, by others with more probability to be Lady E. Hastings,[3] was so

---

[1] In the *Rawdon Papers* there is rather an amusing sketch of Lady Conway's household, written by her husband to Sir G. Rawdon, to dissuade him from sending his daughter, Lord Conway's niece, to live with them. 'In my family all the women about my wife, and most of the rest, are Quakers, and Mons. Van Helmont is governor of that flock; an unpleasing sort of people, silent, sullen, and of a reserved conversation, which can be no ways agreeable to your daughter, nor for her advantage. These and all that society have free access to my wife, but I believe Dr. More, though he was in the house all the last summer, did not see her above twice or thrice.' (p. 251.)

[2] See *Serious Proposal to the Ladies for the advancement of their true and greatest Interest, by a lover of her sex* (published 1694.)

[3] See Miss Strickland's *Lives of the Queens of England: Mary Beatrice*

pleased with the proposal that she purposed giving 10,000*l.* for the erection of a college in which it might be carried out. But Bishop Burnet 'buzzed into the ears' of this great lady a sort of 'No Popery' alarm, and so wrought upon her feelings that, 'as she was zealously attached to the Church of England,' she abandoned her benevolent intention. Hence the scheme fell through for want of funds; but poor Mrs. Astell was not allowed to rest in peace. An atrocious libel, reflecting upon her personal character, and ridiculing her 'Platonic notions' (she was a vehement anti-Platonist!) appeared in the 32nd number of the 'Tatler,' and the attack was renewed in the 63rd number. The papers are manifestly written under an entire misconception, and would not be worth noticing but for the fame of the periodical in which they appeared. Everything we hear of Mrs. Astell gives us the idea of one who lived a most blameless life, and was valued intellectually, perhaps beyond her merits, by her contemporaries. Dean (afterwards Bishop) Atterbury,[1] her near neighbour at Chelsea, John Norris of Bemerton,[2] Dean Hickes,[3] Henry Dodwell,[4] all agree in praising her highly, and it would be difficult to discover a single hint which would lead one to suppose that her reputation as a most Christian-minded woman was undeserved.

Susanna Hopton (1627–1709) resembled in many respects Mary Astell. Both were what would now be called advanced churchwomen; both were intelligent and learned beyond the average of women of their day, both had many friends and correspondents among the clergy, and both

---

of Modena, vi. 245; Ballard's *Memoirs of British Ladies: Mary Astell,* p. 307. Also *Tatler,* No. 37, note in the edition of 1797.

[1] See *Memoirs and Correspondence of Bishop Atterbury,* by Folkestone Williams, i. 169, containing an interesting letter from Atterbury to Smalridge about Mrs. Astell.

[2] See *Letters concerning the Love of God between the Author of the Proposal to the Ladies, and Mr. John Norris.*

[3] See his Letters to Dr. Charlett, Master of University College.

[4] 'That admirable gentlewoman, Mrs. Astell.'

wrote devotional works of considerable repute. But Susanna Hopton was perhaps in rather a higher social position than Mary Astell; at any rate, she was more richly endowed with this world's goods. Dr. Hickes and Dr. Spinckes have both given us brief, but very vivid, sketches of her life and character; and of course she figures conspicuously in Ballard's 'Memoirs of Learned British Ladies.' From these sources, and from her own writings, which evidently reflect the writer's own mind, it is easy to form a definite picture of the good lady. She is described by Spinckes as 'a person of quality, estate, and figure in her country, the ingeniously inquisitive, and truly devout and pious relict of R. Hopton, Esq., who had been one of the Welsh judges in the reigns of Charles II. and James II.'[1] In her early years she had been allured into the Church of Rome, but she came back to the Church of her baptism, more strongly convinced of its excellence than ever, and she never wavered in her opinion again to the end of her long life. Hickes writes of her as 'one whose house is a temple, and whose family is a church or religious society, and whose hands are daily lifted up to Heaven, with alms as well as prayers; one who religiously observes all the orders of the Church, and for the great ends for which they are enjoyned; in a word, one who is a great ornament to our communion in this degenerate age.'[2]

Damaris Cudworth (1658–1708), daughter of Ralph Cudworth, the great author of the 'Intellectual System,' wife of Sir F. Masham, and friend of John Locke, who died in her house, deserves a passing notice as a pious and learned lady. As might be expected in a disciple of Locke, she was a churchwoman of a different type from that of the last two ladies, but she *was* a churchwoman, and, so

---

[1] See Spinckes' Preface to *A Collection of Meditations and Devotions*, in three Parts (published 1717).

[2] Preface to *Devotions in the ancient way of Offices, &c.* See also Hickes' *Letters*, passim, especially vol. ii. pp. 119 and 129.

far as can be ascertained, a very worthy one. Locke held her in the highest admiration and esteem, and her kind attention to that great man is one of the many amiable traits in her character.[1]

Ken's 'Good Virgins,' the two **Misses Kemeyse**, in whose retreat at Naish House the deprived bishop often sought refuge when the gaieties of Longleat drove him from that hospitable seat, or when the rules of his Church suggested a 'retirement into the desert out of the noise and hurry of the world,'[2] ought not to be forgotten. Ken was attracted not only by the solitude of Naish House, but by his esteem for the good old maiden ladies who owned it. They, in their turn, had the deepest reverence for Ken, and relieved, through him, many of the deprived clergy. One of them, who was a recipient of their bounty, Thomas Smith, has drawn a pretty picture of their life. 'The private seat,' he writes to Ken, 'of the good ladyes hath better pretence to the title of a "Religious House" than those so-called in Popish countries. . . . These good ladyes are happy under your conduct, and are, by an uninterrupted course of piety, elevated above all the gaudy pompes and vanities of the world, and enjoy all the comforts and satisfactions and serenity of mind, to be wished for and attained on this side of Heaven, in their solitude.'[3]

The 'Matchless Orinda' may fairly claim a place among eminent churchwomen, though certainly not so prominent a one as the epithet attached to her name would imply. The 'matchless Orinda' was known to prosaic mortals as **Mrs. Katherine Philips**, *née* Fowler (1631-1664). Brought up as a Presbyterian, she became a staunch churchwoman and royalist by conviction, at a time when such a change was anything but beneficial to her worldly pros-

---

[1] See Professor Fowler's 'Locke,' in the *English Men of Letters* series, pp. 62 and 106.
[2] Ken's *Prose Works*, edited by Round, pp. 96-99.
[3] Ken's *Prose Works*, ut supra.

pects. She was born and passed her childhood within the sound of Bow Bells, but on her marriage with a Welsh gentleman, Mr. Philips (the Antenor of her poems), she went to live in the more poetical region of South Wales. Here she made the acquaintance and won the esteem of her neighbour at Golden Grove, Jeremy Taylor, who paid her the high honour of dedicating his 'Discourse on the Nature, Offices, and Measures of Friendship' 'to the most ingenious and excellent Mrs. Katherine Philips.' 'Most ingenious and excellent' we may allow her to have been, though we cannot admit her to be 'matchless,' and though we may think her ingenuity to be rather perverted in her high-flown advocacy of platonic friendship in her poems; but all her influence, which for a time was very great, was exercised in behalf of what was pure and good, and she was an excellent Christian and churchwoman.

Mrs. Evelyn, the wife of John Evelyn, was a wife worthy of such a husband. This is evident from incidental notices in the famous 'Diary,' and is confirmed by the lady's own 'Letters,' and by the 'Character' of her, as sketched by Dr. Bohun, her son's tutor. 'The memory,' writes Dr. Bohun, 'of her virtues and benefits made such deep impression on her neighbours of Deptford and Greenwich, that if any should bring in another report from this, or what was generally received among them, they would condemn it as false, and the effect of a slanderous calumny.' She herself gives us an excellent sketch of what she considered to be the province of a pious wife and mother, though it would hardly satisfy the advocates of women's rights. 'We are willing,' she writes to Dr. Bohun, 'to acknowledge all time borrowed from family duties is misspent; the care of children's education, observing a husband's commands, assisting the sick, relieving the poor, and being serviceable to our friends, are of sufficient weight to employ the most improved capacities amongst us.'[1] In

---

[1] The *Letters of Mrs. Evelyn, with her Character by Dr. Bohun*, will be

these unpretentious but useful duties she was content to spend her blameless life, proving a good helpmate to her famous husband, whom she survived about three years.

There are some ladies whose piety is only known to us from the fact of their funeral sermons having been preached by famous divines, and therefore preserved. Such were **Lady Cutts**, who died at the early age of eighteen, and of whom a full biography is given in one of Atterbury's famous sermons;[1] and **Lady Marow**, whose funeral sermon Bishop Hough preached in 1714. It concludes, after a long panegyric, thus: 'They who knew the Lady Marow will subscribe to what I have said concerning her; and, I apprehend, will think the character rather short and defective, than that I have exceeded it;'[2] **Lady Brooke** (1602-1683), daughter of the famous royalist T. Culpepper, and wife of Sir R. Brooke; but, apart from the fact that funeral sermons are not very satisfactory testimonies, these ladies are rather too shadowy beings to be adduced as instances of female piety.

There is, however, one class of churchwomen who must not be omitted, namely, the wives of clergymen. The popular opinion that the clergy of this period married, as a rule, wives of a low social standing, may be incorrect. But waiving that question for the present, it is clear that the clergyman's wife, as such, was not so prominent a feature in clerical life as she is at present. She generally appears, when she appears at all in clerical biographies, simply as the helpmate of her husband. Thus, **Anne Nelson**, daughter of the rector of Haugham in Lincolnshire, who married Robert Sanderson, is sufficiently described, according to the notions of Sanderson's biographer, as 'such a wife as was suitable to his own desires; a wife that made his life happy

found appended to the 4th volume of Evelyn's *Diary*, Bray's edition, 1852.

[1] Sermon VI. in Atterbury's *Sermons*, 8th ed., 1766.

[2] See *Life of Rev. John Hough, D.D., successively Bishop of Oxford, Lichfield and Coventry, and Worcester*, by J. Wilmot, p. 78.

by being always content when he was cheerful; that divided her joys with him, and abated of his sorrow, by bearing a part of that burden; a wife that demonstrated her affection by a cheerful obedience to all his desires during the whole course of his life; and at his death too, for she survived him.'[1] **Mary Caning**, who became the wife of Robert Frampton, afterwards Bishop of Gloucester, is briefly referred to by Frampton's contemporary biographer as one who 'understood the grounds of religion as thoroughly as most. And as few could talk better of it than she, so yet fewer there are that so conscientiously reduced their knowledge to practice, and was thereby a yoke fellow worthy such an husband.'[2] **Bridget Gregory**, who married Bishop Bull, is described, while yet living, by Bull's biographer, as 'in all respects a fit consort for a clergyman, as being in her own nature sufficiently provident, and yet well disposed to all manner of good works, out of a true principle of love to God and goodness. Her attire was very plain and grave; her chief diversion was the care of her family; and her main ambition was to please her husband, to whom she was always a complying and obedient wife.'[3] He then proceeds to describe her self-denying labours in behalf of the temporal and spiritual condition of the poor; but all was done in the strictest subordination to her husband's authority.

It is the same with **Mrs. Mary Patten**, who was married to the saintly Bishop Wilson in 1698. During the short period of her married life, which was barely seven years, she was the most sympathising and helpful of companions. The good bishop mentions in his catalogue of 'special favours,' 'October 27, 1698, I was married to M. Patten, an excellent woman;'[4] and then tells us of 'her great modesty

---

[1] Izaak Walton's *Life of Dr. Robert Sanderson*.
[2] *Life of Robert Frampton, Bishop of Gloucester*, edited by Rev. T. Simpson Evans, from an old MS. Memoir, pp. 109–10.
[3] Nelson's *Life of Bull*, p. 69. [4] Keble's *Life of Bishop Wilson*, i. 121.

and meekness of spirit, her remarkable dutifulness to her parents and love to her relations; her singular love to himself, her tender affection for her children, in performing all the offices of a kind and pious mother; her peculiar care of her family, and the prudence and mildness with which she governed it; the great humility of her conversation with all sorts of persons; her great compassion for the poor and miserable, and her cheerful concurrence with him in relieving them.'[1] This is an ample catalogue of virtues, but it will be observed that they are all of the domestic sort. Nor do any of the exquisite prayers which, *more suo*, he wrote on the occasion of her last illness and of her death, from which the above description is taken, give us any other impression.

Still more strikingly is the point we are noting brought out in the life of **Elizabeth Blake** (1661-170$\frac{3}{9}$), the third wife of Bishop Burnet, who appears to have been really a remarkable woman. She was the eldest daughter of Sir R. Blake, and married at the age of seventeen Mr. Berkeley of Spetchley, the match being brought about by Bishop Fell. That distinguished prelate, and the still more distinguished Stillingfleet, were most intimate with her, and expressed the very highest opinion both of her intellectual and moral character. Of her intellectual powers we have ample evidence in the devotional work which she published anonymously, and which will be noted in its proper place; and her piety, generosity, and humility were equally conspicuous during her married life and her seven years of widowhood. And yet, Thomas Burnet, the bishop's son, describes the marriage of such a woman with his father in terms which would be applicable to the selection of a nursery governess. 'The assiduous attention which he was obliged to, whilst he was preceptor to the Duke (of Gloucester), and the tender age of his children, made it requisite to look out for a proper mistress to his family. He fixed

---

[1] See Stowell's *Life of Bishop Wilson*, p. 54.

upon Mrs. Berkeley, a lady of uncommon degrees of knowledge, piety, and virtue,' &c.[1]

All these, be it observed, were ladies of gentle birth. And so was a still more remarkable woman than any of them, **Susanna Annesley** (1669-1742), the faithful wife of Samuel Wesley. She was the daughter of Dr. Annesley, a near relation of the Earl of Anglesey, and the minister of S. Giles', Cripplegate, from which he was ejected by the Bartholomew Act. Thus she was brought up a nonconformist, but became a staunch churchwoman by conviction before she was thirteen years of age. The many readers of the many lives of John Wesley must have been struck with the marked individuality of his mother's character. She impressed herself upon her three famous sons, whose early education, as, indeed, that of all her numerous family, was entirely under her charge, more strongly than their father. The very style of writing which was common to all three brothers, Samuel, John, and Charles, closely resembles that of their mother; plain good sense, expressed curtly and even bluntly, but in thoroughly pure and idiomatic language, belongs to them all. Mrs. Wesley was a well-educated woman, with a strong and even masculine mind. She showed, too, a masculine spirit in her brave struggles with poverty; but there was in her no lack of feminine delicacy, and she was ever content to be simply the rector's wife, though she was clearly the stronger character of the two. She did not always agree with her husband, for while *he* wrote in defence of the Revolution, *she* sympathised with the nonjurors; but she was faithful to her marriage vow of obedience, and was as admirable a wife as she was a mother. But her life and letters are, or might be, so well known, that it is needless to dwell

---

[1] See *Life of Bishop Burnet*, by Thomas Burnet, Esq., prefixed to Burnet's *History of his Own Times* (edition of 1815). For an account of Mrs. Elizabeth Burnet, see the *Memoirs* of her by Thomas Goodwyn, D.D., Archdeacon of Oxford (afterwards Archbishop of Cashel), prefixed to her *Method of Devotion* (2nd edition, 1709).

longer upon her.¹ But for the fame of her great sons, this very remarkable woman would have probably passed into oblivion. And in other rectories, besides Epworth, may there not have been Susanna Wesleys? She is not spoken of as a phenomenon, and there is no reason to suppose that in her generation there were not many who followed her, though perhaps 'haud passibus æquis.'

¹ See Dr. Adam Clarke's *Memoirs of the Wesley Family*. *The Mother of the Wesleys*, by Rev. — Kirk. *Susanna Wesley*, by E. Clarke, in the *Eminent Women* series. *The Women of Methodism*, by A. Stevens, LL.D. Southey, Tyerman, &c.

CHAPTER IV.

RESTORATION OF ORDER.

A DIFFICULT task, no doubt, lay before the restorers of Church order after the return of the king. The havoc which had been made with the fabrics, the long disuse in public of the order and ceremonies of the Church of England, the perplexity of men's minds amid the din of contending parties when there were almost as many sects as worshippers,[1] might well make many feel as Basire felt when he said ' it would take up a whole man to reform the parsons and repair the churches.'[2] Nevertheless, if the majority of the nation, clergy and laity, had set themselves, shoulder to shoulder, to restore order externally and internally, the work would soon have been done. Unfortunately this was not the case. Many able and pious churchmen, both lay and clerical, have been noticed, and many more might be added to the list, and these men in time made their influence felt. But there were also many, both clergy and laity, who were very far indeed from helping to strengthen the hands of the Church. It has been said, and, it is to be feared, with great truth, that the Church had to begin her work with a clergy of whom at least three-fourths were alien to her doctrine and discipline.[3] The penal Acts were a direct encouragement to men of loose principles to conform, and a discouragement to men of tender consciences. They excluded a Howe, a Baxter, and a Bates, and retained a

---

[1] See Henry Rogers' *Life and Character of John Howe*, p. 64.
[2] See *Correspondence of Bishop Cosin* (Surtees Society), Part II.
[3] *Church Quarterly Review*.

Parker, a Cartwright, and a Wood. There were very many conformists who were not churchmen at all, except in name.[1] With such a clergy it was not likely that Church order would be restored rapidly, even if the laity had been staunch. But, though doubtless the laxity and viciousness which belonged to the Court and its purlieus have been attributed too generally to the country at large, still the contemporary complaints of a general looseness of morals are too numerous and trustworthy to be disregarded. The reader, therefore, must expect to find in this chapter indications of only a very gradual progress.

To begin with the fabrics. The condition of the Cathedrals must have been appalling indeed when the king returned. S. Paul's is described as a loathsome Golgotha.[2] The choir had been turned into horse barracks for the Oliverian troopers, and saw-pits had been dug within its enclosures.[3] When Bishop Hacket went to Lichfield 'he found sorrow and pity in himself to see his Cathedral Church lying in the dust. At S. Asaph the postmaster had kept his horses and oxen in the nave. At Exeter they made the church a common jakes.'[4] The accounts of

[1] Take the following contemporary definition of Latitudinarians: 'Persons that had no great liking for the liturgy or ceremonies, or indeed the government of this church, but yet had attained to such a largeness and freedom of judgment, as that they could conform, though without any warmth or affection for these things.' (Appendix to Birch's *Life of Tillotson*, by J. B. [that is, John Beardmore, Tillotson's pupil at Clare Hall].). This is not a fair description of all 'Latitudinarians,' but it is applicable to many 'conformists.' Dean Granville complains of 'the nonconformity or rather semi-conformity of the clergy (who did with zeale more than enough and sometimes too bitterly inveigh against nonconformists), which engendered that brood which are the authors of our misery, and their forwardness to dispense, throughout the nation, with the Church discipline as they pleased, rubricks of Liturgy,' &c. (*Remains of Dean Granville*, Surtees Miscellanea, Part I., p. 136.) See also Part II., p. 42. Also, *Life of Bishop Frampton*, edited by Rev. T. Simpson, p. 133; South's *Sermons*, passim; *Life of Bishop Hacket*, &c. &c.

[2] *A Character of England*, &c., by John Evelyn, published 1659.

[3] *Sir Christopher Wren and his Times*, Elmes, p. 224.

[4] *Traditions and Customs of Cathedrals*, by Mackenzie Walcott, p. 6.

Canterbury,[1] Chichester,[2] in fact almost all the Cathedrals except Salisbury are as bad. The parish churches do not appear to have suffered so severely as the Cathedrals, which were the objects of the Puritans' special aversion, but the accounts of them are sad enough. Thus Archdeacon Basire reports of Northumberland in 1662 : 'The Fabricks of many Churches and Chappells are altogether ruinous and in great decay, and cannott be gotten repaired without visitations. In many churches there be neither Bibles, Books of Common Prayer, surplisses, fonts, Communion Tables, nor anything that is necessarie for the service of God.'[3] In 1665 he does not appear to have found matters much improved,[4] and four years later he 'did visit as many churches as he could, sundry of which were scandalously ruinous.'[5] In 1671 the author of the 'Answer to the Grounds &c. for the Contempt of the Clergy' writes: 'You might ride through a street remarkable for nothing so much as that haply the church is not thakt so well as most of the houses.' In 1677 Evelyn rode through Suffolk, and found 'most of the Houses of God in this county resembling rather stables and thatched cottages than temples in which to serve the Most High.'[6] In 1686 the commissioners appointed by Bishop Lake to inquire into the condition of parish churches in Sussex report a most

The whole of this work deserves careful attention from those who desire to know the state of the Cathedrals.

[1] See Kennet's *Register*, 162, and Lathbury's *History of the Convocation of the Church of England*, p. 298.

[2] *Diocesan Histories—Chichester*, by W. R. W. Stephens (S.P.C.K.), p. 221, &c.

[3] From Hunter's Collection of MSS., ii. 68, quoted in Granville's *Remains*, Part I., p. 251. See also Basire's letter to Bishop Cosin, in 1661, in *Correspondence of Bishop Cosin*, Surtees Society, Part II., p. 87.

[4] At S. Nicholas, the mother church of Newcastle, the roof was so bad that it rained in upon the aldermen when they were receiving the Holy Communion. The chancel at Ilderton was ruinous ; at Ingram the body of the church was ruinous, 'covered with sodds'; at Shilbottle the Minister had no gown, and the chancel no windows. And so forth.

[5] *Correspondence of Isaac Basire*, edited by Darnall, p. 280.

[6] *Diary*, ii. 113.

grievous state of things;[1] in the same year Bishop Turner complains of 'the sordidness of so many country churches' in the diocese of Ely;[2] and even so late as 1697, the Bishop of Lincoln tells his clergy that some chancels 'lay wholly disused in more nasty manner than any cottager would keep his own house.'[3] But sad as these accounts are, it will be observed that most of the things complained of might have been easily remedied, and in many cases they certainly were. Thus Bishop Turner, in the letter already quoted, gratefully owns that 'having found very many of the churches very sadly dilapidated, or, at least, mightily out of repair, he had now pleasing accounts from many places of the care already taken to repair them.' The mere enumeration of Sir Christopher Wren's achievements is sufficient to shew that the work of church building and restoration was actively carried on. 'From 1666 to 1711 he designed and built fifty-three parish churches in London, besides reparations and additions to many others, repaired and added to the Cathedrals of Salisbury, Chichester, Westminster Abbey &c.'[4] It must of course be remembered that the Fire of London, in which eighty-nine churches were destroyed, necessitated much of this work; but on the other hand, it did not include the most active part of our period, the latter part of the reign of Queen Anne, when Wren, though still living, was laid by, while it did include the reign of James II., during which church building was almost at a standstill.[5] Lichfield Cathedral was practically rebuilt,

[1] See *Diocesan History of Chichester*, ut supra, p. 238.
[2] See *Letter to the Clergy of the Diocese of Ely*, by Bishop Turner, before his Visitation, 1686.
[3] *Visitation Charge*, 1697.
[4] See *Sir Christopher Wren and his Times*, by James Elmes, p. 265, and Lucy Phillimore's, *Sir Christopher Wren*, Appendix II., p. 338, where a full list of the churches &c. built by Sir C. Wren is given.
[5] 'There are few examples,' writes White Kennet, 'of piety to parish churches in the reign of James II., because of the just apprehension of danger, and threats of destruction to the Church by law established.' (*Case of Impropriations*, &c., published 1704, p. 308.)

M

mainly through the noble exertions of Bishop Hacket, whom his grateful fellow-citizens therefore called 'a second Cedda.'¹ 25,000*l.* were spent on Exeter Cathedral during Dr. Seth Ward's short incumbency of the see; and a large sum was expended, though with very questionable taste, on Salisbury, when he was Bishop of Sarum. S. Paul's was entirely rebuilt, and in fact, most of the Cathedrals were made more or less decent, and this implies the expenditure of a vast sum of money.

With regard to the parish churches, we can only gather what was done from incidental notices; but these are sufficient to show that the work was very considerable. Thus the two excellent Lords Digby, Simon and William, spent large sums in church building and repairing at Coleshill, Overwhitacre, and Sheldon;² Dr. Busby 'built a handsome church at Willan.'³ All Saints', Oxford, was built from a design of Dean Aldrich, and 'esteemed a finished specimen of his acknowledged skill in architecture.'⁴ The Man of Ross's liberality in regard to the fabric of his parish church is historical. We read of a new church at Ingestre built by the 'pious and generous Walter Chetwynd, Esq.,' in 1677;⁵ of a new church (Christ Church) near Paris Garden, Southwark, erected in 1670 at the sole expense of Mr. George Marshall, an inhabitant.⁶ But it would be wearisome to go on with the list; let us rather observe, that from what we know of the churches that were built, it is obvious that there was no stinting of money. Take, for instance, the noblest of all the monuments of the period, new S. Paul's. Besides the parliamentary aid, which must have

---

¹ Letter from the Corporation of Lichfield to Elias Ashmole in 1666. See *Memoirs of the Life of that learned Antiquary, E. Ashmole, Esq., drawn up by himself by way of Diary.*
² See *Life of Rawlet* (by Dr. Bray).
³ *Case of Impropriations* &c., p. 345.
⁴ See *Life and Literary Remains of Dean Bathurst* (1711), p. 71.
⁵ *Case of Impropriations* &c., 297.
⁶ White Kennet's *History of England*, iii. p. 286.

been considerable,[1] Bishop Compton issued an address to the country at large, which was nobly responded to, especially by the wealthier clergy. The work was thirty-five years in progress (1675–1710), and, when completed, was worthy of a great nation. Other churches built at the same time in London, such as S. Mary-le-Bow, of which the Londoners of the time were immensely proud,[2] and S. James's, Piccadilly, were very costly, as, indeed, were all Wren's churches. We then come to the famous Act of 1710 for the building of fifty-two new churches within the bills of mortality. The project was cordially recommended by Convocation[3] and warmly taken up by Queen Anne; and the Bill passed Parliament without opposition. The veteran Wren gave the benefit of his advice, though he was too old to undertake so vast a work. The Commission was formed, and everything seemed to be going on in the most satisfactory manner. But alas! Robert Nelson shewed a sad prescience when a year or two later he uttered a warning voice, reminding his rich fellow-countrymen that the work was 'only *begun*, not *done*.'[4] It never *was* done. Of the fifty-two projected churches, only twelve were built, and three or four others repaired; the work languished, and was quietly suffered to drop altogether; but on the twelve that were built no expense was spared.

From the fabrics we pass on to the services which were performed within them. To begin with the Sacraments. One of the disorders against which good churchmen waged incessant war, was the administration of Holy Baptism in private houses without any urgent necessity. Pepys con-

[1] An Act was passed for levying a duty of 3s. a chaldron on all coals brought into the port of London, half of which was to be applied to the rebuilding of S. Paul's and other parish churches from 1670 to 1687.

[2] 'It lifts up its head,' writes Paterson, 'above and excells most of the churches in London, and perhaps in Europe.' (*Pietas Londinensis*, published 1714.)

[3] See Lathbury's *History of Convocation*, p. 410.

[4] *Address to Persons of Quality: Ways and Means of Doing Good* (1715).

stantly refers to these private christenings in terms which intimate that they were the rule, not the exception.[1] Bishop Compton made 'the shameful disuse of public baptisms' one of the chief subjects of conference with his clergy in 1683.[2] It is related of Sherlock of Winwick, as a proof of his exceptional firmness, that he would never baptize in houses, or except as the rubric directs,[3] and Bull's similar conduct at Suddington is spoken of in similar terms.[4] Dean Granville complains of one of his curates' 'complaisance with the rich about privately baptizing, which,' he adds, 'was quite the contrary to my method, who, if I had made an exception at all, would have made it for the poor.'[5] Articles of Visitation generally include a question on this subject, as being one of the evils of the day.[6] It was not an evil easily eradicated. So late as 1703 we find the Lower House of Convocation complaining of the neglect of parents to bring children who had been privately baptized to church. Later still, Bishop Bull warns his clergy in the diocese of S. David's against private baptisms.[7] It should be noted that it was not mere carelessness on the part of the minister which caused this irregularity. In the first place, there was a difficulty in persuading some people who 'had as mean an opinion of the baptismal waters as Naaman had of those of Israel,'[8] to have their children baptized at all, and clergymen might act on the principle, that if the mountain would not come to Mahomet, Mahomet must go to the mountain. Again, the old disputes about the sign of the cross and sponsors had not yet died out, so

---

[1] See *Diary*, passim.
[2] *Episcopalia, or Letters of Henry Compton, Bishop of London, to the Clergy of his Diocese*, 1686.
[3] Memoir prefixed to Sherlock's *Practical Christian* (6th edition, 1713).
[4] Nelson's *Life of Bishop Bull*, pp. 94 and 184.
[5] *Remains*, Part II., pp. 159-60.
[6] See, *inter alia*, Bishop Hacket's *Articles of Visitation* in 1668.
[7] Nelson's *Life of Bull*, p. 259.
[8] *Representation of the State of Christianity in England*; an interesting and racy anonymous tract published in 1671.

there was a temptation to cut the Gordian knot by not performing the rite in church at all. Dean Sherlock thinks that this was the origin of the evil custom.[1] There was also an encouragement to the practice from quite an opposite direction. In the time of the troubles, churchmen who desired to have their children baptized according to the rites of the Church, were forced to have the Sacrament administered at home, the churches not being available; and the habit formed by necessity lived on when the necessity no longer existed. And finally, there was the feeling of parents that it was a grander thing to have the christening at home, that it 'saved charge and trouble,'[2] that consideration was thus paid to 'the softness of mothers who would not expose an infant to the air, except,' adds our informant with sly humour, 'it be to send it to nurse.'[3]

There was at least equal disorder to be remedied in the administration of the other great Sacrament of the gospel. If in the later days of the Commonwealth public baptism had fallen into disuse, there was almost a total cessation of the Holy Communion in churches.[4] Indeed, before the civil war broke out there had been great laxity about the celebration of the Holy Communion. Even George Herbert's model country parson, 'touching the frequencie of the Communion, celebrates it, if not duly once a month, yet at least five or six times in the year, as at Easter, Christmas, Whitsuntide, afore and after harvest, and at the beginning of Lent,' and the writer clearly contemplates the possibility of its being celebrated even less frequently.[5] It is obvious

---

[1] See his *Practical Discourse of Religious Assemblies*, published in 1681, in which he also says that 'Public baptism is now very much grown out of fashion, most people looking upon it as a very needless and troublesome ceremony,' &c., p. 192.
[2] Sherlock, *ut supra*.   [3] *Ibid.*
[4] See Perry's *History of the Church of England*, ii. p. 221.
[5] *A Priest to the Temple, or the Country Parson*, &c., chap. xxii., 'On the Sacraments.'

that after the great wave of puritanism had passed over the country, there would be still greater difficulty in establishing frequent Communions. And we have abundant evidence that such was the case. When Bull was at Suddington, good churchman as he was, 'he could only bring the Holy Communion to seven times in the year,' 'and this,' adds his biographer, 'was oftener than was usual in little villages.'[1] Dean Granville, who laid the very greatest stress upon frequency of Communion, could, in his early years at Sedgfield, only venture to insist upon his curates celebrating upon the four great Festivals and at least five other times during the year, though afterwards (1679), he succeeded in establishing a monthly Communion.[2] The writer of a 'Representation of the State of Christianity in England,' gives a most grievous account of the infrequency of Communions and the paucity of communicants in 1674. Anonymous tracts are not to be relied on, but more trustworthy authorities tell a similar tale. Even in 1694 Evelyn declares that 'unlesse at the four greater Feasts, there is no Communion hereabouts.'[3] He is referring especially to Wotton, but his language implies that the same neglect occurred in other parishes. Sir Jonathan Trelawney, when Bishop of Bristol, says of two villages in his diocese, Elberton and Littleton, 'in one the Sacrament has not been administered since the Restoration, in the other very seldom.' This must have been written between 1685 and 1689; he adds, 'I never saw so ill churches or such ill parishioners,' so let us hope that such extreme neglect was exceptional.[4] But Bishop Turner of Ely is informed in 1686, that, 'at Little Gransden there is but Communion twice a year:'[5] and even at a large place like Dedham, in Essex, where there was a most devoted and hardworking vicar, Mr. Burkitt, the Holy Communion was administered only once in every

---

[1] Nelson's *Life of Bull*, p. 93.
[2] *Remains*, Part I., p. 129-133.   [3] *Diary* for May 6, 1694.
[4] Trelawney's letter to Archbishop Sancroft.
[5] See Miss Strickland's *Lives of the Seven Bishops*, p. 184.

two months.¹ Archbishop Sancroft, in his Injunctions to the clergy of his Province in 1688, is content with requiring that 'in greater towns the clergy should administer the Communion once every month, and even in the lesser too, if communicants may be procured, or, however, as often as they may.'² There was, no doubt, a steady improvement as Church principles by degrees permeated through the country. Dean Sherlock, while deploring, in 1681, the neglect of the Lord's Supper, yet adds, 'With joy we now observe more frequent and numerous Communions than have been for many years last past.'³ In the same year Dr. Comber wrote to Dr. Granville, 'If we consider how terribly this Sacrament was represented, and how generally it was laid aside in the late times, we might wonder how monthly Communions should be so well attended on by the people as they are, and this was as large a step as could be in prudence expected for the first twenty years.'⁴ Dr. Comber is referring especially to the Cathedrals, and in these a further step was soon made very generally. In the same year, Patrick, then Dean of Peterborough, tells us, 'The archbishop required, according to the rubric, that we should have a Communion every Sunday in Cathedral Churches.' Dean Granville was most persistent and indefatigable in the matter;⁶ and, largely owing to his exertions, the custom became established, but not without opposition,—and sometimes on the part of those who ought to have been the first to encourage it.⁷ The same rule was adopted in several London

---

¹ *Life of Rev. Mr. William Burkitt*, by N. Parkhurst (published 1704).
² Quoted in D'Oyly's *Life of Sancroft*, i. pp. 320-5.
³ *Practical Discourse of Religious Assemblies*, p. 205.
⁴ Granville's *Remains*, Part II., p. 86.
⁵ *Autobiography of Simon Patrick*, p. 99.
⁶ Comber's biographer calls the 'procuring a weekly Sacrament in all the Cathedrals throughout the kingdom, Dr. Granville's great affair.' (*Memoirs of Dean Comber, by his great-grandson*, p. 180.) See Granville's *Remains*, Part I., Introduction, pp. xxxii and xxxiii; Part II., p. 125, and *passim*.
⁷ Thus Dr. John Lake, when Bishop of Bristol, met with great opposition

churches. Beveridge, who made S. Peter's, Cornhill, a model parish in every respect, was one of the first to revive this primitive practice.[1] S. Martin's in the Fields, S. Andrew's, Holborn, and several other churches followed the example, so that in 1714, Paterson, in his 'Pietas Londinensis,' could specify twelve churches which had the weekly Communion. This does not, of course, include the chapels of the nonjurors. At the chapel in Great Ormond Street, which Robert Nelson frequented, there was a celebration, 'every Sunday, Good Friday, and other solemn occasions.'[2] But, as a rule, the monthly Communion was the limit even in the London churches. John Scott, Rector of St. Giles' in the Fields, who would certainly take a high standard of churchmanship, assumes this. 'It is,' he writes, 'at most but once a month you are invited.'[3] When there was a weekly celebration it was frequently due to the private efforts of the 'Religious Societies.'[4]

Turning to the number of communicants we have cheering accounts from several sources. Evelyn tells us of 'neere a thousand devout persons partaking of the Holy Communion' in S. Martin's in the Fields, at one service in 1688.[5] At Dr. Horneck's church (the Savoy Chapel), 'the number of communicants held a great proportion to that of

---

from the Dean when he tried to establish the weekly Communion in the Cathedral.

[1] He writes to his parishioners, 'God, in His providence hath so ordered it that you live in a place where this Holy Sacrament is actually celebrated every Lord's Day, and may be so, if there be occasion, every day in the year.' (*The Great Necessity and Advantage of Public Prayer and Frequent Communion*, p. 538.) Dean Granville, when in London, 'went to Dr. Beveridge's for the satisfaction of receiving the Sacrament, which he celebrates weekly in his parish church.' (*Remains*, Part I., p. 174.)

[2] See Secretan's *Life of Nelson*,' p. 175.

[3] *Christian Life*, vol. i. p. 313.

[4] See Josiah Woodward's *Account of the Rise and Progress of the Religious Societies in the City of London*, &c., 4th edition, 1712.

[5] *Diary*, iii. 252. Let us hope they were all 'devout persons,' but it is fair to add that S. Martin's was a great church for persons qualifying for office by communicating.

his auditors,' and those auditors were very numerous, for 'a vast crowd there was that followed him, and such a collection of most devout and conformable persons as were hardly to be found elsewhere; it was no easy matter to get through the crowd to the pulpit.'[1] The members of the Religious Societies frequented in great numbers the weekly communions which were established by their means.[2] In a little village near Leeds we hear of 'above a hundred communicants on Good Friday, and near as many on the following Easter Day;'[3] and there is an interesting letter, dated May 25, 1714, from Dr. Hickes to Dr. Charlett, Master of University College, Oxford, in which the writer says, 'I think you were wrong not to assist the parish priest for want of a surplice, the want of a surplice being a sufficient excuse in foro ecclesiastico et conscientiæ, for administering the service without one, *especially in a large Communion; where it was charity both to priest and people to assist.*'[4]

In most of these instances, however, especial pains had evidently been taken.[5] On the whole, the frequency of, and attendance at, the Holy Communion appear to have been two of the least satisfactory points in connection with the restoration of Church order. Facts certainly do not bear out the theory, held by two of our most eminent historians,[6] that the practice of 'occasional conformity'

---

[1] See *Life of Rev. Anthony Horneck*, by Bishop Kidder.
[2] See Josiah Woodward's *Account of the Rise and Progress of the Religious Societies in the City of London*.
[3] See Ralph Thoresby's *Diary*, April 3, 1713.
[4] *Letters from the Bodleian*, edited by Bliss, p. 286.
[5] Horneck, we are told, 'took indefatigable pains on these occasions, but was encouraged to do so from the great success his labours met with.' (Kidder's *Life*.) Mr. Plaxton, the clergyman of the village near Leeds was 'very commendably serious and industrious in his cure, and had brought his parish into an excellent order' (Thoresby's *Diary*); and the young men belonging to the Religious Societies would naturally attend the Communions established at their own expense.
[6] Earl Stanhope (*Reign of Queen Anne*, p. 90) and Dr. Hallam (*Constitutional History of England*, vol. iii. p. 248.) Every recommendation of bishops and others to hold more frequent Communion clearly implies that

and the concessions made to conciliate Puritan communicants were conducive, even to the increase of numbers at that holy rite.

From the very commencement of our period, the question of concessions to the scruples of the Puritans had been a moot point. On the eve of the Restoration Peter Gunning refused the Holy Communion to a member of parliament at S. Margaret's, Westminster, who did not, and would not, kneel to receive it.[1] Some years later, Bishop Frampton stopped a clergyman from taking the sacred elements round to the pews, but all were not so strict as Gunning and Frampton.[2] There were, no doubt, many nonconformists, as Edmund Calamy told Burnet,[3] who desired to shew their friendliness to the Church by occasionally partaking of the Holy Eucharist, before the Test Act passed; but these, for the most part, wished to do so standing, and remaining in their own pews; and many clergy, from an amiable desire to conciliate, connived at the practice. The Test Act of 1673, which forced nonconformists either to abstain from seeking any public office or to become occasional conformists, of course increased the number. This Test Act is just one of those many Acts which were intended far more for the convenience of the State than for the benefit of the Church. It originated in the panic which arose from the marriage of the Duke of York with a Romanist, and his Romish tendencies generally, and it may possibly have been good policy to pass a measure 'for preventing dangers which might happen from popish recusants.'[4] Perhaps, also, the measure in question

there were immense difficulties owing to the extreme paucity of attendance. See, *inter alia*, Sancroft's *Injunctions*, quoted above; Nelson's *Life of Bishop Bull*, *Life of Dean Comber*, tract on *The Present State of Religion in England*, &c.

[1] MS. Journal of an M.P., Saturday, May 25, 1661, quoted in Lathbury's *History of Convocation*, p. 297.

[2] *Life of Bishop Robert Frampton* (Evans), p. 139.

[3] *Account of My Own Life* (1671–1731), by Edmund Calamy, i. p. 473.

[4] See Tindal's *Continuation of Rapin*, vol. xiii. p. 115.

may have been the only one that could be effectual for the purpose; because, as the doctrine of transubstantiation was an article of faith, the Pope could grant no dispensation to Romanists to take such a test.[1] But all this is looking at the matter from a purely political point of view. As affecting Church order, the Test Act had most disastrous effects; it tended either to perpetuate disorder, or to place consistent clergymen in an awkward predicament. It is recorded, for example, as an instance of the uncharitableness of Dr. Hooke, vicar of Halifax, that 'he would grant no certificates but to kneelers,' one of the first instances (1673) of the Test Act being brought to bear against nonconformists. The rule, it is added, was generally dispensed with by the clergy of that time.[2] Even a bishop (Croft of Hereford) boldly advised the clergy to dispense with the rule, but it should be added that the book in which he did so called forth much disapprobation.[3] As a matter of fact, the rule *was* dispensed with in towns where Puritanism was strong; Bishop Cartwright records with conscious pride that 'at Northampton, they all came to the altar at my invitation, who had never done it before, all but two men, one of whom clapped on his hat and walked out.'[4] But the connivance was not successful, even as regards numbers, while it tended to keep up irregularities which in reality were much more than formal.

The unsuccessfulness of the attempt to draw people to Holy Communion by indulging their scruples is all the more strongly marked when we contrast the infrequency of celebrations and the paucity of attendance at them, with the frequency of the other Church services. The number

[1] *History of England, principally in the seventeenth Century*, by Leopold von Ranke, iii. 339.
[2] Hunter's *Life of Oliver Heywood*, p. 257.
[3] The book was called, *The Naked Truth, or True State of the Primitive Church, by an Humble Moderator* (Herbert Croft, Bishop of Hereford), published 1675.
[4] *Diary of Thomas Cartwright, Bishop of Chester*, 1686-7 (Camden Society), p. 12, and *note*.

of week-day services and the good attendance at them must have been among the greatest encouragements to the restorers of Church order. Immediately after the Restoration Bishop Cosin set himself vigorously to carry out the rubric about daily prayer in every part of his diocese, and succeeded, as only a strong man could have succeeded, to a very remarkable extent.[1] Archdeacon Basire warmly seconded his chief's efforts: and Cosin's son-in-law, Granville, also archdeacon, did the same, and set the example by strictly requiring of his curates at Sedgfield and Easington,[2] 'that the Mattins and Evensong shall be (according to the rubrick) said dayly, in the chancells of each his parish churches, throughout the year, without the least variation.' In a curious document respecting the church expenses at Newcastle, one item is, 'for candles in winter for the daily prayer.'[3] Ralph Thoresby attended church regularly twice every day at Leeds,[4] and we find from incidental notices that, when he was travelling, he was still able to keep up his habit, at least in market towns.[5] But daily services were also not uncommon in country places. Isaac Milles walked every day to read the service in his parish church at Highclere, and tolled the bell himself.[6] Johnson of Cranbrook 'read the prayers every morning in his church, when at home.'[7] At Southwell 'the prayers were said three times every day,'[8] 'at Brecknock and Carmarthen twice.'[9] It was not unusual for pious people to leave bequests to

[1] See Vita Joannis Cosini, among the *Vitæ quorundam Eruditissimorum et illustrium Virorum*, T. Smith, 1707.

[2] *Remains*, Part II., pp. 129-133.

[3] See Ambrose Barnes' *Remains*, Appendix.

[4] See *Diary* for January 1, 1711, and *passim*.

[5] December 30, 1708. 'Stamford; got to church to forenoon prayers (Thursday);' and so forth. See *Diary*, passim.

[6] See *Life*, &c.

[7] See *Life of Rev. J. Johnson, Vicar of Cranbrook*, by Rev. T. Brett, 1748.

[8] *Tour of Great Britain* (Defoe).

[9] Nelson's *Life of Bishop Bull*, pp. 273-5.

parishes, on condition that daily service was performed, thus shewing that it was a duty that might be fairly expected to be done. Morley did this for Farnham,[1] Beveridge for Barrow and Mount Sorrell.[2] Bishops were in the general habit of insisting strongly upon the daily service in their Charges and Pastorals. Sancroft,[3] Sharp,[4] Patrick,[5] Stillingfleet,[6] all do so; and Bishop Turner uses terms which are so forcible that they are worth quoting. 'Have,' he writes to the clergy of his diocese, in 1686, 'as the rubrick directs, morning and evening prayer every day of the week in your church ... if by any means in the world you can prevail with at least a few of your parishioners, which sure cannot be wanting in most parishes, where there are either some devout gentry and persons of quality, or at least some piously disposed people ; and to all such I could almost kneel, begging them to do their parts towards so good a work, perhaps the best and the most public good they can ever do in the places where they live ; and where there are either poor widows, who may well afford to be at prayers for those whose pensioners they are ; or children taught by a schoolmaster or mistress, there it is very hard if some little daily congregation might not be found, would but the minister attempt and labour at it with as much application and zeal as the thing itself mightily deserves.'[7]

The practical and devotional works of the period insist upon the duty of daily worship in terms which would have been absurd if opportunities for daily worship had not

[1] See White Kennet's *Case of Impropriations*, p. 294.

[2] *Life*, prefixed to the *Theological Works of William Beveridge*, in the Library of Anglo-Catholic Theology.

[3] See Sancroft's *Articles* of 1688.

[4] See *Pastoral Letter of Archbishop Sharp*.

[5] See *Letter to the Clergy of the Diocese of Ely*, 1692.

[6] See Bishop Stillingfleet's *Ecclesiastical Cases, relating to the Rights and Duties of the Parochial Clergy* (1698), p. 45.

[7] *Letter to the Clergy of the Diocese of Ely, before his Visitation*, by Bishop Turner, 1686.

been general. Beveridge and Patrick, the most popular devotional writers of their day, assume over and over again that such worship was accessible,[1] and urge it strongly, as they could do with a particularly good grace, since they had both, the one at S. Peter's, Cornhill, the other at S. Paul's, Covent Garden, faithfully carried out the Church's rule themselves, and with eminent success. Nelson, in his 'Practice of Piety,' gives as one rule, 'Attend the daily services of the Church,' thus implying that they were generally accessible. And so they were. At S. Martin's in the Fields (owing to the benevolence of that pious layman, Dr. Willis) and at S. Paul's, Covent Garden, besides the ordinary daily services at 10 and 3, which were well attended by people of leisure, there were early and late services at 6 a.m. and 8 p.m., for the benefit of people of business and domestic servants, both of which were well frequented.[2] Chamberlayne tells us that there were 'prayers thrice every day at the King's Chappell,'[3] and Hutton that the same custom prevailed at S. Andrew's (Holborn ?) in 1708.[4] A great impetus was given to daily worship in the London churches by the members of the Religious Societies, who not only supported the services with their purses, but took care that there should be a congregation by their constant attendance.[5] An anonymous writer in 1709, says 'it is a great ease and comfort to good Christians within these cities of London and Westminster and the suburbs, that in most churches there be constant prayers morning

---

[1] See Beveridge's *Great Necessity and Advantage of Public Prayer*. Patrick's *Discourse concerning Prayer*; *Work of the Ministry*; *Treatise of Repentance*, &c.

[2] See *Autobiography of Simon Patrick*, p. 20, and *Life of Henry Hammond*, prefixed to his *Practical Catechism*, in the Library of Anglo-Catholic Theology, p. cx. *note*.

[3] *Angliæ Notitiæ*, p. 135.

[4] Hutton's *New View*, ii. 118, quoted in Plume's *Life of Bishop Hacket*, Mackenzie Walcott's edition, p. 29, *note*.

[5] See Josiah Woodward, *ut supra*.

and evening. These are supported by particular benefactions or voluntary contributions.'[1] 'Most churches' is rather too strong an expression; but when Paterson published his ' Pietas Londinensis ' in 1714, he could specify sixty-five out of two hundred and four churches in which there were daily prayers, while at the great majority of the remainder there were at least prayers on Wednesdays and Fridays. The 6 a.m. prayers seem to have been especially well attended, though, if the ' Guardian ' is to be trusted, not always in the most reverent fashion.[2] Even as early as 1664 they existed, for Pepys records, ' July 14, 1664. In Fleet Street, hearing a psalm sung, I went into S. Dunstan's and there heard prayers read, which, it seems, is done there every morning at 6 o'clock.' This part of our subject may be appropriately concluded with the words of one who more, perhaps, than any other man, contributed to the revival of this pious and canonical practice of daily prayer: ' Blessed be God,' writes Beveridge, ' He hath opened the eyes of many, especially in this city [London], who now see the things that belong to their everlasting peace, and therefore are as constant at their public devotions daily as at their private business.'[3]

Another point of Church order for the restoration of which vigorous efforts were made during the whole of our period was public catechising, according to the fifty-ninth canon. The Low Church bishops insisted upon this duty as strongly as their High Church brethren; Burnet,[4] Tenison,[5]

---

[1] *Defence of the Church and Clergy of England*, p. 31.
[2] See No. 65, by Steele.
[3] *The Great Necessity and Advantage of Public Prayer and Frequent Communion*, p. 494.
[4] See *A Discourse of the Pastoral Care*, pp. 187-8.
[5] Among the Injunctions he drew up in the name of the king (1695), to be given to the Bishops and rest of the Clergy, No. 14 is that *Catechising be duly performed according to the 59th Canon*, and he enlarges upon the duty.

and Compton,[1] no less than Ken,[2] Turner,[3] Beveridge,[4] and Patrick.[5] But there was considerable difficulty in carrying it out. The Puritan party in the Church regarded no service as complete without a sermon, and could by no means be persuaded that 'catechising is often the best and most useful sort of preaching,' and that 'the sermon ought not to jostle this out.'[6] As a protest against this excessive love of sermons, others preferred the prayers and nothing else; and hence catechising found opponents from opposite quarters. And then, if the ministers were ready, the people were not. 'One might,' says a writer often quoted, 'as well prevail with some masters of families to sacrifice their charge to Moloch, as to send them to church to be catechised.'[7] 'As to catechising,' writes Bishop Stillingfleet to Archbishop Tenison in reference to the king's Injunctions in 1694, 'it would be very well to have a warm injunction about it; but what if people will not send their children?'[8] Dean Sherlock, though he is of opinion that 'no great good can be expected till public catechising be revived,' admits that the fault lay mainly with the people, who would not send their children and servants.[9] Still there was clearly a marked advance in this as in other matters, as time went on. In the early years after the Restoration

---

[1] See *Episcopalia, or Letters of Henry, Bishop of London, to the Clergy of his Diocese*, 1686. In First Letter, 1679, he says 'the want of catechising has left the Church without a foundation.'

[2] See Hawkins' *Life*, prefixed to Ken's *Prose Works*, ed. by Round, p. 7.

[3] *Letter to the Clergy of the Diocese of Ely before his Visitation*, by Bishop Turner, 1686.

[4] See *Life*, prefixed to *Private Thoughts*; also *Church Catechism explained for the use of Diocese of S. Asaph* dedicated to the Clergy of the Diocese.

[5] See *Work of the Ministry represented to the Clergy of Ely* (1698), p. 52.

[6] See a tract entitled *A true Notion of the Worship of God, or a Vindication of the Service of the Church of England* (published 1673).

[7] *Representation of the State of Christianity in England*, 1674.

[8] *Miscellaneous Discourses of Bishop E. Stillingfleet*.

[9] *Practical Discourse of Religious Assemblies*, p. 197 (published 1681).

the tone of the advocates of catechising is more despondent than it is later on. Thus, the king's 'Directions concerning preachers' in 1662 can only express a faint hope that 'the afternoon's exercise' might sometimes be catechetical. A year or two later both Granville and Basire complain that catechising 'hath been shamefully neglected.'[1] Pepys in 1663 records with evident disgust: 'Mr. Milles preached a sleepy sermon on catechising, which, I perceive, he means to introduce.' Sherlock of Winwick writes in a desponding tone on the subject in 1661.[2] Lancelot Addison in 1674 'cannot but with deep resentment observe that since the time God turned again our captivity, and restored this Church to the free use of His ordinances, catechising has met with but cold entertainment from those by whom it ought to have been most lovingly caressed.'[3] But eight years later, Thoresby who still retained the Puritan's love of sermons, 'could hear of no sermon after dinner throughout the country,' and so was forced to go and hear 'the town minister catechise,' and was much pleased with what he heard;[4] and in 1704 Beveridge, writing to the clergy of his new diocese (S. Asaph) to urge catechising, adds, 'not as if I thought this duty had been neglected among you; for I have heard to my great comfort that it is generally practised throughout the diocese every Lord's day.'[5] Samuel Wesley in 1709 required his curate to catechise at Epworth every Sunday, as a matter of course;[6] though a few years earlier he had complained that 'the people had grown too proud, and thought themselves too wise to be satisfy'd, or "put off," as they'd be ready to call it, with catechising.'[7] Catechising in Lent had been very

[1] Granville, *Remains*, Part II., p. 17.
[2] See *Catechism of the Church of England paraphrased*, by R. Sherlock.
[3] *The Primitive Institution*, &c. p. 77. [4] *Diary*, Nov. 12, 1682.
[5] Dedication of the *Church Catechism explained* &c., to the Clergy of the Diocese.
[6] See Tyerman's *Life and Times of S. Wesley*, p. 367.
[7] *Athenian Oracle*, p. 33.

general from the commencement of our period, and it became more and more usual on every Sunday afternoon, as years rolled on.

Another point of order to which great attention was paid was the regulation of what were called the 'Pulpit Prayers.' If it be thought that an exaggerated importance was attached to this point, it should be remembered that a considerable number of the clergy after the Restoration, being 'conformists' rather than churchmen, were inclined to indemnify themselves for using a service which they disliked, by expatiating at their own sweet will in 'conceived prayers' before and after sermon; they would even curtail the service in order to gain time for this more congenial exercise. One clergyman in the diocese of Gloucester had the audacity to excuse himself to Bishop Frampton, (of all men in the world!) for such curtailment on the plea that 'the length of the service hindered him from praying in the pulpit so long as he would.'[1] It should be remembered, too, that this was an old grievance, dating from before the time of the Rebellion.[2] It was evidently a subject that required very delicate handling. We find, immediately after the Restoration, the bishops arguing that the liturgy was no grievance, because 'ministers are not denied the use and exercise of their gifts in praying before and after sermon, although,' they add rather feebly, 'such praying be but the continuance of a custom of no great antiquity.' In 1661 a committee was appointed in the Lower House of Convocation 'to compile a prayer before sermon;' and in the same year the Upper House unanimously agreed[3] to authorise one form of prayer before and after sermon; but the matter,

---

[1] *Life of Bishop Frampton* (Evans), p. 134.

[2] See Heylin on *Bidding Prayer*, written 1637.

[3] Lathbury (*History of Convocation*, p. 288), says 'almost unanimously,' but the *Journal of the Upper House* says, 'Reverendi Patres *unanimi* consensu et assensu in votis dederunt pro unicâ formâ Precum tam ante quàm post Sermonem sive orationem prædicatam, usitandâ et observandâ per ministros intra Provinciam Canterburiensem.'

writes Kennet, was 'afterwards dropped upon prudential reasons.'[1] The 'prudential reasons' were probably a desire to give scope for what many, both ministers and people, valued highly, 'the conceived prayer.' Sometimes the prayers before and after sermon were longer than the whole church service. Even so late as 1675, a published sermon has a 'prayer before sermon' prefixed to it, four pages long. A Dr. Samwaies complains to Dean Granville that many are 'so passionately addicted to a sermon ushered in with a private prayer, that they will not endure to be present at our assemblies till that prayer be begun.'[2] There was of course a strong feeling also on the other side. Bishop Cosin, who generally managed to carry his point, almost banished the pulpit prayers from the diocese of Durham.[3] Dean Granville calls Bidding of Prayer 'the very criterion of a true Church of England man,'[4] and devoted himself to substituting it for the pulpit prayers with an energy only second to that which he shewed in establishing the weekly celebration in every Cathedral. At his persuasion, Beveridge adopted the Bidding Prayer at S. Peter's, Cornhill, and Beveridge's reputation was so great that the precedent was sure to be followed by many. The Dean of Westminster (Steward) wrote a tract with the significant title, 'The old Puritan detected,' the object of which was to put a stop to pulpit prayers, and which made a considerable sensation. There were, however, many whose churchmanship was unimpeachable, who regularly used pulpit prayers. For instance, Bishop Wilson's prayers before sermon were especially admired when he preached in London, particularly when he prayed for those who never prayed for themselves.[5] Evelyn tells us that Archbishop Sharp's prayer before sermon when he preached at the Temple in 1696 was one

---

[1] *Register*, 576.   [2] Granville's *Remains*, Part II., p. 80.
[3] *The Dead Man's real Speech*. Funeral Sermon on Bishop Cosin, by Archdeacon Basire.
[4] *Remains*, Part I., p. 179.   [5] Cruttwell's *Life*, p. 58.

of the most excellent compositions he ever heard.¹ Bishop Hacket 'never practised Bidding of Prayer before sermon.'² Prayers before and after sermon composed by Jeremy Taylor are still extant. Like almost all Church questions of the seventeenth century, it became mixed up with politics. The fifty-fifth canon required that the sovereign should be prayed for with his name and titles; and this frequently became a test of loyalty. In 1687, when the clergy were alarmed about Romanism, Bishop Cartwright, who was a tool of James II., tells us that on one occasion he admonished the clergyman 'to amend his prayer in which he gave not the king his titles, and to be wary of reflecting so imprudently as he did upon the king's religion;'³ and that on another he 'chid Mr. Turner for his extempore prayer.' In 1695 Archbishop Tenison wrote to the bishops of his Province that 'they should require their clergy not to leave out the king's titles;'⁴ and in 1706, Bishop Kennet, at his Visitation at Huntingdon, hopes the clergy 'will pray for the Princess Sophia in their pulpit prayers.' A little earlier a correspondent of the 'Athenian Oracle' inquires why, in the pulpit prayers, the name and titles of the king were neglected, and receives in reply a snub, to the effect that 'either the gentleman cannot go to church, or goes where there is a Jacobite minister.'⁵ Pepys, in the early part of our period,⁶ and the 'Spectator,' towards its close,⁷ make some rather captious remarks on the introduction of other names into the pulpit prayers, as if it were done for ostentation. In the Church revival of Queen Anne's days, the Bidding Prayer came more into use, to the great disgust of more than one Low Church

---

¹ *Diary* for April 26, 1696. ² Plume's *Life*, p. 100.
³ *Diary of Thomas Cartwright, Bishop of Chester*, 1686-7 (Camden Society), p. 30.
⁴ See Kennet's *History of England*, iii. p. 714.
⁵ *Athenian Oracle*, p. 406.
⁶ *Diary*, March 166¾, also Dec. 23, 1666.   ⁷ No. 312.

bishop;[1] but by the close of the reign the custom of using either a collect, and the Lord's Prayer, or a short prayer of the nature of a collect, had become pretty general, and continued to be so all through the eighteenth century.

The disuse of chancels, especially when there was no celebration, was another disorder which required to be rectified. From an interesting tract written in 1683, it would appear that it was 'the custom of most parish churches to read the second service at the desk.'[2] The writer combats the reasons given for so doing, among others the very ridiculous one that 'it is indecent for the priest to go out of the desk to the altar with his surplice on.' A furious reply, which makes up by strong language for weak arguments, immediately appeared, declaring that the custom was general since the Reformation, that the Bishop of London did not disapprove of it, and that 'Protestants were jealous of such needless motions, passes and repasses,' and thought them 'papistical.'[3] Among many disorders complained of in the diocese of Exeter about the same time, one was that the 'Communion Service in very many churches was not read at the Table.'[4] The Bishop of Lincoln (Gardiner), in his Visitation Charge in 1697, implies that in his diocese the chancels were often not used even when there was a celebration, for he appeals to his clergy whether they did not 'find great inconvenience in consecrating in so strait a place as an alley of the church,

---

[1] See *Life of Bishop White Kennet*, p. 127, and Bishop Trimnell's *Visitation Charge at Norwich* in 1710.

[2] *Parish Churches turn'd into Conventicles* by serving God therein otherwise than according to the Church of England; in particular by reading the Communion Service or any part thereof in the desk; or Plain Reasons for the reading of the second service, where there is no Communion, at the Altar or Holy Table, in an Epistle dedicated to all Clergy who read it at the desk, by Rd. Hart, 1683.

[3] *Parish Churches no Conventicles* from Ministers reading in the desk when there is no Communion, by O.U. An answer to the pamphlet [above] pretended to be written by R. Hart, but really by T. A., Barrister-at-law. 1683.

[4] See *Tanner MSS.*, 29, 71.

and delivering the bread and wine in narrow seats, over the heads, and treading upon the feet of those that kneel.' It need scarcely be said that the position of the Holy Table was an old subject of discussion, as the last rubric at the commencement of our Communion Service still shews. The Holy Table itself was sometimes treated with painful irreverence. Bishop Cosin, in the Articles of Inquiry at his Visitation in 1662, asks the churchwardens, 'Are you confident that none sit, lean, or lay their hats upon the Communion Table?'[1] Dean Granville put two boys in the Correction-house for playing at cards on the Communion Table[2] in 1681, and the story of the people who stood upon the Communion Table at Canterbury to look at the Princess Mary is another illustration.

This last point is part of a larger subject,—that of irreverent behaviour in church generally. But in dealing with the subject we must be upon our guard against applying the standard of the nineteenth century to the habits of the seventeenth. For instance, it seems very sad to think that the restorers of Church order had to wage incessant war against the habit of wearing the hat during divine service, or at any rate, during parts of it.[3] But it must be borne in mind that the hat was not infrequently worn indoors during the seventeenth century. Pepys evidently considered it an unnecessary piece of strictness to insist upon the bare head in church, for he tells us contemptuously how he heard 'a simple

---

[1] Bishop Cosin's *Works*, vol. iv. (Library of Anglo-Catholic Theology.)
[2] *Remains*, Part II., p. 70.
[3] One of the articles of inquiry at Bishop Hacket's second Triennial Visitation in 1668 is, 'Do your parishioners behave reverently in church, men and youths with their hats off?' Bishop Cosin, in his *Primary Visitation of Durham Cathedral*, 1662, speaks of 'some who come into the quire in their furre and nightgowns, and sit with their hats on their heads at the reading of the lessons.' In 1689 King William 'gave great offence because he would wear his hat in church, and if he ever uncovered it during the Liturgy, always resumed it when the sermon began.' See also *Life of Bishop Lake*, who pulled off the people's hats in York Minster during divine service.

fellow [in a sermon], exclaiming against men's wearing their hats on in church.'¹ Again, in no part of the seventeenth century was the reverence due to sacred places recognised to anything like the same extent that it is now. The mere mention of 'Paul's Walk' is a witness of this.² When, then, we read of 'the ill custom of walking in the body of York Minster during divine service,'³ of the vergers at Westminster Abbey ordering the organs to strike up to put a stop to Isaac Barrow's inordinately long sermon,⁴ or of half the congregation at S. Lawrence Jewry taking fright at the odd and slovenly appearance of the same great preacher, and rushing out of church with a loud clatter,⁵ or of the Holy Communion at Whitehall being interrupted by 'the rude breaking in of multitudes zealous to hear the second sermon by the Bishop of Bath and Wells' (Ken),⁶ or of Burnet 'rising from his knees, sitting down in his stall, and making an ugly noise with his mouth' when poor King James was prayed for, in December 1688,⁷ or of Burnet himself being interrupted while preaching by loud 'hums' of applause, we must not suppose that such conduct implied the same degree of irreverence that it would do now. Bad behaviour in church was, however, a recognised evil⁸ which the restorers of Church order endeavoured, and not without success, to remedy.

¹ In *Diary* for Nov. 17, 1661. Also *Diary* for Jan. 21, 16⁶⁰/₆₁.

² 'It was the fashion of those times (James I.) and did so continue till these (1658), for the principal gentry, lords, courtiers, and men of all professions, not merely mechanicks, to meet in S. Paul's Church by 11, and walk in the middle isle till 12, and after dinner from 3 to 6; during which time some discoursed of business, others of news.' (Osborne's *Traditional Memoirs of the reigns of Elizabeth and James.*) See also *Microcosmography*, by Bishop Earle, 1628, on *Paul's Walk*, pp. 116-9.

³ *Life of John Lake, Lord Bishop of Chichester.*

⁴ See *Life of Seth Ward, Bishop of Salisbury*, by Dr. Pope (1697), p. 148.

⁵ *Id.* p. 139.   ⁶ Evelyn's *Diary.*

⁷ *Correspondence of Henry Hyde, Earl of Clarendon*, ii. 218.

⁸ See Bishop Cosin's and other prelates' *Visitation Charges and Articles of Inquiry*, passim; Atterbury's *Sermons*; *Diary of Bishop Cartwright*; Swift, Sermon on *Sleeping in Church*, vol. viii. in Scott's edition, &c.

Church Psalmody was naturally a point which attracted considerable attention in connection with the restoration of Church order. No part of the church furniture had suffered more severely in the devastation of the Puritans than the organs. The erection of an organ in the chapel of S. John's College, Oxford, was considered a decisive proof of Laud's popish tendencies,[1] and Milton was quite an exception among the Puritans in his love of this species of church music.[2] Even churchmen were not quite agreed upon the point. Jeremy Taylor gives but a reluctant permission to the use of organs in churches.[3] Stillingfleet was of opinion that 'harmonious voices were sweeter when unaccompanied,' and that 'fiddles and flutes, and harpsichords even, in some people's opinion, could never be accommodated to purposes of devotion.'[4] But he adds, 'I see no objection to the thing itself' (instrumental music), and some years later (1698, the 'Dialogues' were in 1686), he defended 'the use of organical music in the public service against the charge of its being a Levitical service.'[5] It was more frequently charged with having a popish tendency. Both charges were answered, it need hardly be said, with immense learning, by Henry Dodwell in his treatise 'Of the Lawfulness of Instrumental Musick in Holy Offices,' written in 1698, owing to a dispute

---

[1] See Dean Hook's *Life of Laud*, p. 42.   [2] See *Il Penseroso*.

[3] See his *Ductor Dubitantium*, and Heber's *Life*, prefixed to his edition of Taylor's *Works*, p. cclxxxviii. The passage is quoted and answered in the preface to Dodwell, *Of Instrumental Music*, p. 69 &c.

[4] See *On the Amusements of Clergymen and Christians in general*; three *Dialogues between a Dean and a Curate*, by E. Stillingfleet, Lord Bishop of Worcester, 2nd Dialogue. The Bishop (then Dean) is speaking of singing at home, but his objections seem quite as applicable to the church.

[5] Bishop Stillingfleet's *Ecclesiastical Cases relating to the Rights and Duties of Parochial Clergy*, p. 382. But even here he speaks rather hesitatingly, and without any enthusiasm in favour of the practice. 'The use of organical music in the Public Service, if it intends to compose and settle, and raise the spirits of men in the acts of worship, I see no reason can be brought against it. They who call it a Levitical service can never prove it to be any of the Typical Ceremonies, unless they can shew what was represented by it.'

which had arisen on the setting up of a new organ at Tiverton in 1696. In the same year Gabriel Towerson preached a sermon 'concerning vocal and instrumental music in the church' at the opening of a new organ at S. Andrew Undershaft. The erection had evidently met with opposition, for, after speaking of vocal music, the preacher proceeds, 'I must not expect to pass on so smoothly while I deliver my opinion concerning that singing and making melody which is attended with that of musical instruments.'[1] The reintroduction of the organ into churches was gradual. Within a month of the Restoration, Pepys records, 'This day the organs did begin to play before the king;'[2] and on November 4, 1660, 'To the Abbey, where the first time that I ever heard the organs in a Cathedral;' and on April 4, 1667, 'To Hackney. Here I was told that at their church they have a fair pair of organs which play while the people sing, which I am mighty glad of, wishing the like at our church in London, and would give 50*l.* towards it.' But the organ was not the only instrument that was used in churches. We hear of cornets in Westminster Abbey in 1667, of fiddlers in red vests in the same church, of wind music at Durham,[3] and of the fiddlers being expelled by the queen (Mary) from S. James' Chapel Royal in 1689. By the time of Queen Anne, the lawfulness, and even the desirableness, of instrumental music in church was fairly established; and we hear little or nothing on the subject during that reign.

But another difference of opinion in connection with Church psalmody arose, on the publication of the New Version of the Psalms, and the quasi-authorisation of its optional use given by the King in Council in 1696. Of course, with good churchmen this would be a very questionable

---

[1] He also refers to the 'Levitical' objection. 'Foreign writers, especially Calvin, look on Instrumental Music as a rudiment of the Law,' &c.

[2] *Diary* for June 17, 1660.

[3] See *Traditions and Customs of Cathedrals*, by Mackenzie Walcott. p. 145.

authority, Convocation never having been consulted. But apart from this irregularity, the question was discussed on its own merits. Beveridge threw all the weight of his very great authority into the scale of the old Version, partly because it *was* old, partly because it was more intelligible to the common people, and partly because it had been conferred with the Hebrew, which the new had not been.[1] The struggle between the two Versions lasted far beyond the limits of our period, but it is curious to observe that few people found fault with the *poetry* of Tate and Brady. Beveridge indeed seems to have thought that it was only *too* good. 'The style,' he says, ' is brisk and lively, and flourished here and there with wit and fancy,'—an objection in which he will not carry many modern readers along with him. Samuel Wesley evidently considered the new infinitely superior to the old as a composition, but tells his curate at Epworth that 'they must be content with their grandsire Sternhold.' He agrees with Beveridge that the common people would understand it better, ' for,' he adds caustically, ' they have a strange genius at understanding nonsense.'[2] Tom Brown, who may be supposed to represent a certain type of lay opinion, has some doggerel verses on the two versions which begin with apostrophising Sternhold and Hopkins with more force than politeness as

> Ye scoundrel old bards and a brace of dull knaves,

and end

> I'm not such a coxcomb, 'stead of new psalms to learn old,
> Or to quit Tate and Brady for Hopkins and Sternhold.[3]

The idea of any ' tertium quid' seems to have entered into no man's thoughts. With the exception of Jeremy Taylor and

---

[1] *Defence of the Books of Psalms collected into English Metre, by Sternhold and Hopkins, with Critical Observations on the late New Version, compared with the old*, by W. Beveridge, late Bishop of S. Asaph, 1710.

[2] See his Letter to a Curate, inserted in Tyerman's *Life and Times of Samuel Wesley*, pp. 382-7.

[3] See *The Works of Mr. Thomas Brown*, iv. p. 64.

Dean Hickes, no writer suggests the use of hymns, and it is doubtful whether even Taylor meant them to be used in the public service;[1] at any rate, his own spiritual songs are not all adapted for that purpose, though he *did* write 'eucharistical hymns.' Anthems, of course, were used in the Cathedrals and the Chapels Royal, but in the parish churches the choice lay simply between the old and new versions, and the balance of opinion was decidedly in favour of the old. The attachment of churchmen to Sternhold and Hopkins is curious, considering that the version was the offspring of Puritanism; but it was quickly deserted by its parent and adopted by his foe.

The difficulties connected with Church psalmody which met the restorers of Church order were not confined to the introduction of instrumental music, and the choice between the old and the new versions. Dean Sherlock in 1681 refers with great regret to the 'universal practice of sitting when we sing the Psalms,'[2] a slovenly habit which it appears to have been very hard to change. Then, again, having got their organs and other instruments back again into church, the performers seem to have been inclined to run riot with their newly regained treasure. The 'Spectator' complains that the solemn thoughts suggested by the sermon were driven out of his head by the merry jig notes which followed on the organ;[3] and Jeremy Collier is probably alluding to similar exhibitions when he says, ' Church Music must have no voluntary Maggots, no military Tattoos, no light and galliardizing notes. Religious harmony must be moving, but noble withal; grave, solemn and seraphic; fit for a martyr to play, and an angel to hear.'[4] Perhaps it

[1] Taylor wrote to Evelyn in 1656, 'It is a thousand pitties but our English tongue should be enriched with a translation of all the sacred hymns which are respersed in all the rituals and church bookes,' and so forth, but does not directly urge their use in public worship. See *Life*, prefixed to Heber's edition of Jeremy Taylor's *Works*, p. lvi.
[2] See *A Practical Discourse of Religious Assemblies*, p. 178. [3] No. 338.
[4] *Essays upon Moral Subjects*, by Jeremy Collier; *Of Musick*.

is hypercritical to find fault with a voluntary before the first lesson, which the 'Spectator' thinks a laudable custom;[1] but it was surely utilising psalmody for purposes for which it was never intended when 'before sermon a long psalm was set which lasted an hour while the sexton gathered his year's contribution through the whole church;'[2] and though Pepys thought it a 'jest' to hear 'the clerk begin the 25th Psalm which hath a proper tune to it, and then the 116th, which cannot be sung to that tune,'[3] and 'mighty sport to hear our clerke sing out of tune though his master sits by him, that begins and keeps the time aloud for the parish,'[4] yet one does not go to church to find jests or enjoy mighty sport. Such contretemps were perhaps natural on the revival of an unfamiliar practice; but one may sympathise more with the satisfaction with which the other diarist, Thoresby, records on October 3, 1708, that 'a new order of singing was begun this day in the parish church [Leeds], to sing a stave betwixt the daily Morning and Communion Service, as has long been done at London.' Bishop Bull writes to the same effect in the same year.[5]

The restorers of Church order had considerable difficulty about that old bone of contention, the surplice. In October, 1660, its use in Cathedrals, Collegiate Churches, the Chapels Royal and College Chapels was enjoined by Royal Declaration, but in parish churches it was left to the option of incumbents. And even after the Act of 1662, there was evidently some timidity about adopting it. Pepys tells us, in October, 1662, how 'Parson Milles has got one to read with surplice on,' and adds, 'I suppose himself will take it up hereafter, for a cunning fellow that he is.' Bishop Turner

---

[1] No. 630.
[2] Pepys' *Diary* for January 6, 16$\frac{60}{61}$. A similar entry occurs on January 5, 166$\frac{1}{2}$.
[3] *Diary* for January 5, 166$\frac{1}{2}$.
[4] *Diary* for November 13, 1661. [5] See Nelson's *Life of Bull*.

is informed that 'the clergyman of Little Gransden, before Mr. Oley died, never wore the surplice, except on Communion days, and that was but twice a year.'[1] Dean Granville complains of his curate at Kilkhampton in Cornwall 'officiating without the surplice to please the dow-baked people of that country;'[2] and among his archidiaconal[3] articles of visitation one question for the churchwardens was, 'Doth your minister wear the surplice?' Even a bishop, Croft of Hereford, wrote in 1675, 'to be zealous for the surplice is not wise;'[4] and a far more strict prelate, Bishop Smalridge, while he defends the use of the surplice, does so in terms which shew that it was a question on which there was a diversity of opinion.[5] On the other hand, the surplice was not unfrequently worn in the pulpit. In the diocese of Durham it was usual from the time of Bishop Cosin downwards.[6] One of the arguments used in favour of reading the second service at the desk, was, that 'it was indecent to go to the altar and back, with the surplice still on, to the homily or sermon (which, being part of divine service, is performed with the surplice on),' &c.[7] Even as late as 1722, Ralph Thoresby, now a distinct churchman, has this odd entry: 'Mr. Rhodes preached well [at Batley], *though in his surplice.*'[8]

To turn from the inanimate to the animate. Three classes of officers, besides the parochial clergy, require notice in connection with restoration of Church order.

---

[1] See Miss Strickland's *Lives of the Seven Bishops*, p. 180.

[2] *Remains*, Part II., p. 159.

[3] Granville was Archdeacon of Northumberland as well as Dean of Durham.

[4] See *The Naked Truth, &c.* It is fair to add that this work gave great offence.

[5] See *Sixty Sermons*, by Bishop G. Smalridge, 1719.

[6] See Low's *Diocesan History of Durham* (S.P.C.K).

[7] See *Parish Churches turned into Conventicles* (1683); also *Parish Churches no Conventicles*, in answer to the above (1683). The latter argues that 'preaching is appointed to those in Cathedrals, not Parish Churches.'

[8] Ralph Thoresby's *Diary* for June 17, 1722.

Lecturers had been a thorn in the side of the Church before the Rebellion. They had been used in fact as the thin end of the wedge which split the Church. Dating from a period anterior to the Reformation, they had acquired additional prominence in the early part of Charles I.'s reign by the purchase of a number of lay impropriations which were legally vested in feoffees; these feoffees established a number of lectures, nominally to form a 'preaching ministry,' but really to upset the order of the Established Church.[1] These lecturers were practically independent of the parochial ministers; Bishop Wren found them in the diocese of Norwich 'set up without the knowledge of the Ordinary, and observing no Church order at all.'[2] Archbishop Laud strove to check them;[3] but this was no easy task. Among other things, they succeeded in ousting from many churches the good old custom of catechising in favour of afternoon sermons, an order of Parliament in 1641 having allowed parishioners to 'maintain a conformable lecturer,' to whom the parson should give way 'on Sunday afternoons, unless he would preach himself.'[4] In 1630 Heylin, in a sermon preached at Oxford on the Parable of the Tares, says the 'planting of pensionary lecturers in so many places will bring forth those fruits that will appear to be a Tare indeed; tho' now no wheat be accounted fairer,' and declares that their object is 'to cry down the established clergy, undermine the public liturgy,' and so forth.[5] From the Articles of Visitation of the

---

[1] See Jeremy Collier's *Ecclesiastical History*, vol. viii. p. 59. Also Heylin's *Sermon on the Parable of the Tares*, ut infra.

[2] See Archbishop Laud's certificate to the King on Bishop Wren's Visitation of the Diocese of Norwich in 1634, quoted in Marsh's *Memoirs of Archbishop Juxon and his Times*, pp. 24-25.

[3] See *Life of Laud*, in Dean Hook's *Lives of the Archbishops of Canterbury*, vol. xi. pp. 180, 181, 188.

[4] See Perry's *History of the Church of England*, vol. ii. p. 132.

[5] See the sermon quoted in White Kennet's *Case of Impropriations*, &c., p. 198.

Restoration period, it is clear that the subject of lecturers was one that required to be closely looked into. Bishop Cosin, in his primary visitation (1662), makes, as one would expect from him, very strict inquiries about them.[1] Bishop Hacket in his second visitation (1668), asks, 'Doth your parish maintain a lecturer? Is he a vertuous and orthodox divine? Is he licensed by the bishop? Doth he read the full service of Common Prayer once a month at least, wearing a surplice?'[2] and Sheldon and others made vigorous efforts to regulate them.[3] The extreme love of sermons which survived the Restoration naturally added to the popularity of the lecturers. The author of the 'Ladies' Calling' complains that 'people will hurry to a Lecture, though it be at the remotest part of the town, but let the bell toll never so loud for the canonical hours of prayer, it will not call the nearest of the neighbourhood.' Allestree, when he became Canon of Christ Church, rendered most useful service, by undertaking one of the lectures of the city and striving to bring back the people into the old ways by this popular method, while he gave the salary of the lecturer to the poor.[4] Of course the Puritan party, inside and outside the Church, were anxious to retain the office of lecturer, and Baxter, among his proposed terms of union in 1673, required that 'lecturers should not be obliged to read the service, or at most that it be enough if once in half a year they read the greatest part of what is appointed for that time.'[5] Equally of course, strict churchmen objected to these free lances in the Church,

---

[1] See Bishop Cosin's *Works*, vol. iv. (Library of Anglo-Catholic Theology.)
[2] Articles of Inquiry concerning matters ecclesiastical, exhibited to Ministers, Churchwardens, and Sidesmen of every parish within the Diocese of Lichfield and Coventry, in the second Triennial Visitation of John, Lord Bishop, 1668.
[3] See Hook's *Church Dictionary*. Art. 'Lecturers.'
[4] See Bishop Fell's *Life of Allestree*.
[5] See White Kennet's *History of England*, iii. p. 298.

who were quite independent of her laws, and were for ever cavilling at her offices and officers. 'If,' writes Wharton, 'I would recommend myself to a city lectureship, I should have a chance of success if I inveighed against pluralities, and accused the clergy of negligence and covetousness.'[1] Perhaps we may think that the inveighing against pluralities was not in itself an unprofitable or superfluous work, and certainly the lecturers were sometimes useful. Patrick speaks with gratitude of his 'congregation at Covent Garden, and patron, the Earl of Bedford, kindly paying a lecturer for him;'[2] and the 'preaching of a lecture on the first market day of every month in all the great towns in Cheshire'[3] must have been, if duly regulated, a very seasonable exercise. In fact the work of lecturers generally required to be regulated rather than abolished.

A more humble, but more ancient and regular office than the lecturer's, was that of the 'reader' in parish churches, of whom we hear much during our period. Readers are one of the five minor orders in the Church of Rome; in the Church of England they are, of course, no separate order; they were simply an inferior kind of curate who did the mechanical work of reading the service while the great man reserved his energies for the pulpit. There seems to have been an odious and ridiculous notion that it was derogatory to the dignity of a great preacher to read the prayers,[4] and this, it is to be feared, rather than the real necessity of such help, was the cause of the employment of so many readers. The office of reader was, in fact, the lowest rung in the ecclesiastical ladder, and one can hardly wonder that it was badly paid and lightly esteemed. Bramhall, in answer to some contemptuous remarks of Baxter, declares that he has 'great respect for the

---

[1] *Defence of Pluralities*, p. 7.
[2] *Autobiography of Simon Patrick*, p. 80.
[3] Archbishop Nicolson's *Correspondence*, i. 165.
[4] See, *inter alia*, Nelson's *Life of Bull*, p. 85.

poor readers,' but his attitude is evidently that of a superior patting an inferior on the back, rather than of a man defending his brother and his equal.[1] Swift, when he draws an imaginary portrait of an undeservedly unfortunate clergyman, makes him begin his ecclesiastical career as reader in a parish church at 20*l.* a year,[2] and readers are said to have been so badly paid that they used to combine the duties of several churches, rushing, when the sermon commenced, to begin prayers at another church.[3] But, unlike the present day, there was then so great a superfluity of clergymen that even a reader's place was eagerly sought. Thus Dr. Kennet writes to an intimate friend, holding out a hope, but evidently as a great favour, that he might offer the post to his son if he was qualified for it;[4] and Dr. Willis left a salary for a reader to read the prayers at S. Martin's in the Fields, evidently under the impression, which turned out to be correct, that there would be no difficulty in supplying the place.

The domestic chaplain had no connection as such with the services of the parish church, and will therefore be better dealt with in relation to the social life of the period. But there was another functionary who certainly occupied a more important and prominent position than he does at the present day. The parish clerk, who set the psalm, and often, it would seem, selected it, who was invested in black gown and bands,[5] and who, in point of emolument, if the 'Athenian Oracle' is to be trusted, had twice as good a place as the reader,[6] might well be thought to hold a desirable

---

[1] See *Bishop Bramhall's Vindication &c. against Baxter* (1672), pp. 161-2.

[2] *Essay on the Fates of Clergymen.* Swift's *Works*, Scott's edition, vol. vii. p. 237.

[3] See Perry's *History of the Church of England*, ii. p. 240.

[4] In the unpublished MSS. of White Kennet, in the British Museum, to which my attention was kindly directed by R. Garnett, Esq.

[5] 'The stiff parish clerks with their bans and their gowns.'
(T. Brown, 'Verses on Sternhold and Hopkins &c.,' *Works*, iv. 64).

[6] See *Athenian Oracle*, p. 406.

and responsible post which was keenly competed for. An interesting letter from John Lake (afterwards Bishop of Chichester) when he was incumbent of Prestwich, to a friend who 'made interest with him for the appointment of parish clerk,' shews what a valuable piece of patronage it was considered.[1] Swift, in his companion picture of the undeservedly lucky clergyman contrasted with the undeservedly unfortunate one referred to above, describes Corusodes as 'selling the clerkship of the parish when it became vacant.'[2] Stackhouse, in suggesting remedies for the 'miseries of the inferior clergy,' wishes that 'the ancient custom were revived of admitting none but men in Holy Orders to be parish clerks.'[3] Without grudging these functionaries their comfortable profits, one may be thankful that the odious custom of supplying what was lacking by means of 'clerk ales' was not so common after, as it had been before the Rebellion.[4]

This leads us to the subject of the supply of ways and means generally. Our countrymen of the seventeenth and eighteenth centuries appear to have had a wonderful faith in the efficacy of 'Briefs.' And yet that faith scarcely seems to have been justified by results. Now and then the brief was responded to with extraordinary liberality. When Mr. Bowyer's printing-house was burnt down in 1712, the brief brought in 1,400*l.* or 1,500*l.*[5] The brief for the

---

[1] The letter is quoted in Miss Strickland's *Lives of the Seven Bishops*, p. 109.
[2] *Essays on the Fates of Clergymen*, ut supra.
[3] *Miseries and Great Hardships of the Inferior Clergy in and about London, and a modest Plea for their Rights and better Usage, in a Letter to the Bishop of London*, by T. Stackhouse, 1737.
[4] See Bishop Pierce's curious letter, *Canterbury's Doom*, pp. 142-3. 'There is great reason for clerk ales for the maintenance of parish clerks: for in poor country parishes the people, thinking it unfit that the clerk should duly attend at the church and not gain by his office, send him in provision and then come and feast with him, by which means he sells more ale, and tastes more of the liberality of the people, than their quarterly payments would amount to in many years.'
[5] According to Nichols (*Literary Anecdotes of the eighteenth Century*,

French Protestant refugees in 1682 realised more than 40,000*l*. But these were exceptional cases. Bowyer was a very well-known man, and his disaster called forth much sympathy.¹ By their generosity to the French Protestants the English uttered a silent but very emphatic protest against the Romanising tendencies of King James and his creatures. But, as a rule, the briefs were not warmly welcomed, and one can hardly wonder, for a royal mandate is not the right instrument for stimulating Christian charity. Here again, the State stepped in, and in its professed desire to help the Church, was really a hindrance to her work. Besides the obvious objection that it was putting charity upon a wrong footing, the number of briefs became a nuisance;² and the objects for which they were issued were often of a very questionable character. Losses by fire were perhaps legitimate causes; but when we find so right-thinking, and generally, judicious a churchman as Archbishop Sharp, offering to procure a brief for the payment of Mr. Wesley's debts;³ when we hear of a brief being granted to rebuild a play-house that had been burnt down;⁴ when we learn that there were uncomfortable suspicions about briefs being farmed, and that these suspicions could not be satisfactorily repelled;⁵ that they 'encouraged parishioners to let

i. 60), 'a clear amount of 1,514*l*. 13s. 4¾*d*.,' according to others, 1,400*l*. (See Secretan's *Life of R. Nelson*, sub finem.)

¹ Thoresby, *Diary*, February 3, 171⅔. 'Mr. Bowyer's house burned. Hope he may obtain a brief.' Nichols' *Literary Anecdotes*, vol. i. p. 60 &c., shew that there was strong sympathy with Bowyer on all sides.

² Pepys (*Diary*, June 30, 1661) 'observes the trade of briefs is come now up to so constant a course every Sunday, that we resolve to give no more to them;' a not unreasonable complaint, if it be true that the brief was read for fifteen consecutive Sundays for the same object, the relief of some persons who had suffered from a fire in S. Dunstan's in the West.

³ See Tyerman's *Life and Times of Samuel Wesley*, p. 234. Mr. Wesley had too much self-respect to accept the offer.

⁴ See Noble's *Biographical History of England*, i. 93.

⁵ All that Dr. Wells (*The Rich Man's Duty to contribute liberally to the Building &c. of Churches*) can say in answer to the objection that briefs for the rebuilding of Churches are farmed, is, 'If they are, do not give liberally, but give something;' and, 'How does he know it is farmed? Is it suspicion?' &c.

their churches run to ruin in hopes of getting a brief at last for them; that the costs of repairing churches were much over-reckoned in briefs; and that the money was misspent;'[1] we need not be surprised at the system not working well. Briefs for churches, we are told, brought in 'in large parishes not more than 4s. or 5s.; in smaller 1s. or 2s. Some rich people give 6d., others think it a piece of mere imprudence and weakness to give anything. Those who give nothing or too little to briefs for churches, give likewise nothing or too little to briefs for the poor;' but in justice to our ancestors, we must admit that the very small sums generally given to briefs, especially for churches, cannot be altogether regarded as 'a sad proof of the decay of piety.'[2] Political causes may explain the suspicion with which Bishop Ken's efforts to raise a little money for the distressed nonjurors were received by the Privy Council; but it surely shewed a strange confusion between the functions of Church and State, to object to his appeal as 'an usurpation of ecclesiastical jurisdiction, as infringing on the king's rights and of the nature of a brief.'[3] It is curious that the vigorous revival of Church feeling did not suggest the adoption of the weekly offertory, but it is clear that a fair trial was never given to that system. Nelson speaks of Bull's as quite an exceptional case when he established the offertory, 'which is too much neglected in country villages.'[4] Bishop Cosin writes to the Vice-Chancellor of Cambridge about 'the money thrown into the basons at the church doors' for the sufferers from the Plague in 1665,—a plan with which the elders among us were familiar in our youth, but which is now happily very rare. When the offertory *was* adopted, the results were wonderfully encouraging. Patrick was evidently quite embarrassed by the large sum it brought in at S. Paul's,

---

[1] *Rich Man's Duty &c.*, ut supra. All the answer given to these objections is, that supposing they are all true, it is not a good reason for not giving.

[2] *Rich Man's Duty &c.*, ut supra.

[3] *Life of Ken*, by Hawkins, p. 31. [4] *Life of Bull*, p. 94.

Covent Garden;[1] and the amount of voluntary offerings for missionary work was very large, considering the infancy of the undertaking.

The ritual of the period varied from a correctness which would satisfy the most rigid observer of forms in the present day to a slovenliness which would shock the most lax. For instance, the custom of bowing to the East according to the fortieth Canon was far more usual than it is now. Churchmen like Laud and Morton had advocated it before the Rebellion,—the latter having most clearly distinguished it from the Roman adoration to the altar, in a phrase which is almost epigrammatic: 'We bow, not to the Table of the Lord, but to the Lord of the Table.' But after the Restoration it became much more general than it had been before. Bishop Croft of Hereford speaks of it as an ordinary use in 1675, and desires it to be given up, only on the same principle as that on which he would have conceded the surplice, kneeling at the Lord's Supper, the cross at Baptism &c.[2] The 'Athenian Oracle,' (that is, Samuel Wesley,) justifies it most sensibly, and in terms which shew that it was the rule, not the exception.[3] An anonymous writer in 1670 promises an objector to all Church order, that 'he shall not knock his shins when he bows towards the altar.'[4] An anonymous rhymester of about the same date, writing of Church customs which were general, if not universal, says—

> I quarrel not with him that bows the knee
> Towards the East, although the altars bee
> Mere stumbling-blocks to some, they're none to me.[5]

---

[1] 'Having very often great Communions, and sometimes large offerings, I was very solicitous how to dispose of so much money; it was too much to relieve the poor, and I told the churchwardens it was not intended to lessen their rates, &c.' (*Autobiography of Simon Patrick*, p. 90.)

[2] See *Naked Truth*, ut supra.   [3] See *Athenian Oracle*, iii. p. 483.

[4] See *A Private Conference between a rich Alderman and a poor Country Vicar, &c.*, p. 16. Hickeringill (*The Black Nonconformist*, Works, ii. p. 87) objects, among other things, to 'cringing to the east, to the altar.'

[5] *An Apology of the Author of The Asse's Complaint against Balaam.*

A writer in 1687 tells us that at Carlisle Cathedral 'all bowed towards the altar,'[1] and we have contemporary evidence that this was general at Cathedrals.[2] Dr. Edward Lake, in a devotional work written in 1677, strongly urges his readers, 'after receiving, to arise and make their reverence to the altar.'[3] Joseph Bingham, who was far from being an extreme man, is decidedly in favour of the practice;[4] and White Kennet, in his earlier days, recommends it to his 'Christian Scholar.'[5] Of course the practice also met with strong opposition, as the above quotations intimate; indeed the opponents sometimes invoked the strong arm of the law; we read of the church of All Hallows', Barking, being 'presented for innovations, as bowing to the East;'[6] but the custom was still generally retained.

On the other hand there were instances of extreme irreverence which would now shock all but the utterly godless. It has been already told how the Princess Mary thought she was in a Dutch church because the people of Canterbury stood on the Communion Table to look at her, and how Dean Granville sent some boys to the House of Correction at Durham for playing at cards on the Communion Table. Among the Articles of Inquiry at Bishop Cosin's first Visitation at Durham, one is, 'Doth anyone put his hat on the Communion Table?'[7] and Articles of Visitation shew that similar inquiries were seasonable at a later period.

At the east end itself we find the same strange contrasts. On the one hand altar lights were by no means unusual. Among the princely gifts which Bishop Cosin

---

[1] Story's *Journal*, p. 4.
[2] See Granville's *Letters*, ii. p. 95. Mackenzie Walcott's *Traditions and Customs of Cathedrals*, p. 136.
[3] See Lake's *Officium Eucharisticum*. [4] See *Works*, vol. ii. p. 543, &c.
[5] See *infra*, Chapter on Devotional Works.
[6] *Entring Book*, March 1681, quoted in Dr. Stoughton's *Church of the Restoration*, ii. 183.
[7] Bishop Cosin's *Works* (Library of Anglo-Catholic-Theology), vol. iv.

presented to the chapels at Auckland and Durham were two large silver candlesticks, gilded and embossed, three feet high, to be placed upon the altar;[1] Bishop Fuller of Lincoln says he 'will give them [at the Cathedral] a paire of faire brass candlesticks,' not, be it observed, because they had none already, but because 'they have a pitiful paire of ordinary brasse candlesticks upon the Altar, which (he says,) I am asham'd to see, and can indure no longer.' He seems however to anticipate a little opposition, for he adds, 'I find in the Inventory of church utensils, before they were imbezilled, a paire of copper candlesticks guilt. Why may I not give the like?'[2] Hickeringill's objections to the church service in 1682 include 'lighted candles on the altar;'[3] and a picture of S. Paul's of about the same date represents altar lights. In another picture of the coronation of William and Mary, we see twenty-eight lights burning on the altar, and eight on the re-table, and the author of the 'Asse's Complaint against Balaam' writes of them as of an ordinary use.[4]

On the other hand it was by no means universal after the Restoration to have the altar railed in at the east end of the chancel. In a picture of 1670,[5] the altar is at the entrance of the chancel, with the communicants kneeling round it at some little distance. It is not till 1678 that Evelyn records, 'now was our Holy Table placed altar-wise;' and it was not till 1687 that Bishop Cartwright commanded the churchwardens at Liverpool to 'set the Communion

---

[1] 'Duo magna candelabra argentea et dupliciter deaurata, tres pedes alta, opere celato fabricata, et super Altare, sive Mensam Dominicam, quotidie locanda.' (*Correspondence of Bishop Cosin* (Surtees Society), Part II., p. 71.)

[2] Bishop of Lincoln to Dean Sancroft, quoted in Granville's *Remains*, Part I., p. 217, *note*.

[3] *The Black Nonconformist* (Hickeringill's *Works*, ii. 87).

[4] 'As for the harmless Tapers, let them burn,
Yet when the bridegroom wakes her from her urn,
These will not serve the sleeper's turn.'

[5] Frontispiece to *The Devout Communicant Exemplified*.

Table altar-wise against the wall.'[1] Dean Prideaux, a cautious but sound churchman, speaks very doubtfully about altar rails, approving of them himself, but implying that there was great opposition to them, which in some cases it might be well to conciliate.[2] Bishop Sparrow speaks of the 'Holy Table or Altar being anciently placed towards the upper or east end of the chancel,' and strongly approves of the arrangement, but clearly speaks of it as not being at that time general.[3]

'For greater ornament and decency,' writes Dean Prideaux in 1701, 'are added in many churches, paintings and altar-pieces.'[4] The latter were often very elaborate, especially in the London churches. At S. Michael Royal, College Hill, was 'an altar-piece of singular beauty, carved by Grinling Gibbons in right oak.'[5] At S. Bartholomew the Great, Smithfield, when it was 'beautified' in 1696, 'the altar-piece was a very spacious piece of architecture,'— whether it was tasteful or appropriate is another question.[6] At the Savoy Chapel the altar was 'beautified with portraits of the twelve Apostles at large.'[7] Ambrose Barnes, a strong dissenter, writing from Newcastle, complains of 'new altar-pieces fitter for the play-house than for the house where

---

[1] *Diary of Thomas Cartwright, Bishop of Chester*, for September 21, 1687.
[2] *Directions to Churchwardens for the faithful Discharge of their Office*, by Humphrey Prideaux, Dean of Norwich and Archdeacon of Suffolk, 1701.
[3] See *Rationale upon the Book of Common Prayer*, pp. 28-9.
[4] *Directions to Churchwardens &c.*, ut supra.
[5] See *Sir C. Wren, his Family and his Times*, by Lucy Phillimore, p. 272.
[6] The reader must judge for himself. 'It was painted of a stone colour in perspective. It consists of four columns and two pilasters with their entablements of the Doric order. The intercolumns are the Commandments, and lower are the Lord's Prayer and Creed, all done in gold letters upon black. Over the Commandments, and under an arching pediment is a glory, with the word Jehovah done in Hebrew characters.' And so forth. (*New View of London*, i. p. 142.)
[7] Paterson, *Pietas Londinensis*. He calls it 'S. Mary-le-Strand, or the Savoy.' The present S. Mary-le-Strand was not rebuilt till after 1714, when Paterson wrote, but the Savoy Chapel was used as the parish church for the parishioners, and hence was sometimes incorrectly called 'S. Mary-le-Strand.'

God is worshipt, some of them contrived with carved work resembling the lighted tapers of a mass board.'[1] Paintings were of a most varied description. The sacred monogram,[2] the Holy Ghost in the form of a dove, Moses and Aaron, Moses with horns,[3] texts of Scripture, the angel Gabriel, and, what appears strangest of all to our views, Queen Elizabeth and King Charles I;[4]—the former, no doubt, as the champion of Protestantism against Romanism, the latter as the champion and martyr of the Church of England against Puritanism. The queen and the king did not, as might perhaps be the case in the present day, represent the Low and High Church parties respectively. Hearne, who was of course distinctly a high churchman, records with evident approval that at 'S. Peter's in the East, Oxford, on the north wall is painted Queen Elizabeth, lying at full length in her robes, with a crown on her head.'[5]

It was, perhaps, from something of the same kind of feeling, that is, not pure Erastianism, but as a sort of symbol of 'our happy establishment in Church and State,' that the king's arms were ordered to be set up in churches. Certainly, Bishop Hacket was no Erastian; and among his Articles of Inquiry in 1668, one question is, 'Are the king's arms set up?' It is by no means intended to justify the custom, but we should, in common fairness, strive to place ourselves in the position of the churchmen of the period. To them the sovereign was the common barrier against a foreign potentate at Rome on the one hand, and against republicans at home, who had already upset the Church, on the other; and the royal arms were the visible emblem of this barrier. About setting them up *somewhere* in the church, no question seems to have been raised; but when

---

[1] *Memoirs of Ambrose Barnes* (Surtees Society).   [2] *Ibid.*
[3] Bishop Barlow's *Cases of Conscience*, 'Case of setting up images in churches,' in which much curious information will be found. Moses was represented with horns, owing to a mistranslation of Exodus xxxiv. 30, 'Facies Mosis erat cornuta,' in the Vulgate.
[4] See Paterson's *Pietas Londinensis*.   [5] *Reliquiæ Hearnianæ*, vol. i.

they formed, as they sometimes did, part of the altar-piece,[1] the inappropriateness *did* seem to strike some. In the 'Athenian Oracle,' there is an interesting protest against their being 'set up above the Commandments of God in the place of most holy Christian worship, like the cherubims in the most holy place of the temple on the ark of God;' and it is added that 'at S. Peter's, Cornhill, S. Martin's, and other churches where there are and were persons as observant of ceremonial and episcopal order as any, they have been placed elsewhere.'

Pews cannot certainly be reckoned among the *ornaments*, but they were a painfully conspicuous part of the furniture, of the church during our period. It may be true, as Dean Hook says,[2] that they owed indirectly their height and general obstructiveness to Puritanism, but it cannot honestly be said that the restorers of Church order did much to abate the nuisance. Bishop Hacket complains of 'great men being content to set up new pews for their own use, but sticking at all other new (church) building.'[3] Sir Christopher Wren was so far before (or behind) his age as to 'wish that there should be no pews, but only open benches,' but he felt that his wish could not be gratified, for he says, 'there is no stemming the tide of profit of pew-keepers; especially since by pews in the chapel of ease, the minister is chiefly supported;' he is therefore content with the very modest suggestion, in reference to the design of Queen Anne's fifty new churches, that 'a church should not be so filled with pews but that the poor may have room enough to stand and sit in the alleys; for to them equally is the gospel preached.'[4] Even such correct churchmen as Cosin and Granville recognise the system. From a letter of the

---

[1] In the description of the altar-piece at S. Bartholomew the Great, quoted above, the climax is, 'above the pediment are the queen's arms,' &c.

[2] *Church Dictionary*: 'Pews.'

[3] Plume's *Life of Hacket* (Walcott's edition), p. 88.

[4] *Sir C. Wren*, &c., Phillimore, p. 311.

former, we find that he was sorely exercised concerning his daughter's seat in Sedgfield church;[1] and among the offences taken notice of at an archidiaconal visitation of the latter, one is 'the intruding into Mrs. Hackman's pew.'[2] We read of Bishop Cartwright 'sealing a confirmation of Mr. Oldfield's two seats in the gallery at Manchester at 44s. per annum;'[3] and Defoe, in his 'History of the Plague,' speaks of 'people locking themselves up into separate pews.'[4] If this 'locking up' is to be taken literally, it was a survival from the pre-Rebellion period, for Bishop Earle, in his amusing 'Microcosmography,' describes the 'she precise hypocrite as knowing her place in Heaven as perfectly as the pew she has a key to.'[5] But we must not conclude that wherever pews are mentioned, precisely the same thing was meant as we mean. Pepys speaks of his wife 'sitting in Lady Fox's pew at the play,'[6] and Bishop Sparrow of the 'reading pew in parish churches.'[7] What we call 'pews' simply were called sometimes 'closed pews,' sometimes 'privy closets;' and there are few, if any, indications during our period of any serious inclination to return to the good old plan of keeping churches unencumbered with these invidious and unsightly appendages.

The regulation of notices in church was a subject which required and received attention from the restorers of Church order. There was one pious and interesting custom, the disuse of which we may regret, viz. the sending in of 'tickets for intercession.' Thoresby frequently refers to this custom in his diary;[8] and Tom Brown thus describes it—'I peeped into a fine church on my way to Fleet Street. Here, before sermon began, the clerk (in a slit stick contrived for that purpose) handed up to the desk a number of

---

[1] Bishop Cosin's *Correspondence* (Surtees Society), p. 273.
[2] *Remains*, Part II., p. 4.
[3] *Diary of Thomas Cartwright, Bishop of Chester*, for March 26, 1687.
[4] P. 81.   [5] P. 96.   [6] *Diary*, vol. v. p. 114.
[7] *Rationale upon the Book of Common Prayer*, p. 28.
[8] See vol. i. p. 434; ii. pp. 19, 42, &c.

prayer-bills, containing the humble petitions of divers devotees for a supply of what they wanted, and the removal of their afflictions.'[1] But matters of a more secular nature than intercession were wont to be noticed in church. The author of the 'Clergyman's Vade Mecum' protests with good reason against the publishing of 'hues and cries and enquiries after lost goods' in church;[2] and though it was sanctioned by act of parliament[3] that 'persons newly come to be inhabitants might at their request be published after divine service,' the custom was not a very seemly one. The reading of the king's proclamation against vice and immorality four times every year was very usual in churches: and so good a churchman as Bishop Patrick strongly approves of it, and gives most elaborate directions to his clergy how they are each time to improve the occasion.[4] Dean Granville, who above all things prided himself upon his rubrical correctness, yet thought there would be nothing unseemly in advising the people, between the Nicene Creed and the sermon, as to how they should vote at a parliamentary election.[5]

This chapter must not be concluded without a word about the services of those conscientious churchmen who were only prevented by scruples about the oaths from worshipping at the national altars. It is difficult to ascertain much on the subject, for the nonjurors were obliged to keep their meetings secret, since those meetings were liable at any time to be interrupted, the worshippers brought before a magistrate, the oaths tendered to them, and a fine imposed.[6] To prevent the intrusion of any spy, it is said that a watchword was agreed upon each week by the 'faithful remnant.' It need scarcely be said that the services

---

[1] *Works of Mr. Thomas Brown*, iii. p. 69.   [2] Pp. 280-1.
[3] 3 and 4 William and Mary, c. 12.
[4] See *Letter of the Bishop of Chichester to his Clergy*, 1690. Also Defoe's *Account of the Societies for the Reformation of Manners*, 1699, p. 68.
[5] *Remains*, Part I., p. 197.
[6] See *English Church in the eighteenth Century*, i. pp. 56-7.

at these nonjuring assemblies were precisely similar to those at any well-regulated church, with the omission, of course, of the name of the sovereign. The question about the 'usages' was of later date. In London there was, we know, a chapel in Great Ormond Street, which Robert Nelson, who lived in that street, regularly attended, as also did 'my neighbour the Dean' (Hickes) when he was at home. Here the Holy Communion was celebrated 'every Sunday, Good Friday and other solemn occasions.' The minister was Dr. Marshall, to whom Nelson left a small legacy 'in regard of his constant attendance at the Eucharistical Sacrifice.'[1] There was probably also daily service here, for Thoresby, visiting his friend Dr. Hickes on a weekday, 'found him at his nonjuring conventicle.'[2] There was another chapel in Fetter Lane, at which it seems not improbable that Nathaniel Spinckes officiated, for 'he lodged at a glazier's in Winchester Street, near London Wall,'[3] in the neighbourhood. There was in Broad Street 'a nonjuring congregation to which Jeremy Collier preached.' The bishop's chapel at Ely House, Holborn, was naturally used for the services of the nonjurors, so long as Bishop Turner had the power of opening it to them. Lord Clarendon attended the service there on January 30, 1690, and heard 'Mr. Leslie make a most excellent sermon;' there were, he tells us, 'about three score people present — a great auditory at this time.' This does not seem an overwhelming congregation, but perhaps there were more on Sundays. At any rate the Bishop of S. Asaph (Lloyd) was sent to inform Bishop Turner that the king had been told of the great concourse of people that resorted to his chapel, and therefore he advised him to shut it up; the advice not being taken, the same prelate went the next week to his brother of Ely, and 'told him plainly he must let no more

---

[1] Secretan's *Life of Nelson*, p. 175.
[2] Thoresby's *Diary* or May 18, 1714.
[3] See an interesting letter from R. Nelson to Pepys, appended to Pepys' *Diary*, v. 422.

company come to his chapel,' 'so that I perceive,' adds Lord Clarendon bitterly, 'all people are to have liberty of conscience but those of the true Church of England.' The irrepressible bishop, however, was not so easily put down; for, some months later, Lord Clarendon writes, 'I went to the Communion at Ely House, where I found the Bishops of Ely, Gloucester (Frampton), and Peterborough (White), all nonjurors.'[1] There was another place of meeting for the nonjurors in Goodman's Fields at which Dr. Welton, who had been rector of Whitechapel, officiated, and where a congregation of 300 or 250 was wont to assemble.[2] In the country, the nonjurors generally worshipped in private houses; and as many of the laymen who sympathised with them were men of rank and wealth, there would be no difficulty in finding sufficiently large chapels in their private houses to accommodate the small congregation that would assemble in them. This, we know, was the case at Shottesbrook, where Mr. Cherry and Mr. Dodwell maintained between them a nonjuring chaplain, Mr. Brokesby, who conducted the services daily at Shottesbrook Park.[3] The private chapel at Longleat, at which Mr. Harbin, the domestic chaplain of Lord Weymouth, officiated, was devoted to nonjuring services until the accession of Queen Anne, when Lord Weymouth accepted office, and, to the great grief of Ken, was obliged to have the prayers for the sovereign used. At Oxford, Hearne tells us,[4] 'the nonjurors had the Sacrament at Mr. Sheldon's chambers at Christ Church, who finds all the necessaries for it.' The same plan was doubtless adopted in all parts of the country; and probably there was no cathedral or parish church in the kingdom where more orderly services were carried on than in the private chapels or rooms in which this little remnant met for the worship of God.

[1] See Lord Clarendon's *Diary*, ii. pp. 302, 303, 304, and 425.
[2] See Palin's *History of the Church of England*, &c., p. 420, and Lathbury's *History of the Nonjurors*, pp. 252, 256-7.
[3] See *Life of Mr. Henry Dodwell*, by Francis Brokesby. p. 542.
[4] *Diary* for September 14, 1705.

CHAPTER V.

RELIGIOUS AND PHILANTHROPICAL SOCIETIES.

An important feature in the Church life of the period, and a sure symptom of its vigour, may be found in the many Societies which were then founded and flourished. Among the earliest were those which were called simply

The Religious Societies. The origin of these was very humble.[1] About the year 1678, a few young men in London of the middle class were deeply impressed by the stirring preaching of Dr. Horneck at the Savoy Chapel, and the morning lectures of Mr. Smythies at S. Michael's, Cornhill, which were specially designed for the young. As good churchmen, these young men consulted their clergyman; thus it happened that several met at the same house on the same errand, and, being kindred spirits, naturally formed an acquaintance with one another. It is said that the existence of some clubs of Atheists, Deists, and Socinians suggested to them the idea of banding themselves together in what they called 'Societies.'[2] Probably they were advised to do so by their clergy, especially by Dr. Horneck and Mr. Smythies, the former of whom is called by one who knew the circumstances thoroughly their 'father.'[3] The Societies were conducted most strictly on the lines of the Church's teaching. None were to be admitted as

---

[1] See *A Short Account of the several Societies set up of late years, &c.* published about 1700.
[2] See Dr. Josiah Woodward's *Account of the Rise and Progress of the Religious Societies.*
[3] Dr. Woodward, *ut supra*.

members except young men above sixteen years of age who had been confirmed. They were to choose a clergyman to direct them, and their meetings were to be strictly devotional. They were to use no prayers at their meetings except those of the Church, and 'none that peculiarly belong to the minister, as the absolution.' The minister whom they chose was to 'direct what practical divinity was to be read.' After prayer and reading they were 'to have liberty to sing a psalm,' and after all this was done, if there was any time left, 'they might discourse with each other about their spiritual concerns,' but this was 'not to be a standing exercise which any should be obliged to attend unto.' After many other excellent practical rules, the last is that they were to 'love one another, when reviled not to revile again, speak evil of no man, wrong no man, pray, if possible, seven times a day, keep close to the Church of England, &c.'[1] They were to meet once a week, and at every meeting 'consider the wants of the poor,'[2] and each member was to bring a weekly contribution proportionate to his means.' The accession of James II. caused some change in their proceedings. Owing to the dread of Romanism, private meetings began to be suspected. So the Societies changed for a time their name to 'Clubs,' as having a less suspicious sound, and 'instead of meeting at the private houses of the members, met at some public house.' Some of the members shrank back for fear of being involved in a charge of Romanism, but others gave themselves to the work with all the more zeal, thinking rightly that the best way of opposing Romanism was by stimulating the zeal and piety of English churchmen. Seeing 'the daily Mass celebrated at the Chapels Royal and other public places,' they determined to provide counter attractions. They commenced by procuring a daily service at S. Clement Danes, 'where they never wanted a full and affectionate congregation.' They

---

[1] See Bishop Kidder's *Life of Rev. Anthony Horneck, D.D.*
[2] Woodward, *ut supra*.

next set up a monthly evening lecture in the same church 'to confirm communicants in their holy vows,' and at this lecture 'the most eminent divines about the city used to preach.'[1] Soon after the Revolution a new rule was made, 'that everyone should endeavour to bring in one other at least into the Society.' This tended wonderfully to increase their numbers. So, also, did the hearty support of the dignitaries of the Church, who at first, not perhaps unnaturally, looked with some suspicion upon the new movement. Was it not like setting up a Church within a Church? Would it not lead to schism—to faction—to spiritual pride? Such rumours were in the air; in fact the case was so misrepresented to the bishops, that the Societies wisely determined 'to address an Apology to the Bishop of London' (Compton), that is, they sent what we should now call a 'deputation' to his lordship, for we are told that he dismissed them with 'God forbid that I should be against such excellent designs.' There is no doubt that the countenance given by the Diocesan, and by the Archbishop of the Province (Tillotson), greatly increased the popularity of the Societies, and this was further promoted by the interest which the queen took in them;[2] but the credit of leading them into, and keeping them in a right channel, must unquestionably be given to those clergymen who personally directed them; first and foremost to Dr. Horneck, who was not only their chief originator, but also, as his biographer tells us, 'had the care of several societies of young men;'[3] then to Dr. Beveridge, whose great name was of itself sufficient to keep any scheme afloat; then to Mr. Smythies, and a little later, to Dr. Bray, 'to whose memory most of the Religious Societies in London owed grateful

---

[1] Woodward, *ut supra*.

[2] 'Our late gracious queen,' writes Defoe, 'took great satisfaction in these Religious Societies.' (*Account of the Societies for the Reformation of Manners*, p. 16.)

[3] Kidder's *Life of Horneck*.

acknowledgments, being in a great measure formed on the plans he projected'; [1] and finally to Dr. Woodward, who defended and helped them with his pen. These were the men who prevented enthusiasm from degenerating into fanaticism, and kept it well within the sober limits of the Church of England. In 1710 there were no less than forty-two Religious Societies in London and Westminster, besides a great number in the various large towns in the kingdom. One of their most ardent supporters was Robert Nelson, who took them as a text for one of his appeals to 'Persons of Quality,' arguing that 'if a few persons, on no account considerable, and whose names are hardly known,' could do so much to promote the life and spirit of Christianity, 'Persons of Quality' might surely do much more.[2]

Let us see what the Societies *had* done. Their contemporary historian is fully borne out by other testimony when he affirms that 'it is evident even to demonstration that their zeal hath in many places given new life to the celebration of the Lord's Supper, public prayers, singing of psalms &c.'[3] The experiment commenced at S. Clement Danes was extended far and wide. Daily public prayers, celebrations of the Holy Communion every Lord's day and other festival, and preparation sermons or lectures for the Holy Communion, were, with the permission of the incumbent, established in very many churches at the cost of the Societies. A very common notice in 'Pietas Londinensis' is, 'prayers &c. provided by a Religious Society.' Great stress was laid upon the Holy Communion, not only as the central service of the Church, but also as 'the best means to prevent men from apostatising by confirming their vows and relieving their spiritual strength.'[4] Not only did their members not apostatise themselves, they also prevented

---

[1] *Public Spirit Illustrated in the Life and Designs of Dr. Bray* (published 1746).
[2] See *A Representation of the Ways and Methods of Doing Good*, appended to *An Address to Persons of Quality* (published 1715).
[3] Woodward, *ut supra*. [4] Woodward.

many others from doing so. We learn from quite an independent source that they ' promoted family religion ' (which in the reaction against Puritanism had rather fallen into disuse in favour of public prayer), brought many Quakers to Holy Baptism, and preserved many from Popery.[1] Their works of charity were various and extensive. They ' visited the poor at their houses and relieved them, fixed some in a way of trade, set prisoners at liberty, furthered poor scholars in their subsistence at the University,'[2] contributed largely to Dr. Bray's missionary projects, and were greatly instrumental in establishing nearly one hundred charity schools in London, as well as others in the country. But all was subservient to the extension and improvement of public worship, and so successful were they in this, the main part of their work, that, in the language of a historian who wrote a little time after their collapse, ' Prayers were set up in so many places and hours [in London] that devout persons might have that comfort every hour of the day, and there were greater numbers and greater appearance of devotion at prayers and sacraments than had been observed in the memory of man.'[3]

Of course their success was to a great extent owing to the fact that they harmonised thoroughly with the general feeling. They had not to create the demand before they offered the supply. There was a strong devotional spirit abroad, which could find vent only in one direction. The nation's experience of Puritanism on the one hand, or Romanism on the other, was too recent to allow it to tolerate for one moment anything that savoured of either. The Religious Societies supplied additional opportunities of devotions of a purely Anglican type, and therefore they carried the town, we may almost say the nation, along with them. But none the less is it to their credit that they alienated no

---

[1] *Angliæ Notitiæ*, by John Chamberlayne, Part III., continuation of Edward Chamberlayne's (the father's) work, p. 310.
[2] Woodward. [3] Tindal's *Continuation of Rapin*, vol. xiv. pp. 437-8.

one by their extravagance or inconsistency. After they had been thirty-two years in existence, their historian could call attention with perfect truth 'to the humble and inoffensive behaviour,' as well as ' to the blooming piety of the orthodox and sober persons' who composed them.¹ They did *what* they did, and enough has surely been said to show that it was very considerable, without the slightest ostentation, without even letting their names be known. They were content to work quietly on under the direction of their clergyman, looking for, and finding their reward, not in the praise of men, but in the really useful results which they achieved. Among their warmest supporters was the rector of Epworth, Mr. Wesley. A 'Letter concerning Religious Societies' (1699),² and a 'Sermon preached to one of the Religious Societies' (1698), full of most seasonable advice to its members, are still extant. There is no doubt that the father handed down his sentiments on the subject to his more famous son, and that John Wesley intended his Societies to be an exact repetition of what was done by Beveridge, Horneck, and Smythies sixty-two years before,³—in fact he himself constantly refers to his ' going to a Society.' How it was that the Methodist Societies took a different course is a very interesting, and, to a churchman, a very sad question, but it does not come within the scope of this work.

One word must be added on the causes of the collapse of the Religious Societies. One cause was that old, old trouble which has so often interfered with the progress of Church life, and never more than during the period with which this work is concerned, the mixing up of politics with religion. The Societies came to be suspected of Jacobite tendencies. They were especially charged with using their influence over

---

¹ Woodward.

² This letter is appended to his *Pious Communicant rightly Prepared*, and the sermon is among a collection of Spital Sermons and others of the date bound up in one volume.

³ Tyerman's *Life and Times of Samuel Wesley*, p. 226.

the charity schools for political purposes; the charges against them on this score were very vague, but they were quite sufficient, in the sensitive state of men's minds, to cast discredit upon them. Then, again, it is to be feared that the clergymen of the second generation of the Societies' existence were not men of so high a type spiritually as their predecessors, and as it was of the essence of the Societies to take their tone entirely from the clergy who had the exclusive direction of them, this told sadly to their disadvantage. But the chief cause of all was that they became confused with another class of Societies, from which they were in reality perfectly distinct, though the same individuals were often members of both, and though the two kinds are frequently grouped together, not only by later historians, but also in contemporary records.[1] This latter class of Societies we have now to consider.

The Societies for the Reformation of Manners were first formed in 1692 with the laudable aim of checking the prevalent immorality by bringing offenders under the arm of the civil power. They were set on foot by five or six gentlemen of the Church of England, and these were soon joined by others, both churchmen and dissenters. They proceeded upon the principle of a division of labour, one Society, composed of lawyers and magistrates, devoting itself to the work of putting the laws into force and of getting subscriptions to the expenses of prosecutions, another, composed of tradesmen, to the suppression of debauchery in the streets, another, to the somewhat invidious task of informers, and so forth. In 1691, before the Societies were formed, the gentlemen who had the design in view, induced the queen, through the medium of Bishop Stillingfleet who had great influence over her, to issue royal letters

---

[1] Even the title of Woodward's work is confusing: *An Account of the Rise and Progress of the Religious Societies, and of their endeavours for the Reformation of Manners.* Of course he clearly distinguishes between the two in the body of his work.

admonishing the magistrates to do their duty. Magistrates' orders were sent all over the kingdom, and 'blank warrants lodged for the case of informers' &c.[1]—a very hazardous proceeding. Archbishop Tillotson took the matter up warmly, and so did his successor, Archbishop Tenison, who issued a circular letter to his suffragans, begging them to urge their clergy to help on the good work. The contemporary evidence is too strong to permit us to doubt that a considerable effect was produced. Within ten years from their formation, a contemporary declares that they 'had prospered to a degree exceedingly great, beyond what human wisdom did or could expect;' that 'more than twenty thousand persons had been convicted of swearing, cursing, and profanation of the Lord's day in and about London and Westminster,' and that 'about three thousand lewd and disorderly persons had been punished within the same limits.'[2] In 1705 Bishop Compton publicly testified in the House of Lords to the beneficial effects they had produced in the suppression of vice.[3] Defoe affirmed in 1699 that 'they had proved so exceedingly serviceable in the work of Reformation that they might be reckoned a chief support to it.'[4] Dr. Woodward writes to the same effect. Mr. Disney, about 1708, writes in rapturous terms about the 'glorious success' of the Societies.[5] Mr. Bradford, rector of S. Mary-le-Bow, afterwards Bishop of Carlisle, declared in a sermon in 1709 that 'they had not been without considerable effect.'[6] Robert Nelson writes

---

[1] Woodward.

[2] *A Short Account of the several Kinds of Societies set up of late years*, &c. This must have been written about the close of the seventeenth century, for it speaks of the rise of the Religious Societies 'about twenty years since.'

[3] See Rapin (*Tindal's Continuation*), vol. xvi. p. 208.

[4] *Account of the Societies for the Reformation of Manners*, &c.

[5] *Essay upon the Execution of the Laws against Immorality and Profaneness*, by J. Disney, Esq. (afterwards the Rev.). Robert Nelson thought this work 'unanswerably convincing.'

[6] The sermon is in a volume containing a collection of *Spital Sermons*

strongly about their effectiveness, and so does Bishop Bull.[1]

It has been thought desirable to quote this contemporary evidence (which might have been multiplied to a much greater extent), because some later historians have given a different impression, and they are borne out by one great man at least, Dean Swift,[2] and by several anonymous writers,[3] but the weight of contemporary evidence preponderates overwhelmingly in favour of their effectiveness.

That they should have raised great opposition is certainly not surprising. It is one thing to promote religion and virtue by moral persuasion and example, quite another to call in the strong arm of the law. From the time of the Athenian 'sycophants' downwards, the very name of 'informer' has had an odious sound about it. Defoe is most unjust in insinuating that the great men who held aloof from the Societies were instigated by mere timidity and over-caution.[4] This certainly was not the case with Archbishop Sharp, who tells us plainly enough his reasons for hesitating about joining the Societies, and very weighty reasons they are. Bishop (afterwards Archbishop) Nicolson, again, who is much less guarded in his opposition to the Societies, cannot possibly be suspected of timidity;[5] and still less can Dr. Sacheverell, one of their most vehement opponents, whose faults lay in quite a different direction. The fact is, the Societies, well meant and probably effective as they were, seem to have committed the converse of an error which was very prevalent at the time. The penal laws against nonconformists are an instance of the State

---

and Sermons for the Charity Schools, preached in the first few years of the eighteenth century.

[1] See Nelson's *Life of Bull*, pp. 208 and 290.

[2] See Swift's *Project for the Advancement of Religion and Reformation of Manners.* (Swift's *Works*, Scott's edition, vol. vii. p. 99.)

[3] See, inter alia, *Reformation of Manners. A Satyr.* 1702.

[4] *Account of the Societies for Reformation of Manners.*

[5] See Archbishop Nicolson's *Correspondence*, pp. 146, 171-7, &c.

interfering in the province of the Church, these Societies are an instance of the Church interfering in the province of the State. No such objection can be raised against the other Societies which were formed at this period.

The Society for Promoting Christian Knowledge is the mother of several of these, but she herself may be called the daughter of the Religious Societies, inasmuch as it was the spirit awakened by these Societies which, more than anything else, called her into existence,[1] and moreover these Societies interested themselves largely in procuring subscriptions for her.[2] The Society however would never have been established but for the indefatigable and self-denying efforts of one man, Dr. Bray. He it was who first endeavoured, in more ways than one, to gain help from public sources, and failing this, determined to set on foot a voluntary Society. He it was who drew up the plan of the Society, and on March 8, 169⁸⁄₉ (a memorable date), met four other Christian men, all laymen, and virtually established it. The names of these notable five were, Francis, Lord Guildford, Sir Humphrey Mackworth, Justice Hook, Colonel Maynard Colchester, and, last but not least, Dr. Thomas Bray. The first resolution at this first meeting had reference to the design of 'erecting catechetical schools in every parish in and about London;' then Dr. Bray was requested to lay before the Society his scheme for promoting religion in the Plantations; then the five members agreed to contribute 12*l*. towards the printing of good books to be circulated among the poor, steps having been previously taken for founding lending libraries in America. In 1701 the Earl of Marlborough applied for and received from the Society books for the troops under his command; and about the same time Admiral Benbow and Sir G. Rooke began to distribute the Society's books in the fleet. But it was not until 1705 that the Society agreed to set apart a portion of

---

[1] See Perry's *History of the Church of England*, iii. p. 90.
[2] See *Angliæ Notitiæ*, Part III., pp. 310-5.

its funds to furnish the poor in the country with Bibles and Prayer Books at a cheap rate.

It will thus be seen that the Society at first embraced within its province what afterwards became the work of several other associations; and nothing shews the courage, let us rather say the faith, of this little band of men more than the contrast between the magnitude of their designs and the smallness of the company engaged in them. The sixth member elected was John Chamberlayne, the first secretary of the Society; then others quickly followed; but at the first eight meetings (which were held weekly), only five members were present. Well may the Jubilee Tract, published 150 years later, be entitled 'Great Success from small Beginnings.'

To this tract (which gives a full account of the rise and progress of the Society), and to other easily accessible works, the reader must be referred if he desires to fill up this very meagre sketch of the first beginnings of this grand old Society.[1] It can here only be noticed in connection with the Church life of the period; and one point strikes us especially in this connection. It is pleasing to observe the names of men of all parties in the Church among the earliest and warmest supporters of a Society which was designed for the *whole* Church, not any one section of it exclusively. We hear of Tenison and Burnet and Kidder and Fowler and Kennet joining with Patrick and Lloyd and Thomas Wilson and R. Nelson and S. Wesley, all apparently in perfect harmony. In fact, one of the most interesting features in the early history of the S.P.C.K. is the varied characters and tastes of its supporters. Though of a strictly Church type, it was not composed of a clerical clique, that is, of clergymen who had no interests beyond what may be

---

[1] Jubilee Tract; *Great Success from small Beginnings. An Account of the five original Members of the S.P.C.K.* T. B. Murray, 1849; Anderson's *History of the Colonial Church; Public Spirit Illustrated in the Life and Designs of Dr. Bray; Historical Notices of the Missions of the Church of England, &c.*, E. Hawkins, 1845, &c. &c.

termed the technicalities of their profession, and of laymen rather more clerical than the clergy. Both clergy and laity were men of wide and general interests. Among the first five members were a famous lawyer, a knight and a soldier; and among the earlier supporters were William Melmoth, a bencher of the Temple, Blackmore, the physician, Strype, the antiquary, Gilbert White, the naturalist, John Evelyn, of 'Silva' fame, and Ernest Grabe, the universal scholar. As another instance of the width of their sympathies, it may be mentioned that they opened a correspondence with some foreigners distinguished for their active piety,—Francke of Halle, Osterwald of Neufchatel, Jablonski of Berlin, and others.[1]

It is difficult to describe the early work of the Society (which, by the way, for the first ten years of its existence was called the Society for *Propagating* Christian Knowledge), without entrenching upon provinces which originally belonged to it, but afterwards became the work of separate organisations. By slow degrees the work which is now specially connected with the Society became its chief work. In 1709 a preacher places first of all among the objects of the Society, to 'dispense plain and useful books among the common people.'[2] How its other work was deputed to other associations will be seen when we notice its various daughter Societies.

The Society for the Propagation of the Gospel in Foreign Parts was the eldest and most important of them. On Dr. Bray's return from Maryland in 170?, he found that the various designs of his newly-founded Society were too extensive for any one association. He therefore proposed the establishment of a separate Society whose object should be to propagate the Gospel throughout the foreign possessions

---

[1] See Anderson's *History of the Colonial Church*, ii. p. 409.

[2] Sermon at S. Sepulchre's Church, preached June 16, 1709, being the Thursday in Whitsun-week, the anniversary meeting of children educated in Charity Schools in and about the cities of London and Westminster, by S. Bradford, Rector of S. Mary-le-Bow.

of the British Empire. The work had already engaged the attention of Convocation, and would probably have been carried out by that body; but, as a matter of fact, the credit of procuring a royal charter for constituting the new Society a body corporate, belongs primarily to Dr. Bray, and then to Archbishop Tenison and Bishop Compton, who pressed on the matter in a way that perhaps no private clergymen could have done. These three names, Bray, Tenison, and Compton, are *the* three which stand foremost in the floating of this great missionary effort; and to these we may add a fourth, that of Humphrey Prideaux, whose weighty appeals to the primate six years earlier, no doubt contributed to secure Tenison's hearty services.[1] The 27th of June, 1701, is a memorable date, as the date of the first meeting of the Society at Lambeth under the Archbishop's direction; the names of those present shew how closely it was connected with the S.P.C.K., of which it was simply an offshoot. The self-same men were the supporters of both; the older Society deputed some of its functions to a separate corporation; that was all. It is necessary to bear this fact in mind, when estimating the significance of what seems a grievous oversight in these early missionary efforts. From a churchman's point of view, a Church without a bishop is a body without a head. What were our pious forefathers about when they established this sort of acephalous organisation for propagating the Gospel on distinctly Church principles, for they certainly *did* intend to act on Church principles? We have ample evidence that the originators and first workers clearly recognised the necessity of providing episcopal supervision. ' 'Tis a dismal thing,' writes one of the earliest missionaries in Pennsylvania, ' to consider how much the want of a bishop amongst us has retarded the progress of the true religion in America.'[2]

[1] Letter to Archbishop Tenison on his first promotion to the Archbishopric, January, 169$\frac{4}{5}$, quoted in *Life of Dean Prideaux*, p. 159.
[2] *Memorial on the State of the Church in Pennsylvania, most humbly*

'I am very glad,' writes another, in 1709, 'to find that the members of the Honourable Society are convinced that a head is necessary to the body, but, if he don't make haste he will come too late.'[1] 'You can neither well believe,' writes another missionary in the same year to the secretary of the Society, 'nor I express, what excellent services for the cause of religion a bishop would do in these parts [Rhode Island]. These infant settlements would become beautiful nurseries, which now seem to languish for want of a father to oversee and bless them.'[2] Governor Nicholson of Virginia wrote to the same effect to the Archbishop of Canterbury. And the subject was, almost from the very first, mooted at home. In 1703 the question of a suffragan bishop for America was discussed. In 1709 a plan was half-formed for sending a bishop to Virginia, Dean Swift, of all men in the world, being the man destined for the post. A memorial was presented to the queen on the subject in 1709,[3] and another in 1713. At the May meeting in 1712 it was formally resolved that 'it is very expedient to establish bishops and bishoprics in America.' In fact it has been truly said that 'the Church seemed on the point of attaining the object at which she had so long aimed, but the queen's death soon afterwards put an end to arrangements.'[4] If it be thought that the founders of the Society were somewhat slow and deliberate, considering the importance of the matter, it should be remembered that a Society which was, (as has been said) simply the offshoot of another Society, would naturally be tentative in its efforts at first; that thirteen years are, after all, not a very long period in the life of a Church which already numbered nearly as many cen-

offered to the Venerable Society for the Propagation of the Gospel, by Rev. E. Evans, who was sent by the Bishop of London as missionary to Philadelphia in 1700.

[1] Rev. — Talbot, quoted in Hawkins' *Historical Notices of the Missions of the Church of England in the North American Colonies*, p. 144.

[2] Rev. J. Honeyman, quoted by Hawkins, p. 166.

[3] See Anderson, iii. 73-4.   [4] Hawkins, p. 380-3.

turies; and that the earnest churchmen who founded the Society and meant to found bishoprics in connection with it had not the faintest conception of the change that was coming over the spirit of the Church. On the contrary, many of them anticipated halcyon days when the long talked-of 'Protestant succession' became an accomplished fact. Even after the accession of George I., Archbishop Tenison had so much faith in the project that he left 1,000*l.* towards it in his will. Little did the originators dream that what they had all but accomplished would have to wait not very far short of another century before it took a tangible shape!

Our concern, however, is with what the Society did, not with what it did not do. From the beginning its work was twofold, viz., as the charter expresses it, 'to provide learned and orthodox ministers for our loving subjects,' and 'to make other such provision as may be necessary for propagating the gospel in those parts;' or, as Dr. Willis, the preacher of the first anniversary sermon, in 1702, more fully states it: 'the design is, in the first place, to settle the state of religion as well as may be among our own people in the foreign Plantations; and then to proceed, in the best methods they can, towards the conversion of the natives.' Bishop Burnet spoke to the same effect in his sermon in 1703. A singular interest is attached to these early anniversary sermons. We learn from the first of them, that the Romanists had made capital out of the apathy of the English Church as contrasted with their own vigour in the Plantations, and Dean Willis 'wishes we could give the best answer by denying the matter of fact.' Bishop Williams of Chichester refers to the same subject in the sermon of 1706. In 1707 Bishop Beveridge speaks most hopefully of the work of the Society in his very eloquent anniversary sermon; but the sermon which appears to have produced the greatest effect was that of Bishop Fleetwood, in 1711, which was circulated far and wide.

The income of the Society during the first thirteen

years of its existence did not exceed 1,000*l.* a year on an average. As to the proportions contributed in different parts of the country, a Lincolnshire man may be pardoned for noticing with some pride that Lincolnshire held the first place, with Devonshire not far behind. A Lincolnshire landowner, Sir E. Turner, and a Lincolnshire clergyman, Mr. Adamson, vicar of Burton Coggles, were mainly instrumental in introducing the system of 'deputations,' that term meaning, not, as now, persons deputed to advocate the claims of the Society, but persons deputed to receive subscriptions. Among laymen who took an active part in the working of the Society, besides those mentioned in connection with the S.P.C.K., were Sir John Chardin, the great traveller, and Nicholson, Governor of Virginia; and among the clergy, Simon Patrick, Bishop of Ely, whose deep interest in the Society was, it has been suggested,[1] one reason why all Bishops of Ely are *ex officio* constituted members by charter, Bishop White Kennet, and Mr. Burkitt, vicar of Dedham. Queen Anne 'put new life into its work' at her accession,[2] and continued to interest herself greatly in it all through her reign. She appointed a day (Trinity Sunday), when 'a general collection should be made every year for the funds of the Society,' and issued a Royal Letter in 1713, which brought in the goodly sum of 3,060*l.*[3]

Parochial Libraries sprang directly from the missionary zeal of the indefatigable Dr. Bray. When he was appointed the Bishop of London's commissary for Maryland in 1696, his first effort was to procure books for the clergy who were to serve abroad, for he thought that as these clergy 'were likely to be of the poorer sort, they would be ill able to procure even the most necessary books for themselves.' The reasonableness of his appeal was generally recognised,

---

[1] Anderson, iii. 30. [2] See *Angliæ Notitiæ*, Part III., p. 340.
[3] It has not been thought necessary to give authority for all the facts mentioned in the sketch. They may be found in any popular history, such as Anderson's, Hawkins', &c.

but some objected that the poor clergy in England were in equal need of books, and that their wants ought to be supplied first. This objection only opened out a fresh field for Dr. Bray's activity. Without in the least relaxing his efforts in behalf of the Plantations, he 'thought it well to hit the nail that would drive,' and threw himself with characteristic energy into another scheme, the object of which was to establish parochial and lending libraries in every deanery throughout England and Wales, libraries for students about to take Holy Orders, and libraries for schools poorly endowed. In 1697 he published a tract which shewed that he was ready with his plan in all its details.[1] This was quickly followed by another especially addressed to the clergy,[2] and in 1702 he again returned to the charge.[3] The tracts were so effective that it is worth while quoting a passage or two. 'For our younger gentry,' he writes, 'I cannot but think it would tend extremely to furnish their minds with that useful knowledge as will render 'em serviceable to their families and countries, and will make 'em considerable both at home and abroad, and will keep 'em from idle conversation and the debaucheries attending it, to have choice collections of such books dispersed thro' all the kingdom, and waiting upon 'em in their own parlours, as will ennoble their minds with principles of virtue and true honour, and will file off that roughness, ferity, and barbarity which are the never-failing fruits of ignorance and illiterature.'[4] Addressing the clergy he writes: 'The truth is, there are a sort of writers which are traditionally handed down from one old study to another, who are not such a good-humoured and inviting society as to make one delight much in their conversation. But what man of spirit or education, had he a Justin Martyr, a Tertullian

[1] *An Essay towards promoting all necessary and useful Knowledge, both divine and human, in all parts of His Majesty's Dominions.*
[2] *Bibliotheca Parochialis; or a scheme of such theological heads as are requisite to be studied by every Pastor of a Parish.*
[3] *Bibliotheca Catechetica.*   [4] *An Essay &c.*, ut supra.

or Cyprian; a Sanderson, a Hammond or Tillotson come to visit him, would leave such men of sense for the society of the sons of Belial!'[1]

The good man's efforts were not in vain. The names of Lord Digby (Bray's faithful friend and patron),[2] the Earl of Thanet, Viscount Weymouth, and, of course, Robert Nelson, are conspicuous among those who helped both with money and counsel.[3] One of the first to recognise the usefulness of the scheme was Bishop Wilson, who as early as 1699 began to found, with the help of Dr. Bray, lending libraries in the Isle of Man, and succeeded in establishing sixteen in that small island.[4] The success was not quite so great in proportion in the neighbouring island of Great Britain, but it was fairly encouraging. Sixty-seven libraries are said to have been established, and the matter assumed such importance that in 1709 a Bill was passed in Parliament 'for the better preserving of parochial libraries;' and before Dr. Bray's death, a Society was formed under the title of the 'Associates of Dr. Bray,' which still exists.[5]

Charity Schools. It will be remembered that the very first object specified as the design of the S.P.C.K. in 1698 was the education of the poor; and most nobly was this design carried out by the Society during the sixteen years of its history with which this work is concerned. But though the Society gave a most powerful stimulus to the work, it cannot be said to have originated it, nor even the particular form

---

[1] *Bibliotheca Parochialis.*

[2] He founded two libraries, at Coleshill and Overwhitacre. (See *Life of Rawlet*.)

[3] See *Account of the Designs of the Associates of the late Dr. Bray*, 1769. Nelson recommends the scheme to 'persons of quality' in his *Ways and Means of Doing Good.*

[4] Cruttwell's *Life of Bishop Wilson*, p. 59.

[5] Tenison, when rector of S. Martin's in the Fields, was a precursor of Bray; he founded there the first free library in the kingdom in 1684, and, with the help of Sir C. Wren, raised a suitable building for it. The valuable library was sold in 1861, and the money applied to middle-class education. (See Evelyn's *Diary* for Feb. 15, 168¾; Phillimore's *Life of Sir C. Wren*, p. 226 and *note*.)

of it which comes under the denomination of charity schools. The Christian education of all classes had been recognised as a duty before the S.P.C.K. called attention to it. Tillotson, for instance, frequently enforces it in his sermons. And charity schools in which children were not only educated gratis, but maintained and clothed in uniform, and put out as apprentices, were not unknown before 1698. It is difficult to determine the parish to which the honour of having the first charity school belongs. Bishop Smalridge maintains that 'the Blue Coat School belonging to the new church in Westminster [S. Margaret's], erected in 1688, being the first of its kind, may modestly challenge some sort of precedency by right of primogeniture.'[1] Bishop White Kennet declares 'it is no small honour to the Parish of S. Botolph, Aldgate, that here was first laid the foundation of these charity schools.'[2] The school at S. Martin's in the Fields, founded by the joint exertions of Tenison (then rector of the parish) and Patrick (then at S. Paul's, Covent Garden), because the Romanists had founded a free school in the precincts of the Savoy, also puts in a claim to the honour.[3] And, passing from London to the country, we find Bishop Ken setting up many schools in all the great towns of his diocese for poor children,[4] which must, of course, have been before the Revolution. Without settling the question of precedency, it is clear that several charity schools were set up[5] before the S.P.C.K. was even thought of. But the whole credit of turning an exceptional into a very common

---

[1] *The Royal Benefactress*; sermon preached at S. Sepulchre's on the Thursday in Whitsun-week, at the Anniversary Meeting of the promoters of Charity Schools.

[2] *The Christian Scholar.*

[3] See Narcissus Luttrell's *Brief History of State Affairs from September, 1678, to April, 1714*, i. 437. Also Bishop Patrick's *Autobiography*, p. 128, and Secretan's *Life of Nelson*. It appears that the schools in S. Martin's and at S. James', Westminster, were opened on the same day (April 23, 1688).

[4] Hawkins' *Life*, prefixed to Ken's *Prose Works*.

[5] See *Survey of the Cities of London and Westminster*, by R. Seymour, Book I., chap. xiii. (published 1734).

case belongs to the Society. The members at once began to set themselves to this branch of their work with wonderful energy and success. In 1704 the happy thought occurred of assembling all the children of the charity schools in and about London for an anniversary service, on the Thursday in Whitsun-week. This service was at first held at S. Sepulchre's, till the church became too small to hold them all. The procession of the children in their uniforms, and the active part they took in the service, were new sights and proved very attractive. But here again there had been previously isolated instances of such services, for Kennet in 1701 writes of the S. Botolph schools, 'These pretty children in walking by pairs and singing by consort, do naturally strike upon the eyes, and win upon the hearts of good-natured Christians.'[1] The anniversary preachers frequently allude to 'this pleasing sight of this beautiful assembly,' 'the comely order of this procession,' and so forth;[2] and readers of the 'Spectator' will remember the well-known passage in which Steele speaks of 'the gentleman in the pulpit pleading movingly in behalf of the poor children, and they for themselves much more movingly by singing a hymn.'[3] Steele thinks that the scheme was not so well taken up as it deserved to be;[4] but others thought differently. Atterbury, e.g., speaks of it as 'an admirable design which had met with deserved success.' Bishop Bull told the clergy of S. David's 'that the plan had been blest with great success in many parts of the kingdom, especially London;'[5] and the general tone of the anniversary preachers is that of thankfulness, not despondency. And surely with reason, if statistics may be trusted. In 1704 there were fifty-four schools in and about London, and 2,131

[1] *The Christian Scholar.*

[2] See a collection of Anniversary Sermons of Charity Schools in the British Museum.

[3] No. 430. There are three papers (294, 380, 430) advocating the cause of charity schools, all by Steele.

[4] *Spectator*, No. 294.   [5] Nelson's *Life*, p. 284.

children present at the first anniversary service.[1] In 1707 there were about 3,000 children at the anniversary, and in 1709 between three and four thousand, while in 1712 there were 117 schools in London and Westminster. When the Georgian era set in, the progress was less rapid, owing partly to the general sluggishness of the time, and partly to the fact that the schools began to be suspected of being nurseries of Jacobitism.

The scheme extended to all parts of the country. At Cambridge it appears to have been particularly successful. It was set on foot in 1703, and was so warmly taken up by the University authorities that before the end of the year enough money had been gathered to give a free education to 260 children, and the number quickly rose to 300.[2] Oxford was far behind her sister University. In 1707 we find R. Nelson, in a letter to the Master of University College, expressing himself 'much concerned that charity schools were not yet set up in the University,' and a few weeks later 'hoping to find a way of addressing the Vice-Chancellor about the charity schools.'[3] In 1705 Thoresby tells us 'the new charity school in this town [Leeds] was finished and furnished with forty children decently clothed in blue, and wholly maintained.'[4] Bishop Bull strongly urged his clergy to 'set up charity schools in their several parishes.'[5] And, not to weary the reader with further details, it will suffice to add that at the close of 1712 there were 500 such schools in different parts of the country.[6]

An interesting feature in the scheme is the connection between the promoters of the charity schools at home and

[1] *Jubilee Tract, S.P.C.K.*

[2] See *An Account of the Charity Schools at Cambridge, appended to a Sermon preached on S. Paul's Day*, 170$\frac{1}{5}$, by W. Whiston, Professor of Mathematics.

[3] See *Letters from the Bodleian*, edited by Bliss, 1813, pp. 168 and 170. The first letter from Nelson to Dr. Charlett is dated Ascension Day, 1707; the second, July 12, 1707.

[4] *Diary*, i. p. 463.   [5] Nelson's *Life*, p. 283.

[6] See Secretan's *Life of R. Nelson*.

men of kindred spirit abroad. At first England was the receiver. Professor Francke sent over two Germans from Halle[1] to help in establishing catechetical schools in England; these two men attended, by special request, one of the earlier meetings of the S.P.C.K., and the result was that several pious foreigners became masters of our first charity schools.[2] Presently, however, England became the giver. English charity schools won such a reputation that an account of them was translated into German, and schools were founded, to some extent on their model, in Hesse, Sweden, Denmark, Russia, and Switzerland.[3]

The Corporation of the Sons of the Clergy is a Society which may be fairly said to have been founded during our period, for though the institution dates back as early as 1655, it was not incorporated by charter until 1678. It received its name because sons of clergymen were its earliest promoters, and its object was, and is, to relieve the necessities of clergymen and their families, especially their widows and orphan children. The well-known 'Festival,' still held annually, dates from the time of the Rebellion, and the royal charter was granted twenty-three years later, in consideration of the great sufferings of many of the clergy for their loyalty and adherence to the Church. Nelson recommended it among his 'Ways and Methods of Doing Good,' and Atterbury preached on its behalf one of his most eloquent sermons, from which it would appear that the congregation was then exclusively composed of sons of the clergy.[4]

Queen Anne's Bounty. On February 6, 170$\frac{3}{4}$, Queen Anne signalised her birthday by announcing to the House of Commons that she had been pleased to remit the arrears

---

[1] See *Pietas Hallensis*.
[2] Anderson's *History of the Colonial Church*, iii. p. 565.
[3] See Perry's *History of the Church of England*, iii. p. 135.
[4] *Sermon before the Sons of the Clergy at their Anniversary Meeting at S. Paul's*, Dec. 6, 1709. Several paragraphs begin, 'Ye are the sons of the clergy,' &c.

of Tenths to the poor clergy, and that she would henceforth make a grant of the whole of her revenue from First Fruits and Tenths to the augmentation of poor livings. The gift was a very handsome one, amounting to sixteen or seventeen thousand a year, and the benevolence of the bountiful queen is none the less because it would be more correct to call it 'Queen Anne's justice,' than 'Queen Anne's bounty.' But it was unquestionably an act of justice, for the appropriation of the money by the crown was, in plain words, downright robbery. In the days of the crusades, the Popes exacted the first-fruits of every living (that is, the whole of the first year's income), and the tenth of every succeeding year, towards the expenses of those costly expeditions. When the crusades came to an end, the tax did not come to an end with them, it being still found useful for the papal exchequer. When Henry VIII. threw off the papal yoke, he calmly appropriated this source of revenue to the use of the crown; Queen Mary restored it to the Church, but it was resumed by Queen Elizabeth in the very first year of her reign, and to the crown it went ever after. The fact that it was used as a convenient fund out of which 'to gratifie servants and friends' by no means mended matters, especially if, as Burnet intimates, these servants and friends were sometimes of a very questionable character. Robbing Peter to pay Paul is bad enough, but robbing Peter to pay people who were the very reverse of Paul is worse. Burnet may be pardoned a little boastfulness in his account of the matter, if he really had the large share to which he lays claim in bringing about the gracious and graceful act.[1] At any rate, the royal sacrifice was not made in vain, if the gratitude of the people counts for anything. White Kennet declared that it 'redeemed our

---

[1] Mr. Palin (*History of the Church of England*, chap. xi. p. 260), to whom the very name of Burnet is like a red rag to a bull, will not admit Burnet's exclusive claim; and it certainly would be odd if Archbishop Sharp, at any rate, the queen's unfailing counsellor, had not some hand in the matter.

happy Reformation from the only reproach that had been cast upon it,'—and much more to the same effect.'¹ Atterbury, 'that it was an act unequalled by any prince since the Reformation,'²—and this was the general tone in which it was spoken of.

The same spirit of charity which led Christian churchmen to found these various Societies, also led to the foundation of hospitals and other kindred institutions. The two great retreats for our veteran soldiers and sailors date from this period, Chelsea Hospital being founded by Charles II., carried on by James II., and perfected by William III.; Greenwich by William and Mary in 1694. Trinity College Hospital near Mile End was founded in 1695; Aske's Hospital, by R. Aske, haberdasher, who died in 1681; Morden's College, Blackheath, was founded by Sir John Morden in his life-time, 'for merchants fallen into decay, being honest, sober, and discreet members of the Church of England.' Its 'generous and truly Christian founder was present at its consecration,' and died in 1708. Ironmongers' Hall was founded by Sir Robert Geffryes in 1681; he died in 1703;³ and Edward Colston, whose memory is still deservedly honoured every year at his native Bristol, and who was a staunch churchman (as indeed were all the others above mentioned) formed most of his charitable schemes before the close of our period.

[1] See *Case of Impropriations &c.*, p. 356.
[2] Sermon VIII., on the Queen's Accession, March 170¾.
[3] See a *Survey of the Cities of London and Westminster*, by R. Seymour, 1734.

CHAPTER VI.

PREACHING OF THE PERIOD.

THE reaction against Puritanism which marked the Restoration era did not extend to one religious exercise. The people still loved to hear sermons. The mania for sermons is one of the commonest complaints of Church writers during the first twenty years of our period. The sermon 'jostled out catechising;' people 'began to learn at the wrong end, and ran to the Lecture before they had been at the Catechism;' and 'so they have been very opinionative, according to the impression which the affectionate noise of the last sermon has made upon their minds.'[1] 'That erroneous and superstitious conceit of sermons which obtains so much among the vulgar has almost cast all other religion out of doors.'[2] 'This last age has brought in such a partiality for preaching, that prayer seems comparatively (like Sarah to Hagar) despicable in their eyes; so that if they can but come time enough for sermon they think they have discharged the weightier part of the law and of their own duty.'[3] Without a sermon 'the worship of God is counted lame.'[4] 'Preaching is now thought to be the principal part of a clergyman's duty; nay, so infatuated are the people of this nation with reference to this ordinance, that

---

[1] Lancelot Addison's *Primitive Institution &c.*, p. 152 (published 1674).

[2] Ralph Bathurst to Seth Ward, soon after the Restoration. (See *Life and Literary Remains of Ralph Bathurst*, p. 56.)

[3] *The Ladies' Calling*, p. 269 (published about 1665).

[4] *A True Notion of the Worship of God, or a Vindication of the Service of the Church of England* (published 1673).

they seem to imagine that the main, if not the whole of a parish minister's business is to preach, and that the people have little else to do besides to sit in great ease and state, and to hear and judge how well the parson preaches.'[1] Even so late as 1681, Dean Sherlock declares that 'a great many, who have little other religion, are forward enough to hear sermons;' and complains that they 'come to church when the service is half over, and think there is no great hurt in it neither, if they do not lose the sermon.'[2]

When we read of 'the lack of sermons,' it is fair to remember that this crusade against the excessive craving for them was going on. Sir T. Browne, for instance, records in 1662 that 'he had the luck to meet with a sermon at Buxton, which he could not have done half a year earlier.'[3] Howe speaks in 1671 of 'finding there was no sermon in the parish church at Holyhead,' and being 'allowed to occupy the pulpit morning and afternoon, to the great delight of a crowded congregation.'[4] Thoresby tells us that Dolben was 'much honoured as a preaching bishop,'[5] as if such a being were rare; and as late as 1689 Patrick found there was 'but one sermon in the afternoon in all the churches in Cambridge.'[6] But we must not too hastily infer that this lack of sermons was due simply to laziness or incompetence; it is quite as likely that it may have sprung from an unwillingness to pander to a morbid taste. It is clear that the many remonstrances against the excessive craving for sermons were not without effect. Glanvill of Bath wrote a 'Defence of Sermons,' in which he complains that people had run into the opposite extreme to that of the puritanical sermon-lovers; and one of the indictments of White Kennet (1710)

---

[1] A contemporary of Isaac Milles (who was born in 1638), quoted in *Life of I. Milles*, p. 24.
[2] *Practical Discourse of Religious Assemblies*, pp. 66 and 186. (See also South's *Sermons*, vol. iii. p. 522.)
[3] *Tour in Derbyshire* (Sir T. Browne's *Works*, i. p. 30).
[4] *Life and Character of John Howe*, by Henry Rogers, p. 172.
[5] *Diary*, i. p. 172. [6] *Autobiography*, p. 164.

against the High Church movement is, that 'people had begun to think that Common Prayer without sermon (at least in the afternoon) was the best way of serving God.'[1]

The love of sermons, however, survived the Restoration for many years. And the sermons that people loved were both long and abstruse. A sermon then *was* a sermon, not like the brisk little sermonette of our degenerate days, but a solid affair, of at least an hour's duration, and plentifully interspersed with Greek and Latin, and even Hebrew quotations. These scraps of the learned languages were valued, not simply on the 'omne ignotum pro magnifico' principle, but as marks to distinguish the scholarly and authorised divine from the illiterate and amateur preacher. Whether the latter had ever been really popular seems very doubtful. Of course no open objection could be made against the military preacher who had a remarkably effectual way of enforcing attention, when he stood with his little pocket Bible in one hand and his sword in the other. But there is evidence enough to shew that, when the people could have their way, they preferred a preacher who was learned and who would display his learning. When poor Pocock, one of the first scholars in Europe, strove to adapt himself to the capacities of his rustic congregation at Childrey during the Rebellion, he only won contempt for his pains. 'Our parson,' they said to one of the vicar's Oxford friends, 'is one Mr. Pocock, a plain, honest man, but, master, he is no Latiner.'[2] No exception seems to have been taken against the erudite discourses which Jeremy Taylor delivered to the villagers at Golden Grove during the same period. And when the Church was restored with the Monarchy, the people looked upon it as their positive right to be regaled, if not edified, with sermons which had a good sprinkling of foreign languages in them. 'If,' complains Eachard in 1670, 'the minister's words be such as the

---

[1] See *Life of Bishop White Kennet*, p. 127.
[2] *Life of Dr. Edward Pocock* (Twells), p. 95.

constable uses, his matter plain and practical, such as comes to the common market, he may pass possibly for an honest, well-meaning man, but by no means for any scholar, whereas if he soars aloft in unintelligible huffs, preaches points deep and mystical, and delivers them as dark and fantastical; this is the way, say they, of being accounted a most able and learned instructor. Others there be, whose parts stand not so much towards tall words and lofty notions, but consist in scattering up and down and besprinkling all their sermons with Greek and Latin; neither will they rest here, but have at the Hebrew also to a company of farmers and shepherds.'[1] And his opponents justify instead of denying the facts. Barnabas Oley, who held a country living where he constantly preached and was most popular, doubts 'whether we do ill, although it be in our country churches, to sprinkle a little Latin and Greek sometimes about our sermons.'[2] Another answer says 'it may be convenient for the minister to quote out of the learned Greek or Latin, though nobody understands it, to distinguish himself from such who preach in English altogether at Conventicles.'[3] So late as 1711, Addison speaks of 'the natural love of Latin which is so prevalent among our common people,' and tells the amusing story of the two rival preachers in a country town, 'one of whom being well-versed in the Fathers, used to quote every now and then a Latin sentence to his illiterate hearers, who found themselves so edified by it, that they flocked in greater numbers to this learned man than to his rival. The other, finding his congregation mouldering every Sunday, and hearing at length what was the occasion of it, resolved to give his parish a little Latin in his turn, but being unacquainted with any of the Fathers, he digested into his sermons the whole book of " Quæ Genus " and " As in Præsenti ; " and the result

---

[1] *Contempt of the Clergy*, p. 37.
[2] *Answer to Eachard's Contempt of the Clergy* (published 1671), p. 60.
[3] *Vindication of the Clergy, in answer to Eachard*.

was that in a very little time this thickened his audience, filled his church, and routed his antagonist.'[1] But Addison was describing a thing of the past; Swift, writing about the same time, says correctly, that 'he had outlived it.' In fact so marked a change took place in the character of sermons in this and other respects during our period, that they really might be divided into two heads, 'the old style' and 'the new style.' This will appear when we enter into details.

It is remarkable that the very time when church writers were inveighing against the excessive love of sermons was the time when the reputation of church preachers was highest. Never has the Anglican pulpit been more nobly filled than it was when Jeremy Taylor, Isaac Barrow, Robert South, Thomas Ken, and other modern Chrysostoms of the same date occupied it. Let us begin with the first mentioned.

Jeremy Taylor, strictly speaking, hardly comes within the category of *English* preachers during the Restoration period: for his sermons in England and Wales were preached before that event. The return of his sovereign from exile only led to his own splendid exile. But the Englishman in Ireland was an Englishman still; and we cannot afford to give up to our sister Church one of the greatest of all our English preachers. May we not say, *the* greatest? Where can we find an equal combination of copiousness of matter, tenderness of piety, richness of illustration, majestic dignity and sweet melody of language? It has been objected that he is too gorgeous in his language, too abundant in illustration, above all, too profuse in his quotations from the learned languages. That is a matter of taste; but it should be noted that though Taylor's language is gorgeous, it is never tawdry or bombastic,— though his illustrations are numerous and varied, being drawn from all sorts of sources, from classical history and

---

[1] *Spectator*, No. 221.

mythology almost as often as from the Fathers and the early history of Christianity,—they are never inapposite; though his quotations abound, they always seem to flow naturally from his almost inexhaustible fountain of knowledge, and are never dragged in to parade his erudition. He very often translates them, and, when he does not, they may always be passed over by the unlearned reader without losing the thread of the discourse.

The subjects of his sermons are almost always the plain practical duties of daily life. 'If any man *will* do His will, he shall know of the doctrine, whether it be of God,'—this, the text of one of his greatest sermons, really furnishes the key-note to his teaching; and it would be difficult to select a better specimen of his style and matter and general tone of mind (though not of his richness of illustration and quotation), than the following passage from that sermon, which was preached before the University of Dublin: 'I am in a school of Prophets and Prophets' sons, who all ask Pilate's question, What is Truth? You look for it in your books, and you tug hard for it in your Disputations, and you derive it from the Cisterns of the Fathers, and you enquire after the old wayes and sometimes are taken with new appearances, and you rejoyce in false lights, or are delighted with little umbrages, and peeps of Day. But where is there a man, or a Society of men, that can be at rest in his enquiry, and is sure he understands all the truths of God? Where is there a man but the more he studies and enquires, still he discovers nothing so clearly as his own Ignorance? This is a demonstration that we are not in the right way, that we do not enquire wisely, that our Method is not artificiall. If men did fall upon the right way, it were impossible so many learned men should be engaged in contrary parties and opinions. We have examined all wayes but one. All but God's way. Let us, (having missed in all the other) try this: let us go to God for Truth; for Truth comes from God only, and his wayes are plain, and his sayings are true, and his promises Yea and Amen; and if we miss the Truth, it is because we will not find it: for certain it is, that all that Truth which God hath made necessarie, he hath also made legible and plain, and, if we will open our eyes, we shall see the Sun, and if we will walk in the Light, we shall rejoyce in the light; only let us withdraw the curtains, let us remove the impediments and the sin that doth so easily beset us; that's God's way. Every man must in his station do that portion of duty which God requires of him, and then he shall be taught of God all that is fit for him to learn; there is no other way for him but this.

Isaac Barrow ranks next to Jeremy Taylor among the great preachers of the Caroline period,—in some respects, perhaps, even above him. 'Barrow,' writes Hallam, 'was not so extensively learned as Taylor, who had read rather too much, but was inferior perhaps, even in that respect, to hardly anyone else, and was above him in closeness and strength of reasoning.'[1] And again, 'Barrow's sermons display a strength of mind, a comprehensiveness and fertility which has rarely been equalled.'[2] His mathematical training, no doubt, gave an argumentative turn to Barrow's sermons, which make them very different from Taylor's, but they are wanting in that exquisite tenderness, and that almost musical rhythm of language which render Taylor's so fascinating. Like Taylor, he dwells chiefly on the plain, practical duties of life, and avoids deep questions of controversy, sharing the reaction from the controversial spirit of Puritanism. Those who blame Barrow for being too cold and ethical a preacher should make allowance for this reaction. Le Clerc calls his sermons rather treatises and disputations than harangues; and perhaps there is some truth in the remark. But in their way they are wonderful productions. It is said that he would write and re-write them three or four times: and perhaps what they

[1] *Literature of Europe*, iii. 269.   [2] *Id.* p. 295.

gain in carefulness and accuracy, they may lose in fire and energy by the process. Even in those days of long sermons, they sometimes provoked rebellion by their inordinate length; and a prejudice against the uncouth and slovenly appearance of the preacher had to be overcome before they could be appreciated by the hearer.[1] The reader of them should be warned that in the popular edition, the editor, Tillotson, has altered, modernised,[2] and subdivided to such an extent that we do not get Barrow as he was in the pulpit. This, however, has been rectified in Mr. Napier's excellent edition.[3] It is impossible to give a fair specimen of Barrow, for his strength lies in his consecutive train of powerful reasoning, to which no detached passage can possibly do justice. It would necessarily be but a brick from Babylon.

Widely different from either of the above is the third great preacher of the Restoration period, **Robert South**. He was like them both in this respect; that he sought to turn men's attention from the discussion of profound questions and the analysis of their own experiences to the plain, practical duties of life. But here the resemblance ends. He purposely avoided the ornate style of Taylor. In fact it is probable that he actually alluded to Taylor in this passage: '"I speak the words of soberness," said S. Paul; and, "I preach the Gospel, not with the enticing

---

[1] It is needless to quote the story of the vergers at Westminster Abbey causing the organs to blow him down, because he preached so long that they would have no time to shew the chapels; of the stampede at S. Lawrence Jewry, when he appeared in his untidiness in the pulpit; of his Spital sermon which lasted three and a half hours,—especially as some of these stories are not quite accurate.

[2] E.g., 'avoce' is changed into 'divert,' 'meliorate' into 'improve,' 'oscitant' into 'heedless,' 'extund' into 'invent.'

[3] Published in 1859 by the Cambridge University Press, with an admirable notice of Barrow's life and academical times, by Dr. Whewell. This was the first appearance of Barrow as he was; his MSS. were found at Trinity College, and were most competently edited by Rev. A. Napier. May I venture to refer the reader to my article on Barrow in *The Dictionary of National Biography* for further information?

words of man's wisdom." Nothing here of "the finger of the North Star;" nothing of "nature's becoming unnatural;" no starched similitudes introduced with a "Thus have I seen a cloud rolling in its airy mansion," and the like. The Apostles, poor mortals! were content to take lower steps, and to tell the world in plain terms that he who believed should be saved, and he who believed not, should be damned.' And so far from avoiding controversy, he sniffed the battle from afar, and, let his text or subject be what it might, hardly ever preached a sermon without dealing some shrewd blows to his adversaries on the right hand and on the left. He hits hard, but he hits fair, and straight from the shoulder; and, if some of his utterances startle us, we must remember that our forefathers were not so mealy-mouthed as we are, and that congregations were used to hear a spade called a spade, even in the pulpit. Let us take as a specimen his sermon on 'The Scribe Instructed unto the Kingdom of Heaven,' which naturally calls forth his racy wit against the illiterate preachers. The gospel scribe ' was not to be inspired, or blown into the ministry, but to come to it by mature study and labour.' 'He was to fetch his preparations from Industry, not Infusion.' ' All were took up and busied, some in pulpits, and some in tubs, in the great work of preaching.' ' Whosoever pretends to be a preacher, must know that his business is to *persuade*, and that without the helps of human Learning, this can hardly be done to any Purpose. So that, if he finds himself wholly destitute of these, and has nothing else to trust to, but some groundless, windy, and phantastick notions about *the Spirit*, he would do well to *look back*, and taking his *Hand* off from this *Plough*, to put it to another, much fitter for him.'[1] This was in 1660; and thirty years later he returns to the charge: 'Amongst those of the late *Reforming Age*, all learning was utterly cryed down, so that with them the best Preachers were such as could not *read*,

[1] *Sermons*, vol. iv. Sermon I.

and the ablest *Divines* such as could hardly *spell* the letter. None were thought fit for the *Ministry* but *Tradesmen* and *Mechanicks*, because none else were allowed to have the *Spirit*. Those only were accounted like *St. Paul*, who could *work with their Hands*, and in a Literal Sense *drive the Nail home*, and be able to *make a Pulpit* before they *Preach'd* in it . . . Latin was with them a mortal Crime, and Greek instead of being owned for *the Language of the Holy Ghost* (as in the New Testament it is) was look'd upon as the Sin against it, so that, in a word, they had all the *Confusions of Babel* amongst them, without the *Diversity of Tongues*.'[1]

Before quitting South, it is only fair to shew how hard he could hit on the opposite side. Thus of pilgrimages: 'A man, it seems, cannot be a Penitent, unless he also turns Vagabond, and foots it to Jerusalem, or wanders over this or that part of the world to visit the shrine of such or such a pretended Saint; Thus that which was *Cain's* Curse is become their religion. He that thinks to expiate a sin by going barefoot, does the penance of a goose,' &c. . . Of scourgings: 'Let them Lash on never so fast they are not at all the nearer to their journey's end; they may as well expect to bring a cart, as a soul to Heaven by such means.'[2] He is equally severe against the Freethinkers,[3] against Trimmers,[4] against Covetous persons;[5] but as our quotations have already run to a great length, it must suffice to refer the reader to the sermons themselves for proof of this.

The sermons of the three above-named divines rank among the standard works of our literature, which can be said of very few sermons of any era; but the preachers were not so much sought after in their life-time as several others. The reputation of **Ken** as a preacher stood at least as high as any of the three. We hear how 'the Bishop of Bath and

---

[1] Sermon on 1 Cor. xii. 4, 'Now there are diversities of gifts, but the same Spirit,' preached at Westminster Abbey, 1692.
[2] Vol. i. Sermon I., on Prov. iii. 17, 'His ways are ways of pleasantness.'
[3] See *Sermons*, vol. ii. pp. 13-4; i. p. 560.
[4] Vol. vi. p. 35.   [5] Vol. i. p. 164.

Wells preached at S. Martin's to a crowd not to be expressed, nor the wonderful eloquence of this admirable prelate;'[1] how 'the Holy Communion at Whitehall was interrupted by the rude breaking in of a multitude zealous to hear the second sermon by the Bishop of Bath and Wells;'[2] how 'Ely Chappell in Holborn was mightily thronged when Dr. Kenn preacht;'[3] how 'he made almost all who heard him preach weep;'[4] how Charles II. (who knew a good sermon when he heard it, though he did not take much heed to practise what he heard) would say, 'I must go and hear Ken tell me of my faults;' how the Princess Anne wrote to Bishop Turner to keep 'a place for her at his chapel in Holborn,' when Ken preached, as she 'had a great mind to hear him.' There are (so far as I know), only three of Ken's sermons extant; but they are enough to shew that his popularity as a preacher was well-deserved. They are very plain, but very eloquent, and make us wish that we had more specimens of the preaching of this most saintly and courageous man.

Another preacher whose reputation was deservedly high was **Bishop Stillingfleet**. Pepys, who was by no means inclined to overestimate preachers, speaks of 'walking to the Rolls Chapel to hear the great Stillingfleet preach,' and of 'going to Whitehall to hear the famous young Stillingfleet who did make a most plain, honest, and good grave sermon in the most unconcerned and easy, yet substantial manner that ever I heard in my life.' He also informs us that 'the Archbishop of Canterbury, the Bishop of London, and another, believe he is the ablest young man to preach the Gospel since the Apostles.'[5] His sermons are but little known now, but they are well worth studying. There is a fire and energy about them which one would hardly have expected from the cool, lawyer-like mind of the great prelate. As a specimen of

---

[1] Evelyn's *Diary*, i. p. 638.   [2] *Id*. i. p. 647.
[3] Narcissus Luttrell's *Diary* for March 1686-7.
[4] Samuel Wesley's *Letter to a Curate*.   [5] Pepys' *Diary* for April, 1665.

his style, let us take a passage from his singularly powerful and seasonable sermon preached before the House of Commons at S. Margaret's, Westminster, immediately after the Great Fire of London. He personifies London, and makes the city appeal to his congregation. 'Can you look upon my ruines with hearts as hard and unconcerned as the stones which lie in them? If you have any kindness for me or for yourselves, if you ever hope to see my breaches repaired, my beauty restored, my glory advanced, look on London's ruines and repent. Thus would she bid her inhabitants not weep for her miseries, but for their own sins, for if never any sorrow was like her sorrow, it is because never any sins were like to their sins.'[1] Or take again the following passage from his sermon preached before the 'merry monarch' and his scoffing courtiers in the spring of 1667, on the text, 'Fools make a mock of sin;' in which one hardly knows whether to admire most the eloquence or the moral courage of the preacher. 'Is the chair of Scorners at last proved the only chair of infallibility? Must those be the standard of mankind, who seem to have little left of humane nature, but laughter and the shape of men? Do they think we are all become such fools to take scoffs for arguments, and raillery for demonstrations? ... Methinks, among persons of civility and honour, above all others, religion might at least be treated with the reverence and respect due to the concernments of it; that it be not made the sport of entertainments, nor the common subject of plays and comedies. For is there nothing to trifle with but God and his service? Is wit grown so schismatical and sacrilegious that it can please itself with nothing but holy ground? Are prophaneness and wit grown such inseparable companions, that none shall be allowed to pretend to the one but such as dare be highly guilty of the other?'[2]

---

[1] *Twelve Sermons by Bishop Stillingfleet*, published 1696. Sermon I., text, Amos iv. 11.

[2] *Id.* Sermon II.

Archbishop Dolben almost rivalled in popularity the two last-named preachers. When he preached at Westminster Abbey as dean, people crowded to hear him, and he was immortalised by Dryden in his 'Absalom and Achitophel,' as:

> Him of the Western Dome, whose weighty sense
> Flow'd in fit words, and heavenly eloquence;

and after he had attained the mitre, Thoresby tells us that he 'was much honoured as a preaching bishop.'[1] The disinterment of the few sermons he has left from their graves in the British Museum, thoroughly accounts for their popularity. There is one that was preached before the king, August 14, 1666, 'the day of Thanksgiving for the late victory at sea,' which is a most admirable one; it is very clear and plain, with no quotations, written in a pure and terse style, without a word of flattery to his royal hearer, and with something of the downright abruptness of the soldier about it, and gains considerable force by utilising the preacher's military experience. Witness the following extract. 'Courage! break off your sins by repentance; live a Christian, devout and holy life, and pray earnestly for God's gracious favour and succour, so shall you serve the king as considerably as any Volontier in the Fleet. Here is a project to raise an army easily, speedily, without charge or trouble, and such an one as, could I see formed, I should be much tempted to despise all our enemies.[2] No age or sex but are fit to be listed in it. The impotent old man on his couch, the lady in her closet, the sick and weak upon their beds, without danger or fatigue at sea, every one in their own station, where infirmity or tenderness hath ranked them, may fight, and certainly be victorious. Whoever can but mortifie a lust, forsake a sin, kindle an ardent love to God in his heart, shed a tear, send up a prayer, a sigh, or a groan to Heaven, may thereby without any other Artillery, reach and

---

[1] *Diary*, i. p. 172 (May 1, 1684).
[2] Observe the seasonable allusion to the much-vexed question as to the maintenance of a standing army.

gall the enemy at what distance soever. By the secret, invisible influence of your devotions, you may strengthen the hearts and hands of your friends. While your hearts are right with God, and you hold up pure hands in Prayer, (like Moses in the Mount), theirs will be victorious in battail. . . . Truly you are too unkind, if, while your countrymen fight for you, you will not pray for them. While they patiently endure toil, sickness, wounds, nay lose their lives, you will not amend yours,' &c. Dolben's sermons are so striking and so little known that another specimen may not be superfluous. The following is from a Good Friday sermon at Whitehall 1666, from S. John xix. 19. The preacher's purpose is 'not to lament the shame and cruelties, but to celebrate the triumphs and glory of Christ's Passion, to do Homage to the King of sufferers and adore the majesty of our Lord's abasement.' The subject is argued out most admirably at great length, and in a very racy and practical fashion. 'Do you own and accept Christ for your King? I know you are apt enough to admit his other relations to you; everyone hearkens willingly to the tidings of a Mediator and Saviour. 'Tis pleasant enough to think of a Sacrifice considerable enough to atone for our sins. Of such a High Priest entered within the vail, interceding in our behalf at God's right hand, who will surely be heard when he prays, and who hath already obtained eternal redemption for us. Nay, we can take well that he be a King too, provided that his kingdom is not of this world, so he trouble us not with it in this world, pretend not to govern us till we come to Heaven. 'Tis not amiss that he be powerful enough to overcome our enemies, &c. Tell me now, I pray you, what temptation had the Jews, why they should not be as good Christians as we upon their own grounds, if this be all? What carnality of theirs would have resisted the proposition of such a sacrifice to expiate their sins? Why should not a Pharisee be content that he might have an Advocate always pleading for him at the Throne of Grace? What could move the grossest dreamer in the Sanhedrim to refuse a reversion of eternal glory in Heaven, after the enjoyment of those present felicities which he desired on earth. There is something surely more than this, in the accepting and acknowledging Christ for our king, or else the Jews would have accepted him too. The duty of a subject to a Prince is expressed in one word, Obedience;' and he works out the idea in every detail.

There are few more striking instances of the fickleness of fame than may be found in the fate of **Tillotson's** sermons. From 1664, when he was made preacher at Lincoln's Inn, and shortly afterwards, Camden Lecturer at S. Lawrence Jewry, for at least a century his fame as a preacher was unrivalled. He was 'wonderfully admired and loved as preacher at Lincoln's Inn;' and his 'Tuesday lectures at S. Lawrence were much frequented by all the divines of the town, and a great many persons of quality and distinction.'[1] The clergy came to form their style, and in fact 'his sermons were so well heard and liked, and so much read, that all the nation proposed him as a pattern, and studied to copy after him.' Indeed, 'he was not only the best preacher of the age, but seemed to have brought preaching to perfection.'[2] What is especially remarkable is that the intense odium which he incurred by taking Sancroft's place does not seem to have in the least diminished the value which was set upon his sermons. High churchmen as well as low swelled the chorus of praise. Bevill Higgons, whose dislike of the whole school to which Tillotson belonged was extreme, yet owns that 'by the study of the ancients and the classic authors, whom he had made his models, he had form'd a stile and acquired a just way of thinking, with a simplicity and easiness of expression before his time unknown in England. This justly gave him the

---

[1] *Lives and Characters of the Protestant Bishops of the Church of England*, by J. Le Neve (published 1720), p. 223. Also Birch's *Life of Tillotson*, pp. 28-9.

[2] Tindal's *Continuation of Rapin's History of England*, vol. xiv. p. 144.

character of an excellent preacher. I wish from my heart I could speak as well of him in respect to his religion and politics.'¹ Atterbury, who was the very antithesis of Tillotson, says that 'in his poor opinion Dr. Tillotson wrote and reasoned as justly as any man of his time;'² and as Tillotson wrote nothing but sermons, it is to these that the remark must apply. Bishop Bull, a moderate high churchman, recommended Tillotson's sermons 'as well-known and approved of all' to the attention of the clergy of S. David's in his Charge of 1708;³ and Bull's biographer, whose opinions need not be specified, recommended them to his nephew. Samuel Wesley affirms in good prose that Tillotson 'brought the art [of preaching] near perfection;' and in bad verse:

> 'Twas music, poetry and rapture all,
> The sweets of his orac'lous words to share;
> As soft they fell as balmy dew-drops fall,
> As smooth as undisturb'd ethereal air,
> One word you cannot take away;
>   Complete as Virgil's, his majestic sense,
> To twenty ages of the world shall stay
> The standard his of English eloquence.⁴

The writer of a contemporary biography is of opinion that Tillotson 'taught by his sermons more ministers to preach well, and more people to live well, than any since the Apostles.'⁵ The copyright of the sermons after Tillotson's death fetched the (for that time) enormous sum of 2,500*l.*,⁶ and for about half a century they seemed likely to verify

---

¹ *Remarks on Burnet's History of his Own Times*, vol. ii. p. 125 of the Historical Works of Bevill Higgons, Esq.
² Preface to vol. ii. of Atterbury's *Sermons*, p. xli.
³ Bull's *Works* (published 1846), vol. ii. p. 21.
⁴ Quoted in Tyerman's *Life and Times of Samuel Wesley*, p. 192.
⁵ *Life of the Rev. William Burkitt*, p. 32.
⁶ See *Tatler*, No. 101. The writers (Steele and Addison) describe Tillotson as 'the most eminent and useful author of the age we live in,' and say 'the sale of his immortal writings brought her' (his widow) 'in a very considerable dowry; though it was impossible for it to be equal to their value.'

the prophecy of immortality which the two great essayists uttered concerning them;[1] whereas 'now,' as Hallam says, 'they are bought almost as waste paper, and hardly read at all.'[2] What is the cause of this utter collapse? Hallam seems to attribute it to a want of vigour and vivacity in his style; but surely that would have injured their effect in the delivery more than in the perusal of them in cold blood. The defect seems to me to lie at least as much in the matter as in the style. Let anyone purchase the two huge folios (they can be bought uncommonly cheap) and carefully read the sermons, and he will probably wonder, not that the virtue has gone out of them, but that it was ever supposed to be in them. Sermons, of all compositions, can never be immortal when the preacher seems to have no particular message to deliver. And beyond a general impression that it is more prudent on the whole to believe the Gospel, in a modified sort of way, than not, what impression does Tillotson convey? No one would ever dream now of quoting him as an authority on any point of divinity; among other reasons, because it is extremely difficult to ascertain what his precise views were. His popularity appears to me to have arisen, partly from the fact that he hit the popular taste for a simpler, a smoother, and above all, a shorter style of sermon than had been customary, partly from the well-earned reputation of the man for piety, charity, and general amiability, and partly perhaps from the charm of his delivery, about which he evidently took great pains, for he was in the habit, as he told Dr. Maynard, his predecessor at Lincoln's Inn, of 'writing every word before he preached it, and then getting it by heart.'[3] Be this as it may, the prediction of his admiring biographer, that the sermons would be 'the best model for all succeeding ages' has proved singularly incorrect.[4] In fact the simple villagers of Keddington who 'did not

---

[1] *Tatler*, ut supra.   [2] *Literature of Europe*, iii. p. 297.
[3] See Wordsworth's *Ecclesiastical Biography*, vol. iv. p. 718.
[4] Birch's *Life of Tillotson*, p. 20.

relish' the sermons and complained that they did not hear the Gospel, showed that they had greater insight than these learned London clergy who flocked to 'form their minds' on the model of the popular preacher.

A similar fate has overtaken another admired preacher in his day, Tillotson's great friend, **Archbishop Sharp**. Samuel Wesley ranks Sharp as a popular orator above even Tillotson and Stillingfleet.[1] Burnet described him to the Prince of Orange on the eve of the Revolution, as 'one of the best preachers in England.'[2] His 'incomparable preaching' as well as his high character evidently helped to win Ralph Thoresby over to the Church.[3] When rector of S. Giles' in the Fields, still more than when Dean or Archbishop, he was generally known as an excellent popular preacher.[4] And his fame was not quite ephemeral. The published sermons had passed through nine editions before the middle of the eighteenth century; and they are still extant and well worth reading; they are, like himself, plain, practical, thoroughly real and earnest, rather than brilliant; and there is more definiteness about them than there is about Tillotson's; but there is no particular reason why they should take a place among the standard sermons of our literature—and they have not.

The great preacher in the later part of our period was, of course, **Dean Atterbury**. His sermons have not fallen into the oblivion to which Tillotson's, Sharp's, and Stillingfleet's have been consigned. They still occupy a place in the shelves of most theological libraries,—whether they ever come down from those shelves is another question. By the year 1766 they had reached an eighth edition, a con-

---

[1] See *Letter to a Curate*.

[2] Letter to the Prince of Orange, quoted in *Diary of the Times of Charles II.*, ed. by Blencowe. *Correspondence of the Times of James II. and William III.*, vol. ii. pp. 281-7.

[3] See *Diary*, i. p. 313 &c.

[4] See *Life of Kettlewell*, p. 69, and Carwithen's *History of the Church of England*, iii. p. 281.

siderable success when it is remembered that with the advent of the Georges, the preacher's theological and political views went completely out of fashion. But, oddly enough, some of the most fervid panegyrics of Atterbury's sermons come from people who differed most widely from his politics and theology. It was a dissenter (Doddridge) who called him 'the glory of English orators.' It is in a paper of which the editor was a pronounced Whig that 'the oratory, the soft and graceful behaviour, and captivating person' of the Tory dean is immortalised.[1] It is poor John Dunton,—a very erratic churchman, if a churchman at all,—who celebrates Atterbury's 'eloquence and mighty sense of the worth of souls.'[2] It is Stackhouse, certainly not a high churchman, who remarks, 'Among the great preachers of our age no one that I ever knew had happier talents than Dr. Atterbury.'[3] And yet Atterbury is perfectly outspoken; all his sermons are those of a strong churchman, but they are also those of a polished man of the world, not of a mere theologian. They are not for one moment to be compared with those of Taylor, Barrow, and South, the great preachers of the earlier part of our period, but in their way they are finished performances.

Another famous preacher, whose sermons are still known, was **William Beveridge.** 'Beveridge,' writes his contemporary, R. Nelson, 'had a way of touching the consciences of his hearers that seemed to revive the spirit of the Apostolic age.' And Beveridge's biographer in our own day takes a similar view of his sermons. 'Their great beauty,' he writes, 'is a tender and pathetic earnestness, a strong and affectionate appeal to the heart and conscience;' and then, after contrasting him with Barrow, he adds epigrammatically, 'it is not every reader who can reason and investigate with Barrow, but all can feel with Beveridge.'[4]

---

[1] *Tatler*, No. 66. [2] *Life and Errors of John Dunton*, p. 368.
[3] *Life of Bishop Atterbury*.
[4] Hartwell Horne's *Memoir of Bishop Beveridge*.

All this is perfectly true; but there is also another excellence in the sermons which, combined with great simplicity and earnestness, gives them a peculiar value. No preacher sets forth better in their full and due proportion, evangelical doctrine and apostolical order. 'Evangelicals' (in the technical sense of the term) claim Beveridge as their own; and his sermons are truly evangelical, with much more of the gospel in them than many of his day; at the same time they have a most distinctly Church tone, and in fact insist far more strongly and far more persuasively than, say, Atterbury's do upon all those observances on which high churchmen lay most stress.[1] He who would catch the spirit of the English Church could not do better than read and digest the sermons of Bishop Beveridge.

The name of Beveridge naturally suggests that of **Simon Patrick.** Dunton says that he was called *par excellence* 'the preaching bishop,' a title which, if it was really applied to him, conveys a most undeserved reproach upon his brother prelates.[2] Burnet especially recommended him to the Prince of Orange as 'a great preacher;'[3] and when he was at S. Paul's, Covent Garden, his preaching was almost as attractive as Beveridge's at S. Peter's, Cornhill. But we have to take Patrick's preaching power very much upon trust, for his sermons which are extant are not fair specimens. The first is that which he preached while hardly more than a boy, over the grave of his guide, philosopher, and friend, John Smith, the Platonist, and is appended to the magnificent discourses of that extraordinary young man. Almost any sermon would suffer from such a

---

[1] See, e.g., his *Sermons on the Ministry and Ordinances of the Church of England*, in which he dwells strongly on the doctrine of the Apostolical Succession, on the duty of fasting in Lent, in the Ember Weeks, and on every Friday throughout the year.

[2] *Life and Errors of John Dunton*, p. 363. He adds that 'were all others like Patrick in that respect, the dissenters would have no colour to complain that "these bishops sermonize so seldom."' They had certainly no colour to complain as it was; the bishops preached incessantly.

[3] Letter to Prince of Orange &c., *ut supra*.

juxtaposition; much more one which bears evident traces of the rawness of youth. Mr. Mullinger thinks 'there is no more pathetic production in all literature;'[1] but the pathos (as Mr. Mullinger himself seems to intimate) is due rather to the circumstances of its delivery than to its own intrinsic merit; several of Patrick's sermons only come down to us as they have been digested into devotional treatises; and sermons transmuted into treatises are obviously no fair specimens of sermons.

Bishop Burnet is another famous preacher whose powers we must take mainly upon trust. Everyone knows Lord Macaulay's vivid description of the preacher being often interrupted by the deep hum of his audience, and, when he had preached out the hour-glass, of the congregation clamorously encouraging him to go on until the glass had run off once more.[2] His sermons were, as a rule, preached without note, but there are at any rate four sermons still extant, which certainly do not *read* well. They are mainly political, and the whole style as well as tone is not elevated, nor are they by any means free from gross flattery to his royal master.[3]

Judging by results, **Dr. Horneck** must have been one of the most effective preachers of his day; for to him above all others the remarkable movement resulting in the Religious Societies already described is due. Evelyn heard him, and calls him 'a most pathetic preacher.'[4] Wood tells us 'he was a frequent and florid preacher, and very popular in London and Westminster;'[5] Kidder that 'he preached

---

[1] *Cambridge Characteristics in the seventeenth Century*, p. 91, *note*.
[2] *History of England*, i. p. 413.
[3] In a sermon preached before King William at Whitehall on December 2, 1697, the day of Thanksgiving for Peace, he compared William to Solomon, and shows how superior the former is. In another he writes: 'The reign of Saul and the charms that were in Jonathan had, no doubt, given the family a great root. But the divine design that was upon David had broke through all that, and had turned the hearts of the whole nation as one man to him.' Then William is shown to be as David, James and his son as Saul and Jonathan.
[4] *Diary* for March 18, 168⅔.   [5] *Athenæ Oxonienses*, iv. p. 141.

with great vehemence and ardour, with mighty force and conviction. He spake the sense of his soul, and entered into the hearts of his people. . . . His fame grew, and among his auditors were some of the highest rank, and a very great number of truly devout and pious persons."[1] Birch speaks of 'his prodigious popularity on account of his reputation for piety and his pathetic sermons, his church at the Savoy being crowded by auditors from the most remote parts, which occasioned Dean Freeman to say that Dr. Horneck's parish was much the largest in town, since it reached from Whitehall to Whitechapel.'[2] The samples of his sermons which remain fully bear out this reputation. The 'Happy Ascetic' is a most powerful set of sermons.

The name of **Mr. Smythies** as a preacher is naturally associated with that of Dr. Horneck, on account of the great effect which the preaching of both produced upon the young men of the metropolis. His sermons give one the idea of a most impressive preacher; the way in which he analyses his text, picking his subject to the very bone, reminds one a little of Bishop Andrewes, but his style is essentially modern.[3]

Perhaps an adventitious interest is attached to the preaching of **Samuel Wesley** from the fact of his being the father of the man whose preaching woke up England, and the father was not unworthy of the son. Among a batch of sermons preached before the Religious Societies, by far the most racy and energetic is the one preached by the rector of Epworth.[4]

Dr. Richard Lucas was a very popular preacher in his day, and his sermons, when hunted out from the shelves

---

[1] *Life of Rev. Anthony Horneck, D.D.*, by Bishop Kidder.
[2] *Life of Tillotson*, p. 213.
[3] See a Sermon by William Smythies, Curate at S. Giles', Cripplegate, on Galatians vi. 2.
[4] A Sermon concerning the Reformation of Manners, preached at S. James' Church, Westminster, and afterwards at S. Bride's, to one of the Religious Societies, by S. Wesley, 1698.

on which they have accumulated the dust of many generations, shew that his reputation was thoroughly well deserved. In fact they are so good that a specimen must be given. The following is from a sermon on 'I will not fear what man can do unto me.' 'For what can he? His tongue can wound our reputation or his arm our body; he can plunder and rifle us of our estate and fortune, he can deprive us of our liberty, and of life itself. Not to take notice that he can do none of these things unless God permit, what doth all this amount to? "He can wound our reputation;" i.e. he can fight with the air, for reputation is but a popular breath; he can fasten imaginary words upon an imaginary man, for reputation is generally nothing else but the picture of a man drawn by the fancies and opinions of the vulgar. "He can rob us of our estates;" i.e. he can clear our way to Heaven of all that rubbish which doth but trash and clog us on our journey. "He can deprive us of our liberty;" i.e. he can confine us to the happy necessity of entertaining ourselves with wise and holy thoughts and of being entertained by Heaven. Finally, "he can kill the body;" i.e. he can throw down these mud walls which will be built up of marble; he can deliver us from the troubles and evils of this life and send us the speediest way into the joys and glories of a better; this is all vain man can do.'[1] All the rest are in the same quaint, racy style; both matter and language very plain, but the subjects all argued out most exhaustively.

Bishop Hooper of Bath and Wells is another preacher whose sermons, when disinterred from their graves, give one a most favourable impression; they were republished in 1855, and are, therefore, it may be presumed, better known than Dr. Lucas'. They fill two large volumes. Many of them were preached before royalty, but there is not the slightest

---

[1] See *Twenty-four Sermons preached on several Occasions, by R. Lucas, late Vicar of S. Stephen, and Prebendary of Westminster.* Sermon VI., preach't before the Queen, being the Monthly Fast, June 14, 1693.

taint of flattery in them. As might be expected from the friend of Bishop Ken, their tone is markedly church, but they are written in a most charitable spirit.[1]

The sermons of **Bishop Smalridge**, the 'Favonius' of the 'Tatler,' have also been republished in our own day. They somewhat resemble Hooper's, but are not of so distinctly a church type nor yet so evangelical; their great merit is the singularly luminous and smooth style in which they are written.[2]

Sir William Dawes, Bishop of Chester, and afterwards Archbishop of York, had the reputation of being the best preacher of his day.[3] Two large 8vo. vols. of his sermons are still extant; they are very good, plain sermons, their plainness being evidently studied. In many respects they remind one greatly of Archbishop Sharp's, and exactly correspond to his biographer's description of them; 'plain and unaffected, adapted to every common comprehension, and, as much as possible, divested of all appearance of learning;' but they must have required the 'majestic appearance and melody of voice' which the biographer also notices, to make the preacher what he is called on the same authority, 'the most compleat Pulpit Orator of his age.'[4]

Zachary Cradock, Provost of Eton and Canon Residentiary of Chichester, 'was admired in his own time for his uncommon talents of discoursing from the pulpit with the greatest copiousness and vivacity, without notes or preparation.'[5] It is therefore scarcely fair to judge of his powers by his only two printed sermons, which are well

---

[1] See *The Works of the Right Rev. G. Hooper, Bishop of Bath and Wells*, new edition, Oxford, 1855.

[2] *Sixty Sermons by G. Smalridge, sometime Bishop of Bristol and Dean of Christ Church* (new edition, 1852). Also *Twelve Sermons by Bishop Smalridge on different Occasions* (published 1717).

[3] See Perry's *History of the Church of England*, iii. p. 198.

[4] See *The whole Works of Sir William Dawes, late Archbishop of York*, in 3 vols. 8vo., with preface giving an account of the life of the author, published 1733.

[5] Birch's *Life of Tillotson*, p. 61.

enough expressed and argued out, but not very remarkable.[1]

Bishop Frampton had the rare honour of meeting with the approbation of Pepys, who speaks most enthusiastically of his preaching;[2] but I do not know of any of his sermons being extant.

The Cambridge Platonists stood as far apart in their preaching as in their lives from their contemporaries. The greatest preacher among them, John Smith, died, at an early age, before the Restoration. But Whichcote preached to appreciative audiences in London for more than twenty years after that date. Worthington was preaching his thoughtful and exquisitely worded sermons at S. Bennet Fink, 'till the church and parish were laid in ashes'[3] by the Fire of London, and in 1670 was lecturer at Hackney; Rust was carried off to Ireland by his friend and patron, Jeremy Taylor, whose pulpit eloquence he almost rivalled; Norris of Bemerton, the last survivor of the band, published sermons on the 'Beatitudes' which were so popular that they passed through fifteen editions by 1728. But, as a rule, the sermons of the Platonists must have been 'caviare to the general;' they are far too subtle and refined for the popular taste; none but the most highly educated could have appreciated their almost unrivalled beauty.

The general impression derived from a careful study of the sermons of the period is that the standard was high; and on the whole it certainly seems to have been so regarded by contemporaries. 'We have,' writes Glanvill of Bath in 1678 '(blessed be God), plenty of learn'd and most excellent preachers, as many, I believe, as any age or nation ever had;'[4] Edward Chamberlayne writes of the London clergy about the same time: 'These have for a

---

[1] See *Two Sermons preached before King Charles II.*, by Z. Cradock.

[2] *Diary* for January 20, 166$\frac{6}{7}$.

[3] Preface to Worthington's *Great Duty of Self-Resignation to the Divine Will*, by E. F. (that is, no doubt, Edmund Fowler).

[4] *A Reasonable Defence of Preaching, and the way of it,—a Dialogue.*

long time had the most excellent way of sermonising in Christendom; insomuch as divers divines of foreign Reformed Churches have come hither on purpose to learn their manner of haranguing in the pulpit;'[1] and John Chamberlayne, son of the above, wrote in 1707: 'The English are a people that are extremely taken with oratory, and they have the best sort of it in the greatest perfection, that of the Pulpits.'[2] Eachard, while ridiculing some kinds of preaching, admits that 'it is nothing but perfect madness, ignorance, and stupidity not to acknowledge that the present Church of England affords as considerable scholars and as solid and eloquent preachers as are anywhere to be found in the whole Christian world.'[3] Addison calls the sermons of his day 'the best sermons in the world,' though he thinks they are spoiled by the apathetic delivery of them;[4] and further testimony might be quoted to the same effect.[5] Of the three best known diarists of the period, Pepys, Evelyn, and Thoresby, two give a most favourable account of the sermons they heard. Thoresby always speaks of them with approbation; and Evelyn, besides constantly referring to the excellence of individual preachers, affirms roundly, that 'of plain, practical discourses, this nation, or any other, never had greater plenty or more profitable, I am confident.'[6] Pepys, on the contrary, gives us but a very indifferent account of the sermons

---

[1] *Angliæ Notitiæ*, Part II., p. 201. [2] *Angliæ Notitiæ*, Part III., p. 310.
[3] *Observations upon the Answer to the Grounds and Occasions of the Contempt of the Clergy.*
[4] *Spectator*, No. 407.
[5] E.g. the anonymous writer of *A Serious Enquiry into the Present State of the Church of England*, &c., in a letter to Dr. Atterbury, 1711, says: 'We are famed all over the world for this talent in the pulpit.' Lady Masham, whose testimony ranks high, owing to the very superior minds with which she was brought into contact, wrote in 1696: 'There cannot anywhere be found so good a collection of discourses on moral subjects as might be made of English sermons written by divines of our Church.' (*Discourse concerning the Love of God.*)
[6] *Diary*, July 15, 1683.

he heard. But then it must be remembered (1) that he had a way of going about from church to church, hearing part of a sermon here and another part there,¹ so that the impression he carried away with him must have been that of a mosaic rather than a sermon; (2) that when he did keep his seat at one church, he frequently slept all through the sermon; and (3) that when he kept his eyes open they were not always fixed upon the preacher, but wandered about to see what beauties there were among the congregation.² All this, to say nothing of the minor distraction of seeing Lady Batten or some one in the seat which his wife ought to have had,³ detracts a little from the value of his evidence, though, as he is by far the most racy diarist of the three, it is much better known than that of the other two.

Dr. Birch claims for Tillotson the credit of having 'brought back both purity of language and force of reasoning in place of the older style of sermon,' which he is pleased to describe as 'oppressed with an unnecessary mixture of various languages, affected wit, and puerile rhetorick.' The honour, however, of having brought about a change which was thought to be so much for the better was attributed to others besides Tillotson. Salmon declares it was 'the justness of the king's (Charles II.) taste that occasioned that Reformation in Pulpit Oratory which

---

¹ 'November 9, 1662, Lord's Day. Called in at several churches.' 'June 26, 1664. Called at several churches.'

² 'May 26, 1667.—At S. Margaret's, Westminster. Did entertain myself with my perspective glass up and down the church, by which I had the great pleasure of seeing and gazing at a great many very fine women; and what with that and sleeping I passed away the time till sermon was done.' 'December 25, 1664.—To Mr. Rawlinson's church, and a very great store of fine women there is in this church.' 'April 17, 1664.—Slept soundly all the sermon.'

³ 'March 15, 1663.—Up with my wife first time to church, where our pew was so full that I perceive we shall be shut out.' 'March 3, 1662.—My wife and I to church and seated ourselves, she below me, and by that means the precedence of the pew which my Lady Batten and her daughter takes is confounded,' &c.

Burnet so justly admires;'¹ Granger affirms that Bishop Lloyd of S. Asaph 'was a principal reformer of the language and method of sermons;'² and as a matter of fact, South preached in the plain style long before Tillotson's influence could have permeated through the country. But at any rate, Tillotson may be taken as a typical representative of the new style, as his predecessor at Canterbury was of the old. Or rather, both were extreme specimens of their respective styles. It would be difficult for a mere reader of the sermons of both to realise that Sancroft and Tillotson were contemporaries. Whether the change was so entirely for the better as the jubilant tone in which contemporaries speak of it would imply, may be doubted. If the new fashion was, as Evelyn declares it was, 'a far more profitable way,'³ there is no more to be said, for the design of all sermons is to be profitable. But assuredly, if we regard them from a purely literary point of view, the sermons of the old style were far superior to those of the new. No names are so great as those which were noticed first in this chapter; the descent from Jeremy Taylor to the best of the Queen Anne preachers is great;⁴ and there is reason to think that the desire to be plain sometimes led the preacher to be grovelling.

The change, also, in the length of the sermons was not altogether to their advantage as compositions. The required brevity no longer admitted of the exhaustiveness of a Barrow and an Andrewes, or the splendid elaborateness of a Jeremy Taylor. The ancient canonical measure of the hour, of which the hour-glass in the pulpit was the visible reminder, is spoken of, almost as a matter of course, as the proper length for the sermon, both before the Rebellion

---

¹ *An Impartial Examination of Bishop Burnet's History of his Own Times*, i. p. 544 (published 1724).

² *Biographical History of England*, iii. p. 288.

³ *Diary* for July 15, 1683.

⁴ This, at least, is my opinion; Prof. Mahaffy (*Decay of Modern Preaching*, p. 83) seems to rate the Queen Anne preachers as the highest of all.

and after the Restoration.¹ But there was afterwards a disposition on all sides to shorten it. Tillotson's sermons could not have taken more than half an hour to deliver. Burnet, in his 'Pastoral Care,' advises clergy not to preach for more than half an hour.² Granville, who was the very antipodes of both, desires his curate to shorten the sermon to half an hour rather than miss one iota of the prayers.³ Atterbury's sermons were much within the hour, and so were Sharp's.

Another change which met with doubtful, or at least with varying success, was the substitution of unwritten for written sermons. The latter were usual at the Restoration, being the natural result of the reaction from the Puritans, who trusted to the immediate inspiration of the Holy Spirit; they were also necessary when it was thought expedient to compose learned sermons to accentuate the contrast between the trained divine and the illiterate amateur. But by degrees they became less common. Dean Comber hardly ever wrote out any sermons, having always adhered to the plan of preaching from notes which he began as soon as he took priest's orders.⁴ There are conflicting accounts about Tillotson,⁵ but there is no doubt that Burnet preached without book, and recommended the practice very strongly—in fact, rather offensively—to all clergymen.⁶ Samuel Wesley, among his instructions to his curate at Epworth, tells him, instead of reading his sermons

---

¹ 'Here I might spend *the hour* with much delight.' (Sancroft.)
'The parson exceeds not an hour in preaching.' (George Herbert.)
'We sit an hour at a sermon.' (*Art of Contentment*, by Lady Pakington.)
'I did purposely contract my meditations, and express them under the ancient canonical measure of an hour.' (Isaac Basire.)

² Pages 222-3.

³ *Directions to the Curates of Sedgfield and Easington*, 1669. Granville's *Remains*, Part I., pp. 129-133.

⁴ *Memoir by his great-grandson*, p. 361.

⁵ See Wordsworth's *Ecclesiastical Biography*, sub nomine.

⁶ See *Pastoral Care*. Where he tells those who read the sermon that 'this would not be endured by any nation but ours.'

to repeat them from memory. In 1674 the Duke of Monmouth, as Chancellor of the University of Cambridge, censured 'in the king's name' the use of the MS. in the pulpit, and the Duke of Ormond, as Chancellor, did the same at Oxford, being strongly supported by Dr. Bathurst, President of Trinity, among others.[1] But in his charge in 1695, Bishop Sprat is bold enough to protest against extempore preaching. On the whole there was then as now, and as always ought to be, no general rule for a duty which some can perform best with, and some without a MS.

---

[1] See Dr. Stoughton's *Church of the Restoration*, ii. p. 255. See also *Life of Isaac Milles*: 'Extempore preaching was then (about 1674) the practice of the generality of the clergy' (p. 32). Also Swift's *Letter to a young Clergyman*.

CHAPTER VII.

DEVOTIONAL AND PRACTICAL WORKS.

FROM the beginning to the end of our period there was one work which was valued far above all others by churchmen of every type. That was *The Whole Duty of Man*. It was published about three years before the Restoration, anonymously but under the sanction of the great name of Dr. Hammond. Mr. Garthwait, the bookseller, with whom the sealed MS. had been left, consulted Dr. Hammond about its publication, and requested him to write a preface if he approved. Dr. Hammond replied in a letter full of commendation, which is usually printed with the book in lieu of a preface. The aim of the work is expressed in the title which is rather an ambitious one. It runs thus: 'The Whole Duty of Man laid down in a plain and familiar way, for the use of all, but especially of the meanest reader.' It contains seventeen chapters, 'one whereof being read every Lord's Day, the whole may be read through thrice every year;' and then follows a remark which has now a slightly ludicrous sound, reminding one of an advertisement of patent pills—'Necessary for families.' An author who expects his book to be read through three times every year, must indeed rate its value highly, but the result proved that he did not overrate it. The book very soon took its rank next to the Bible and Prayer Book, indeed it was frequently coupled with the two in a way in which no one would have dreamed of coupling any other book. Nelson, in his 'Ways and Means of Doing Good,' 'recommends Persons of Quality to disperse Bibles, Prayer Books, and "The Whole Duty of Man."' It was a common requirement from teachers of the newly founded charity schools that they should teach 'Church principles of religion as laid down in the Catechism, and by the help of "The Whole Duty of Man."' One item of Dodwell's 'Advice to a young Man on his susception of Holy Orders,' was to 'persuade every family in his parish to read "The Whole Duty of Man" according to the method of the partition therein prescribed,' that is, three times through every year. Bishop Bull advised 'poor ministers in his diocese who were incapable of preaching in any tolerable manner, to read now and then a chapter or section out of "The Whole Duty of Man" in lieu of a sermon.'[1] It was sometimes chained in churches to be read aloud there.[2] The 'Athenian Oracle' thinks it 'the best book in the world that ever was printed, next to the Bible, and the authors the best writers next to those who writ by inspiration' (p. 64). William Whiston says that his father often told him that after the Restoration all profession of seriousness would have died out but for Hammond's 'Practical Catechism' and 'The Whole Duty of Man.' Eachard advises readers of books about 'experiences, getting of Christ, and the like, to change them all away for "The Whole Duty of Man."'[3] This last quotation points, no doubt, to one cause of its appreciation. 'It was popular,' says Canon Bowles, 'as succeeding to the Fiduciary system,' and for the same reason it was 'vituperated by a certain class of pietists;'[4]—that is, by the Evangelical school in the eighteenth century. One can quite understand the objections which were raised by them against it, but it cannot be fairly said that a holy life is not

---

[1] *Charge to the Clergy of S. David's*, 1708. Nelson's *Life*, pp. 102 and 214.
[2] A chained copy is still to be seen in the interesting library at Wimborne Minster.
[3] *Observations upon the Answer to Grounds for the Contempt of the Clergy*, p. 240.
[4] Bowles' *Life of Ken*, i. p. 48.

recommended on Christian motives in 'The Whole Duty of Man.' The doctrine of the Atonement, e.g., is most distinctly stated, though of course it is not put so prominently forward as it afterwards was by the Evangelical school. After the Restoration its popularity extended beyond the limits of rigid churchmen. Thomas Gouge, a benevolent nonconformist, 'procured it to be translated, with the Bible, Liturgy, and other good books into Welsh;'[1] and Armstrong, a friend and supporter of the unfortunate Duke of Monmouth, and therefore presumably favourable to Protestant dissent, read it on his way to Tyburn.[2]

When one turns from what was said about the work to the work itself, a feeling of disappointment is, perhaps, inevitable. In beauty of thought and expression it is not for a moment to be compared with Taylor's 'Holy Living,' and 'Holy Dying,' nor, in strength of argument and general intellectual power, with Law's 'Serious Call.' It is simply a well-written, old-fashioned statement of Church doctrine, and a recommendation of a Christian life based on strictly Church principles, with occasionally a dignified, but never scurrilous, reflection on the modes of religious life during the Rebellion. The three branches of man's duty, ' to live soberly, righteously, and godly in this present world ' are the main burden of the work.

The interest in the book was probably increased by the curiosity which prevailed respecting its authorship. In this respect it rivalled the 'Junius' Letters' of the next century. Dorothy, Lady Pakington, Archbishop Sterne, Archbishop Sancroft, Archbishop Frewen, Bishop Fell, Bishop Henchman, Dr. Allestre, Dr. Hammond, Dr. Chaplin, Mr. Fulman, Mr. Abraham Woodhead, have all been mentioned as probable authors, the first two, especially the former, having the most suffrages; but the opinion of the elder Disraeli is probably correct, that 'the modesty of the author made him

---

[1] Birch's *Life of Tillotson*, p. 89.
[2] See Von Ranke's *History of England*, iv. p. 197.

(or her) effectually conceal all the possible clues to identity.'[1]

The question became further complicated by the publication of several other works under the name of 'the Author of the Whole Duty of Man,' which it is all but certain were not written by that author. These are, *The Causes of the Decay of Christian Piety*, a severe diatribe against the immorality of the Restoration period, which was evidently a bitter disappointment to the anonymous author who had expected halcyon days when the cloud that had hung over the Church was rolled away; *The Gentleman's Calling*, which combats the odious but fashionable notion that immorality and irreligion were characteristics of the fine gentleman; *The Ladies' Calling*, a much needed protest against the levity which prevailed, especially in the higher circles; and *The Art of Contentment*, which, in its latest edition, is boldly attributed to Lady Pakington, though the evidence of the authorship is by no means complete. Judging from internal evidence, none of these works appear to be written by the same author as the 'Whole Duty'; none of them, certainly, attained anything like the same popularity, though they were, no doubt, all extensively read in their day.

Infinitely superior to 'The Whole Duty of Man,' but

---

[1] Those who wish to pursue the curious question of the authorship of the work may be referred to the following works: — *The Art of Contentment*, by Lady Pakington, ed. Rev. W. Pridden; Editor's Preface, vol. xvii. of *Englishman's Library*; Bishop Fell's *Life of Henry Hammond*, prefixed to the edition of the *Practical Catechism* (Library of Anglo-Catholic Theology, Part LI.); Curwithen's *History of the Church of England*, iii. p. 18; *Reliquiæ Hearnianæ*, Diary for February 6, 170$\frac{6}{7}$, August 5, 1706; *Notes and Queries* for January 21, 1882; *Life of Dr. Humphrey Prideaux*, p. 19; Granger's *Biographical History of England*, iii. p. 253; Ballard's *Memoirs of British Ladies* (Dorothy, Lady Pakington); Hickes' Preface to his *Anglo-Saxon and Mæso-Gothic Grammar*; *Athenian Oracle*, i. pp. 63–4; *The Christian Religion as professed by a daughter of the Church of England* (Mary Astell); Bowles' *Life of Ken*. Most of these take different views. The *British Museum Catalogue* mentions the work under the heads of Lady Pakington and Archbishop Sterne, and no others.

not nearly so popular as that or several other books which will come before us, were Jeremy Taylor's devotional works. Bishop Heber, indeed, thinks that they were universally popular,[1] and so they were in comparison with the 'Ductor Dubitantium,' with which he is contrasting them; but if either the warmth and abundance of testimony, or the extent of sale is a criterion, they scarcely held the place they ought to have held, viz. in the very foremost rank of their kind. Highly educated men no doubt rated them at their proper value. John Scott, e.g., refers to the 'Holy Living and Dying' as 'an incomparable treatise,'[2] but the very beauty of their style was a hindrance to their general acceptance. We have seen in the matter of preaching that there was a strong and growing tendency to value plainness and even homeliness of style, and the same tendency is observable in regard to that kind of literature which approaches nearest to sermons. Posterity however has duly redressed the balance, and while the 'Whole Duty of Man' and many other immensely admired works in their day are now almost forgotten, Jeremy Taylor is still read by thousands. Indeed, he is so well known that it is not necessary to dwell on him. *The Golden Grove, or Prayers for every day in the Week*, the *Holy Living* and the *Holy Dying*, *The Great Exemplar, or Life of Christ*, and *The Marriage Ring*, are deservedly the most popular of his devotional works; and it is creditable to the taste of the English nation that it has shown and still shows a due appreciation of one who was the greatest of English devotional writers as he was the greatest of English preachers.

The reaction against the excessive love of sermons, and in favour of catechising, naturally produced or revived a large number of catechetical treatises. First among these, both in date and importance, was Hammond's *Practical*

---

[1] Heber's *Life of Jeremy Taylor*, prefixed to his edition of the *Works*, p. xcvi.

[2] Preface to *The Christian Life*.

Catechism, which the writer drew up 'for his own private convenience out of those materials which he had made use of in the catechetic institution of the youth of his parish.'[1] He happened to shew the MS. to Dr. Potter, Provost of Queen's College, Oxford, who was so impressed with its value that he persuaded him to publish it anonymously, and generously offered to undertake the whole care and charge of the first edition (1644). Thus we owe to a kind of accident one of the most valuable works on the subject which has ever been published. The work came into great request after the Restoration, and is still well known.

A more original, if not a more valuable treatment of the same topic, may be found in Bishop Ken's *Exposition of the Church Catechism, or Practice of Divine Love*. It was composed for the benefit of the diocese of Bath and Wells, and its object is to shew that the love of God is the central thought of the whole Catechism. The argument of the whole work is thus ingeniously summed up: 'If I seriously desire the love of God, I must first expel all contrary loves out of my heart, and then consider the motives and causes that excite it; the former is taught in the *vow of baptism*, the latter in the *Creed*. When divine love is once produced my next care is to put it in *practice*, and that is, by bringing forth the fruits or effects of love, which are all contained in the *Ten Commandments*. When the love of God is produced in my heart, and is set on work, my last concern is to preserve, and ensure, and quicken it; it is *preserved* by prayer, the pattern of which is the Lord's Prayer; it is *ensured* to us by the Sacraments which are the pledges of love, and more particularly it is quickened by the Holy Eucharist which is the feast of love, so that the plain order of the Catechism teaches us the rise, the progress,

---

[1] Bishop Fell's *Life of the Author*, prefixed to the sixteenth edition of Hammond's *Practical Catechism* (Library of Anglo-Catholic Theology), p. xxxi.

and the perfection of divine love, which God of His great mercy give me grace to follow' (p. 4).

Another excellent treatise on the same subject is Simon Lowth's *Catechetical Questions*, &c. (1673). The author was vicar of Tylerhurst, near Reading, and his little book is evidently the production of a working clergyman who knew what was wanted in a parish. It is simply an amplification of the Church Catechism, and is plain, clear, and definite in its Church principles. For practical purposes it is one of the best, if not the best, that will come before us.

The *Catechism of the Church of England paraphrased*, by R. Sherlock, Rector of Winwick (1661), like the preceding, clearly grew out of the exigencies of a hard-working parish priest. The author was encouraged to publish it by the commendation of the great Hammond, whose judgment was certainly not at fault; it is an excellent paraphrase, and passed through ten editions in as many years.

Dean Comber's *Explanation of the Church Catechism* (1666) is not now so well known as his 'Companion to the Temple,' but his biographer seems to imply that it was considered his chef-d'œuvre in his own day.[1] The plan of it was 'so laid that all the answers are "Yes" or "No"'— not a very happy plan, one would think, for eliciting youthful intelligence.

Lancelot Addison's *Primitive Institution, or a Seasonable Discourse of Catechising* (1674), deserves notice, if for no other reason, as the work of the father of one who was the greatest prose writer of our period. It is not a catechetical treatise, like the others, but an earnest recommendation of the duty of catechising, and is interesting, among other reasons, because the father's quiet humour frequently reminds us of his greater son. 'Religion began when God was Adam's catechist.' 'The penmen of disputation seem to have intended rather the Defamation than the Conviction of each other; and to have been of opinion

---

[1] *Memoirs of Dean Comber, by his great-grandson*, p. 215.

that men were to be refuted, as Mercury of old was worshipt, by throwing dirt and stones in their face.' 'Catechising has met with but cold entertainment from those by whom it ought to have been most lovingly caressed. In most places it has been looked upon rather as a Foreigner than a Native of the Church, and as fruits of their mouth never in season but for a few days in Lent;' and so forth. Was not Lancelot the true father of Joseph?

Dr. Thomas Marshall, rector of Lincoln College, Oxford, drew up at the request of his diocesan, Bishop Fell, *Notes of Catechism*, to be used by ministers of the diocese in catechising children,[1] but the work does not appear to be extant.

And last, but not least, we have Bishop Beveridge's *Church Catechism Explained* (1704), which has the advantage of having been written by one who had had one of the largest and most successful experiences as a parish priest of any clergyman in his day. It was dedicated to the clergy of the diocese of S. Asaph, for whose special use it was drawn up by their new bishop; but it has been found most useful to the whole of that National Church of which its writer was a distinguished ornament.

This is by no means an exhaustive list of the catechetical treatises of our period, but it may suffice to shew that the subject was one which occupied a very important place in the minds of churchmen.

Another effect of the restoration of the Church with the Monarchy was a demand for practical works on the Sacraments, especially on the Holy Communion, and the demand was met with a corresponding supply. Perhaps the most remarkable of these treatises was Dr. Edward Lake's '*Officium Eucharisticum*, &c.; A Preparatory Service to a Devout and Worthy Reception of the Lord's Supper, with a Meditation for Every Day in the Week (1673).' Dr. (afterwards Archdeacon) Lake had been tutor and chaplain

---

[1] See *Athenæ Oxonienses*, iv. p. 170.

to the Princess Mary, and chaplain to the Duke of York. Perhaps his connection with two successive sovereigns may have lent an adventitious interest to his little work; but its intrinsic merit was great, and so was its popularity. It passed through fifteen editions in twenty years and fifteen more in the next fifty, so that the Oxford republication of it in 1843 is the thirty-first edition. The editor of Lake's 'Diary' is surprised that the tutor of the future Queen Mary, and the friend of Dr. Compton, 'the Protestant Bishop,' should have put forth a work which certainly advocates advanced Church views without compromise or disguise. But surely there is no need of surprise. The Princess Mary, left to her own inclinations, was one person; the Queen Mary, under the influence of King William, quite another. And Dr. Lake was as truly 'Protestant,' that is, anti-Roman, as Dr. Compton,—or, say, Dr. Littledale. In no one point does he go beyond the fair limits of the English Church. He does not profess to be original. 'I cannot,' he says to the reader, 'say it is mine, but a collection, and recommends itself unto thee, clothed in the language, not of any private conception (of such the world is already full enough), but of primitive Liturgies;' but the directions for self-examination are Dr. Lake's own, and they are very searching and very striking.

The next most popular treatises on the Sacraments were those of Bishop Patrick. One of these is called *A Book for Beginners, or a Help to Young Communicants*, which gives one the impression of having been written, as of course it was, by a man of great experience in parochial work. Its elementary nature may be gathered from the fact that the first chapter contains 'directions for such as cannot read,' and the writer desires 'their masters or mistresses, or some good neighbour or relation, to be so charitable as to read to them their duty about the matter.' The little work is thoroughly adapted for such very rudimentary intelligences, and reminds one of Bishop Oxenden's simplest works, which many parish priests have found so very acceptable among the poor and uneducated in our own day.

It is characteristic of the transition through which Bishop Patrick's mind passed, that this elementary work was the product of his later days. When much younger he had written a far more elaborate treatise on the same subject, entitled *Mensa Mystica* (1660). It is full of Greek and Latin and even Hebrew quotations, and a strong vein of Platonism runs through it. It is written in the quaint style of the earlier part of the seventeenth century. Patrick also wrote a Baptismal treatise, entitled *Aqua Genitalis, a Discourse concerning Baptism*, which is the substance of a sermon preached at All Hallows' Church, Lombard Street, but much enlarged. This too, especially the preface, is full of Platonism.

That deservedly popular writer on practical subjects Robert Nelson, published a sacramental treatise, entitled *The Great Duty of frequenting the Christian Sacrifice*, in 1706. Like everything which this good man wrote it is plain and to the point, and contains some good 'Practical Devotions for the Altar.'

Another exceedingly good Sacramental treatise is Lancelot Addison's *Christian's Manual*. It consists of two parts (1) 'The Catechumen, or the young Person's account of his knowledge in Religion, before his admission to the Lord's Supper. (2) An Introduction to the Sacrament, or a short, plain, and safe way to the Communion Table.' It is as plain and practical as Patrick's 'Young Beginner,' but indicates (what one would have hardly expected) a more advanced type of churchmanship, and it contains, what is indeed rare, some really well-written prayers.

The Pious Communicant rightly prepared, by Samuel Wesley, Rector of Epworth (1700), is chiefly remarkable for a very spirited rendering of the whole of the Great Hallel (Psalms 113-118), 'which,' says the writer, 'was the Paschal Hymn sung by the Jews at the Passover, and by our Saviour and his apostles at the Institution of the Lord's Supper; and any of them, as they are here turned into metre, may be sung, either in private, or by a family, before or after the Sacrament.' This work is also notable for its marked Church tone, which is also conspicuous in an 'Appendix on Baptism.'

William Smythies' *Unworthy Non-Communicant* (1683), is a work that deserves the most respectful consideration, owing to the extraordinary success which the writer met with in drawing young men to the Holy Table. Its main object is to shew that 'there is generally more danger in unworthy neglecting than in unworthy receiving.' It is all addressed to non-communicants, and is practically a long, plain, stirring, but rather stern sermon.

Gabriel Towerson published in 1686 a book *Of the Sacraments in general*, which was really a part of his 'Exposition of the Church Catechism,' but was published separately. It is of the old-fashioned High Church type, strongly anti-Roman, and full of references to the Fathers. It is too learned for a popular treatise, at least in the present day.

If this professed to be an account of all the Sacramental treatises of the period, many others would have to be noticed, and, above all others, Johnson of Cranbrook's *Unbloody Sacrifice*; but books like this, immensely valuable as they are, would come more properly under the head of controversial, than of practical and devotional writings.

Of course the Sacraments hold a conspicuous place in those practical works which treat of public worship generally. By far the most popular of these was Dean Comber's '*Companion to the Temple*, or An Essay on the Daily Offices of the Church' (Part I., 1672). It is a sort of paraphrase of the Liturgy, and, as its alternative title indicates, strongly recommends daily service. Without disparagement to an excellent book, one cannot but feel that its seasonableness, as coming soon after the Restoration of the Common Prayer, accounts for its extraordinary popularity. It is said that a London clergyman purposed having the three volumes chained in his parish church, and that the Dean of S. Paul's was accustomed to 'buy a dozen at a time to bestow, as it is believed, on the ministers he prefers in the citie.'[1] Comber's biographer complains that 'Wheatly borrowed his best parts from hence.'[2] Be this as it may, the later has now practically superseded the earlier work.

William Sherlock's *Discourse of Religious Assemblies* (1681) is not a paraphrase or explanation of, but a persuasive to attend the Church services. It is a particularly sensible and interesting work, and well deserved to be republished, as it has been in our own day. Still more popular was the same writer's *Practical Discourse concerning Death*, which went through thirty editions in a very short time, and has lately been republished.[3] In spite of the enthusiastic praise which Addison lavished upon it,[4] it does not seem to me to be so powerful a work as the one noticed above.

John Scott's *Christian Life* is also extolled by Addison as one of the finest and most rational schemes of divinity that is written in our tongue or any other.[5] The praise is not exaggerated, but when this work is termed a 'rational scheme,' we must remember what Scott meant by 'reason.' It was 'the noblest principle of our nature, that by which we are raised above the brutes, yea, by which we are allied to angels, and do border upon God Himself' (vol. i. p. 49). 'He that follows this reason sits above the clouds in a calm and quiet æther, and with a brave indifferency hears the rowling thunder grumble and burst under his feet' (p. 68). 'That light of reason which shineth in human and angelical

---

[1] *Memoirs of Dean Comber, by his great-grandson*, p. 93.   [2] *Id.* p. 67.
[3] Under the able editorship of Rev. H. Melville, Vol. XI. of the *Englishman's Library*, 1840.
[4] *Spectator*, No. 289.   [5] *Spectator*, No. 447.

minds, being rayed forth and derived from Him, He must have it in Himself in perfection' (ii. p. 247). In fact, Scott meant by reason what the Platonists meant by it, and he differed as widely as possible from those who were afterwards called 'rationalists;' he was, indeed, distinctly a high churchman. What a beautiful description this is of the baptized Christian: 'In our Baptism, wherein we gave up our names to Christ, we became denizens and freemen of Heaven. All the difference between them and us is only this, that we are abroad, and they at home; we are on this, and they on the other side of Jordan; we in the acquest and they in possession of the heavenly Canaan. . . . Shame will it be to us not to copy their behaviour, we who are below stairs in the same house' (i. p. 174). We are strongly reminded of the refined thoughts and exquisite language of the Cambridge Platonists all through this treatise. Only Scott was more practical. The exigencies of his position brought him down from the clouds. A resident fellow of Christ's or Emmanuel can afford to dwell in sublime abstraction; a hard-working parish priest cannot. Scott was rector of S. Giles' in the Fields at a time when religious controversy seemed likely to put in the background the importance of a religious life, and 'he thought a discourse of the Christian Life, which is the proper sphere of Christian zeal, might be a good expedient to take men off from these dangerous contentions.'[1] He succeeded in drawing a very beautiful and attractive portrait of such a life; in fact, next to Jeremy Taylor, no writer has expressed such refined thoughts in such refined language as Scott has in his 'Christian Life.' The only drawback is that it is too long; the three thick volumes might with advantage have been condensed into one.

If the 'Christian Life' is too long, another and still more popular work on the same subject, Rawlet's *Christian Monitor*, falls into the other extreme. Its compass is

---

[1] Epistle dedicatory to the Bishop of London.

rather that of the modern tract than of the solid volumes of the seventeenth century. But it was specially written for the poor, whose limited capacity for reading the writer knew well from his experience in his parish in Newcastle. It is admirably adapted for its purpose, being written in the simplest of simple language. Its circulation was enormous. It passed through twenty-five editions before the close of the seventeenth century. Granger tells us that 'it had been oftener printed than any other tract of practical divinity,' and that 'one clergyman at Reading had distributed near ten thousand copies, chiefly among soldiers.' Rawlet wrote several other devotional works, but none of these require special notice.

While Scott's 'Christian Life,' and Rawlet's 'Christian Monitor,' are almost forgotten, a work which is infinitely inferior to both, but especially the former, is still well known and sometimes read. Beveridge's *Private Thoughts* really consists of two works, written at different times; but they are now generally published together as two parts of the same work. The first is entitled in full, 'Private Thoughts upon Religion, in twelve articles, with practical resolutions grounded thereupon;' it was written when the author was only twenty-three years of age, and was intended simply for his own satisfaction and establishment in the Christian faith. The second is called 'Private Thoughts upon a Christian Life.' Both, but especially the former, bear evident traces of having been written by a very young man. There is a positiveness about all things human and divine, an airy way of settling the most difficult questions, which is characteristic of youthful enthusiasm before it is toned down by age and experience; but it should be added that there is the freshness as well as the rawness of youth about the work; and this, together with the evident earnestness and reality of the writer, may have tended to keep it alive. Indeed it is the best known of all Beveridge's writings, and the author has suffered in consequence; for those who depreciate Beveridge as a writer (and they are many) are probably thinking especially of this, his juvenile effort. This is rather hard upon this really good writer, because neither part of the 'Private Thoughts' was published until after his death; and it is doubtful whether he ever intended to give them to the world.

Bishop Patrick's sacramental treatises have been noticed, but these by no means exhaust the list of his practical works. His *Discourse concerning Prayer* (1686) quite accords with the spirit of the times in urging the daily service of the Church as of greater obligation and efficacy than family, or even private prayer. It was reprinted in 1840 under the editorship of the Rev. F. Paget. The editor calls it an appropriate companion to Patrick's *Treatise of Repentance and Fasting* (1686); and rightly describes both as 'characterised by the same dutiful love to the Church, and the same desire to inculcate a strict obedience to her ordinances,' and as 'designed to lead men to the "old paths" of Catholic truth and Scriptural antiquity.'[1] Patrick's *Work of the Ministry represented to the Clergy of Ely* (1698), also re-edited in 1841 by W. B. Hawkins, is particularly interesting as giving the experience of a veteran in ministerial work who had been one of the most successful clergymen of his day. *The Devout Christian instructed how to pray*, is simply a book of family prayers, with private prayers for almost every conceivable occasion appended, and does not require much notice; but the *Advice to a Friend*, published under the initials 'S.P.' in 1673, is a singularly beautiful tract in Patrick's early style, before his Platonic tincture had worn off, and is really worthy of being bound up, as it has been, with Jeremy Taylor's 'Contemplations of the State of Man in this Life and in that which is to come.'[2] But perhaps the most

---

[1] Paget's preface to *Discourse concerning Prayer*.
[2] They are bound together in one volume in Pickering's *Christian Classics*, 1847.

notable of all Patrick's practical works is *The Parable of the Pilgrim*, the idea of which is exactly the same as that of 'Bunyan's Pilgrim's Progress,' only of course it is conceived and worked out from a churchman's point of view. But for the fortunate insertion of the date '1663' in the original letter to the friend to whom it was written, it might have been suspected that the rector and future bishop had condescended to borrow from the tinker; for the work was not published until 1668, by which time the 'Pilgrim's Progress' had probably appeared. But there is no need for supposing that either Patrick borrowed from Bunyan or Bunyan from Patrick. The idea is sufficiently obvious to have occurred spontaneously to both. It must be admitted that the unlettered Bunyan is far more successful than the lettered Patrick. The latter makes the fatal mistake (for an allegorist) of giving us all moral and very little story. He also confuses the allegory with the application, and, truth to tell, is utterly deficient in fancy.[1] One can as little wonder that Patrick's 'Pilgrim' is, from a literary point of view, dead, as that Bunyan's is alive, and likely to live as long as the world lasts. And yet Patrick had some of the elements of successful writing in this department. His style is quaint, easy, and clear, and his mode of telling his story is very pleasing.

Among the devotional works of our period, a conspicuous place belongs to reprints of earlier works which had, of course, found no favour during the Rebellion, but now came into demand again. To this class belong many of Jeremy Taylor's works, and also the exquisitely beautiful 'Contemplations' of Bishop Joseph Hall. George Herbert's 'Country Parson' re-appeared in 1675 with a most interesting preface by Barnabas Oley. Oley, indeed, had been

---

[1] The defects are pointed out with a kindly hand by Thomas Scott in his 'Introductory Essay' to his edition of the *Pilgrim's Progress* (1828), p. xviii., &c., where the writer also discusses the question of the dates of the two works.

brave enough to write a preface to the edition which was put forth in 1652, when the sentiments must have been odious to the dominant party. But his later preface is peculiarly interesting as illustrating the immense value which was set upon the immortal picture by the clergy of the time.[1] Bishop Cosin's *Devotions* falls under the same category, for though the writer survived the Restoration several years, it was originally published in 1627, and during the Rebellion met not only with neglect but vituperation. Its author's name afforded scope for a vile pun; it was called 'cozening devotions,' and was accused of cheating the devout reader out of the truth. But after the Restoration it was widely read.[2] Bishop Brian Duppa's *Holy Rules and Helps to Devotion* is another book of the same sort, but it does not appear to have been so popular after the Restoration as any of the above mentioned, for it did not reach a second edition until 1818. It is a plain, and very spiritual little work, full of Latin quotations, and contains some good prayers, and questions for self-examination. *Christian Consolations* really belongs to the same class; for, though it was not published until 1671, it was written many years earlier. Bishop Heber attributes it to Jeremy Taylor, but Alexander Knox plainly shews that this is wrong. The writer was probably Bishop Hacket; it is boldly attributed to the latter in the new edition which appeared in 1840. The book is written in the quaint style of the early part of the seventeenth century; it is purely practical, but has a more decidedly Church tone than Bishop Duppa's work. Broadly speaking, we may place Sir Thomas Browne's *Religio Medici* among the reprinted practical works of the Restoration period. How far Sir T.

[1] 'All the clergie of mine acquaintance, and, I verily believe, all the old clergie of the nation, as well as my poor self, do long to see ourselves and our younger brethren conform to that idea of a clerk which the noble, holy Herbert hath pourtraied in this book.'

[2] See *Vita Joannis Cosini*, by T. Smith, p. 8. Also Granville's *Remains*, pp. ii., 65, 6.

Browne may be regarded as a churchman has been seen in the sketch of his life.[1] At any rate the work found favour among churchmen, and disfavour among the puritans; for it was written in 1633-5, passed into neglect during the Rebellion, and became extraordinarily popular after the Restoration; at least if imitation be the best test of popularity as well as the sincerest form of flattery.[2] Another reprint which found favour was Bishop Andrewes's *Devotions*. They were re-translated out of the original Greek and Latin[3] and published by Dean Stanhope in 1675, and the original translation of 1648 by 'R.D.' [Richard Drake] was republished in 1692. They are too well-known to require notice.

To return to the works which were actually written during our period. Dr. Richard Lucas was as eminent for his devotional writings as for his preaching. His *Practical Christianity*, or an Account of the Holiness which the Gospel enjoins, is a plain, earnest work, in which all controversial topics are carefully avoided. The reason given for their avoidance is the converse of that usually given; it was not that he thought, as Nelson, for instance, thought, that the love of controversy drew men away from practical religion, but that the want of practical religion betrayed men into the errors which provoked controversy. Feeling that 'no kind of discourses contribute more to the peace and welfare of Church and State than those practical ones which aim at implanting real goodness in the minds of

---

[1] See *supra*, p. 177.

[2] These are some of the imitations—at least of the title: *De Religione Gentilium*, 1663; *Religio Stoici*, 1665; *Religio Clerici*, 1681; *Religio Laici* (Dryden), 1682; *Religio Laici* (Blount); *Religio Jurisprudentis*, 1685; *Religio Militis*, 1690; *Religio Bibliopolæ*, 1694; *Religion of a Prince*, 1704; *Religion of a Gentleman*, 1710. It is fair to say that two of the imitations appeared before the Restoration: *De Religione Laici* (Lord Herbert), 1645; *Religio Jurisconsulti*, 1649.

[3] The first part was originally in Greek, the second in Latin. The Manual of devotion for the sick was in Greek; large portions of the Greek were transcriptions from Liturgies of the Eastern Church.

men,' he keeps this object steadily in view, and shews (1) 'the necessity of being religious,' (2) 'the motives which the Gospel proposes to Holiness,' (3) 'the temptations to sin, and their remedies,' (4) 'the three general instruments of holiness, or preservatives against sin,' these being Sacraments, prayers, and fastings. The whole subject is systematically worked out in very well-written language.

Another little work of Dr. Lucas' is called *Christian Thoughts for every day of the Month*, which gives first the thought (e.g. for the first day 'Of faith'), then the application, then two sentences, one from the Bible, another from a Christian Father. *Divine Breathings of a Pious Soul thirsting after Christ*, in a Hundred Pathetical Meditations, is attributed to Dr. Lucas; but if it be his, it is singularly unlike his acknowledged writings, being ornate and rapturous, while they are particularly plain and calm.[1]

But a far more interesting and finished work than any of the above is Dr. Lucas' last composition, *An Enquiry after Happiness*. The circumstances of its composition lend a peculiarly melancholy interest to it. They cannot be better stated than in the writer's own touching words 'To the Reader':—'It has pleased God that in a few years I should finish the more pleasant and delightful part of life, if sense were to be the judge and standard of pleasure; being confined (I will not say condemned,) by well-nigh utter blindness, to retirement and solitude. I thought it my duty to set myself some task which might serve at once to divert my thoughts from a melancholy application on my misfortune, and might be serviceable to the world. Like one that truly loves his country, when no way else

[1] All the three works are bound together in a single volume, in the edition of 1746 (the 7th); but the last with a separate pagination. It is published anonymously but signed 'Christopher Perin, who gave them [*The Divine Breathings*] as being found among the writings of an eminent divine.' How the eminent divine was identified with Dr. Lucas is not shewn, but in the title to the whole volume it is boldly said that the *Breathings* are by the same author as *Practical Christianity*, which was beyond question the composition of Dr. Lucas.

is left him, he fights upon his stumps; so will I ever, in the remains of a broken body, express, at least, my affection for mankind, and breathe out my last gasp in their service.' The good man's labours in the midst of his infirmity were not in vain. His book is an exceedingly well-written book, full of plain truth plainly stated in an easy, scholarly style. It is conspicuous as much for its marked good sense as for its earnestness. It takes three different kinds of life, (1) the gentleman's, (2) the tradesman's, (3) the contemplative, and shows how religion can give happiness in each; it then dwells on 'the ways of prolonging life, viz. (1) by cheerfulness, (2) by asking God to do so.' The second volume, which seems originally to have been a separate publication, is entitled 'Religious Perfection,' and it is particularly refreshing to those who have studied the fierce but very feeble controversies which raged some years later respecting 'perfection,' 'assurance,' 'final perseverance,' &c., to turn to a work which was written before these painful disputes broke out, and which deals with its subject in a less pretentious but more satisfactory way. We can well understand how the whole work should be admired (as it was) by such competent judges as Dean Stanhope, Alexander Knox, and Bishop Jebb.

In the interesting correspondence between the two last-named eminent men, several other devotional works of our period are highly commended. Scougal's *Life of God in the Soul of Man*, is said by Mr. Knox to 'contain perhaps the finest view of practical religion, the most removed from coldness on the one hand and overheat on the other, that is to be found in the Christian world.'[1] The reader who is first introduced to the work with such a flourish of trumpets will probably feel a little disappointment when he reads it.

---

[1] See a letter from Knox to Jebb (1801), quoted in Bishop Jebb's Introduction to his edition of Bishop Burnet's *Lives, Characters*, and an *Address to Posterity* (1833), p. xxii. The work is also recommended by Susanna Wesley to her son John.

Not but what it is a well-written, well argued-out piece, but it bears evident traces of having been written, as it was, by a very young man;[1] and devotional works, of all works, require the experience which nothing but age can bring. Bishop Burnet's *Conclusion to the History of his Own Times* is also recommended by Mr. Knox as 'containing in a small compass as fine a view of Christianity as almost ever was composed,'[2] and Jebb to whom the recommendation was given, quite endorses it, declaring that 'Bishop Burnet's short but exquisite conclusion to his "Address to Posterity" can never be antiquated. So long as the English language lasts, it will be read and re-read with fresh improvement and delight.'[3] It is fully admitted that there is much that is earnest and excellent in the practical writings of Burnet, which are infinitely more valuable than his History, but even these are defaced by that unfortunate propensity, which amounted in Burnet almost to a mania, of depreciating his brother clergy. Nothing of this kind can be objected to the next two writers whom Mr. Knox commends. He does not exaggerate when he declares that 'Archbishop Leighton's writings, in sublime piety, and often in genuine strokes of natural but most exalted eloquence, are not excelled but by the sacred writers;' but they scarcely fall under the category of what is popularly meant by devotional works. So far from exaggerating, he might have praised even more highly than he does, Worthington's *Great Duty of Self-Resignation to the Divine Will*, a perfect little gem of twelve pages, which for beauty both of thought and language, is equal to the best of the Platonists' writings. Though it now appears in the form of a single devotional work, it is really the substance of several sermons preached for the most part at S. Bennet Fink's; one of the most striking of these, that on the resignation of Job, was preached there on the very

---

[1] Scougal was a Scotch Episcopalian clergyman, who died in 1675, at the age of twenty-eight.
[2] *Introduction* (ut supra), p. xxi. [3] *Id.* p. ii.

Sunday when the Great Fire broke out which laid both the church and parish of S. Bennet Fink in ashes.[1]

Several other devotional works of the period were originally sermons. Such were several of Bishop Patrick's works already noticed. Such was Mr. Smythies' *Benefit of Early Piety, recommended to all young Persons*. It is addressed chiefly to young men, and one reads it with special interest owing to the extraordinary success which the author met with in dealing with this most important class. Like all Mr. Smythies' writings, it takes rather a severe view, but it is eminently practical and good, and became so popular that it reached a fifteenth edition in 1729. Such was Dr. Horneck's *Happy Ascetick*, a singularly powerful appeal in behalf of a Christian life, which one also reads with peculiar interest owing to the peculiar success of the author in dealing with souls. Such too was Bishop Gunning's *Paschal or Lenten Fast*, which is a sermon preached before King Charles II., with enlargements.

We have touched upon the devotional work of one Platonist; let us turn to another, a far more voluminous writer, of the same school. Norris of Bemerton almost rivals Patrick in the number of works, all more or less practical, which he put forth. All, judging from the number of editions through which they passed, were popular in their day; but it must suffice here to notice the most famous. His *Letters concerning the Love of God*, 'a correspondence between himself and a gentlewoman' [Mrs. Astell], are interesting as representing in miniature the famous controversy between Fénélon and Bossuet. And though the gentleman is not a Fénélon nor the lady a Bossuet, the letters are well worth reading. Norris is a worshipper of Malebranche, and presents the great French idealist's thoughts on 'pure, disinterested love' in an English dress, but it must be confessed that the comparison is not in favour of our own

[1] See the Preface to the *Great Duty, &c.*, signed 'E. F.,' that is, no doubt, Edward Fowler, afterwards Bishop of Gloucester.

countryman. He had previously (1689) addressed a letter to another lady, 'the excellent lady, the Lady Masham,' which is practically a devotional work, and a very good one. It is entitled *Reflections upon the Conduct of Human Life*, in which he argues, after the manner of his master, against the too great love of human learning, and advises 'the renunciation of all studies merely curious,' fearing, no doubt, that 'the excellent lady's' connection with two such master minds as Cudworth and Locke would lead her to value intellect too highly. In 1702 Norris published a treatise *On Religious Discourse in Common Conversation*, in which he argues in an earnest, sensible manner against the avoidance of religious conversation for practical and not controversial purposes, even among good people. But perhaps the most striking of all his works is that entitled *Reason and Religion*, or 'Grounds and Measures of Devotion considered from the nature of God and the nature of Man, in several Contemplations, with exercises of Devotion apply'd to every Contemplation.' He tells us in the preface that it was 'intended for the pious entertainment of more refined and elevated understandings, so many excellent works having been written lately for the use of the ordinary and unlearned.' He certainly knew his own powers when he addressed himself to the more educated; for, like all the Platonists, his thoughts were too subtle and his language too refined for the multitude. His mind was elegant rather than strong; but more conspicuous even than his elegance is the deep vein of earnest piety which runs through all his writings.[1]

Most of the writers hitherto mentioned have been clergy-

[1] They fill no less than thirteen 8vo. volumes. Among his other practical works are (1) *A Discourse concerning Worldly and Divine Wisdom*; (2) *The Importance of a Religious Life considered from the happy Conclusion of it*; (3) *Religious Singularity displayed: shewing the Necessity of Practising that great Christian Virtue*; (4) *Practical Treatise concerning Humility*; (5) *Treatise concerning Christian Prudence*; (6) *Account of Reason and Faith*.

men; but it has been seen that the part which laymen took in the Church life of the time was large, and some of the best practical works come from the pens of the laity. In the very year of the Restoration, Robert Boyle published *Some Motives and Incentives to the Love of God, pathetically described in a Letter to a Friend*, which passed through many editions and was translated into Latin. In 1690 the same pious layman published *The Christian Virtuoso*, shewing that by being addicted to experimental philosophy a man is rather assisted than indisposed to be a good Christian,—a seasonable work calculated to dispel the foolish prejudices which some had conceived against the Royal Society on the ground that it tended to irreligion or popery. *The Practice of Piety* was another practical work written by Boyle.

If circulation be a test of merit, few practical works rank higher than *The Great Importance of a Religious Life*, by the pious lawyer, William Melmoth. It was first published in the commencement of the eighteenth century, and before the century closed had passed through twenty-eight editions. Its latest edition (1849) affirms that no less than 150,000 copies were sold in the first forty years of the present century. The work itself hardly seems to account for this extraordinary demand. It is simply a plain, sensible appeal in behalf of a religious life, written, as one would expect from a lawyer, in an argumentative style. Its theology is that of Tillotson, whom the author frequently quotes with approbation.

Strictly speaking, perhaps one ought not to reckon the great judge, Sir Matthew Hale, among the devotional writers of the period, because his *Contemplations* were designed solely for his own use, and were never intended to be published. But as a matter of fact, this posthumous work is one of the most touching devotional works of the time. The 'Tractate on Afflictions and True Wisdom' and that 'On Humility,' in especial, have hardly been surpassed by any writer.

Nor must we forget to notice the great names of Joseph Addison and Richard Steele among the laymen who wrote on practical religion. Those, however, who are only acquainted with their exquisite 'Saturday papers' in the 'Spectator,' which in one sense must certainly be accounted as devotional pieces of a very high order, will be sadly disappointed when they turn to the works of the same writers on exclusively religious topics. Two more trite and vapid treatises than Steele's *Christian Hero*, and Addison's *Evidences of Christianity*, were never written. The latter was composed when Addison was failing, and Tickell tells us he 'was more assiduous than his health could well allow.' If the loss of a valuable life was hastened for so unsatisfactory a result, it is all the more provoking, but the fact is, both Steele and Addison mistook their vocation when they attempted this kind of work.

The most famous and useful of all the lay writers on practical subjects was Robert Nelson. It is hardly necessary to describe his *Festivals and Fasts*, with which everybody is, or ought to be, familiar, and which has never been superseded by any other work of the kind. Equally excellent in its way is his *Practice of True Devotion*, which was written because the author thought the prevalence of religious controversies drew men away from 'the solid and substantial part of religion, the spirit and life of devotion.' The good man, therefore, treats his subjects entirely from a practical point of view, carefully avoiding all controversy. His *Address to Persons of Quality*, and his *Representation of the Ways and Means of Doing Good*, which is a sort of supplement to it, are two of the most stirring and sensible addresses ever published, and doubtless contributed in no slight degree to help on the many charitable and religious enterprises which adorned the reign of Queen Anne quite as much as the literary masterpieces and military successes which shed a lustre upon that era. The merits of Nelson as a writer are not due to any particular genius, but simply to his thorough reality, his earnest piety, and his plain, practical common sense. The works thoroughly reflect the character of the man, and it is to be hoped that they will never pass into oblivion so long as true religion of the true Church of England type is valued by Englishmen.[1]

It was not the fashion of the day for ladies to appear in print. But several devotional works published anonymously are known to have been written by ladies. Susanna Hopton was one. Three of her works were edited by Nathaniel Spinckes, under the title of *A Collection of Meditations, in Three Parts*. They were originally all published separately, and consist of—(1) *A Hexameron*, or 'Meditations on the six days of Creation.' (2) *Meditations or Devotions on the Life of Jesus Christ*. (3) *Daily Devotions and Thanksgivings*, which first came out in 1673, 'by a humble penitent.' But the most notable of her works is *Devotions in the ancient way of Offices*, with psalms, hymns, and prayers for every day of the week, and every Holiday in the year. It was published in 1701 by Dr. Hickes, who tells us that 'it had four editions unreformed from Roman Catholics, five as it was reformed by Dorrington, while this is a second in a new reform.'

Mary Astell's anonymous practical works were much admired. Her *Christian Religion as professed by a daughter of the Church of England* (1705), is exactly described by its title. It is a book of the old-fashioned Church type, advocating strongly, but temperately, all the doctrines of the Church, including non-resistance, and is very emphatic against Romanism. Her *Serious Proposal to Ladies* has been noticed in the sketch of her life; and the *Letters concerning the Love of God* have been mentioned in the account of her correspondent John Norris' works. They are full of pertinent inquiries, showing that the writer must certainly have been a very intelligent lady; but they are

---

[1] An excellent account of all his works will be found in Secretan's *Life of Nelson*. His sacramental treatises have already been noticed.

not quite so extraordinary productions as her enthusiastically admiring antagonist would have us believe.[1]

Elizabeth Burnet, third wife of the Bishop of Sarum, was the author of one devotional work which is well worthy of notice. It is entitled, *A Method of Devotion, or Rules of Holy and Devout Living*. As one would expect from the wife of Bishop Burnet, she writes from a Low Church point of view; but as one would *not* expect from that relationship, she writes with the most unaffected diffidence. The Method 'was put together for private use, and is very defective from the low capacity of its compiler, and was published to excite such as are better qualified to do something more perfect of this sort, and in the meantime to give a little assistance to young and ignorant persons.' Strange language from a Mrs. Burnet! and quite an unnecessary apology for her publication. The book is an excellent one; full of plain, practical rules, those on the employment of time being particularly good. It was intended for the writer's own sex, and two of the meditations in especial—one 'for the Beautiful,' the other 'for the Deformed,' are most interesting. The whole work strikes one as being remarkably real and natural, and gives a most favourable impression of the writer. After her death 'it was thought fit,' says the editor, Archdeacon Goodwyn, 'to put the name of the author, which her modesty did not suffer her to consent to while she lived.'

Another lady who wrote on devotional subjects was Damaris, Lady Masham, the daughter of Cudworth and friend of Locke. In 1696 she published *A Discourse concerning the Love of God*, which she probably wrote under the inspiration of Locke, and which took the opposite view from

---

[1] 'Madam,' he writes, 'I should never be able to express the value I set upon your letters, either as to their ingenuity or their piety. The former of which might make them an entertainment for an angel, and the latter sufficient (if possible) to make a saint of the blackest devil;' with much more in the same extravagant style.

that of John Norris. In 1705 she published another devotional work, entitled *Occasional Thoughts in reference to a Virtuous and Christian Life*,—both anonymously.

Devotional works specially intended for clergymen were not very numerous during our period. Burnet's 'Pastoral Care,' and Herbert's 'Country Parson,' of course fall under this head. The only other two that need be noticed are Nathaniel Spinckes' *Sick Man Visited*, and Samuel Wesley's *Advice to a young Clergyman*. The former is in the form of a dialogue, and describes six visits from the minister to his sick parishioner, followed by some meditations, and no less than sixty-three prayers, 'proper for the use of the sick on different occasions,'—the whole work being written in a very touching and homely style. The latter was addressed by Mr. Wesley to his curate at Epworth, and gives advice as to the conduct of Church service, parish work, books for private reading, which any young clergyman might study with advantage in the present day.

If this professed to be an exhaustive account of devotional works, several others would require notice. 'The Poor Man's Help and Young Man's Guide,' by William Burkitt, the excellent incumbent of Dedham; 'The Rich Man's Duty to contribute to the Building of Churches,' by Dr. Wells, rector of Cottesback, which has been republished at Oxford with a preface or advertisement by J. H. N.; 'The Duties of the Closet,' by Sir William Dawes, a marvellous performance considering that the author was only twenty-one years of age when he wrote it; 'Fair Warnings to a Careless World,' by Dr. Josiah Woodward; 'A Discourse concerning Lent,' by George Hooper, afterwards Bishop of Bath and Wells; and perhaps also those biographies which were plainly written for a practical object, such as Bishop Burnet's Lives of Justice Hale, John, Earl of Rochester, and Robert Boyle, and many others, would demand attention. But as this only professes to be a typical sketch, it must suffice to add a few words on a form of literature in which devotional writers frequently express their thoughts, viz. Sacred Poetry.

A few words will be all that is required; for, to say the truth, sacred poetry did not rise to a high level during our period. Even from those from whom great things might be expected, great things have not come. For example, whose expectations would not be raised high, if they heard for the first time of four volumes of 'Poems Devotional and Didactic' by the writer of the immortal Morning, Evening, and Midnight Hymns? But such expectations would be doomed to disappointment. Abstract the dross, and the residuum of true poetry in Bishop Ken's four volumes would shrink to a very small compass. They were published posthumously, and the sanguine editor hopes that 'while it is found valuable as a collection of sacred poetry, it may add something to the popularity even of the author of the three hymns.' It certainly does nothing of the kind. The majority of the poems are tame and flat, without anything distinctive or even quaint in them. There is no unreasonableness in the complaint of 'the absence of all discrimination on the part of the editor who committed most impartially to the press the entire unsifted mass of the bishop's poetical papers.' One of the best pieces is 'The Christian Pastor,' a few lines of which may be quoted:

> Give me the priest these graces shall possess,
> Of an ambassador the just address,
> A father's tenderness, a shepherd's care,
> A leader's courage which the Cross can bear,
> A ruler's awe, a watchman's wakeful eye,
> A pilot's skill the helm in storms to ply,
> A fisher's patience, and a labourer's toil,
> A guide's dexterity to disembroil,
> A prophet's inspiration from above,
> A teacher's knowledge, and a Saviour's love.

The true spirit of poetry which breathes in Jeremy Taylor's prose writings might have made us regret that he had not turned his attention to verse, had he not unfortunately done so. Certainly the 'Festival Hymns' appended to the 'Golden Grove' should rather make us thankful that the best preacher and devotional writer of his day,—almost of any day,—did not exhaust his energies in work which was not congenial to him. The irregular Pindaric metre in which they are written is not, perhaps, suited for hymns. But that is not all. The divine afflatus is wanting,—that indescribable something which every person of taste recognises when it is there and misses when it is absent, which is necessary to constitute true poetry. George Herbert's rhythm is as rough and irregular as Taylor's, but in reading the slightest fragment of the former one feels 'that is a true poet,' in the latter one does not. It is hardly necessary to quote extracts, for the world has not ranked Taylor among its poets, and the world in this respect has not done him injustice. His prose is most poetical, his poetry most prosaic.

The same may be said in a minor degree of John Norris, but the contrast is not so violent; for his prose is immeasurably inferior, and his poetry perhaps a little superior to Taylor's. It can, however, scarcely be called devotional poetry, being mostly dedicated to the praise of a retired life.

Bishop Patrick, whose prose, curiously enough, does not give the slightest indication of a poetical mind, wrote sacred poetry which is by no means contemptible. There is unquestionable merit in some of his poetical translations from the ancients. Let us take as a specimen the following translation from Aquinas 'Upon the Morning we are to receive the Holy Communion:'—

> O wondrous night! Strange Supper of the Lord!
> I come, said He, to do thy will,
> I must all Rites, all Promises fulfill.
> For his selected twelve the Sacred Board
> With his own type, the Paschal Lamb, was spread,
> All He their dark Forefathers would afford,

With a plain sallad, and no pleasant bread,
When on the dusky type the twelve had fed,
With his own hands he deals his body for a dole,
So deals it to them all, that each receives the whole.

The following original 'Hymn before Lent' has been borrowed and adapted, but neither acknowledged nor improved, in modern collections.

> Hallelujah to our King!
> That's the song good angels love!
> Hallelujah, sweetly sing
> All the souls of saints above;
> There they sing, and singing, stay
> In God's Courts an endless day.
>
> In eternal hymns of praise
> Great Jerusalem on high
> Tunefully her voice does raise,
> All her sons in bliss reply;
> Thus they sing, but we must weep,
> Exiles, whom the heathen keep.
>
> Ah! unworthy we, unfit!
> Hallelujah should not sing,
> Guilty souls must intermit,
> And no Hallelujahs bring.
> Now the solemn time comes in,
> To lament for every sin.
>
> O Bless'd Three One! then let us pray,
> And beg Thy mercy now we may,
> Beg that we may observe one high
> Perpetual Easter in the sky,
> And to Thy praise the song may sing
> Of Hallelujah to our King.[1]

Addison's hymns are too well-known to need quoting; but Samuel Wesley deserves mention, if for no other reason, for his sheer industry in the department of sacred poetry. 'The noted poet, Mr. Wesley,' as Thoresby calls him,[2] did

---

[1] See *Poems upon Divine and Moral Subjects*, original and translations, by Bishop S. Patrick, and other eminent hands (1719).

[2] *Diary* for September 10, 1724.

not reach a very high level. His heroic poem on the Life of Christ, which gained him the living of Epworth, can only be called a 'great work' in point of size. Perhaps the best of his numerous poetical performances is the spirited translation of the Great Hallel appended to his 'Pious Communicant.' The following rendering of a part of Psalm 116 is a fair sample :—

> Yes, all those vows which in my straits
>   Unto the Lord I made ;
> Shall now be at his Temple Gates
>   Before his People paid.
> His Priests shall mix their Hymns with mine
>   His goodness to record,
> And all Jerusalem shall joyn
>   With me to praise the Lord.

The following, from Psalm 118, is surely superior to either the Old or the New Version :—

> Blessèd be he who'll Blessings bring,
> Pardon and Grace from Heaven's high King.
> We, who from his high Altar bless,
> Will for his people ask success ;
> He from the confines of despair,
> Has rais'd us to the Lightsome Air.
> Let the crown'd victims haste away,
> And thousands after thousands slay,
> Wash the broad courts with sacred gore,
> Till Bashan's Fields can send no more, &c.

Much of the rest of his sacred poetry rises to this level, and it is a little too severe upon his literary work to say, 'he made ample amends for his bad poetry by his good life.'[1]

William Rawlet published in 1687 'Poetic Miscellanies,' which are at any rate not contemptible. Witness the following 'Hymn on the Ascension Day :'—

> Art thou ascended, blessed Lord, on high ?
> And do I on this earth still grovelling lye,

[1] Granger's *Biographical History*, vol. iii. p. 330.

In muddy, sensual, fading pleasures drown'd,
Where pain and grief, horrors and hell are found ?
O pity, dearest Lord, some pity take
On a poor, fainting soul, for thy Name's sake.
Help, Lord, Lord help, to Thee I lift mine eyes,
Stretch forth thy helping hand, and make me rise ;
O raise my sinking soul above the mud
And dirt of low delights, which flesh and blood
Relish and crave ; let my exalted mind
Its pleasure in thy love and service find.
Keep my soul mindful of its heavenly birth,
That it may Heaven-ward tend, wean'd from this Earth.
By all my falls upon this slippery ground,
Grant that I nearer may to Heaven rebound,
And let all streams of comfort here below,
Up to the Fountain lead me, whence they flow.

Dean Comber also sacrificed to the Muses. His best piece, the 'Elegy on the Death of Mary, Queen of England,' is most pathetic and striking, but it can hardly be ranked among devotional poetry. Susanna Hopton wrote at least one hymn, which is so quaint and so little known that it may be quoted in full.

Sweet Jesu, why, why dost Thou love
  Such worthless things as we ?
Why is thy Heart still towards us,
  Who seldom think on Thee ?
Thy Bounty gives us all we have,
  And we thy gifts abuse,
Thy bounty gives us e'en thy Self,
  And we thy Self refuse.
My soul, and why, why do we love
  Such worthless things as these ?
These that withdraw us from the Lord,
  And His pure eyes displease.
Break off, and be no more a child,
  To run and sweat and cry ;
While all this stir, this huge concern,
  Is only for a Fly ;
Some silly Fly that's hard to catch,
  And nothing when 'tis caught ;
Such are the Toys thou striv'st for here,
  Not worth a serious thought.

> Break off, and raise thy manly eye
>   Up to the joys above;
> Behold all those thy Lord prepares
>   To woo and crown thy love.
> Alas! dear Lord, I cannot love
>   Unless Thou draw my heart,
> Thou, who thus kindly mak'st me *know*,
>   O make me *do* my part.
> Still do thou love me, O my Lord,
>   That I may still love Thee,
> Still make me love Thee, O my God,
>   That Thou may'st still love me.
> Thus may my God, and my poor soul,
>   Still one another love,
> Till I depart from this low world
>   T' enjoy my God above.
> To Thee, Great God, &c.   (Doxology).[1]

Dean Hickes inserted several hymns in the 'Devotions in the ancient way of Offices' noticed above, some of which are good. John Mason's 'Songs of Praise' (1683) were deservedly most popular. Henry Vaughan wrote sacred poetry of very great beauty, but it scarcely comes under the head of 'devotional works.'

Other good Christians essayed to write sacred poetry, which it would be cruel to their memory to quote. Sir Richard Blackmore had entered upon his career as the rival of Milton in the domain of Christian epics before our period closed; Sir Matthew Hale poured forth his soul every Christmas day in verse which speaks more for his piety than for his poetry; Henry More wrote pious verses, which are, of course, like everything that emanated from that refined mind, full of beautiful ideas; but these would have been better expressed in prose. In short, it is hard to find any addition worth mentioning to the exceedingly meagre list given above of the devotional literature produced in a metrical form. A low, or rather a false,

---

[1] Hymn appended to *The Sacrifice of a Devout Christian, or his Preparation for, and Reception of, the Blessed Sacrament*, at the end of the *Hexameron*.

standard of sacred poetry prevailed, a curious illustration of which may be found in the fact that Tate and Brady's version of the Psalms, much as it was criticised, never seems to have been objected to on the ground that it was deficient in poetical inspiration; on the contrary, it was more than once objected to as being only too good. The lack is all the more remarkable because the prose of the period is full of the poetical spirit; and also because the preceding half-century was singularly rich in sacred poetry. Whom can we place on a level, or anything near on a level, with George Herbert, John Donne, Francis Quarles, Richard Crashaw, Abraham Cowley, Robert Herrick,[1] or any of 'that serried throng of poets militant who gave in their allegiance to Laud, and became ornaments, and then martyrs, of the High Church party,'[2]—to say nothing of the great Puritan poet who towered far above them all? Indeed, an apology would be needed for touching upon the devotional poetry at all, were it not obviously necessary, in common fairness, to point out the barrenness as well as the fertility of the soil.

[1] I am aware, of course, that the three last survived the Restoration, but their poetry, both in date and spirit, belongs to the earlier era distinctly.

[2] E. W. Gosse, in a most interesting article on 'Richard Crashaw,' in the *Cornhill Magazine* for April 1883, and since republished in his *Seventeenth Century Studies*. See also Professor Henry Morley's admirable little selection of *Cavalier and Puritan Song*, 'The King and the Commons,' especially his Introduction.

CHAPTER VIII.

THE CHURCH AND SOCIAL LIFE.

In discussing the relation of the Church to social life, an obviously important but exceedingly difficult question occurs at the threshold of the inquiry. What was the social position of the officers of the Church,—the clergy?

The most contradictory answers have been given both by contemporaries and by writers of our own day to the question. Everybody knows Lord Macaulay's description of the social position of the clergy in the latter part of the seventeenth century; and everybody ought to know that the accuracy of that description has been much disputed.[1] But is it possible to generalise at all about the social position of a body of men drawn from such widely different classes, and possessed of such widely different talents, as the English clergy have always been? Let any one attempt to make such a generalisation about the clergy of our own day, concerning whom he has, presumably, access to far more information than he can have concerning the clergy of any past generation, and he will soon find what a hopeless task he has set himself. But in dealing with the case of the clergy of the period we are considering, the difficulty is increased tenfold, not only by the distance of time, but also by a combination of circumstances which have now ceased to exert anything like the same influence which they exerted then. The far greater prevalence of

[1] See Mr. Macaulay's *Character of the Clergy in the latter part of the Seventeenth Century*, &c., by Rev. Churchill Babington; also Mr. Gladstone's Review of Trevelyan's Life of Macaulay (*Gleanings*, vol. ii.).

pluralities vastly widened the gulf between different classes of clergy, and that in a twofold way. It made the great prizes of the Church better worth having, but on the other hand, when two or three pieces of preferment were held by one man, those left open were of course proportionately fewer, and a vast number of clergy lived and died without the slightest chance of rising above the rank of stipendiary curates. Those who were taunted with the plebeian rank of the clergy could retort, with perfect truth, by enumerating a whole host of patrician names. The Granvilles, the Comptons, the Breretons, the Booths, the Montagues, the Crewes, the Norths, the Bathursts, the Annesleys, the Finches, the Grahams, the Fernes, the Trelawneys, and many other noble families, all had their representatives among the clergy. 'In short,' writes Jeremy Collier most truly, ' the Priesthood is the profession of a gentleman. . . . The honour of the family continues, and the heraldry is every jot as safe in the Church as 'twas in the State.'[1] So also Wood speaks of Holy Orders as 'the readiest way for preferment for the younger sons of noblemen.'[2] Very probably; but the selfsame reason which made the ministry an eligible profession for these sprigs of nobility made it an ineligible one for vast numbers of the clergy.

Again, the law of supply and demand will, of course, always affect the social status of the clergy. The complaint *now* is, that the demand exceeds the supply; it *then* was, that the supply exceeded the demand. Eachard affirms that ' we are perfectly overstocked with professors of divinity, there being scarce employment for half of those who undertake that office;'[3] and his adversaries, who demurred to

---

[1] *Short View of the Profaneness and Immorality of the English Stage*, p. 88. See also Zachary Cawdrey's *Discourse of Patronage*, published 1675. 'The nobility and gentry have dedicated some of their own sons to the ministry.' Also Chamberlayne's *Angliæ Notitiæ*, Part I., p. 246, and Part III., p. 249, where lists of patrician clergy are given.

[2] *Athenæ Oxonienses.* Account of Bishop Compton.

[3] *Grounds and Occasions of the Contempt of the Clergy &c.*, p. 105.

almost all his statements, never attempted to deny this. Tenison, when he was rector of S. Martin's in the Fields, found 'thirty or forty young men in Holy Orders in his parish,' more or less at a loose end.[1] These superfluous clergy found employments which have now all but disappeared, and which, while they were exercised, tended to increase the number of clergy of a lower grade. 'Readers' in parish churches are a thing of the past; 'lecturers' are now merged in incumbents or stipendiary curates; 'governors' of young men of quality are exchanged for private tutors, who are not necessarily clergymen, or who, if they are, generally combine parochial with their tutorial work; and finally, the domestic chaplain pure and simple, except as an honorary officer, has well-nigh disappeared.

But the domestic chaplain was so conspicuous a feature in the period we are dealing with, and exercised so much influence on social life, that he must not be so summarily dismissed. It has been customary to represent him as having been little better than a menial servant. Everybody knows the story in the 'Tatler' (No. 255) of the chaplain who, instead of retiring when the sweetmeats came in, 'continued to sit out the last course, and was informed the next morning by the butler that his lordship had no farther occasion for his services;' and of the chaplain in the 'Guardian' (No. 163), who was bold enough 'to maintain his post at the dessert, and every day to eat tart in the face of his patron.' Oldham's lines are supposed to represent the normal condition of the domestic chaplain:

> Diet, an horse and thirty pounds a year
> Besides th' advantage of his Lordship's ear,
> The credit of the business, and the state
> Are things that in a youngster's sense sound great,
> Little the unexperienced wretch does know
> What slavery he oft must undergo:
> Who, though in silken scarf and cassock drest,
> Wears but a gayer livery at best.

[1] See Evelyn's *Diary* for February 15, 168$\frac{3}{4}$.

> When dinner calls, the implement must wait,
> With holy words to consecrate the meat,
> But hold it for a favour seldom shewn
> If he be deign'd the honour to sit down.

Eachard places him still lower, implying that for 10*l*. a year he might be expected to do the work of a groom as well as of a chaplain;[1] and an execrable doggrel of the period entitled 'The Chaplain's Petition to the Hon. House for Redress of grievances' (1693), gives us, if possible, a still lower opinion of the office. From these and such like sources Lord Macaulay and others have drawn their familiar descriptions of the domestic chaplain. Yet surely there is another side to the picture. When we turn from satire to history, it is remarkable to observe how many clergymen of the very highest standing and character were at some period of their lives domestic chaplains. Ken was chaplain to Lord Maynard, Wilson (Sodor and Man) to the Earl of Derby, Sherlock of Winwick to Sir R. Bindlosse, Bray to Sir J. Price, Kettlewell to the Countess of Bedford, Parsons to the Countess of Rochester, Hough to the Duke of Ormond, Samuel Wesley to the Marquis of Normanby. A body which numbered such men as these among its ranks could not necessarily be contemptible. And why should they be? Surely the domestic chaplains had opportunities of doing good among the upper classes which few other men possessed. And that they *did* sometimes do good, the noble and courageous remonstrances which Wilson and Sherlock made to their respective patrons prove. When they combined the cure of the patron's parish with their chaplain's duties, as Ken for example did at Easton, there was no fear of their becoming idle. Moreover, the office of domestic chaplain gave a chance, even now much needed, to young men who had taken their degrees at the University (which they did earlier than they do now), to study divinity and perform quasi-clerical

---

[1] *Grounds and Occasions for the Contempt of the Clergy*, p. 18.

functions before they attained the canonical age for ordination, or when, for other reasons, they desired to put off that all-important step.¹ Chaplains also often instructed the sons of the family, and hence gained an influence over the young squire which lasted through life. In fact, for many reasons, for the last more than all, it is by no means an unmixed advantage that the office of chaplain has fallen into disuse.

Of course the abuses of the office were very sad. It was, for instance, an utterly unreasonable custom and one fruitful of great abuses, that a man should be able to qualify for being a pluralist by becoming a nobleman's chaplain.² And *when* chaplains were treated as satirists tell us they were (and there is doubtless some truth in the accounts), the result inevitably tended to degrade the clerical office. But though it was a delicate post to fill, it might be, and often was, filled with great advantage to social life. Let anyone read Jeremy Collier's most admirable treatise on 'the Office of a Chaplain,'³ or Barnabas Oley's answer to Eachard, quoted above, or, if he prefer a layman's view, Addison's description of Sir Roger de Coverley's chaplain, and he will see what noble work such a man might do.

In estimating the social position, both of chaplains and of the clergy generally, one circumstance which has constantly been overlooked ought to be carefully taken into account. The difference in the external treatment of various ranks was far more marked than it is at the present day. The upper and the upper middle classes were then divided from one another by a very distinct line of demarcation; and on the other hand the tradesman was far less distinctly divided from the professional man than he is now. It was no want of appreciation of his merit which caused Lord

---

[1] See some excellent remarks on this point, probably by Mr. Barnabas Oley, in the *Answer to Grounds and Occasions for the Contempt of the Clergy*, pp. 87-8.

[2] See a very painful instance of this in Pepys' *Diary* for May 29, 1667.

[3] Published in *Essays upon Moral Subjects*, by J. Collier.

Ashburnham to set Locke to take his meals at a side table. It was merely the custom of the day. There was nothing remarkable in the fact that of the two brothers Barrow, one should be a linen-draper and the other a bishop. Nor was it regarded as a very extraordinary rise for the son of a barber, like Jeremy Taylor, to reach the episcopal bench. When, therefore, we read of 'a shopkeeper or artisan' being hardly ready to change places with a clergyman,[1] or of the disgust of a fussy alderman at a clergyman's wife 'by a wilful mistake getting the upper hand of a shopkeeper's wife, whose husband may, within a little time, be an alderman of the town,'[2] we must not suppose that such stories imply as much social degradation of the clergy as they would at the present day.

And least of all must we be misled by the travesties of the clergy in the light literature of the day. Of all the refutations of Lord Macaulay's famous description, none is so damaging as his own explanation of the sources from whence he derived his information. He did not, he says, pay much attention to his censors, because no one was fit to judge of such a question except those who had soaked their minds with the transitory literature of the day. If one who, in the course of business, certainly *has* gone through that edifying process, may venture to give an opinion, it is, that no one is more *un*fit than those who have derived their impressions solely or even mainly from such sources. Let us apply the test to our own times. Will any competent person contend that Mr. Slope, Archdeacon Grantley, Bishop Proudie, Mr. Charles Honeyman, Dr. Crump, and Mr. Hugby are anything but caricatures? And yet Mr. Trollope and Mr. Thackeray are fairness itself when compared with the Wycherleys, the Otways, and the Congreves of the seventeenth century. Why, these latter

---

[1] See *Angliæ Notitiæ*, Part I., p. 212.
[2] See *A Private Conference between a rich Alderman and a poor Country Vicar*, published 1670.

writers had the very best of reasons for decrying the clergy, for, if *they* were right, the clergy's teaching was obviously wrong.¹ But even supposing that the wading through the filth of the Restoration dramas was the best mode of enabling the mind to judge of so serious a subject, still sufficient facts are not furnished from which to draw an induction. For, after all, the allusions to the clergy are very slight and sparse and vague. The 'Saygraces' and the 'Crapes' are mere shadows; you cannot draw any tangible conclusion from their unsavoury characters.

It is, however, admitted that there is other evidence far more satisfactory and conclusive of the 'contempt of the clergy,' a phrase so incessantly repeated that it almost becomes a stock phrase of the time. In fact contemporary testimony is almost unanimous on the point. Complaints come from the most opposite quarters. Burnet, the low churchman, bewails 'the contempt the clergy are generally fallen into.'² White Kennet, of the same school, declares that 'the contempt of the clergy is the sin and shame of this latter age.'³ Defoe, the dissenter, affirms that 'the ecclesiastical power has lost its credit.'⁴ High churchmen all take up the same sad tale. Atterbury laments that 'the clergy are made a by-word and a reproach,' and frequently repeats the lament in different forms in his sermons and charges.⁵ Barnabas Oley, while demurring

---

[1] 'The contempt of religion is ofttimes both the cause and the effect of it [contempt of the clergy]. It is not at all to be wondered at that those who hate to be reformed should hate those whose duty and business it ought to be to endeavour to reform them. Woe be to us if those who are enemies to religion speak well of us!'—Stillingfleet's *Ecclesiastical Cases &c.*, p. 176.

[2] *A Discourse of the Pastoral Care*, Preface, p. xxvi.

[3] Letter from Kennet to Stillingfleet (1698), in *Collectanea Curiosa*, the Tanner MSS.

[4] *Account of the Societies for Reformation of Manners* (1699), p. 113.

[5] See especially his 'Fast Sermon at S. Paul's,' April 9, 1707, *Sermons*, vol. ii. p. 129. Also his sermon before the Sons of the Clergy, Dec. 6, 1709 ii. 265.

to most of the assertions of Eachard, fully admits that his assertion that the clergy are contemned is too true.[1] Peter Barwick complains bitterly of the 'contumely with which even the best clergy are treated;'[2] Bramhall that it has 'become gentile and fashionable for every man who has wit and pride enough, to despise a parson.'[3] Lancelot Addison assumed it as a fact not to be disputed, and wrote a treatise on 'the reasons of the present contempt of the clergy.'[4] Stillingfleet (perhaps the highest living authority on such a point), declares that 'the contempt of the clergy is too notorious not to be observed.'[5] Dr. Bray grounds his appeal for clerical libraries on 'the contempt of the priestly office.' Henry Dodwell, as his biographer tells us, 'resented warmly contempt cast on clergymen.' Edward Chamberlayne, himself a great respecter of the English clergy, affirms that 'they are less respected generally than any in Europe;'[6] and Dean Swift not only protested against the contempt of the clergy,[7] but did more than he has been generally credited with towards removing it.

What were the grounds for this 'contempt of the clergy?' Eachard specifies two, 'the ignorance of some, and the poverty of others.' Let us take the latter point, which was most frequently dwelt upon and certainly the best established, first. In estimating what was a competency for a clergyman, we are helped by the Royal Letter issued to the Bishops, Deans, and Prebendaries in 1660, bidding them 'take due care to provide *sufficient* maintenance for Vicars, or for Curates where vicarages were not

[1] *Answer to Grounds and Occasions &c.*, ut supra.
[2] *Vita Joannis Barwick*, p. 235.
[3] *Vindication &c. against Baxter* (1672).
[4] The full title is: *A modest Plea for the Clergy, wherein is briefly considered the Original, Antiquity, and Necessity of that Calling; together with genuine and spurious Reasons of their present Contempt.*
[5] Bishop Stillingfleet's *Ecclesiastical Cases relating to the Rights and Duties of the Parochial Clergy* (1698), p. 176.
[6] *Angliæ Notitiæ*, Part I., p. 252.
[7] See *Essay on the Fates of Clergymen*, and *Works* passim.

endowed, before granting new leases of rectories, &c.' The amount specified as a sufficient maintenance is '100*l.* or 80*l.* per annum, or more if it will bear it.'[1] White Kennet, nearly half a century later (1704), specifies the same amount.[2] Multiplying this by four, to allow for the altered value of money, we have from three to four hundred a year, about the same as we should now judge a competent average income for a beneficed clergyman.

Now let us see how the case is reported to have stood. Swift estimates the average income of a vicar at 40*l.* a year, declaring 'the maintenance of an Incumbent in most parts of England' to be 'contemptibly small.'[3] Henry Wharton affirmed, at the beginning of the eighteenth century, that 'in this nation are some benefices not exceeding the value of 5*l.* per annum, many hundreds not exceeding 20*l.*, and some thousands not exceeding 30*l.*;'[4] Bishop Burnet, that 'some hundreds of parishes in England pay not 10*l.* a year to their pastors, and perhaps some thousands not 50*l.*'[5] If these statistics be correct, it is no wonder that Chamberlayne wrote in 1684, 'at present the revenues of the English clergy are generally very small and insufficient;'[6] Hickes in 1705, 'there are about ten thousand parish priests, whereof at least two-thirds live meanly or miserably;'[7] White Kennet in 1704, 'of nine thousand benefices, near seven thousand are beneath a competency;'[8] Glanvill in 1678, 'the livings in corporations are generally fallen from what they were before our unhappy troubles a third part at least in their value;'[9] Eachard in 1670, 'I'll

---

[1] See *Case of Impropriations &c.* (White Kennet), p. 254.
[2] *Id.* p. 405.   [3] *On the Bill for Clerical Residence* (Ireland).
[4] *Defence of Pluralities*, p. 185.
[5] *History of the Reformation*, Part II., Preface.
[6] *State of Britain*, p. 269.
[7] *Several Letters which passed between Dr. George Hickes and a Popish Priest.*
[8] *Case of Impropriations*, p. 405.
[9] *Letter to an M.P. on the present State of Ministers in Corporations and great Towns*, appended to his *Essay concerning Preaching*.

assure you that 20*l*. or 30*l*. a year is the portion of hundreds of the clergy of this nation;'[1] B. Oley in his reply to Eachard, 'I wish I could confute that part of your letter which concerns our poverty, but ... there is too much truth in it to be contradicted,'—and many other contemporary writers to the same effect.[2] Most of what has been quoted relates to the beneficed clergy, but when we turn to the unbeneficed, from the stipendiary curate at 30*l*. a year to the hack chaplain at 10*s*. a month, the matter is certainly not mended. It may be perfectly true that 'of the aggregate national income the clerical order had, not a smaller, but a larger share than now,'[3] but pluralities now abolished, large livings now divided, bishoprics now greatly reduced in value, and many other causes, make this statement quite compatible with a vast amount of clerical poverty. This ought not to have been a cause of contempt, for, as Barnabas Oley finely says, 'an holy man in a poor living is in a kingdom, if there be a kingdom of Heaven upon earth, as I believe, I know there is;' but, as a matter of fact, it is to be feared that Juvenal's dictum is true for all ages and all classes:

> Nil habet infelix Paupertas durius in se,
> Quàm quod ridiculos homines facit.

Eachard's second point, the ignorance of the clergy, is by no means so apparent. It is admitted on all hands that the clergy in London and at the Universities were, as a rule, men of great learning and literary industry; and, as Mr. Churchill Babington shews unanswerably, a vast amount of excellent literary work came from country parsonages. He specifies Beveridge, Patrick, Fullwood, Kettlewell,

---

[1] *Contempt of the Clergy*, p. 85.
[2] See, e.g., Dean Granville's *Remains*, Part II., p. 45; Dean Sherlock's *Discourse of Religious Assemblies*, p. 173; *A Dialogue between two Oxford Scholars*, in *Works of Mr. Thomas Brown*, i. 1–13.
[3] Mr. Gladstone: Review of Trevelyan's Life of Macaulay—*Gleanings*, vol. ii.

Towerson, Fuller, Puller, Sherlock of Winwick, and John Norris, as proofs of his assertion.[1] And many more might be added. Thomas Comber wrote his treatise on the Catechism in the country living of Stonegrave, and the first part of his 'Companion to the Temple' in the country living of East Newton;[2] Joseph Bingham 'completed in his country retirement, besides several single volumes, his "Origines Ecclesiasticæ";'[3] Lancelot Addison wrote several works, of repute in their day, in the country living of Milston; Simon Lowth wrote his admirable catechetical treatise in the country living of Tylehurst; Edward Pocock continued his learned labours with greater zest than ever after the Restoration in the country living of Childrey; John Flamsteed prosecuted his invaluable astronomical researches in the country living of Barstow; George Bull wrote all his immortal works in the country livings of Suddington and Avening; Edward Stillingfleet wrote his exhaustive 'Origines Sacræ' and several other works in the country living of Sutton; Samuel Wesley was most active in literary work in the country living of Epworth; William Reeves made his useful translations of Justin Martyr, Tertullian, and other Fathers in the country living of Crawford.

Of course the mere fact of the literary industry of individual country clergy does not disprove the ignorance of the general mass; but there are other circumstances which may lead us to doubt whether their ignorance was a fair ground for contempt.

(1) We have general testimonies disproving the general ignorance of the clergy. Eachard admits that 'the ordinary sort of our English clergy do far excel in learning the com-

---

[1] Mr. Churchill Babington on *Mr. Macaulay's Character of the Clergy in the latter part of the seventeenth Century*. The fact that Beveridge and Patrick were afterwards transferred to London cures does not, of course, affect the fact that much of their literary work was done while they were still country parsons.

[2] *Memoirs of Dean Comber*, p. 67.

[3] *Life of Bingham*, prefixed to vol. i. of his *Works* in 9 vols., p. ix.

mon priests of the Church of Rome.'[1] Atterbury asserts that 'for depth of learning, as well as other things, the English clergy is not to be paralleled in the whole Christian World.'[2] Burnet, who is by no means inclined to overestimate the clergy, admits 'the high reputation for learning of which the clergy of this Church has been so long possessed;'[3] and an anonymous opponent of Burnet points to 'the general character of the order as to parts and learning, which' he thinks 'was never better than at present' (1713).[4]

(2) It is clear that, as a rule, a University degree was always required before a man was admitted as a candidate for Holy Orders;[5] and though a degree might not imply quite so much as it does in these days of examinations, it *did* imply a certain amount of culture; for the Universities were in a better position then than they were in later times when Gibbon, Gray, and others complained of their inefficiency.

(3) Though it may seem inconsistent with what has been said above to appeal to 'transitory literature' as a proof of anything, there is one kind which may at any rate bear out the assumption that the clergy were not such ignoramuses as to deserve the contempt of the nation. The fugitive pamphlets on theological and ecclesiastical topics were written to a very great extent by clergymen; they are

---

[1] *Observations upon Answer to Contempt of Clergy.*

[2] Sermon before Sons of Clergy, vol. ii. p. 269 of *Sermons*.

[3] See his Introduction to *Four Discourses delivered to the Clergy of Sarum*, 1694, p. x.

[4] *The Clergy and present Ministry defended—a Letter to the Bishop of Sarum*, occasioned his new Preface to the *Pastoral Care*.

[5] Bishop Turner publicly announced to the clergy of the diocese of Ely in 1686, 'I will ordain none who hath not taken some degree in one of the Universities of these realms, except by faculty from the Archbishop.' (*Letter before his Visitation*.) Wharton plainly assumes the necessity of a University degree for Ordination. (*Defence of Pluralities*, p. 187.) See also Cardwell's *Documentary Annals*, ii. p. 304, and Mr. Churchill Babington's criticism on Macaulay (ut supra) p. 92.

very numerous, and in point of literary merit, they will certainly bear comparison with a similar class of literature in the present day.

(4) The education of the upper classes was almost exclusively in the hands of the clergy, who must therefore be credited with the training of the refined writers of the Augustan period of English literature.

It sounds like a paradox to assert that contempt for the clergy arose partly from their poverty, but partly also from their prosperity. There is, however, no doubt that such was the case. Owing to the very unequal distribution of Church revenues, both grounds for contempt or dislike existed. 'The envy and malignity,' writes Wharton, 'wherewith almost all sorts of men look upon the possessions of the clergy is unaccountable.'[1] Oley specifies 'envie and the affectation of gallantrie' as two occasions of contempt of which Eachard took no notice.[2] Pepys' strictures on the clergy clearly imply the same spirit.[3] Nor is it to be wondered at. The sudden change from adversity to outward prosperity was sure to provoke such a feeling. And perhaps there was some ground for it in the demeanour, especially of some of the younger divines, who could not carry corn. Swift, staunch defender of his order though he was, complains of 'the pert, pragmatical demeanour of several young stagers in divinity upon their first producing themselves into the world.'[4] Stillingfleet writes in 1676, 'I have lately been much in the country, where I have heard sad complaints of some disorderly clergymen. . . . I heartily wish our bishops would not admit such raw persons to live on the Church.' 'People,' he adds, 'are

---

[1] *Defence of Pluralities*, p. 181.
[2] *A friendly Prosopopœia to the Author of Grounds and Occasions of the Contempt of the Clergie*, in Oley's Preface (1675) to Herbert's *Country Parson*.
[3] See *Diary* for November 9, 1663, and *passim*.
[4] *Argument against abolishing Christianity*, vol. viii. p. 85, of Scott's edition of Swift's *Works*.

ready to believe anything against the clergy they do not love.'[1] And many other testimonies might be given.[2]

And finally, the immorality and scepticism of the Restoration period naturally tended to make those whose very profession was a tacit rebuke to both, objects of contempt. Stillingfleet preached a most powerful and courageous sermon[3] on the subject in 1666 before the king, who sorely needed such plain speaking, which has already been quoted. 'Drolling on serious things,' writes Scott in his 'Christian Life' (ii. p. 99), 'is a humour of the age.' Hobbism was partly the cause, partly the effect of this scoffing spirit. 'Hobbes was,' in the language of one of the most thoughtful of our modern historians, 'one of the greatest opponents of hierarchical influences in the State who has ever existed.'[4] The stage both reflected and kept alive the hostility to the clergy.

But notwithstanding all this, the clergy beyond doubt exercised a considerable influence on the social life of the period. Their circumstances during the Rebellion had forced them into positions in which they were able to learn more of the real mind of the laity than clergymen in ordinary times can do. Many had actually engaged in lay professions. Some, like Dr. Bathurst, had practised medicine,[5] nor was it at all unusual to combine the clerical and medical professions after the Restoration.[6] The bishop of the diocese had, in fact, the power of granting licenses to the clergy to practise medicine. A frequent question in

---

[1] '*Letter to the Bishop of ——*' in Stillingfleet's *Miscellaneous Discourses*.

[2] See, inter alia, *Answer to Grounds and Occasions of Contempt of the Clergy* (1671), p. 42, and Evelyn's *Diary* for May 20, 1681.

[3] Sermon II. of *Twelve Sermons by Bishop Stillingfleet*, published 1696. Text: 'Fools make a mock at sin.'

[4] Leopold von Ranke: *History of England, principally in the seventeenth Century*, iii. p. 573.

[5] See *Life and Literary Remains of Ralph Bathurst, Dean of Wells &c.*, passim.

[6] See e.g. *Diary of Rev. John Ward, Vicar of Stratford-upon-Avon*, arranged by C. Severn, M.D., *passim*, and especially the *Life* prefixed, p. 12.

the Articles of Visitation of the period is, 'Are there any [clergy or laity] who practise Physic, Chirurgery, or Midwifery without license of the Ordinary?'[1]

Many had seen active military service. Dolben had entered as a volunteer into the royal army and had risen by his merits to the rank of major.[2] Compton had been a cornet in the Royal Horse Guards,[3] and 'is said to have been in the field at Edge-Hill fight in his cradle, and to have trailed a pike in Flanders under the Duke of York;'[4] Thomas Marshall, Rector of Lincoln College, had borne arms for the king at Oxford;[5] Bishop Lake had also 'accepted a commission in the army of Charles I., and acquired military reputation in defence of Basing House and Wallingford Castle;'[6] Allestree 'thought it no disgrace to carry a musket and perform all the duties of a common soldier, till the end of the war;'[7] Mew, Bishop of Winchester, had been a soldier for Charles I. in 1642, and afterwards in Scotland for his son; had fought under the Duke of York in Flanders, and had so far retained his military instincts after he had received the mitre, as to engage at Sedgmoor in the thickest of the fight.[8]

Nor was the legal profession one to which the clergy were entire strangers. Bishop Seth Ward, 'for his great skill in the Civil Law and laws of the land was designed by King Charles II. to be Keeper of the Great Seal;'[9] and Bishop Robinson of Bristol actually *was* made Lord Privy Seal. Bishop Stillingfleet was on all sides confessed to

---

[1] See, *inter alia*, Articles at the Bishop of Chichester's (Patrick's) Visitation, 1690.
[2] Granger's *Biographical History of England*, iii. p. 246.
[3] Birch's *Life of Tillotson*, p. 185.
[4] E. Calamy's *Account of his Own Life*, ii. p. 40.
[5] Wood's *Athenæ Oxonienses*, iv. p. 170.
[6] Bowles' *Life of Ken*, ii. p. 148.   [7] Fell's *Life of Allestree*, p. 6.
[8] *Life of Ken*, by a Layman, i. p. 251.
[9] See a curious *Essay on the great Affinity of the two Professions of Law and Divinity, &c. &c.—a Letter from a Clergyman to a Lawyer*; published about 1714.

be as good a lawyer as a divine. 'It does not at all misbecome the clergy,' says the writer of the curious essay quoted above,—a high churchman,—'to study, and be acquainted with the common law.'

The extremely active part which the clergy took,—and were expected to take,—in politics, however undesirable we may think it, unquestionably tended to give them influence over the social life of the day. In the general election of 1690 we are told that in some places the parishioners appeared, with their clergyman at their head, to vote unanimously for the Episcopalian candidates, who were generally successful, and that in London 'the Presbyterian or sectarian candidates failed' mainly owing to the influence of Bishop Compton.[1] Dr. Granville proposed to tell his people how to vote in church.[2]

Another circumstance which brought the clergy into close relation with social life was the thorough harmony of the spirit of the Church's teaching with the popular feeling on the subject of amusements. Nothing had served more to disgust the majority of Englishmen with the Puritans than their discountenance of those recreations which had made England 'merrie England.' The Church had always been a friend to innocent recreation, and the experience of twelve years of Puritan rule naturally tended to emphasise her teaching on this point. One of her greatest preachers thoroughly represented her spirit when he said, 'Christianity is not so tetrical, so harsh, so envious as to bar us from innocent pleasure.'[3] Those who wrote against the selfish, frivolous, and pleasure-loving spirit of the time are most careful to guard against the supposition that they disallowed amusements,—even some which would now be regarded as questionable. No one, e.g., will accuse

---

[1] *History of England, principally in the seventeenth Century,* L. von Ranke, v. p. 90.

[2] See Granville's *Remains,* Part I., pp. 196-7.

[3] Isaac Barrow—Sermon *Against Foolish Talking and Jesting.*

the pious Robert Nelson of being over-lax, either in his principles or his practice; and yet, under certain restrictions, he admits the lawfulness of gambling.[1] Mary Astell, though she was accused of encouraging asceticism in her proposed Protestant Nunnery, declares that her institution would 'not only permit but recommend harmless and ingenious diversions, particularly such as might refresh the body without enervating the mind.' Dr. Wells, in his stirring appeal to rich idlers to divert some of the money they spent upon their pleasures to the building of churches, is careful to add, 'I desire the reader well to observe that I do by no means go about to affirm that a gentleman ought not to please himself at all with horse-racing or hunting &c. They are all very innocent and allowable, when used with due moderation.'[2] Dean Granville, in drawing up the most strict and even austere rules for his household, allows 'playing at cards between All-Hallow Day and Candlemas.'[3] John Scott, who certainly took a very high standard of Christian duty in his 'Christian Life,' admits that 'we are not obliged to be so industrious in our calling as to deny ourselves any moderate refreshments or recreations, which are not only useful, but sometimes necessary to breath our spirits after they have been almost stifled in a cloud of business, and divert our wearied thoughts, which, like the strings of a lute, by being slackened now and then, will sound the sweeter when they are wound up again.'[4] Whether right or wrong, there was certainly a general opinion that the Puritan objection to amusement was founded on other grounds besides those of Christian duty—an opinion which found a vivid expression in the mock controversy on bear-baiting in 'Hudibras' (Part II., Canto I.).

[1] See Preface to the *Practice of True Devotion.*
[2] *The Rich Man's Duty to contribute liberally to the Building &c. of Churches,* p. 144.
[3] *Remains,* Part II., p. 153.   [4] *Christian Life,* i. p. 279.

The part which the clergy themselves might lawfully take in the amusements they did not condemn was a point on which opinions differed. Some even of the higher clergy felt no scruple about joining heartily in recreations which would now be generally considered unclerical. Bishop Juxon, who was universally respected, not only much delighted in hunting, but 'kept a pack of hounds, and had them so well ordered and hunted, chiefly by his own skill and direction, that they exceeded all other hounds in England for the pleasure and orderly hunting of them.'[1] Bishop Seth Ward's partiality to the same amusement is described in a most lively fashion by his biographer. 'Sometimes we by chance chopt upon the dogs, and sometimes by my contrivance, knowing whereabouts they intended to hunt, but however and whensoever it happened, the bishop would ride a ring or two very briskly, but when it came to picking work, or cold hunting, he would leave them and proceed in his Promenade; but first I was sent to invite all the gentlemen to dine with him, whether he knew them or not; and this not once only, but toties quoties, as long as his health permitted.'[2] But the great Stillingfleet thought differently. There is a most interesting pamphlet by Josiah Frampton, expressing Stillingfleet's views on clerical amusements, which, as it is little known, and as the opinions of such a man as Stillingfleet on any subject are valuable, is worth quoting at some length. In 1686, Stillingfleet, then Dean of S. Paul's, was staying at a country house at which Frampton, then a young curate, was also a visitor. 'We were sitting one day,' writes Frampton, 'together after dinner, and the dean began to rally me a little on my attachment to country diversions, on which he knew I had a weak side. I had brought him two young

---

[1] Whitelocke's *Memorials*, p. 24, quoted in Marsh's *Memoirs of Archbishop Juxon and his Times*. See also Dean Hook's *Lives of the Archbishops of Canterbury*, 'William Juxon,' vol. vi. p. 421; also Lord Campbell's *Lives of the Lord Chancellors*, iv. p. 7, *note*. Juxon's hunting days were over before the Restoration, but he clearly represented the mind of that period.

[2] *Life of Seth Ward, Bishop of Salisbury*, by Dr. Walter Pope, p. 74.

partridges that day for his dinner, and he began by expressing his obligation to me for my attention to him, and then asked me some questions which led me to give him an account of my day's exploits. I did not see his drift, and, in the spirit of a sportsman, told him that the late rainy season had made game very scarce, that the two covies from which I had shot the brace I had brought to him were the only birds I had seen the whole day though I had been out from five in the morning till twelve noon, and had walked upwards of fifteen miles. 'Well,' said the dean, with an affected gravity of countenance, 'I only wished to know the extent of my obligation to you; and I find your philanthropy has done more for me in giving me seven hours of your time than I could have done (even were I able to walk as you can) for any man in Christendom. . . . . I have often thought that the clergy have rather impaired the respectability of their character by mixing too much with the amusements of laymen. They not only get into a trifling way of spending their time, but by making themselves cheap they diminish the weight of their instructions.' After dwelling on this point, the dean thus limits clerical amusement: 'It should intend the exercise of the body and the recreation of the mind, and should be suited to the genius of the profession.' By these limits, 'riotous and cruel amusements are excluded, and among these I give the first rank to hunting, which is both, and the next to shooting. To speak plainly, I cordially allow no amusement to a clergyman that has anything to do with shedding blood.' He is then asked about fishing. 'I am afraid,' replied the dean, 'I shall be thought too rigid if I abridge a clergyman of this amusement. Only I absolutely enjoin him not to impale worms on his hook, but to fish either with an artificial fly or a dead bait; if he like fishing with a net I approve it more, but still I cannot bring myself to recommend any *amusement* to him which arises from *destroying* life.' Cock-fighting and horse-racing he absolutely taboos. He does not object to card-playing in itself, but fears 'the lust of it is so great that a clergyman should dread to sanction what has certainly so bad an effect on the manners of the people.' He is next asked about the playhouse. 'What a noble institution,' said the dean, 'have we here! I know of nothing that is better calculated for moral instruction, nothing that holds the glass more forcibly to the follies and vices of mankind. I would have it go hand-in-hand with the pulpit. I should encourage comedy more than tragedy, inasmuch as I should have more hope of curing such vices and follies as require the lash than such as require the gibbet. In my Utopia I mean to establish two theatres, one for the higher, the other for the lower orders of the community. But the drama of the present age has nothing less in its view than good morals; and clergy cannot well, I think, be innocent spectators as the stage is now managed.' The curate then asks him about 'Dancing Assemblies and cheerful meetings of other kinds.' 'As they are at present managed,' said the dean, ' so far as I am acquainted with them, I should hardly allow a clergyman to attend any of them. Put them under my regulations and he may attend them all. Summon an assembly when you please, at some *private* house. *Public* houses always lead to promiscuous company and intemperance. Let the meeting consist of well-educated and well-disposed young people of both sexes, and when the music strikes up and the dance begins, send for me, and I will hobble away as fast as my gouty feet will allow, and if I may be permitted quietly to occupy a corner of the room in an elbow chair, I shall enjoy the scene as much as any of you. To see youth and innocence made happy amidst such amusements as are suitable to them always gives a new joy to my philanthropy; which is as suddenly injured when I see them entangled in pleasures which I cannot but look upon as secret snares for their innocence.' Riding he strongly recommends. 'The very trot of a horse is friendly to thought. It beats time as it were to a mind engaged in deep speculation.' Carpentering and turning are also advised, and then follows a remark which should gladden the heart of clerical tennis-players, as it stamps by anticipation this favourite recreation with the approval of one of our greatest divines. 'Curate: I am afraid, sir, you will laugh at me for being fond of shuttlecock. Dean: Laugh at you! No! I respect the man who invented shuttlecock.'[1]

The Sunday question was another matter on which the teaching of the Church harmonised with popular feeling. There was a very marked difference between the standpoints of churchmen before and after the Rebellion. No attempt was made after the Restoration to reintroduce the Book of Sports; and such books as Heylin's 'History of the Sabbath,' or Bishop White of Ely's 'Treatise of the Sabbath Day,' Dr. Prideaux's (Regius Professor of Divinity at Oxford) ' Doctrine of the Sabbath,' Dr. Sanderson's ' Case of the Sabbath ' in his ' Cases of Conscience,' were succeeded by works which were certainly written from a very different point of view. Not that Sabbatarianism pure and simple was advocated in any of them. They all admitted that the Christian Lord's day was a different thing altogether from the Jewish Sabbath. Worship, not rest, was the key-note of their teaching; but for worship rest was needed, and therefore they pleaded for rest on the weekly Christian festival, rightly associating it (though putting it on a higher level) with other Christian Holy-days. This is the line taken by Jeremy Taylor: 'The Jews had a divine commandment for their day, which we have not for ours; but we have many commandments to do all that honour to God which was intended in the fourth Commandment, and the Apostles appointed the first day of the week for doing it in solemn assemblies. . . . The Gospel Sabbath or rest is but a circumstance and accessory to the principal and spiritual

---

[1] *On the Amusements of Clergymen and Christians in general. Three Dialogues between a Dean and a Curate.* From the MSS. of Dr. Josiah Frampton, bought by Dr. Edwards.

duties.'[1] To the same effect, John Scott: 'As for the Lord's Day, it is instituted, and ever since the Apostles' time hath been observed in the Christian Church as a day of public worship and weekly thanksgiving for Our Saviour's Resurrection. And certainly it must needs be of vast advantage to be one day in seven sequestered from the world and employed in divine offices.'[2] So, Bishop Stillingfleet charges his clergy in 1698: 'The religious observation of the Lord's Day is no novelty started by some late sects and parties among us, but hath been the general sense of the best part of the Christian world, and is particularly enforced upon us of the Church of England, not only by the Homilies but by the most ancient ecclesiastical law among us.'[3] Dean Comber in reply to a clergyman who had consulted him in 1673, gives four sensible 'reasons for observing the Lord's day, though no Sabbath.'[4] Great stress was laid upon the interpretation of the fourth Commandment in the Church Catechism, 'and serve him truly *all the days of my life*.' Thus Hammond, who, though he wrote a little before the Restoration, closely represents the post-Restoration teaching, interpreted the Sabbath rest as ceasing the whole life from sin, and devoting one day in the week to worship.[5] Bishop Sparrow, while carefully distinguishing between the Sabbath and the Lord's day, maintains that there was at least an analogy between the two days, though he rightly lays stress upon the festival character of the latter day, and treats of it in close connection with other Christian festivals.[6]

Without entering into any controversy with one another on the point, different divines clearly held different opinions about the lawfulness, or rather the expediency, of any recreations on the Lord's day, though all agreed that they

[1] *Holy Living. Works*, vol. iv. pp. 214–5.   [2] *Christian Life*, i. p. 293.
[3] *Ecclesiastical Cases &c.*, p. 197.
[4] See *Memoirs of Dean Comber*, p. 70.
[5] *Practical Catechism*, p. 186.
[6] *A Rationale upon the Book of Common Prayer*, p. 67.

were absolutely unlawful during the hours of divine service. Beveridge, at least in his early years, maintained that the Lord's day was profaned by any recreation;[1] Lancelot Addison teaches his catechumen to say, 'The fourth Commandment requires me to keep holy all such days which are separated from a common to a religious use. On the Lord's Day I have been taught that I am forbidden all worldly undertakings and employments, vain sports and recreations, and all actions but those of piety, mercy, necessity, and decency.'[2] Dean Hickes protests against the 'profaners of the Lord's Day, which is set aside for public worship,' and does not limit the profanation to the times of worship.[3] One of Bishop Hacket's questions in his Articles of Visitation in 1668 is, 'Do they engage in bodily labours on Sundays and Holy days?' without any mention of the hours of divine service. Bishop Atterbury recounts with evident approval, that Lady Cutts made the whole of the Lord's day a day of rest.[4]

On the other hand, we have the great name of Bramhall strongly, almost indignantly, on the side of those who permitted Sunday recreations,[5] though he insists upon apostolical, if not divine, authority for the observance of the Lord's day.[6] Two other great names, those of Thorndike and

[1] *Private Thoughts* (vol. viii. of *Works*, in Library of Anglo-Catholic Theology), Part I., p. 356.
[2] *The Christian's Manual*, p. 33.
[3] *Posthumous Discourses by Dean G. Hickes*, published by N. Spinckes, p. 341.
[4] Atterbury's *Sermons*, vol. i. p. 210. Sermon VI., on the Death of Lady Cutts.
[5] 'If Mr. Baxter think that no recreations of the body at all are lawful, or may be permitted on the Lord's Day, he may call himself a catholic if he please, but he will find very few churches of any communion whatsoever, old or new, reformed or unreformed, to bear him company. No, no, even among the churches of his own communion, &c.' (Bishop Bramhall's *Vindication*, &c.' (1672), p. 155.)
[6] 'What was the authority by which this change from the seventh day to the first was made? If not by our Lord's authority, at least by that of the Apostles. It is undeniable the Lord's Day is an apostolical tradition.' (See Dr. Hessey's *Bampton Lectures*, 1860, *Sunday*, Lecture I., p. 14.)

Cosin, are on the same side, both also basing the authority of Lord's day observance on apostolical custom. Simon Lowth only stipulates that there shall be no secular work 'at the appointed times of God's service.'[1] Dr. Edward Lake advised his spiritual protégée, the Princess of Orange, to abstain from card-playing on Sunday, but 'I told her,' he adds, 'I could not say 'twas a sin to do so, but 'twas not expedient, for fear of giving offence.'[2] In fact, it was as a matter of expediency, not as a matter of principle, that most of the Anglican divines, whether pre-Restoration or post-Restoration, regarded this vexed question; they agreed on some sort of observance of the Lord's day; they agreed in thinking that the day was utterly different from the Jewish Sabbath. But they naturally gave prominence to one or other side of the Church's teaching, according to the circumstances by which they were surrounded. When Puritanism was in the ascendant, they protested against Sabbatarianism; when the reaction set in, and the Court and its purlieus set the bad example of Sunday desecration, of which the ghastly account of Charles II.'s last Sunday on earth gives so terrible a picture, they dwelt rather on the positive side of the Church's teaching on the subject. And Puritans themselves, or at any rate nonconformists, modified their utterances on the Sunday question. Dr. Watts takes exactly the same line as the Anglican divines;[3] while Chillingworth actually found some difficulty in conforming because the ante-Communion service implied that 'the fourth Commandment was a law of God binding upon Christians.'[4]

The most striking contrast between the earlier and later Stuart periods in regard to Sunday is to be found, not in

---

[1] *Catechetical Questions*, 1673.
[2] *Diary of Dr. Ed. Lake* (1677-8), p. 22.
[3] See Southey's *Memoirs of Dr. Watts*, prefixed to the *Lyric Poems*. On the Sabbath, p. xxxv.
[4] See Dr. Tulloch's *Rational Theology*, i. p. 285.

the writings of divines, but in royal and parliamentary utterances. James I. insisted on manly exercises on the Sunday, among other reasons, 'lest the youth should grow up unfit for warriors.'[1] Charles I. reissued his father's Book of Sports, 'out of pious care for the service of God,' &c.[2] But Charles II. had hardly been three years upon the throne when a Bill passed both Houses of Parliament 'for the better observance of the Sabbath,' but was mysteriously missing when it should have received the royal assent.[3] Pepys tells us, on September 14, 1662, that 'the Bishop of London had given a very strict order against boats going on Sundays,' and on September 20, 1663, that a proclamation had been read against Sunday travelling. In 1690 Queen Mary 'forbade all hackney carriages and horses to work on Sundays, and had constables stationed at the corners of the streets to capture all puddings on their way to bakers' ovens on Sundays,'[4] but this was outrunning public opinion, and an embryo riot caused the law to be immediately suspended. In 1677 a parliamentary statute prohibited all travelling and trading on the Lord's day, and all through the latter part of our period, magistrates, goaded on by the Societies for the Reformation of Manners, were very active in putting down Sunday desecration.[5] As in many other cases, our divines were more liberal than their lay brethren. The general position taken up by them was more tenable than that either of the Puritans or their antagonists in the early part

---

[1] See Hook's *Lives of Archbishops of Canterbury*: Laud. Vol. xi. p. 40.
[2] Collier's *Ecclesiastical History*, viii. p. 77.
[3] *History of England* continued from Sir James Mackintosh's (Cabinet Cyclopædia), vii. p. 31.
[4] Miss Strickland's *Lives of the Queens of England*: Mary II. Vol. vi. p. 33.
[5] See Disney's *Essay upon the execution of the Laws against Immorality and Profaneness*. 'Seldom,' writes an anonymous pamphleteer in 1711, 'has greater vigilance been used by the civil magistrate to secure a religious observance of the Lord's Day.' (*The Nation vindicated from the Aspersions cast upon it in Representation of the present State of Religion*.)

of the seventeenth century. They steered clear of the Scylla of confounding the Lord's day with the Sabbath, and of the Charybdis of making too light of the sacred character of the weekly Christian festival.

The connection between the clergy and the Royal Society was another point in which the Church very decidedly affected one section at least of the social life of the period. Different writers differ a little as to the origin of this great institution,[1] but all are agreed about this, that distinguished churchmen, lay and clerical, were among its earliest supporters and brightest ornaments; the names of the two Wrens (Matthew and Christopher), John Wilkins, Seth Ward, Robert Boyle, Ralph Bathurst, Thomas Willis, John Pearson, Joseph Glanvill, and Wallis, need only be mentioned to shew this. Indeed, Eachard's opponent did not exaggerate when he affirmed that 'a great part of the discoveries of the Society up to that time (1671) were owing to ecclesiastical persons.'

It is true that there was also some opposition on the part of some churchmen to the new institution. One is sorry to know that the great name of Robert South must be counted among its opponents; he ridiculed it in that very character in which he ought to have been its panegyrist, viz. as Public Orator of the great University where the Society had been nourished in its infancy, if not actually born.[2] The author of 'Hudibras' also, who in his way was

[1] Bishop Sprat (*History of the Royal Society*, 1667) traces its rise to 'some space after the end of the Civil War at Oxford, in Dr. Wilkins his Lodgings in Wadham College.' Dr. Birch thinks 'we may go still farther back for the origin, on the authority of Dr. Wallis, one of its earliest and most considerable members. About 1645, several worthy persons residing in London met weekly,' &c. (See *Diary and Correspondence of Dr. J. Worthington*, p. 216, note. Also Von Ranke's *History of England &c.*, iii. p. 582, Weld's *History of the Royal Society* (1848), i. p. 30.) Professor Craik is no doubt correct in saying there were two Societies, one at Oxford, one, earlier still, in London, during the Commonwealth. The Charter for the Royal Society proper was given in 1672. (See Craik's *Compendious History of English Literature*, ii. p. 158 &c.)

[2] See South's Latin Oration at the opening of the Sheldonian Theatre.

Y

a very strong churchman, reserved some of his shafts of ridicule for the new Society, and the most vehement and extravagant of all its opponents, Henry Stubbs, a Bath physician, grounded his opposition partly on the absurd assumption that the Society 'intended to destroy the established religion, and introduce Popery in its stead.'[1] But these were exceptional cases. The preponderance of Church opinion was certainly on the side of the rector of Bath, Mr. Glanvill, who demurred to the dismal anticipations of his parishioner, and agreed with the thesis of Robert Boyle's 'Christian Virtuoso,' shewing 'that by being addicted to experimental philosophy, a man is rather assisted than indisposed to be a good Christian.' In short, the Church was abreast if not ahead of popular opinion in regard to natural science.

The same cause which rendered it difficult to appraise the social position of the clergy, renders it also difficult to determine the extent to which they mixed in social life. The vast gap which divided different classes of clergy probably accounts for the fact that we have complaints of a diametrically opposite character on this point. On the one hand, e.g., Granville complains in his Visitation Charge, 1675, that 'clergy make themselves too cheap and contemptible by mean conversation at feasts &c., without doing or receiving spiritual advantage, by handling the plough and spade more than the Bible, by frequenting markets and fairs, horse-races and hunting;'[2] and an anonymous writer in 1714 thinks 'it is a thing altogether undecent to see so many preachers of the Gospel haunting and crowding the Parliament Lobbies and Ante-chambers of Lay Assemblies, whispering here and buzzing there, and as busie as bees.'[3]

July 9, 1669, of the members of the Royal Society he says 'Mirantur nihil nisi pulices pediculosos—et se ipsos.'

[1] See Birch's *Life of Robert Boyle*, p. 189 &c.
[2] *Remains*, Part II., p. 20.
[3] *A Letter from one Clergyman to another concerning Ministers intermeddling with State affairs*.

On the other hand Swift 'cannot but think that through a mistaken notion and practice, the clergy prevent themselves from doing much service which otherwise might lie in their power, to religion and virtue, by affecting so much to converse with each other, and caring so little to mingle with the laity. They have,' he says, 'their particular clubs and particular coffee-houses, where they generally appear in clusters; a single divine dares hardly shew his person among numbers of fine gentlemen, or if he falls into such company is silent and suspicious, in continual apprehension that some pert man of pleasure should break an unmannerly jest and render him ridiculous.'[1] To the same effect one of Burnet's opponents writes: 'The clergy would be better qualified for their office if they were more acquainted with the laity and with secular affairs. It is their herding together, and not conversing enough with the world, that makes many of them often judge and act so oddly as they do. Where should the Physician be but with the sick?' &c.[2] These absurdly contradictory indictments may easily be reconciled by supposing that the writers were thinking of very different classes of clergy.

One circumstance which would draw attention alike to the banding together of clerical cliques and the mixing of clergy in unclerical assemblies, was the fact that clergymen were wont to wear in public the canonical habit; that is, the habit prescribed by the 74th Canon. It was of course disused during the Rebellion, but resumed at once on the Restoration, and though at first, as Bramhall complains, 'those who wore canonical habits and walked in cassocks and girdles, were taken for pensioners to his Holiness,'[3] the prejudice soon wore off; laxity, not Protestantism, was

---

[1] *Project for the Advancement of Religion and Reformation of Manners.*
[2] *An Impartial Examination of Bishop Burnet's History of his Own Times,* by Mr. Salmon, ii. p. 733.
[3] *Vindication of himself and the Episcopal Clergy from Presbyterian charge of Popery by Baxter &c.* (1672). Preface.

the cause why the dress was sometimes abandoned. Granville mentions as a proof of the secularity of some of the clergy, that they were 'scarcely distinguished from the laity so much as by their habit.'[1] Stillingfleet thinks 'it argues lightness for a clergyman to wear a lay habit,' and wishes 'he could be obliged to wear a short cassock under his coat.' The canonical dress was clearly the rule. Among some visitation inquiries in 1678, are: 'Doth your parson wear such apparel as is prescribed by the Canon, that is, a gown with a standing collar, and wide sleeves strait at the hands, and a square cap? or doth he go at any time abroad in his doublet and hose? or doth he use to wear any light-coloured stockings? in his journeyings, doth he usually wear a cloak with sleeves, commonly called the priest's cloak?' &c. Eachard complains of 'the young spark tossing his head at a clergyman because he is obliged to wear the same canonical habit.'[2] The custom naturally lingered on longer and was more rigorously observed in London than in the country. Thus, while Trimmell, Bishop of Norwich, declared in 1710 that 'the habit particularly recommended by the Canon was out of use,'[3] Swift, writing about the same time of the London clergy, says: 'the clergy are the only set of men among us who constantly wear a distinct habit from others; the consequence of which (not in reason, but in fact), is this, that as long as any scandalous persons appear in that dress, it will continue in some degree a general mark of contempt. Whoever happens to see a scoundrel in a gown reeling home at midnight (a sight neither frequent nor miraculous), is apt to entertain an ill idea of the whole order.' He thinks it would be 'infinitely better if all the clergy (except the bishops) were permitted to appear like other men of the graver sort, unless at those seasons when they are doing

---

[1] *Remains*, Part II., p. 45.
[2] *Grounds &c. of Contempt of the Clergy*, p. 576.
[3] *The Bishop of Norwich's Visitation Charge*, 1710.

the work of their function.'[1] At the same time Swift himself, 'whenever he went abroad, or gave audience to a stranger, was careful to appear in cassock and gown.'[2] The nonjuring clergy usually walked in the London streets in full canonicals. Dress may seem a slight matter, but it is a straw which shews which way the wind blows; and, especially in connection with social life, it is by no means without significance.

But to pass on to a graver subject. The relation of the Church to social life is obviously affected most deeply by the state of *Church discipline*. The efforts to revive this powerful engine after the Restoration were evidently made in a not very hopeful spirit; but still the mere fact that efforts *were* made, and even the constant iteration of complaints about the decay of discipline, are proofs that it was not entirely dead. And facts prove that it was not. Pepys heard on July 16, 1665, 'a declaration of penitence of a man that had undergone the Churche's censures,' at a church near London. In the church accounts of Gateshead for 1666-7, one entry is, 'A white sheet for pennance, 1s. 6d.'[3] Samuel Wesley gave most strict directions about discipline to his curate at Epworth, telling him to direct the churchwardens to enforce the 90th Canon, and declaring that he had always brought to public penance ante-nuptial and no-nuptial fornicators.[4] 'In the parish register of Wadhurst,' writes the accomplished historian of the diocese of Chichester, 'there is a notice in 1677-8 of an account of ecclesiastical discipline, which is the latest example of the

---

[1] *Project for the Advancement of Religion &c.*, pp. 95-96.

[2] See *Quarterly Review*, No. 306, for April 1882. Art. Jonathan Swift. See also Swift's *Argument against abolishing Christianity*: 'I am very sensible how much the gentlemen of wit and pleasure are apt to murmur and be shocked at the sight of so many daggle-tailed parsons, who happen to fall in their way and offend their eyes.'

[3] See *Appendix on the History of Newcastle and Gateshead*, in *Memoirs of Ambrose Barnes* (Surtees Society), p. 401.

[4] See Tyerman's *Life and Times of Samuel Wesley*, p. 387.

kind I have noticed in this diocese.'[1] Bishop Hacket publicly excommunicated the Dean of Lichfield in 1667.[2] One point was very generally insisted upon; that is, the payment of commutation money for penance. This was rather an evasion of, than a submission to, strict discipline; but still the fact that money was parted with, even to evade it, is a proof that discipline was not quite dead. Archbishop Sharp wrote to a clergyman in 1704 about the money commutation for a penance: 'I would have it *entirely* applied to the use of the Church, and as *notoriously* as her offence to it hath been. If you are of opinion that this fault of hers ought not to be commuted, but that it is for the interest of religion that she should do a personal penance, I pray signify it to me.'[3] Among the articles of inquiry at the Visitation of the Bishop of Worcester (Lloyd) in 1705 are these: 'Are any Commutations of Penance made by any ecclesiastical officer? By whom? For what offences? For what pious uses hath the money been employed?' Bishop Frampton of Gloucester enjoined his clergy 'if any were so obstinate as to refuse to hear the church, to let them know he had authority to deliver such a one to Satan that he might learn not to blaspheam,' and was not afraid to act up to his determination in the case of a powerful peer, Lord Wharton, whom he compelled to pay commutation money.[4] Among the practical agenda of Convocation in 1710 one was: 'The regulating the proceedings in excommunication and reforming the abuses of commutation money.'[5] In 1714 the subject had assumed so definite a shape that a form of

---

[1] *Diocesan Histories* (S.P.C.K.) *Selsey—Chichester*, by W. R. W. Stephens. The notice is, 'July 16. Eleanora Woodgate et Sarah Moore in ecclesiâ parochiali inter divinorum solemnia palam, publicè et solemniter denunciatæ et declaratæ fuerunt pro excommunicatis.' And then 'E. W. et S. M. in ecclesiâ &c. pœnitentiam agebant.'

[2] See Pepys' *Diary* for January 17, 166⅞.

[3] *Life of Archbishop Sharp*, by his son, i. p. 213-4.

[4] See *Life of Robert Frampton*, ed. Evans, p. 165 and 168.

[5] See Lathbury's *History of Convocation*, p. 408, and Wilkins' *Concilia Magnæ Britanniæ*, iv. p. 623.

excommunication was drawn up by Convocation;[1] but the matter, like many other matters, fell through, owing to the death of the queen.

The tone of Church writers on the subject of discipline during our period is not sanguine, but it is not hopeless. Bishop Wilson, indeed, scouts the very idea that it cannot be enforced:—'Discipline impracticable! This cannot be, when it was practised for so many years in the Primitive Church. The commands of Christ cannot be impracticable. That would be to tax him with ignorance or weakness.'[2] The good bishop's regimen in his own diocese shewed that discipline could be made a very real thing indeed; but then, of course, the circumstances of the Isle of Man differed from those of the adjacent Isle of Great Britain. Bishop Turner, in his admirable 'Letter to the Clergy of the Diocese of Ely' (1686), bids them 'labour in sermons and private conferences to make their parishioners deeply apprehend the great and heavy load which the just censures of the Church do lay upon grievous offenders in any kind,' and advises them to read 'my reverend friend Dr. Comber's excellently learned and no very long Treatise of Excommunication.' Dr. Comber has no difficulty in shewing in this work, (1) The divine original of Excommunication; (2) The universal Practice; (3) The ends for which it was instituted; but he complains that 'the Schismatics and Profane, the Atheistical and those who are of most profligate conversations, do all conspire to make the Church's discipline weak and ineffectual,' and his general tone gives one the idea that he thought the conspiracy was successful.[3] Atterbury, in the dedication of his Sermons to his staunch friend Bishop Trelawney, hopes 'by your Lord-

---

[1] The title of the Form was: 'An Exhortation to be read in the church, when the person decreed to be excommunicated is present.' Passages in brackets to be omitted when the person is absent. (See Lathbury, p. 436.)

[2] *Sacra Privata*: Thursday's meditations.

[3] See *A Discourse concerning Excommunication*, by Thomas Comber, Precentor of York (1686), *passim*.

ship's means, and within the circle of your power, to see all proper steps taken towards reviving decayed discipline, and restoring Church Censures to their due force and credit.'

The wish for the restoration of discipline was by no means confined to high churchmen. Archbishop Tenison suggested to King William the necessity of preserving and restoring the discipline of the Church, urged the clergy to have recourse to ecclesiastical censures, and enjoined, in the king's name, 'that no commutation for Pennance should be made but by the express order and direction of the bishop himself, which should be declared in open Court; and that the commutation money should be applied only to pious and charitable uses.'[1] Compton, the Protestant bishop, made Church discipline a subject of one of his very practical letters to his clergy;[2] and, grotesque as it may sound, Defoe, the dissenter, desires, evidently in all sincerity, the restoration of Church discipline.

Of course the efficacy of Church discipline depends upon the value men set upon Church privileges. 'Penances, suspensions, and excommunications,' writes Dean Hickes, 'ought to have no other than spiritual effects;'[3] and Dr. Comber strongly insists upon the same point. Here lay the real difficulty; and the churchmen of our period, being practical men, felt it keenly. Bishop Stillingfleet, who generally contrived to hit the right nail on the head, replied to Archbishop Tenison's Injunction quoted above: 'Suspension and Excommunication doth but drive them out of the Church, and they care very little for coming at it.'[4] Dean Sherlock puts the matter still more strongly: 'Consider wherein the power of the keys consists, which Christ committed to S. Peter and the rest of the Apostles, or what

[1] See *Life of Tenison*.
[2] *Episcopalia, or Letters of Henry, Bishop of London, to the Clergy of his Diocese*. Letter 3.
[3] *Constitution of the Catholic Church*, p. 93.
[4] Letter to the Archbishop about the King's Injunctions, 1694, in Stillingfleet's *Miscellaneous Discourses*.

is the true ancient discipline of the Christian Church. The power of the Church, which is truly spiritual, consists only in letting into the Church, and shutting out. What would those men value Church censures who excommunicate themselves?'[1] 'The Church,' writes Bishop Barlow to R. Boyle, 'having no power to punish any save those of her own body (by Penance, Excommunication, &c.), therefore Papists and Sectaries are not liable to Church censures.'[2] A correspondent of Bishop Nicolson goes a step further. 'As to joining with Dissenters in this specious matter [the Reformation of Manners], I must always look upon them as the real cause why our Church discipline is not powerful enough at present to correct the vices they now complain of. It is they that have taught the people to slight the ecclesiastical censures.'[3] Disney, who took exactly the opposite view from that of the above writer on the Societies for Reformation of Manners, agrees with him as to the fact: 'The discipline of the Church and terror of Penance and Excommunications are at a very low ebb, seldom exercised and little feared.'[4] Robert Nelson, who always took the practical view of things, instead of lamenting the decay of discipline, suggests that as 'the discipline of the Church is at so low an ebb among us, we ought to take the more care to exercise it upon ourselves.' And finally, Johnson of Cranbrook, a very strong churchman, roundly asserts that 'no wise man has any reason to hope that Church discipline can be restored in such an age as this.'[5] On the whole, though there were isolated cases of the enforcement of discipline, it can hardly

---

[1] *A Practical Discourse of Religious Assemblies*, p. 83.
[2] *Cases of Conscience.* 'Case of Toleration in Matters of Religion' (1692).
[3] Archbishop Nicolson's *Correspondence &c.*, p. 165. Letter from Mr. Yates to Bishop Nicolson, March 1699.
[4] *Essay upon the execution of the Laws against Immorality &c.*
[5] *The Clergyman's Vade Mecum*, p. 274. It was published anonymously, but it is pretty clearly ascertained that the author was Mr. Johnson.

be regarded as having exercised much real influence upon social life.

All through our period we hear much of the now obsolete office of 'casuist.' The term 'casuistry' had not then acquired the evil meaning which now attaches to it.[1] It meant, as it is still defined in dictionaries to mean, the dealing systematically and exhaustively with delicate cases of conscience. Such cases must constantly arise; and it is a misfortune that the science which dealt with them—(for it *is* a science[2] demanding great acuteness, thoughtfulness, and training for its acquirement)—should have fallen into disuse. It has been said that casuistry became extinct after the Restoration; and as a proof of its extinction is adduced the flatness of the reception of Jeremy Taylor's 'Ductor Dubitantium,' the work on which he 'bestowed more anxiety and prayer' than on any of his works; the work on which he was content that his fame should rest.[3] But does it quite follow that popular distaste for the subject was the cause of the comparative failure of the work? The treatise is obviously far too long. The grand and florid style, both of language and thought, which made Taylor's sermons and devotional works so impressive, is quite out of place in casuistry, in which lucidity is the one thing needful. Mr.

---

[1] At least it was not *generally* used in a sinister sense, though the works of the Jesuits which probably caused Englishmen to regard it as an 'evasive perversion of reason,' 'a quibbling with God,' already existed. See the excellent 'Note' of Dr. Whewell to his introductory Lecture, in his *Lectures on The History of Moral Philosophy in England*. He appositely refers to Pope as giving instances of both uses of the word:

In a good sense:
   Who shall decide when doctors disagree,
   And soundest *casuists* doubt, like you and me?

In a bad sense:
   Morality by her false guardians drawn,
   Chicane in furs, and *Casuistry* in lawn.

See also Hallam's *Literature of Europe*, chap. iv. § 1, *passim*.

[2] At least in the popular, if not in the technical sense of the term. Hallam's *Literature of Europe*, ii. p. 495, defines it rightly as the instrument for applying the science of ethics.

[3] See Heber's *Life*, prefixed to Taylor's *Works*, p. xcvi.

Hughes is surely right when he pronounces the 'Ductor Dubitantium' 'too complicated, overlaid with words and metaphors; full of overstrained arguments on both sides.'[1] It is, no doubt, as Dr. Whewell calls it, 'a noble work;' any work to which a mind like Taylor's gave its deepest attention could hardly fail to be; but there is no wonder that it was not very popular.[2] The author wrote it, not because he felt that he had a vocation for this kind of writing, but to supply a want. 'Though,' he says, 'in all things else the goodness of God hath made us to abound, and our cup to run over; yet our labours have been hitherto unimploied in the description of the Rules of Conscience and Casuistical Theology.'[3] His countrymen were 'wholly unprovided with casuistical treatises, and were forced to go down to the forges of the Philistines, to sharpen every man his share and his coulter, his axe and his hammer.' This is not quite accurate; the great names of Joseph Hall and Robert Sanderson among writers of casuistry suffice to shew that English churchmen were not 'wholly unprovided with casuistical treatises;'[4] but, of course, in comparison with the Romish Church, the English Church was very scantily provided. And on the other side, the Puritans had paid at least as much attention to casuistry as Anglican churchmen. One of the first Englishmen who 'reduced the science of

---

[1] Hughes' *Biographical Memoirs of Jeremy Taylor*, prefixed to his edition of Taylor's *Sermons*.

[2] See Dr. Whewell's *Lectures on the History of Moral Philosophy in England*, Lecture I., and Hallam's *Literature of Europe*, iii. p. 381 &c., for accounts and criticisms (more favourable than those in the text) of the *Ductor Dubitantium*.

[3] Dedication to the king.

[4] Bishop Hall's *Resolutions and Decisions of divers Practical Cases of Conscience in continual Use among Men*, was published in 1649. Bishop Sanderson's *Cases of Conscience* were first published in 1634; there are only eleven cases altogether in this volume. Bishop Sanderson also published two treatises which, at least, bear upon casuistry; *De Obligatione Conscientiæ* and *De Juramenti Obligatione*. The latter has been edited in our own day with excellent notes by Dr. Whewell, himself Professor of Casuistry at Cambridge.

casuistry into some kind of form and explained it with some accuracy,'[1] was William Perkins, a Puritan in the time of Elizabeth.[2] He was followed by his friend and pupil, William Ames,[3] who says of his master, ' he [Perkins] left many behind him affected by that study [the study of cases of conscience] who by their godly sermons (through God's assistance) made it to run, increase, and be glorified throughout England.' These of course would be Puritans. When Owen was Dean of Christ Church, a 'regular office for the satisfaction of doubtful consciences was held in Oxford,' which irreverent undergraduates called 'the scruple shop.'[4]

After the Restoration there is abundant evidence that the Anglican divines fully appreciated the value of casuistry. Bishops strongly recommended its study to their clergy. Bishop Stillingfleet advised the clergy of the Worcester diocese ' to have a care to qualifie themselves for resolving cases of conscience.'[5] Bishop Gardiner charges the clergy of the Lincoln diocese to the same effect; while his predecessor, Bishop Barlow, was himself 'eminent for his knowledge of casuistry,'[6] as is proved by his admirable 'Cases of Conscience,' a work well worthy to be placed on a level with the 'Cases of Conscience' of his great predecessor Bishop Sanderson. Bishop Sprat, in his advice to the clergy of the Rochester diocese about the sick, says : 'I would persuade you to have some good, sound body of Casuistical Divinity to be always at hand. You can scarce imagine, unless you have try'd it, as, I hope, some of you have, of what unspeakable use this Divine Science of Cases

---

[1] See Hallam's *Literature of Europe*, i. p. 554.
[2] The title of his work is, *The whole Treatise of Cases of Conscience, distinguished into three books, taught and delivered by Mr. W. Perkins, in his Holyday Lectures* (at Cambridge). See Whewell's *History of Moral Philosophy*, Lect. I., p. 2.
[3] *De Conscientiâ, ejus jure et casibus*, published 1630.
[4] See Heber's *Life of Jeremy Taylor*, p. clxx.
[5] See *Life and Character of Bishop E. Stillingfleet* (published 1710).
[6] See *Diary &c. of Dr. Worthington*, p. 126, *note*.

of Conscience will be to you upon any sudden unforeseen emergency in such ghostly visits. Indeed, the being a sound and well-experienced casuist is also a most excellent qualification towards all the other ends of your ministerial office; there being no kind of skill or proficiency in all your theological studies that more becomes a divine of the Church of England, whose highest spiritual art is to speak directly from his own conscience to the Consciences of those under his Pastoral care.'[1]

So far was the study from being out of date, that in 1683 a professorship was founded by Dr. Knightbridge and his brother at Cambridge, 'of Moral Philosophy or Casuistical Divinity,' the holder of which was usually called the 'Professor of Casuistry'; and its usefulness so commended itself to the first professor, Dr. Smoult, that he augmented the endowment.[2] Dr. Horneck 'was frequently addressed to with Cases of Conscience, and sometimes with cases that were very extraordinary.'[3] Archbishop Sharp was referred to 'by many Peers as a faithful Casuist.'[4] Of Mr. Marsh, vicar of Newcastle, who died in 1692, we are told that 'his known abilities in resolving cases of conscience drew after him a great many good people, not only of his own flock, but from remoter distances who resorted to him as to a common oracle, and commonly went away from him entirely satisfied in his wise and judicious resolutions.'[5] And to quote a layman as well as the clergy, Henry Dodwell advises his young minister on the necessity of skill in Casuistical Divinity. 'For,' he writes, 'if you must particularly apply, you must particularly know the state of the conscience you have to deal with.'[6] If Bishop Barlow's

---

[1] Visitation Charge, 1695.
[2] See *Lectures on the History of Moral Philosophy* (p. 12), by Dr. Whewell, when he was the worthy holder of the Casuistry chair.
[3] See Bishop Kidder's *Life of Anthony Horneck*.
[4] *Life*, by son, i. p. 268.
[5] Preface to Marsh's *Sermons*, by John Scott (author of the *Christian Life*). See also *Memoirs of Ambrose Barnes* (Surtees Society), p. 112.
[6] Dodwell's *Letter of Advice for the Susception of Holy Orders*, p. 56.

'cases' may be regarded as typical instances, casuistry certainly took a most practical form; and in this form it bears so obviously upon social life, that it is hoped too much will not be thought to have been said about it in that connection.[1]

Among the heterogeneous matters which are grouped together in this chapter, as all bearing upon social life, may be placed Family Prayer. 'The Puritans,' says a writer of the eighteenth century, 'by long extempore prayers, stuffed with absurd cant &c., brought family devotion into disrepute with many, who instead of reforming the abuse, omitted it altogether.'[2] The proceeding was not a logical one, nor was it at all intended by those who were really anxious to keep alive a religious tone, though of a different kind from that of Puritanism. Thus 'The Whole Duty of Man,' which more than any other work both represented and directed the course of feeling on matters of religion after the Restoration, provided a number of private prayers, but none for families; not because the writer would have family prayer neglected, but 'because the Providence of God and the Church hath already furnished for that purpose infinitely beyond what my utmost care could do. I mean the Publick Liturgy or Common Prayer, which for all publick addresses to God (and such are Family Prayers), are so excellent and useful that we may say of it, as David did of Goliath's sword, "There is none like it."' Pious men of all parties in the Church perceived the danger of neglecting family prayer. Prideaux, when Archdeacon of Suffolk, 'being well-informed that in many families of the clergy Prayers were wholly omitted, morning and evening, made

---

[1] These are some of the titles of Bishop Barlow's cases: *The case of Toleration in matters of Religion. The case of Mr. Collington concerning the validity or nullity of his marriage with Gallicia, her former husband then living. The case ' De Judæis in Republicâ Christianâ tolerandis vel de novo admittendis.'* They are addressed to Hon. R. Boyle, the most practical of men.

[2] *Life of Dean Humphrey Prideaux* (published 1748), p. 62.

this the subject of a Visitation charge.'[1] Burnet records, evidently as a hint to those who neglected the duty, that Sir M. Hale 'used constantly to worship God in his family, performing it himself if there were no clergyman present.'[2] Henry Dodwell urges his young minister to 'persuade masters of families to keep up morning and evening prayers.'[3] 'The first thing,' writes Bishop Bull to the clergy of S. David's, 'that I would recommend to you, and which I do earnestly exhort you to, is, To apply yourselves with great diligence to establish the practice of family devotion in all the families of your respective parishes. . . . I must with some warmth beseech you, to make a particular application to every housekeeper in your several parishes,' &c. He dwells at some length on the point, and gives them a list of tracts urging the duty, which shews that the need of stirring up householders on the matter was keenly felt.[4] In addition to the efforts of individuals, the matter was taken up by public authority. In 1688 'there was provided a family book to be authorised by Convocation; it contained directions for family devotions, with several forms of prayer,' compiled probably by Tillotson;[5] and in the Royal Injunctions of 1694 one article was 'concerning family devotion.' How far these various efforts were successful we have no means of knowing.

Before concluding this chapter, one very important question must be discussed. Did the Church use that influence which she possessed over social life to stem the torrent of immorality which swept over the Court and its purlieus, and, to a less extent, the whole nation, when the revulsion against Puritanism was at its height? The overwhelming difficulties she must have met with in the attempt have been noticed in the introductory chapter; but did she

---

[1] *Life*, p. 69.
[2] *Life of Sir M. Hale*, p. 92.
[3] *Letters &c.*, ut supra, p. 98.
[4] Nelson's *Life of Bishop Bull*, pp. 279-283.
[5] Lathbury's *History of Convocation*, p. 333.

set herself boldly to overcome those difficulties? True *churchmen* did, but mere *conformists* did not, and alas! the latter abounded. But it was fixedness of principle rather than courage that was lacking, where there was a lack. Want of moral courage does not appear to have been a besetting sin of the Church of our period. Indeed, it was not a temptation to which her circumstances rendered her peculiarly liable. Outward prosperity, with all its drawbacks, does not tend to make men sycophants. We have abundant instances of courage in high places.[1] Sheldon, whatever his defects may have been, at any rate set an excellent example in this respect. He remonstrated with King Charles in very strong, not to say rough, language on the irregularity of his life, and by his honest expostulations lost all favour at Court and never regained it. Ken 'was brought into relation with three kings, and had the Christian boldness to rebuke them all.'[2] He replied to the application to receive King Charles' mistress into his lodgings at Winchester, 'Not for his three kingdoms'; he was so notoriously in the habit of uttering plain truths from the pulpit without fear or favour, that King Charles was wont to say, 'I must go and hear Ken tell me of my faults.' He faced the brutal Kirke in his drunken rage and remonstrated with him on his cruelties after the Monmouth rebellion; on the same occasion he met Lord Faversham at Bridgwater, and plainly told him that his doings were 'murders in law'; and he wrote to King James to expostulate with him on 'Jeffreys' campaign.'[3] He bravely preached at Court on the duty of obeying God rather than the king, when the duties con-

---

[1] Mr. Hunter, in his *Life of Oliver Heywood*, says that 'we are not able to judge at this distance of time whether the clergy about Court, or conforming clergy generally, may have been justly chargeable with not having raised the warning voice' (p. 199), but surely the instances cited in the text may enable us to form an approximate judgment.

[2] *Life*, by a Layman, i. p. 403.

[3] See Sir James Mackintosh's *Review of the Causes of the Revolution of 1688* (*Miscellaneous Works* in 1 vol., p. 289).

flicted, and when the sermon was reported to James as being a premeditated insult, and Ken had to give an account of himself to the king: 'If,' he replied, 'his Majesty had not neglected his own duty of being present, my enemies had missed this opportunity of accusing me.'[1] The oft-told tale of the glorious resistance of the Seven Bishops to King James' arbitrary demands, and that of the bold stand of the Fellows of Magdalen generally, and of their President, Hough, the meekest of men, in particular, need only be alluded to, to shew that courage was not lacking when occasion required it. John Sharp, when he was rector of S. Giles' in the Fields, preached boldly against Romanism, in contravention of the express orders of King James, and Bishop Compton refused to suspend him for so doing, at the expense of being suspended himself. The vast majority of the London clergy, Edward Fowler, to his credit, leading the way, and Simon Patrick following next, refused to read the king's illegal Declaration; the clergy of the diocese of Durham refused, almost to a man, to obey the injunctions of their servile bishop, Lord Crewe, on the same matter; indeed, the vast majority of the clergy throughout the kingdom acted in the same bold spirit – out of ten thousand clergy only two hundred consented to read the Declaration. Samuel Johnson sat in the pillory, and was whipped from Newgate to Tyburn for warning 'Protestant officers and soldiers against being instruments of the Court for the destruction of their religion.' Sancroft, feeble and irresolute as he has been termed, had no fear of expostulating with James, when Duke of York, on his change of religion.[2] Courage, too, in boldly rebuking vice in the vicious days of Charles II. was certainly not lacking. Pepys, who is very

---

[1] Bowles' *Life*, ii. p. 138. See also Ken's sermon on the *Reformed Church of Judah* [England], preached at Whitehall in King James' reign against popery.

[2] It is not thought necessary to give authorities in proof of these facts, as they will be found in every popular history, and have never been disputed.

chary of recording anything good of the clergy, specifies at least two occasions on which he heard bold sermons preached against adultery in the presence of the king, who must have felt that the preachers' shafts were aimed against him.[1] On the latter occasion the preacher was Dr. Creighton (Pepys spells him Creeton), who is said by a writer of the next generation to have been one who 'preached boldly against the vices of the times.'[2] Stillingfleet's noble sermon before the same mocking king and his mocking courtiers on the suggestive text, 'Fools make a mock of sin,' has already been noticed, and he was no less bold in his sermon before the House of Commons on the kine of Bashan. A less known man, one Mr. Nuggett, King Charles' chaplain, was not afraid to beard the lion in his den, preaching at Windsor Castle itself a sermon against adultery which must have made the royal adulterer's ears tingle (August 15, 1675). Many of Bishop Hooper's published sermons were preached before royalty, and are full of the most courageous and out-spoken utterances without the slightest tincture of flattery.[3] Archbishop Sharp, in his sermon at Queen's Anne's Coronation, April 23, 1702, began well his important office as her spiritual director, by pointing out her duty most fully and bravely,[4] and all through her reign he pursued the same bold course.

[1] 'April 6, 1662. To Whitehall, and there heard a very honest sermon before the king. He did much insist upon the sin of adultery, which me-thought might touch the king.'

'July 29, 1667. Dr. Creeton before the king preached against the sins of the Court, and particularly against adultery, over and over again instancing how for that single sin in David, the whole nation was undone.'

[2] *Lives of the English Bishops from the Restauration to the Revolution* [by Nathaniel Salmon], published 1733.

[3] The second was before the king at Whitehall, November 5, 1681, in which he avers it was not the part of the Church to flatter the Civil Power; the third before the queen at Whitehall, January 25, 169$\frac{0}{1}$; the fourth before the king and queen at Whitehall, January 14, 169$\frac{3}{4}$; the fifth before the king at Kensington in 1695. (See *Works* in 2 vols., new edition. Oxford, 1855.)

[4] The subject is, 'The duty of Princes to be Nursing Fathers to their subjects.' 'Arbitrariness,' says the preacher, 'is a word fit for none but

Courage of rather a different kind was called for from the clergy on one memorable occasion which, even after this lapse of years, cannot be recalled without a thrill of horror. Conflicting statements may be found as to their behaviour during the Great Plague of London in 1665. On the one hand we are told that 'the English clergy, with a benevolence and a fortitude above all praise, resolved to remain in their stations, and to supply the wretched sufferers with spiritual consolations;'[1] on the other, that 'whilst the Anglican clergy fled, the Presbyterian preachers mounted once more the pulpits.'[2] Defoe, who lived nearer the time, and whose testimony will not be suspected of unduly favouring the clergy, writes, more correctly than either of the above: 'It is true some of the dissenting turned-out ministers stayed, and their courage is to be commended and highly valued, but these were not in abundance; it cannot be said that they all stayed and that none retired into the country, any more than it can be said of the Church clergy that they all went away; neither did all those that went away go without substituting curates and others in their places to do the offices needful and visit the sick as far as it was practicable.'[3] Indisputable facts bear out this statement. It is certain that in some cases the Church pulpits were deserted by their proper occupants, and occupied by the ministers who had been ejected by the Act of Uniformity—all honour to the good men who filled the gap when their services were so sorely needed. But it is equally certain that there were many instances of noble self-sacrifice on the part of the clergy. Archbishop Sheldon again set an excellent example.

God; for *all* his creatures are under laws by which they must be governed.' (See Archbishop Sharp's *Sermons*, vol. ii. pp. 75-85.)

[1] *History of the Church of England*, by J. B. S. Carwithen, iii. p. 114.

[2] *History of England, principally in the seventeenth Century*, Leopold von Ranke, iii. p. 447.

[3] *History of the Great Plague*, p. 272. Mr. Maddox (*Examination of Neal's 4th vol. of History of the Puritans by Grey and Maddox*, 1739) gives a similar account (iv. pp. 315-6).

He firmly continued at Lambeth all the time of the greatest danger,[1] and used his vast influence to procure aid for the sufferers and 'preserved numbers who but for him would have perished.'[2] 'Stayed,' writes Patrick with artless simplicity, 'in my parish during the Plague. When my parishioners returned, they were wonderful kind to me, and I found myself much endeared to them by my stay among those who remained.'[3] There is a most interesting set of letters in the 'Ellis Correspondence' from the Rev. Stephen Bing to Dr. Sancroft, Dean of S. Paul's, 'upon the ravage of the Great Plague.' Mr. Bing was one of the clergy who stayed at his post, and we find in his letters such entries as these: 'The Prayers of the Church are continued, and persons attending.' 'On the last Holy-day we had a sermon, and shall have another on the Fast Day.' 'The Cross [S. Paul's] sermons are continued, and we had on the Fast Day a laudable sermon by Mr. Risden, minister in Bread Street.' 'Mr. Portington [one of the S. Paul's clergy] lies at the point of death, whose turn being to officiate this week, I supply.' 'Dr. Barwick is a constant frequenter at our church, sometimes three times in a day.' 'It is said that my Lord Bishop of London hath sent to those pastors that have quitted their flocks by reason of these times, that, if they return not speedily, others shall be put into their places.' There are also letters from Tillotson to Sancroft in the same collection, shewing that the former was in London during the Plague, and most active in behalf of the sufferers. All the letters are written in July and August, when the Plague was at its height.[4] This was just one of those occasions on which there is no medium between pusillanimity and heroism; those who seized the golden opportunity and shewed the martyr-spirit

---

[1] Grey and Maddox, *Examination of Neal's History of the Puritans*, iv. p. 346.
[2] Carwithen, *ut supra*.   [3] *Autobiography*, p. 57.
[4] See *Ellis' Original Letters*, second series, vol. iv. pp. 24, 25–27, 28, 30, &c

gained such an influence as few can acquire; those who fled were branded with a stigma of cowardice which must have seriously impaired their influence when, the danger over, they returned to their posts.

One great hindrance to the influence of the Church on social life arose from a cause the very opposite to one of the two reasons alleged by Eachard for the 'contempt of the clergy.' The Caroline age is rightly called the golden age of English theology, but that theology would have affected the masses more if it had been of a less precious metal. Jeremy Taylor, Barrow, South, Thorndike, Hammond, Sparrow, Gunning, Stillingfleet, and the rest are constantly quoted as authorities, but I doubt whether their works could be placed with advantage in the hands of 'the general reader.' At a later date the nonjuring divines were mostly refined and cultured men, and their influence was chiefly among the refined and cultured. It is not that the great Caroline divines are difficult to understand, or that they loved to deal with abstruse doctrines. On the contrary, they strove of all things to be practical, but practical, in the sense of influencing the practice of the multitude, they were not. Who would hope to convert a vulgar drunkard or debauchee from his evil ways by putting into his hands a volume of Barrow or Jeremy Taylor? Such writers would be, to use a modern phrase, quite out of touch with him. The difficulty here hinted at has been a difficulty of the Anglican Church, more felt by it than by either the Romanists on the one hand or any of the sects on the other, but never more so than in the latter half of the seventeenth century.

CHAPTER IX.

THE CHURCH AND OTHER RELIGIOUS BODIES.

THE relation of the Church to other religious bodies is too important a feature in the Church life of our period to be altogether ignored; though, as it more concerns religious thought than religious life, and is therefore in some points more suitable for a controversial treatise than for a work of this kind, it will suffice to touch upon the subject lightly.

The first point which naturally suggests itself in this connection is the relationship between the Church and the English nonconformists. And, at the outset, let us frankly acknowledge that, so far as the Church in general, and individual churchmen in particular, fostered or sanctioned that spirit of persecution which unquestionably existed more or less during the whole of our period, and especially the earliest and latest years of it, a grievous fault was committed. But in common fairness several points must be taken into full account, which are far too apt to be overlooked.

(1) It is obviously most unfair to judge the seventeenth century by the standard of the nineteenth.[1] At the earlier date the true principles of religious toleration were most imperfectly understood on all sides. It was generally thought that it was nothing less than a most culpable crime to tolerate error; and error was, of course, any set of opinions with which the holders of power did not happen to agree. How rigorously the Presbyterians, when they were dominant in England, acted upon this principle, and

---

[1] I must apologise for so often repeating this warning; but the necessity meets one at every turn when reading modern histories of that period.

how bitterly they denounced any attempt to ignore it, need not here be specified. The Independents—to their honour be it recorded—were more tolerant, but they made several exceptions to their toleration, and as the Church was one of these exceptions, it was more likely that the remembrance of their toleration would exasperate than conciliate churchmen.

(2) The question as to how to deal practically with the nonconformists was by no means a simple one. It is all very well to suggest in an airy way that they should have been suffered to worship God after their own fashion, while we worshipped Him in ours. But would they have been content with this sort of 'happy family' arrangement? The vast majority, who were Presbyterians, assuredly would not.[1] A very small number of the nonconformists at the Restoration were dissenters. Most of them were as strongly in favour of one National Church as the strictest churchman in the kingdom.

(3) The enormous provocation which the Church had received ought surely to be taken into account. True, it is no sufficient excuse to say that the persecution was only retaliation,[2] for one has yet to learn that revenge is a Christian virtue. But churchmen may at least claim that some allowance should be made for the natural exasperation of men who had seen the most cherished objects of their veneration rudely destroyed and insulted; damage done which was simply irreparable, principles outraged which were in their eyes sacred. When the turn of the wheel again gave them the upper hand, it would have been more than human nature if they could have regarded with favour the claims of those to whose principles they attributed all these disasters.

(4) It ought not to be forgotten that there was a very

[1] For example, the Presbyterians repudiated the 'Declaration of Indulgence.'

[2] This was said. See the *Brief Martyrology &c. of the London Clergy* in the Harleian Miscellany, with the suggestive motto 'Nec lex est æquior ulla.'

real and widespread feeling that both the Church and the Monarchy were still in danger. Whether there were any sufficient grounds for the alarm is another question; but that it was quite genuine, no one who studies impartially contemporary documents can for a moment doubt.

(5) It is most necessary to distinguish between the legitimate results of Church principles, and the acts of politicians whether ecclesiastical or lay,—two things which have been often confounded. A very striking case in point may be found in the marked change for the better in the treatment of nonconformists which resulted from the succession of Sancroft to Sheldon in the primacy. Sancroft was a true English churchman, Sheldon was a statesman in a mitre. When the churchman took the place of the statesman at the helm, the spirit of persecution was arrested.[1] And, as a rule, it was those who were conformists rather than churchmen who were most cruel. One of the most violent writers against nonconformity was the recreant Samuel Parker, whom no one will accuse of being a strong churchman. The prelate who (next to Sheldon) is popularly supposed to have been the most harsh in his treatment of nonconformists, was Bishop Seth Ward, whose churchmanship was of a very lax type. Bishop Sanderson, on the other hand, a model churchman of the very best type, 'signified his concern that some things were carried so high in the ecclesiastical settlement, which,' he said, 'should not have been if he could have prevented it,'[2] and was uniformly mild in his treatment of nonconformists.[3] So was Juxon, a true son of the Church.[4] So was Bishop Ken, the very best representative, perhaps, of Church principles in his own or any age. 'The Church of England,' he said, 'teaches

---

[1] See Wilkins' *Concilia* for a proof of this; a proof all the more striking because it is given by a mere dry statement of facts, without pointing out the significance of them.

[2] See Calamy's *Account of My Own Life*.

[3] See Perry's *History of the Church of England*, ii. p. 370.

[4] See Hook's *Lives of Archbishops*: 'Juxon,' xi. p. 436.

me charity towards those who dissent from me,' and in accordance with that teaching he ever acted. So was Bishop Earle, perhaps the most popular of all the bishops of the Restoration era, and a thorough churchman in the spiritual sense. But the fact is, it was popular feeling that was so strong in favour of suppressing nonconformity. All that was done, was done in accordance with the national will, and was at least as welcome to the laity as to the clergy. It is a well-known fact that the Act of Uniformity and the rest of the 'Clarendonian Code' would have been far less rigorous if they had been framed solely by the House of Lords, where the bishops in the flush of their regained power must have had great weight in such matters. It was in the House of Commons that the greatest intolerance prevailed. We have curious instances of the feeling of bitterness against nonconformity in the diaries of such men as Pepys and Sir John Reresby,[1] upon both of whom the true principles of the Church exercised very small influence. At the same time it is not denied that some churchmen of an unquestionably high type, such e.g. as Cosin, and Patrick in his earlier life, were in favour of harsh dealing with nonconformists. And it is deeply to be regretted that this was the case. The Church could well have afforded to dispense with the aid of the secular arm; nay, as the results of the Toleration Act abundantly proved, her position would have been positively strengthened if it had rested purely on moral and intellectual grounds, not on force.

It is a more pleasing task in dealing with this question of the relationship of the Church to nonconformists, to turn to the many instances of kindness which occurred. As is

---

[1] Sir John calls King Charles' 'Proclamation for the indulgence of tender consciences (1671) the most violent blow that had been given to the Church of England from the day of the Restoration. All sectaries,' he adds in dismay, ' now publicly repaired to their meetings and conventicles; nor could all the laws afterwards, and the most rigorous execution of them, ever suppress these separatists or bring them to due conformity.' (*Memoirs*, p. 174.)

so often the case, individuals were far more kindly and considerate when acting in their individual capacity than when acting as part of a mass. In the Savoy Conference, for instance, according to Baxter, no two men were more bitter against nonconformity than Morley and Gunning; and yet both showed personally great kindness towards nonconformists. Morley, we are told, 'stopped proceedings against Mr. Sprint, an ejected minister, and invited him to dinner, endeavouring to soften down the terms of conformity; and drank to an intermeddling country mayor in a cup of canary, advising him to let dissenters live in quiet, in many of whom, he was satisfied, there was the fear of God, and he thought they were not likely to be gained by rigour or severity.'[1] Mr. J. Farrol, the ejected minister of Selborne, 'was frequently desired to visit his Lordship' (Bishop Morley, in whose diocese of Winchester Selborne lay), 'and upon repeated assurances of being welcome to him, he went, and was very courteously and respectfully entertained by him several times at his table.' 'His Lordship,' it is added, 'was free in discoursing with him upon past times; and he observed that when he spoke of Mr. Dod (the Puritan) who taught him Hebrew and was otherwise helpful to him, he made this addition, "who is now in Heaven."'[2] When Gunning succeeded the eminent Dr. Tuckney in the Mastership of S. John's and Regius Professorship of Divinity at Cambridge, he allowed the ejected divine 'a very considerable annuity for his whole life.'[3] Archbishop Sharp, the one blot in whose character was his advocacy of some of the harsh measures against nonconformity at the close of Queen Anne's reign, was, when rector of S. Giles', so intimate with the nonconforming Baxter, who lived in the parish, that Baxter consulted him on the delicate

---

[1] Stoughton's *Church of the Restoration*, i. p. 478.
[2] E. Calamy's *Account of the Ejected Ministers &c.*, ii. p. 344.
[3] *Athenæ Oxonienses*, iv. p. 140, and Granger's *Biographical History of England*, iii. p. 49.

question of taking a wife.¹ Stillingfleet, who in his public capacity was no friend of nonconformity, yet 'sheltered in his rectory at Sutton one of the ejected ministers, and took a large house which he converted into a school, for another.'² Even Archbishop Sheldon, that arch-enemy of nonconformity, presented to the living of Ashwell Ralph Cudworth, who, 'all through the Commonwealth was in some ways peculiarly associated with Cromwell and his friends,'³ and 'often treated very kindly' Thomas White, the ejected lecturer of S. Bride's, whom he 'protected at the chappel at Ludgate.'⁴ Bishop Seth Ward, another violent opponent of nonconformity, 'always retained a grateful sense of John Howe's kindness,' and on one occasion, if not more, did him substantial service. 'Howe, having preached at the house of a gentleman whom he had been visiting for a few days, found on returning home that an officer from the bishop's court had been to apprehend him, and, not finding him, had given notice that citations were out against Howe and his friend. But the bishop received Howe with the utmost politeness, and treated him as an old acquaintance. Neither Howe nor his friend, after the interview, heard anything more about the process.'⁵ Howe also continued to be on intimate terms with Bishops Stillingfleet, Wilkins, Kidder, Sharp, Tillotson, and other eminent clergymen.⁶ Dr. Watts 'lived on terms of good-will and friendship with some of the most eminent of the clergy,'⁷ and a greater man, Lightfoot, was allowed, in spite of his nonconformity, to continue Master of S. Catherine's, Cambridge, after the Restoration.⁸ Dr. Wrench, fellow of S. John's,

---

[1] See Tyerman's *Life of Samuel Wesley*, p. 230. [2] Stoughton, i. p. 292.
[3] Dr. Tulloch's *Rational Theology &c.*, ii. p. 204.
[4] Calamy, *Account of Ejected Ministers &c.*, ii. p. 31.
[5] *Life &c. of John Howe*, by Henry Rogers, p. 180 &c.
[6] Rogers, p. 215 &c.
[7] *Memoir of Dr. Isaac Watts*, by R. Southey, prefixed to his *Lyric Poems*.
[8] See Worthington's *Diary*, i. p. 54, *note*.

Cambridge, finding at the Restoration a worthy man in his place, would not disturb him.[1] Bishop Laney of Peterborough, in his primary visitation before S. Bartholomew's Day, said very significantly to the assembled clergy, 'Not I, but the law,' and though he had suffered considerably from the Presbyterians at Cambridge in 1644, he could, in the see of Lincoln, 'look through his fingers,' and he suffered a worthy nonconformist to preach publicly very near him for some years together.[2] Edmund Calamy tells us that 'several ministers of the Established Church used to visit at his father's house, and at his grandfather's,'[3]—both, of course, dissenters, and that Mr. Gilbert, an ejected minister, was not only friendly with, but received substantial support from several of the most eminent clergy at Oxford.[4] Ambrose Barnes, a strong dissenter, records how at Newcastle 'Vicar Marsh would step out privately by night, and make him respectful visits, throwing the blame of the rigorous proceedings upon the misfortunes of the times.'[5] Dr. Bridgman, rector of Worthembury, 'acted kindly to Philip Henry, and showed no sympathy with the ruling powers,'[6] and several instances are given of the kindness and forbearance of Bishop Nicolson of Gloucester to nonconformists in his diocese.[7] Of course, those who love to fan the flame of discord may easily find instances of a different mode of treatment; but on the whole it is abundantly clear that the leniency in carrying out the laws against nonconformists forms a pleasing contrast to the harshness of those laws themselves.

When we turn to the Anglican Church's relationship to the Reformed Churches abroad, which were certainly more in sympathy with her home nonconformists than with herself, all is changed. A very marked distinction

---

[1] See Zouch's *Life of Dean Sudbury*, p. 73.　[2] Stoughton, i. p. 488.
[3] *Account of My Own Life*, i. pp. 74 and 89.　[4] *Ibid.* p. 270 &c.
[5] *Memoirs of Ambrose Barnes* (Surtees Society), p. 9.
[6] Stoughton, i. p. 207.　[7] *Ibid.* pp. 291-3.

was drawn between those who lacked episcopal ordination because they could not help themselves, and those who deliberately rejected it, when it was to be had, and by none more than by high churchmen. Bishop Cosin, for instance, whose severity towards nonconformists at home was a blot upon an otherwise fine character, laid great and frequent stress upon this difference. 'I never,' he said, 'refused to join with the French Protestants at Charenton or anywhere else, in all things wherein they join with the Church of England.'[1] He expressly declared his opinion for communicating with Geneva rather than Rome;[2] and drew a synopsis, in parallel columns, of the divergent views of the Roman Catholics and the Reformed Churches, summing up in favour of the latter on every point.[3] In this he strictly followed in the lines of his great predecessor at Durham, Bishop Morton, who was also a churchman of a very stiff type. But 'as for our brethren,' he says in his will, 'the Protestants of foreign churches reformed, the most learned and judicious of themselves have bewailed their misery for want of bishops. And therefore God forbid that I should be so uncharitable as to condemn them for no churches for that which is their infelicity, not their fault. But as for our perverse Protestants at home, I cannot say the same of them, seeing they impiously reject that which the other piously desire.'[4] Dean Granville and Archdeacon Basire naturally followed the lead of Bishop Cosin. 'I would not,' writes the former, 'unchurch the Foreign Protestants. They must conform with us here, and I with them there;'[5] while the latter enters more at length into his reasons for

[1] See *Remains of Dean Granville*, Part II., p. 37.

[2] See *Bishop Cosin his opinion, when Dean of Peterborough and in exile, for communicating rather with Geneva than with Rome &c.*, in two *Letters*, 1684.

[3] See *The State of us that adhere to the Church of England*, by John Cosin, Bishop of Durham. Also his letter to Dr. Richard Watson in Bishop Cosin's *Works*, vol. iv. (Lib. of Angl.-Cath. Theol.), p. 386 &c.

[4] Quoted in Lathbury's *History of Convocation*, p. 293.

[5] See Granville's *Remains*, Part II., p. 36 &c.

'a moderate connivance at inordinate ordinations.'[1] Archbishop Bramhall indignantly denies that 'all or any considerable part of episcopal divines in England do unchurch either all or the most part of the Protestant Churches,' and elucidates the whole matter in his own powerful style.[2] John Scott, in his 'Christian Life,' clearly explains that 'whenever the Divine Providence doth by unavoidable necessity deprive any Church of its episcopacy, it thereby, and for the *present* at least, and whilst the necessity continues, releases it from the obligation of the institution of episcopacy; and therefore so long as it doth not renounce episcopacy, but still continues in communion with other churches that enjoy it, it ought to be looked upon and communicated with as a true member (though a maimed one) of the church catholic;' and then he contrasts this case with that of those who wilfully separate themselves.[3] And Sancroft, in a letter to Dr. Covel, chaplain to the Prince of Orange at the Hague (1678) declares that he will never abandon his efforts in behalf of an union with Foreign Protestants.[4] The above, it will be observed, were all high churchmen; the low churchmen, of course, found no difficulty about the matter.

The sentiments in favour of foreign Protestants found a very practical expression in 1685, when the Revocation of the Edict of Nantes flooded England with French Protestant refugees. The extraordinary sympathy which was shewn with these poor sufferers has already been described; and here, again, none were more active than the high churchmen. Bishop Ken gave them a fine of 4,000*l*.,

---

[1] See *The Dead Man's Speech &c.*

[2] See *Bishop Bramhall's Vindication of himself and the Episcopal Clergy from the Presbyterian charge of Popery by Baxter, in his Treatise of the Grotian Religion &c.*, 1672. Baxter was one of those good men who never know when they are beaten; otherwise this extraordinarily powerful work would have crushed his not very powerful adversary.

[3] *Christian Life*, iii. pp. 312-3.

[4] Letter quoted in Molesworth's *History of the Church of England*, p. 123.

which happened to fall in at the time; boldly preached in their behalf at the Chapel Royal before James II., who of course had no real sympathy with them, though he was forced to receive them favourably; and wrote to his clergy a touching appeal 'to be brotherly kind to strangers, to Christian strangers, whose distress is very great, and is in all respects worthy of our tenderest commiseration.'[1] Turner, Bishop of Ely, high churchman though he was, actually provided for the refugees a chapel at Thorney Abbey, where they might worship without conforming to the Church of England;[2] and Lloyd, Bishop of S. Asaph, undertook, so long as he held the see, to allow a French Protestant 20*l.* a year and his board.[3]

It was, however, not unnatural that in time churchmen began to feel that the refugees, by their settlement in England, virtually swelled the ranks of nonconformists, and hence the learned Bingham addressed to them a characteristically exhaustive argument in favour of their joining the Church of England.[4]

The French refugees, having thriven so well, were followed a quarter of a century later by a swarm of 'poor Palatinates;' the sympathy in behalf of the latter, however, was by no means so unanimous, and an outcry arose that the influx of so many foreigners (chiefly Lutherans), would endanger the Church of England.[5] Still, on the whole, the feeling in favour of foreign Protestants was a marked feature of the whole of our period.

The relation of the Church to Romanists, whether at home or abroad, may be very briefly described. It was from first to last, and from the highest of high churchmen to the most latitudinarian of low, one of deep, uncompro-

---

[1] Ken's *Prose Works* (Round's edition), p. 484.
[2] See Miss Strickland's *Seven Bishops*: 'Turner.'   [3] *Ibid.*: 'Lloyd.'
[4] *A serious Address to the Refugees of the French Church to join in constant and full Communion with the Church of England.* (Bingham's *Works*, vol. ix.)
[5] See Earl Stanhope's *Reign of Queen Anne*, p. 299.

mising hostility. In the reign of James II., when the most systematic and not altogether unsuccessful efforts were made to bring men over to the king's religion, it is computed that for every one that was lost to the Church through Romanism, ten were gained from the ranks of nonconformists who appreciated the zeal of the clergy against popery. And by none was Rome more heartily opposed than by high churchmen generally and nonjurors in particular. Collier, Leslie, Hickes, Ken, Brett, Turner, Sancroft, Fell, Nelson, and countless other names of high churchmen, appear in print as strong anti-Romanists. Perhaps the most powerful body of anti-Roman literature that has ever been published, is that which was written by divines of the Church of England during this period, and afterwards collected by Bishop Gibson for his valuable 'Preservative against Popery.' The few converts who were won over to Romanism were so feeble and for the most part so obviously led by other motives than those of conviction, that they are scarcely worthy even of being termed exceptions that proved the rule. It is true, indeed, that there were periodical and utterly unreasonable panics during which the clergy were suspected of Romanising, notably in 1673 when the Test Act was passed, in 1678 when the infamous Oates Plot was at its height, and in 1680 when the bishops very properly voted against the Exclusion Bill;[1] but the suspicion was never seriously entertained for any length of time.

In fact, all through our period the danger lay quite in another direction; Romanists were cruelly persecuted, and most of all when latitudinarianism was in the ascendant.[2]

---

[1] 'They tore out,' it was said, 'the very bowels of the Church of England.' A lampoon entitled *The Bishops and the Bill* was very popular. Each verse ended, 'The bishops, the bishops, they threw out the bill,' and the last, 'To throw out the bishops who threw out the bill.'

[2] 'After the Revolution,' writes Lord Campbell (*Lives of the Chancellors*, vol. iv.), 'the penal code against Romanists was made far more severe and revolting than it had ever been under Elizabeth or any of the four kings of the Stuart line.' The excellent Lord Somers, a Whig and a latitudinarian in Church affairs, was largely responsible for these laws.

The same excuse, indeed, may be made as was made for the persecution of nonconformists, viz. that political causes contributed far more than theological to bring about the harsh treatment of Romanists, but the fact remains that persecution of, not toying with Rome, was a blot of the period.

There is yet another Church whose chequered fortunes stirred up a deep interest in the breasts of English churchmen. At no part of our period was the Episcopal Church of Scotland in a satisfactory state. After having been cruelly persecuted during the Rebellion, it was re-established under Charles II. on a radically wrong basis, and cruel persecutions were instituted, rather in its name and on its professed behalf, than by the Church itself. The political element was at this time too strong in the Church of England, but it was far stronger in that of Scotland. The bishops who were forced upon Scotland (always excepting the saintly Leighton), were not churchmen at all in the spiritual sense of the term, while the chief instrument in the persecution, Lauderdale, was not a churchman even in name. When the turn of the wheel brought the Presbyterians again into power after the Revolution, the Episcopal clergy were cruelly used, and the sympathy of their English brethren was strongly awakened in their behalf. The 'rabbled' ministers gratefully acknowledged that many of them were saved by the charity of their English brethren from actual starvation; and when Anne succeeded William, it was through the intervention of English churchmen, especially Archbishop Sharp, who used his great influence with the queen, and almost insisted upon her taking the matter up,[1] that the persecution by very slow degrees abated. William III. could hardly be expected to give

[1] 'He spoke earnestly to the Queen about the Episcopal clergy in Scotland, and charged her again upon her conscience (when she made some excuses) with some warmth to take care to put a stop to these persecutions. She said she would.' This was in 1708. (*Life of Archbishop Sharp*, by his son, vol. ii.)

much power or privilege to the Scotch Church, for the clergy were Jacobites almost to a man; but this does not in the least account for its persecution by Presbyterians, who made no secret of the fact that their object was to destroy Prelacy, root and branch. Sympathy with their distressed brethren across the Tweed was of course felt most keenly by nonjurors such as Ken and Nelson, but even low churchmen, like Burnet, were not insensible to their sufferings. A large consignment of Bibles and Prayer Books, chiefly, it would seem, at the instance of Robert Nelson, was sent, both as a practical aid and as a token of intercommunion. The political question does not appear to have had much to do with the sympathy of the English with the Scotch Church; it was the generous sympathy of a prosperous with a distressed sister, with whom she was in the fullest terms of communion; for there does not appear to have been the slightest trace of any doubt about the English and the Scotch Churches being bound closely together all through our period.

The relationship between the English and the Irish Churches need not be dwelt upon. They were in fact one, 'the United Church of England and Ireland.' Several great names form connecting links between the two branches,— John Bramhall, Jeremy Taylor, George Rust, Charles Leslie, Jonathan Swift, and others among the clergy, Robert Boyle and James Bonnell among the laity. The harmony between the two bodies does not appear to have been ever interrupted; but there are no traces of that warm sympathy—circumstances did not occur to bring it out—which, as we have seen, existed between England and Scotland.

In conclusion the reader must be reminded that this only professes to be a sketch of certain phases of Church life. Had it professed to be a complete history of Church life, much would of course have had to be said upon matters which are here touched upon very lightly or not at all.

The work of Convocation, for instance, the schemes of comprehension, the political acts in which the Church was concerned, the controversial writings of the time, are all parts of Church life in its broadest sense, but not in the narrower sense in which the term is used here. But even of what the work professed to do the performance is woefully imperfect. Perhaps, however, it may stimulate some other literary workman to explore the same mine; such an one will find a rich vein of ore which will amply repay his toil.

LIST OF AUTHORITIES QUOTED OR REFERRED TO.

No author is included who has been quoted at second hand. The dates of the editions used have been given for the convenience of those who desire to verify the quotations.

Account of the Societies for Reformation of Manners, (Defoe) 1699
Addison, Joseph, Life of, by Lucy Aikin, 2 vols. 1843
    ,,   ,,   Evidences of Christianity, about 1715
Addison, Lancelot, Primitive Institution, &c. 1674
    ,,   ,,   Christian's Manual, 5th ed. 1700
Advice to Clergy of Diocese of Lincoln, by Bishop Gardiner, 2nd ed. 1697
Advice to the Clergy in six Sermons, by J. Cock, 1664-88
Allestree, Dr. R., Life of, by Bp. Fell, new ed. 1848
Amusements of Clergymen and Christians in general, new ed. 1820
Anderson, J. S. M., History of the Colonial Church, 3 vols. 1856
Angliæ Notitiæ, E. and J. Chamberlayne, 16th ed. 1687
Animadversions on 'The Naked Truth,' 1676
Anniversary Sermons preached before S. P. G. 1845
Answer to Grounds, &c., for Contempt of Clergy (B. Oley ?), 1671
Apology of author of 'Asses complaint against Balaam'
Art of Contentment, by Lady Pakington (?) Ed. W. Pridden, 1841
Ashmole, Elias, Memoirs of, &c., by way of Diary, 1717
Asses complaint against Balaam, L. Griffin, 1663
Astell, Mary, The Christian Religion as professed by a Daughter of the Church of England, 1705
    ,,   ,,   Serious Proposal to Ladies, 1694
    ,,   ,,   Letters concerning the Love of God. Pub. by J. Norris, 2nd ed. 1705
Athenæ Cantabrigienses, from Cole MSS. in British Museum
Athenæ Oxonienses, Anthony à Wood, new ed. Bliss, 1813
Athenian Oracle, 1706

Atterbury, Bp., Memoirs and Correspondence of, G. Folkestone Williams, 2 vols. 1869
" " Life by Stackhouse
" " Sermons, 3 vols. 8th ed. 1766

Babington, Rev. Churchill, Character of Clergy in latter part of 17th century, 1849
Bagehot, W., Biographical Studies, ed. R. H. Hutton, 1881
Baker, T., Memoirs of life and writings, from Papers of Z. Grey, 1784
" " Reflections upon Learning, 6th ed. 1727
Ballard, George, Memoirs of British Ladies, 1775
Barlow, Bp. T., Cases of Conscience resolved, 1692
" " Genuine Remains of, 1693
Barnes, Ambrose, Memoirs of, Surtees Soc. 1867
Barrow, Dr. Isaac, Works, with Life by Whewell, ed. Napier, 1859
Barwick, Vita Joannis, by P. Barwick.—
" " Translation with notes (by Hilkiah Bedford ?) 1724
Basire, Dr. Isaac, Correspondence of, ed. Darnell, 1831
Bathurst, Dean Ralph, Life and Literary Remains of (T. Warton)
Beveridge, Bp. Life of, prefixed to Private Thoughts, ed. of 1825
" " Life pref. to ed. of Works by C. Bradley, 1828
" " Private Thoughts, vol. viii. of Works, Lib. Angl. Cath. Theol.
" " Theol. Works., Lib. Angl. Cath. Theol. 1842
" " Defence of Sternhold and Hopkins' Book of Psalms.
" " Sermons on Ministry and Ordinances of Church of England, new ed. 1837
Bingham, Jos., Works, in 9 vols. with Life prefixed, 1840
Bonnell. James, Life and Character of, by Archdeacon Hamilton, 1707
Boyer's Annals of the Reign of Queen Anne, 2 vols.
Boyle, Hon. R., Birch's Life of, 1744
Bramhall, Abp., Vindication &c., from the charge of Popery, 1672
" " True Notion of the Worship of God, 1673
Bray, Dr. Thomas, Essay towards promoting all necessary and useful knowledge, 1697
" " Bibliotheca Catechetica, 1702
" " Bibliotheca Parochialis, 1697
" " Public Spirit illustrated in the Life and Designs of, 1746
Brewer, J. S. A., English Studies, 1881
Brief Account of the New Sect of Latitudinarians, by S. P. 1669
Brokesby, F., Life of Mr. Henry Dodwell, 1715
Brown, Works of Mr. Thomas, 3 vols. 9th ed. 1760
Bull, Bp., Works, ed. 1846, esp. Charge to clergy of S. David's, in 1708

LIST OF AUTHORITIES

Bull, Bp., Life by R. Nelson, Oxford ed. 1845
Burnet, Bp., History of my own Times, in 4 vols. 1815
    ,,   ,,   Lives of Sir M. Hale, Earl of Rochester &c. new ed. 1829
    ,,   ,,   Four discourses delivered to clergy of Sarum, 1694
    ,,   ,,   Discourse of Pastoral Care, 1692
    ,,   ,,   Four Sermons by, (preached before the King &c.)
    ,,   ,,   Lives, Characters, &c. and an Address to Posterity, ed. Bp. Jebb, 2nd ed. 1853
    ,,   ,,   Visitation Charges, 1704, 1708, 1714
    ,,   ,,   Elizabeth, Methods of Devotion, with Life by T. Goodwyn, 2nd ed. 1709
Burton, Jas. Hill, History of the Reign of Queen Anne, 1880

Calamy, Edmund, Account of my own Life, 2 vols. 2nd ed. 1830
    ,,   ,,   Account of Ejected Ministers, 2nd ed. 1710
Campbell, Lord, Lives of the Lord Chancellors, vol. iii. 1845
Carstares, William, — Storey, 1674
Cartwright, T., Bishop of Chester, Diary of, Camden Soc. 1843
Carwithen, J. B. S., History of the Church of England, 1833
Causes of Decay of Christian Piety, ed. of 1765
Cave, Dr. Wm., Primitive Christianity
Cawdrey, Zachary, Discourse of Patronage, 1675
Chaplains' Petition to the Hon. House for redress of grievances, 1693
Character of England in 1659, (John Evelyn)
Chichester, Life of John (Lake), Bishop of, 1690
Christian Monitor (Rawlet's), 25th ed. 1699
Clarke, Dr. Adam, Memoirs of the Wesley Family, 1823
Clergyman's Vade Mecum, 3rd ed. 1709
    ,,   Advocate, Account of Ill-treatment of Church and Clergy, 1711
Coleridge, S. T., Notes on English Divines, 1853
Collectanea Curiosa from MSS. of Abp. Sancroft (Tanner MSS.), 1781
Collier, Jeremy, Ecclesiastical History in 9 vols., vol. viii. 1841
    ,,   ,,   Essays upon Moral Subjects, 7th ed. 1732
    ,,   ,,   Life of, by F. Barham, Pref. to Eccl. Hist. 1840
    ,,   ,,   Short Account of the Profaneness and Immorality of the Stage, 1730
Comber, Dean Thomas, Companion to the Temple and Closet, 1673
    ,,   ,,   ,,   Discourse concerning Excommunication
Compton, Life of Bishop, (undated)
    ,,   Episcopalia, Letters to clergy of London diocese, 1683 &c.
Correspondence of Henry, Earl of Clarendon, and Lawrence, Earl of Rochester, ed. Singe, 1828
Cosin, Bishop, Correspondence of, Surtees Soc. 1872

Cosin, Bishop, State of us that adhere to Church of England
„   „   Works of, vol. iv., Lib. Angl. Cath. Theol. 1851
Cradock, Zachary, 25 Sermons preached before King Charles II. 1742

Dartmouth, Lord, Notes on Burnet's 'Own Times'
Dawes, Sir W., Abp. of York, Whole Works of, with Life of Author, 1733
'Dead Man's Real Speech,' Funeral Sermon on Bishop Cosin, with a Brief of his life by I. Basire, 1672
Debary, T., History of the Church of England from accession of James II. to 1717, 1860
Defence of Pluralities as now practised in the Church of England (H. Wharton), 2nd ed. 1703
Devotions in the Ancient Way of Offices, 2nd ed. 1701
Discourse of profiting by Sermons, 1683
Disney, J., Essay on execution of Laws against Immorality, 2nd ed. 1710
Dodwell, H., Treatise concerning Instrumental Music in Churches, 2nd ed. 1700
„   „   Letter of Advice for the susception of Holy Orders, 2nd ed. 1680
Dolben, Archbishop, Sermons of
Dunton, John, Life and Errors of, 1818
Duppa, Bishop Brian, Holy Rules and Helps to Devotion, 2nd ed. 1818

Eachard, John, Works of, in 3 vols. 1774
Earle, Bishop, Microcosmography, new ed. P. Bliss, 1811
Echard, Lawrence, History of the Revolution, &c. 1725
Edwards, W. E., Sermon before the Grateful Society (on Colston), 1783
Ellis's Original Letters, 2nd series, 1837
English Poets from Chaucer to Cowper, Chalmers, vol. viii. 1810
Episcopalia, or Letters of Henry (Compton), Bishop of London, to clergy, 1686
Essay concerning Preaching (Glanvill of Bath ?), 1678
Essay on the Great Affinity of the two Professions of Law and Divinity, 1714
Evelyn, John, Diary, 5 vols. 1827

Foulis, H., History of the Plots and Conspiracies of our pretended Saints, 1662
Fowler, Bishop of Gloucester, Visitation Charge, 1707

Fox, C. J., History of the early part of the reign of James II., 1808
Frampton, Bishop of Gloucester, Life, ed. by T. Simpson, 1876
Fuller's Worthies, Nichol's ed. in 2 vols. 1811

GENTLEMAN's Calling, ed. of 1765
Gladstone, Rt. Hon. W. E., on Macaulay, Gleanings, vol. ii.
Godolphin, Mrs., Life of, by J. Evelyn, pub. by Bishop of Oxford, 1847
Government of the Tongue, by author of Whole Duty of Man
Granger, J., Biographical History of England, vol. iii. 1804
Granville, Dean, Remains of, 2 vols. Surtees Soc., 1865
Grey, Zachary, and Maddox, Examination of Neal's History of Puritans, 1737
Gunning, Bishop P., The Paschal or Lent Feast, Lib. Angl. Cath. Theol. 1845

HACKET, Bishop, Memoirs of Life of Archbishop Williams, 1715
    „   „   Articles of Enquiry at Visitation of 1668
    „   „   Christian Consolations, New ed. with account of Author, 1840
    „   „   Life and Death of, T. Plume, ed. by Mackenzie Walcott, 1865
Haddan, A. W., Remains, ed. by Bishop Forbes, 1876
Hallam's Constitutional History, 3 vols. 1854
    „   Literature of Europe, 3 vols. 1843
Hammond, Henry, Practical Catechism, with Life of Author, Lib. Angl. Cath. Theol. 1847
Happy Ascetick, by Dr. Horneck, 1681
Hastings, Lady Elizabeth, Historical Character of, by T. Barnard, 1742
Hawkins, E., Historical Notices of Missions &c., 1845
Hearne, Life of Mr. Thos. from his own MS. copy in Bodleian, 1772
Henry, Philip, Diary, ed. by M. H. Lee, 1882
Herbert, George, Priest to the Temple, with Pref. by B. Oley, 1675
Heywood, Oliver, Hunter's Life of, 1842
Hickes, Dean G., Posthumous Discourses, pub. by N. Spinckes, 1726
    „   „   „   Apologetical Vindication of Church of England, 1686
    „   „   „   Constitution of the Catholic Church, 1716
    „   „   „   Letters with a Popish Priest, 2nd ed. 1715
Higgons, Bevil, Remarks on Burnet's Own Times, Works, vol. ii. 1736
Histoire de la Revolution de l'Angleterre par M. Guizot, 1841
History of England continued from Sir J. Mackintosh, Cab. Cycl. 1836
History of England under House of Stuart, Soc. Dif. Useful Knowledge, 1840
History of the Great Plague, (Defoe), 1756
Holy Time of Christmas defended against Nonconformists, 1676

Hook, Dean, Lives of the Archbishops of Canterbury.
Hooper, Bp. of Bath and Wells, Short Character of, from Mist's Journal, 1730
" " Works of, new ed. in 2 vols. 1855
Hopton, Susanna, A collection of Meditations and Devotions, pub. by N. Spinckes, 1717
Horneck, Dr. A., Life, by Bp. Kidder, 1698
" Dr. A., Summary Account of, in a letter to a friend, 1697
Hough, Bp., Life of, by J. Wilmot, 1812
Howe, John, Life and Character of, by H. Rogers, 1836

IMPARTIAL Vindication of the Clergy of the Church of England, 1680

JOHNSON, John, of Cranbrook, Life of, by T. Brett, 1748
Jubilee Tract, S.P.C.K., Great Success from Small Beginnings, Murray, 1849
Jura Cleri, Apology for the rights of the long-despised clergy, by Philo-Basileus, Philoclerus, 1661
Juxon, Abp., and his Times, Memoirs of, by W. H. Marsh, 1869

KEN, Bp., Prose Works, with Life by Hawkins, (J. T. Round), 1838
" " Life by Canon Bowles, 1830
" " Life by a Layman, 1851
" " Manual of Prayers for use of Winchester Scholars, ed. G. M. (George Moberly), 1840
" " Prayers for the use of all persons who come to the Bath for cure, (Markland), 1849
" " Poems, devotional and didactic
Kennet, Bp. White, Life of, 1730
" " History of England, vol. iii. 1706
" " Case of Impropriations and Augmentation of Vicarages, 1704
" " The Christian Scholar, 5th ed. 1710
" " Unpublished MSS. in British Museum
Kettlewell, John, Life of, 1719
Kidder, Bp. Charge to clergy of Bath and Wells, 1692

LAKE, Bp., Account of the Profession made by, 1690
Lake, Dr. Edward, Diary, ed. P. Elliott, Camden Soc. 1846
" " " Officium Eucharisticum, 31st ed. 1843
Lathbury, T., History of Convocation, 2nd ed. 1853
" " History of the Nonjurors, 1845
" " History of the English Episcopacy from the Long Parliament to the Act of Uniformity, 1836

Lathbury, T., A History of the Convocation of the Church of England, 1842
Le Neve, John, Lives and Characters of Protestant Bishops of the Church of England since the Reformation, 1820
Leslie, Charles, Life prefixed to Theol. Works in 7 vols.
     „   „   Life, by Rev. R. J. Leslie, 1885
Letter from a minister in the country to a gentleman in London on the Reformation of Manners, 1701
Letter from one clergyman to another concerning ministers intermeddling with State affairs, 1714
Letters from the Bodleian, ed. Bliss, 1813
Life of James II. late king of England, 2nd ed. 1703
Lingard, Dr., History of England, vols. ix. and x. 1854
Lives of the English Bishops from the Restauration to the Revolution, 1733
Lloyd, Bp. of Worcester, Articles of Visitation, 1705
London Parishes in 1824
Lowth, Simon, Catechetical Questions, &c. 1673
Lucas, Dr. Richard, Enquiry after Happiness, new ed. 1803
   „   „   „   Practical Christianity &c. 7th ed. 1746
   „   „   „   Sermons in 3 vols. 2nd ed. 1722
   „   „   „   Twenty-four Sermons, 3rd ed. 1735
Luttrel, Narcissus, Brief Historical Relation of State Affairs, in 6 vols. (1678-1714), 1857

Macaulay, Lord, Eng. Men of Letters, J. C. Morison, 1882
   „   „   History of England, 2 vols. 1873
   „   „   Essays, 1 vol. 1872
Mackintosh, Sir J., Miscellaneous Works in 1 vol. 1851
Macpherson, J., Original Papers containing Secret History of Great Britain (1660-1714), 1775
   „   „   History of Great Britain (1660-1714), 1775
Mahaffy, J. P., Decay of Modern Preaching, 1882
Melmoth, William, Great Importance of a Religious Life, new ed. 1849
Milles, Isaac, Life of, new ed. 1842
Miscellanies of the Fuller's Worthies' Library, Dr. Grosart, 1871
Miseries of the Inferior Clergy, by T. Stackhouse, 1737
Molesworth, W. Nassau, History of the Church of England from 1660, 1882
More, Dr. Henry, Life of, by R. Ward, 1710
Mullinger, J. B., Cambridge Characteristics in the 17th Century, 1867

Naked Truth, The, Herbert Croft, Bishop of Hereford, 1675
Nelson, R., Address to Persons of Quality, 1715

Nelson, R., Great Duty of frequenting the Christian Sacrifice, 5th. ed. 1714
„ „ Life of Bishop Bull, 1845
„ „ Secretan's Life of, 1860
„ „ Festivals and Fasts, S. P. C. K. 1823
„ „ Practice of True Devotion, &c., 3rd. ed. 1716
Nichol's Literary Anecdotes of the 18th Century, vol. i.
Nicoll, John, Diary of Transactions in Scotland, 1650–67, 1836
Nicolson, Abp., Correspondence, 1809
Noble, Mark, Biog. Hist. of England, 1806
Norris, John, of Bemerton, on Religious Discourse in Common Conversation, 1702
„ „ Theory and Regulation of Love, 1688
„ „ Reason and Religion, 7th ed. 1724
„ „ Of Human Life, 1689
„ „ Practical Discourses
North, Roger, Examen
„ „ Lives of the Norths (Life of Dr. John North) new ed. 1826

OWEN, John, Orme's Life of, in Pref. to Owen's works, 1826

PALIN, W., History of the Church of England, 1688–1717, 1851
Parish Churches turned into Conventicles, by R. Hart, 1683
Parish Churches no Conventicles, by T. A. 1683
Parker, Samuel, De rebus sui temporis, 1726
Parkhurst, N., Life of Rev. Mr. Burkitt of Dedham, 1704
Paterson, James, Pietas Londinensis, 1714
Patrick, Bishop, Autobiography, new ed. 1839
„ „ Articles of Inquiry at Chichester, 1690
„ „ Advice to a Friend, new ed. 1847
„ „ Book for Beginners, or Help to young Communicants, 17th ed. 1713
„ „ Consolatory Discourses, 10th ed. 1783
„ „ Christian Sacrifice, 5th ed. 1679
„ „ Devout Christian instructed how to pray, 1672
„ „ Letters to his Clergy of Chichester Diocese, 1690
„ „ Mensa Mystica, 6th ed. 1702
„ „ Discourse concerning Prayer, 1686
„ „ On the Work of the Ministry, new ed. by Hawkins, 1841
„ „ Parable of the Pilgrim, 6th. ed. 1687
„ „ Poems, 1719
„ „ Treatise of Repentance and Fasting, esp. of the Lent Fast, 1686

Pearson, Bishop, Minor Theol. Works, with Memoirs of Author, Churton, 2 vols, 1844
Pepys, Samuel, Diary and Correspondence, ed. by Lord Braybrook, 3rd ed. 1848
Perry, Canon, History of the Church of England, 3 vols. 1861
Peterborough, Diocesan History, S. P. C. K., E. A. Poole
Pocock, Dr. E., Life of (Twells), repub. 1726
Practical Christian, The, a Devout Penitent, Sherlock, 6th ed. 1713
Prideaux, Dean Humphrey, Life of, 1748
„ „ Directions to Churchwardens, 3rd ed. 1713
Private Conference between a Rich Alderman and a Poor Vicar, 1670

Ranke, Leopold von, History of England principally in 17th Century, Tr. 1875
Rapin, Hist. of England, Tr., with continuation, by Tindal, 5th ed. 1760
Rawdon Papers, 1819
Rawlet, J., A Brief Account of (Dr. Bray), 1728
„ „ Christian Monitor
„ „ Poetic Miscellanies by, 1687
Reformation of Manners, A Satyr, 1702
Religio Medici, vol. ii. of Works of Sir T. Browne, Bohn's ed. 1852
Remains of T. Hearne (Reliquiæ Hearnianæ), P. Bliss, 1869
Representation of Present State of Religion, 1711
Representation of the State of Christianity in England, 1674
Reresby, Sir John, Travels and Memoirs of, 3rd ed. 1831
Royal Society, History of, by Bishop T. Spratt, 1667
„ „ Weld's History of, 1848
Russell, Rev. M., History of the Church in Scotland, 2 vols. 1834
Russell, Rachael, Lady, Life of, 3rd ed. 1820
„ „ „ Letters of, 3rd ed. 1792

Salisbury, Diocesan History, W. H. Jones, S. P. C. K.
Salmon, N., Impartial Examination of Burnet's Own Times, 2 vols. 1724
„ „ Lives of the English Bishops, from the Restoration to the Revolution
Sancroft, Abp., Life of, by Dr. G. D'Oyly, 2 vols. 1821
„ „ Familiar Letters of, to Mr. North, 1757
Sanderson, Bishop, Works, ed. Jacobson, 1854
Scoones, W. Baptiste, English Letters, 1880
Scott, Dr. John, The Christian Life, 3 vols., 10th ed. 1739
Scougal, H., Works, with Life of Author, new ed. 1765
Secretan, C. F., Memoirs of the Life, &c., of the pious R. Nelson, 1860
Selden, John, Life of, by J. Aikin, M. D. 1812
Selsey—Chichester, Diocesan History, S. P. C. K., Preb. Stephens, 1881

Serious Enquiry into the Present State of the Church of England, 1711
Seventeenth Century Studies, E. W. Gosse, 1883
Sharp, Abp. John, Life of, by his son, ed. T. Newcome, 2 vols. 1825
  „   „ Sermons, 2 vols., 9th ed. 1754
Sherlock, Dean W., Practical Discourse of Religious Assemblies, ed. H. Melville, Eng. Lib., vol. xi. 1840
  „   „   „ Practical Discourse concerning Death
Sherlock, R., of Winwick, Catechism &c. paraphrased, 10th ed. 1672
Short Account of several kinds of Societies, 1700
Sidney, Hon. H., Diary of Times of Charles II., ed. Blencowe, 1843
Skeat's History of the Free Churches
Smalridge, Bishop, Sixty Sermons, new ed. 1852
  „   „ Twelve Sermons, on different occasions, 1717
Smith, John, Select Discourses, 4th ed. (H. G. Williams), 1859
Smythies, W., Benefit of Early Piety, 15th ed. 1729
  „   „ Sermons (detached).
  „   „ Unworthy Non-communicant, 4th ed. 1707
Somers' Tracts, vol. xii.
South, Dr. Robert, Sermons in 6 vols. with Life of Writer (1697-1717)
Sparrow, Bp. A., Rationale upon the Book of Common Prayer, 7th ed. 1722
Spinckes, N., The Sick Man Visited, 4th ed. with life of author, 1731
  „   „ Manual of Private Devotions collected by, 15th ed. 1772
Spital and Charity Schools Anniversary Sermons, A Collection of, in the British Museum
Spratt, Bp., Charge to Clergy of Rochester Diocese, 1695
  „   „ History of the Royal Society, 1667
Stanhope, Earl, Reign of Queen Anne, 4th ed. 1872
Steele, Richard, The Christian Hero, 1700
Stillingfleet, Bp., Life and Character of, 1710
  „   „ Ecclesiastical Cases relating to Rights and Duties of the Parochial Clergy, 1698
  „   „ Primary Charge to the Diocese of Worcester
  „   „ Miscellaneous Discourses, 1735
  „   „ Rational Account of Grounds of the Protestant Religion, new ed. 1844
  „   „ Twelve Sermons by, 1696
Stoughton, Dr. J., Church and State 200 years ago, 1862
  „   „ The Church of the Restoration, 2 vols. 1870
Strickland, Miss A., Lives of the Queens of England
  „   „ Lives of the Seven Bishops, 1866
Sunday, Dr. Hessey's Bampton Lectures, 1860
Survey of Cities of London and Westminster by R. Seymour, 1734
Swift, Works of, in 8 vols. ed. Scott, 2nd ed. 1824
  „ by Leslie Stephen, Eng. Men of Letters, 1882

LIST OF AUTHORITIES

TASWELL, Dr. W., Autobiography (1651–1682) ed. G. P. Elliott.
Taylor, J. J., Retrospect of Religious Life in England, 2nd ed. 1876
Taylor, Bp. Jeremy, Whole Works with Life, R. Heber, 3rd ed. 1839
    ,,   ,, Life of, by R. A. Willmot, 1847
    ,,   ,, Contemplation of State of Man in this Life and that which is to come, new ed. 1847
Teale, W. H., Lives of English Laymen, Eng. Lib. vol. xxii, 1842
Tenison, Abp. Life of, (undated)
Thoresby, Ralph, Diary (1677–1724) ed. J. Hunter, 1830
Thorndike, H., Discourse of Right of Church in a Christian State, new ed. J. S. Brewer, 1841
Tillotson, Abp., Life by Dr. T. Birch, 2nd ed. 1753
    ,,   ,, Sermons, 2 vols. 10th ed. 1735
Tour of Great Britain by a gentleman (D. Defoe), 1724
Towerson, Gabriel, Of the Sacraments in general, 1686
    ,, Sermon concerning vocal and instrumental music in church, 1696
Trelawney Papers, ed. by W. D. Cooper for Camden Soc. 1853
Trevor's Life of William III.
Trimmell, Bp., Charge to clergy of Norwich, 1709
    ,,   ,, Visitation Charge, 1710
True Notion of Worship of God, Vindication of Services of Church &c. 1673
Tulloch, Dr., Rational Theology and Christian Philosophy in 17th Century, 1862
Turner, Bp., Letter to clergy of Ely Diocese before his Visitation, 1686
Tyerman, L., Life and Times of Samuel Wesley, 1866

USHER, Abp., Life of, by J. Aikin, M.D. 1812

VINDICATION of the late Abp. Sancroft from the Reflections of Mr. Marshall, 1717
Vita Joannis Barwick, by Peter Barwick, 1671
Vita Joannis Cosini, T. Smith, 1707

WAKE, Bp. of Lincoln, Primary Visitation Charge, 1707
Walcott, Mackenzie, Traditions and Customs of Cathedrals, 2nd ed. 1872
Walker's Sufferings of the Clergy epitomised, 1862
Walton, Bp. Brian, Life of, by H. J. Todd, 2 vols. 1821
Walton, Izaak, Lives of Herbert, Sanderson, &c. new ed. 1845
    ,,   ,, Life of, by T. Zouch, 1825

Ward, Bp. Seth, Life of, by Dr. W. Pope, 1697
„ „ Some Particulars of the Life, Habits, and Pursuits of, 1879
Ward, J., Vicar of Stratford-on-Avon, Diary arranged by C. Severn, 1839
Ward, A. W., History of Dramatic Literature in Reign of Queen Anne, 1875
Warwick, Mary, Countess of, Autobiography, ed. Croker, Percy, ed. 1848
„ „ unpublished MSS. of, in British Museum
Watts, Dr. I., Memoirs of by Southey, prefixed to Lyric Poems, 1840
„ „ Vol. vi. of Works in 9 vols. 1813
Weld, C. R., History of the Royal Society, 1848
Wells, Dr. E., of Cottesbach, Rich Man's Duty &c. 1840
Welwood, Jas., Memoirs &c. for 100 years preceding 1688, 7th ed. 1736
Wesley, Samuel, the Elder, Sermon concerning the Ref. of Manners, 1698
„ „ The Pious Communicant rightly prepared, 1700
Whole Duty of Man, ed. of 1763
Wilkins' Concilia Magnæ Britanniæ, vol. iv. 1737
Wilkins, Bp. Life of, prefixed to his works, 1708
Williams, J. B., Life of Sir Matthew Hale, 1835
Wilson, Bp. Thos., Sodor and Man, Life of, by J. Keble, 2 vols. 1863
„ „ „ Life of, by Hugh Stowell, 1827
„ „ „ Life of, by C. Cruttwell, 1782
„ „ „ Sermons in 4 vols. 1785
Wood, Anthony à, Life of writer by himself and pub. by T. Hearne, 1772
Woodward, Josiah, Account of Rise and Progress of Rel. Socs. 4th ed. 1712
„ „ Fair Warnings to a Careless World, 1717
Women of Methodism, by A. Stevens, 1866
Worcester, Diocesan History, S.P.C.K. Gregory Smith and Onslow, 1883
Wordsworth's Ecclesiastical Biography, vol. iv. 1853
Worthington, Dr. J., Great Duty of Self-resignation to the Divine Will
„ „ Diary and Correspondence, Chetham Soc. 1847
Wren, Sir Christopher, and his Times, by J. Elmes, 1852
„ „ „ His Family and his Times, Lucy Phillimore, 1881

Zouch, T., Life of Dean Sudbury
„ „ Memoirs of Sir George Wheler
„ „ Life of J. Walton and notices of his Contemporaries, 1825

INDEX.

ACT

ACT OF UNIFORMITY, 345
Addison, Dean Lancelot, 47, 91, 177, 267-8, 303, 306
— Joseph, 136, 267-8
'Address to Persons of Quality' (R. Nelson), 285
'Address to Posterity' (Bp. Burnet) 281
'Advice to a Friend' (Bp. Patrick), 275
Aldrich, Dean, 105, 162
Allestree, Dr. R., 4, 44-5, 191, 310
All Saints' Church, Oxford, 162
Altar Lights, 198-9
— Pieces, 200
— position of, 199
Amusements of clergy, 311-6
Anne, Queen, 14, 64, 83, 163, 222, 338
— state of Church under, 14-15
Andrewes' Devotions, Bp., 278
Anniversary Sermons of S. P. G., 221
'Answer to Grounds and Occasions for Contempt of Clergy,' 300 et seq.
'Aqua Genitalis' (Bishop Patrick), 270
'Art of Contentment, The,' 264
Ashmole, Elias, 9 n., 28, 119-121
Aske's Hospital, 230
Associates of Dr. Bray, 224
Astell, Mary, 146, 148-9, 312
Athenian Oracle, The, 193, 197, 202, 262
Atkins, Sir Edward, 136-7
Atterbury, Bp. F., 85, 248-9, 302, 318, 327
— Lewis, 5

BRAMHALL

Barington, Rev. Churchill, 305
Baker, Thomas, 103
Baptisms, Private, 163-4
Barlow, Bp., 329, 332, 333
Barnes, Ambrose, 200, 348
Barrow, Bp. Isaac, 36
— Dr. Isaac, 38-9, 183, 237-8, 311
Barwick, Dean John, 18
— Peter, 36, 42, 107-8, 303, 340
Basire, Archd. I., 6, 42, 43-4, 172, 177, 349
Bathurst, Dr. Ralph, 6, 260
Baxter, Richard, 191, 346
Bedford, Hilkiah, 91
'Benefit of early piety' (Smythies), 282
Beveridge, Bp., 5, 47, 49, 76-7, 89, 90, 173, 174, 177, 179, 186, 209, 221, 249-50, 274
Bidding Prayer, 179
Bingham, Joseph, 96-7, 198, 351
Bishops for the Plantations, 219-221
Blackall, Bp. Offspring, 86
Blackmore, Sir Richard, 136, 218
Bohun, Dr., 152
Bonnell, James, 135
'Book for Beginners, or Help to Young Communicants' (Patrick), 269
Borage, Timothy, 48
Bowing to the East, 197
Bowyer, the printer, 194
Boyle, Hon. Robert, 46, 113-6, 321
Bradford, Bp. of Carlisle, 211
Bramhall, Abp., 18, 192, 303, 318, 323, 350

B B

BRAY

Bray, Dr. Thomas, 99, 209, 216, 218, 219, 222-4, 299, 303
Brett, Thomas, 104
Briefs, 194-7
Brokesby, Francis, 206
Brooke, Lady, 153
Brown, Tom, 203
Browne, Sir Richard, 108-9
— Sir Thomas, 117
Brownrigg, Bp., 3 n., 6, 19
Bull, Bp., 5, 36, 47, 84, 125, 128, 164, 166, 246, 262, 306, 335
— Mrs., 154
Burkitt, Wm., of Dedham, 101, 106, 222
Burnet, Bp., 67-70, 149, 183, 251, 302, 304
— Elizabeth, 155
— Thomas, 70 n.
Busby, Dr. Rd., 41-3, 44, 87, 108, 162

CALAMY, Edmund, 170
Card-playing, 312, 314
Caroline Age, Theology of, 341
Cartwright, Bp. Thomas, 171, 180, 199, 203
Cases of conscience, (Sanderson), 316, 332
— — — (Barlow), 332
Casuistry, 330-4
'Catechetical Questions' (Simon Lowth), 267
Catechising, Public, 175-8
'Catechism of Church of England paraphrased' (Sherlock), 267
— explained' (Comber), 267
— — (Beveridge), 268
Cathedrals, condition of at Restoration, 159-160
'Causes of Decay of Christian Piety,' 264
Cave, Dr. Wm., 5, 104
Chamberlayne, Edward, 255, 303
— John, 217, 256
Chancels, disuse of, 181-2
Chaplains, domestic, 193, 298-300
Charity schools, 221-8
Charles II., 8-9, 257, 319,
— — state of Church under, 6-10
Chelsea Hospital, 230
Cherry, Francis, 132-3
Chetwynd, Walter, 137, 162
Chillingworth, 319

CONFORMISTS

'Christian Consolations' (Hacket?) 277
— Life, The' (John Scott), 272-3, 331
— Monitor, The' (Rawlet), 273-4
— Virtuoso, The' (Boyle), 284, 321
— Hero, The' (Steele), 285
'Christian's Manual, The' (L. Addison), 270
Christ Church, Oxford, 4
Church services, Attendance at, 171-5
Clarendon, Edward, first Earl of, 41, 118-9
— Henry, second Earl of, 126-7, 205, 206
'Clarendonian Code,' 345
Clergy, of Restoration Period, 16 et seq.
— social position of, 296-302
— superfluity of, 297
— light literature on, 301-2
— conduct of, in Great Plague, 339-341
— contempt for, 302-3
— envy of, 308
— learning of, 305-8, 342
— and amusements, 311-6
— and immorality, 335
— courage of, 336-8
— and Legal Profession, 309
— and Medical Profession, 310
— and Military Profession, 310 et seq.
— scoffers on, 309
— and politics, 311
— poverty of, 303-5
Clerk Ales, 194
Cock, Vicar of St. Oswald's, Durham, 101
Colchester, Col. Maynard, 216
'Collection of Meditations' (Hopton), 286
Collier, Jeremy, 102, 187, 205, 297
Colston, Edward, 137, 230
Comber, Dean Thomas, 90, 259 317, 327
Communicants, Number of, 168-171
'Companion to the Temple' (Comber), 271, 306
Compton, Bishop, 13 n., 65-7, 209, 214, 219, 269, 310, 311, 328, 337
Conformists not Churchmen, 159, 336

INDEX

CONTEMPLATIONS

'Contemplations' (Bishop Hall), 276
Convocation, 13, 326, 335
Conway, Lady, 52, 147
Corporation of the Sons of the Clergy, 228
Cosin, Bishop, 6, 21-3, 53, 88, 172, 179, 182, 191, 196, 198, 319, 349
'Cosin's, Devotions, Bishop,' 277
'Country Parson, The' (G. Herbert), 276
Country parsons, Literary work from, 305-6
Cradock, Zachary, 254
Creighton, Dr., 338
Crewe, Lord, Bishop of Durham, 337
Croft, Bishop of Hereford, 197
Cromwell, Oliver, 4
Cumberland, Bishop, 85
Cutts, Lady, 153, 318

DAILY PRAYER, 172-5
Dancing, The Clergy and, 315
Dartmouth, Lord, 61, 71, 123
Dawes, Sir W., Archbishop of York, 86, 254
Declaration, James II.'s, 337
Defoe, Daniel, 203, 214, 302, 339
Derby, Countess of, 147
'Devotions in the ancient way of offices' (Hopton), 286
'Devout Christian instructed how to pray' (Patrick), 275
Diaries of the Period, 132-3, 256-7
Digby, Lady Frances, 144
Digby, Simon, Lord, 93, 99, 123-4, 162
Digby, William, Lord, 124, 162
Discipline, Church, 325-330
'Discourse concerning the Love of God' (Lady Masham), 287
'Discourse concerning Prayer' (Patrick), 275
'Discourse of Religious Assemblies' (Sherlock), 272
Disney, J., 214, 329
Dodwell, Henry, 84, 129-132, 184, 206, 262, 303
Dolben, Archbishop, 4, 33-4, 44, 243-5, 310
Dress of the Clergy, 323-5
Dryden, John, 57, 74, 213

GRABE

'Ductor Dubitantium' (Jeremy Taylor), 330
Duppa, Bishop Brian, 6, 18

EACHARD, 256, 262, 303, and passim
Earle, Bishop, 26-7, 203, 345
'Ellis Correspondence,' 340
'Enquiry after Happiness, An' (R. Lucas), 279
Epworth Rectory, 95
Evelyn, John, 24, 109-111, 166, 199, 218, 256
Evelyn, Mrs., 140, 152-3
'Evidences of Christianity' (Addison), 285
Exclusion Bill, 352
Excommunication, 327, 329
'Exposition of the Church Catechism' (Ken), 266-7

FAMILY PRAYER, 334-5
Fell, Bishop, 4, 30-32, 44, 45, 87
Fell, Dean Samuel, 31, 44
'Festivals and Fasts' (Nelson), 285
Fifty-two new churches, Project for, 163, 202
Fire of London, 161, 242, 282
Fishing, Clergy and, 314
Fitzwilliam, Dr. John, 102, 147
Flamsteed, John, 306
Fleetwood, Bishop, 221
Fowler, Bishop, 52, 86, 337
Frampton, Bishop, 84, 170, 255, 326
Frampton, Josiah, 313-6
Frampton, Mrs., 154
Frewen, Archbishop Accepted, 17
French Protestant Refugees, 195, 350-1
Fuller, Bishop of Lincoln, 199
Fuller, Thomas, 18
Fullwood, Archdeacon, 49, 104

GARDINER, Bishop of Lincoln, 181, 332
'Gentleman's Calling, The,' 264
Glanvill, Joseph, of Bath, 105, 255, 322
Godfrey, Sir Edmondsbury, 117
Godolphin, Mrs., 24, 140
'Golden Grove, The,' 265
Grabe, Dr., 104

GRANVILLE

Granville, Dean Denis, 88 91, 164, 166, 167, 177, 182, 189, 311, 312, 322, 324, 349
'Great Duty of frequenting the Christian Sacrifice' (Nelson), 270
'Great Duty of Self-Resignation to the Divine Will' (Worthington), 281
'Great Exemplar, The' (Taylor), 265
'Great Importance of a Religious Life' (W. Melmoth), 284
Greek Church, 43, 218
Greenwich Hospital, 230
'Grounds and Occasions for the Contempt of the Clergy,' 299 et seq.
'Guardian, The,' 298
Guildford, Francis, Lord, 216
Gunning, Bishop Peter, 4, 23–25, 89, 170, 346

Hacket, Bishop, 3n., 4, 27–9, 162, 180, 201, 202, 318
Hale, Sir Matthew, 116-7, 335
Hall, Bishop Joseph, 6, 18, 331
Hammond, Dr. H., 5, 18, 39, 89, 122, 261, 317
Hastings, Lady Elizabeth, 144-6
Hat worn in church, 182-3
Hearne, Thomas, 132-3, 201, 206
Henchman, Bishop, 35
Herbert, George, 38
Hewitt, Dr., 4
Hickes, Dean, 87, 91-2, 169, 187, 301, 318, 328
Higgons, Bevill, 245
Hobbism, 51, 309
Holy Communion, Infrequency of, 165
—— Weekly, in Cathedrals, 167
—— Kneeling at, 170
'Holy Living' and 'Holy Dying' (J. Taylor), 265
'Holy Rules and Helps to Devotion' (B. Duppa), 277
Hook, Justice, 216
Hooper, Bishop (Bath and Wells), 47, 80-1, 253-4, 338
Hopton, Susanna, 149-150
Horneck, Dr. Anthony, 48, 97-9, 168, 207, 209, 251, 333
Hough, Bishop, 87, 299
Hourglass in Pulpit, 258

LEIGHTON

Howe, John, 52, 347
'Hudibras,' 312, 321
Hunting, Clergy and, 313
Hymns, Want of, 186-7

Incomes of the Clergy, 303-5
Independents, The, 343
Instrumental Music in Church, 184-5
'Irenicon' (Stillingfleet's), 75
Irish Church, 354
Ironmongers' Hall, 230
Irreverent behaviour in church, 182-3

James II., 337, 351 and passim
—— state of the Church under, 10-11
Jebb, Bishop, 280
Johnson, John, of Cranbrook, 102, 172, 329
Johnson, Samuel, 337
Juxon, Archbishop, 5, 17, 313, 344

Kemeyse, The Misses, 151
Ken, Bishop, 47, 70-74, 80, 92, 183, 196, 240-1, 299, 337, 344, 350
Kennet, Bishop White, 85, 92, 180, 193, 198, 222, 302, 304
Kettlewell, John, 48, 92-4, 144, 299
Kidder, Bishop, 79-80
Killingbeck, Vicar of Leeds, 101, 134
King, Bishop of Chichester, 113
King's arms in churches, 201
Knightbridge, Dr., 333
Knox, Alexander, 280
Kyrle, John ('Man of Ross,'), 118-162

'Ladies' Calling, The,' 191, 264
Lake, Bishop, 82-3, 150, 194, 310, 319
Lake, Dr. Edward, 198, 269, 278-80, 319
Lancy, Bishop, 348
Latitude-men, 50
Lecturers, 4, 190-2, 298
Leighton, Archbishop, 281, 353

Leslie, Charles, 101-2, 205
'Letters concerning the Love of God' (Norris), 282, 286
'Life of God in the Soul of Man,' (Scougal), 280
Light Literature on the Clergy, 301-2
Lloyd, Bishop of Worcester, 47, 83, 205, 326, 351
Lloyd, Bishop of Norwich, 86
Locke, John, 31, 46, 76, 301
Lowth, Simon, 49, 306
Lucas, Dr. Richard, 101, 252-3

MACAULAY, Lord, 68, 74, 299, 301
Mackworth, Sir Humphrey, 216
Magdalen College and James II., 337
Marow, Lady, 153
'Marriage Ring, The' (J. Taylor), 265
Marsh, Dr., Vicar of Newcastle, 101, 333, 318
Marshall, Dean, Rector of Lincoln College, 46-7, 310
Mary II., Queen, 94, 185, 213, 269, 320
Mary-le-Bow, Church of S., 163
Masham, Lady, 150
Maynard, Lord, 136
Maynard, Lady Margaret, 144
Melmoth, William, 137, 218
'Mensa Mystica' (Patrick), 270
'Method of Devotion, A' (E. Burnet), 287
Mew, Bishop of Winchester, 310
Milles, Isaac, 47, 100, 172
Milner, Vicar of Leeds, 101, 134
Morden's College, Blackheath, 230
More, Dr. Henry, 51, 125, 147
Morley, Bishop, 5, 25-6, 71, 80, 113, 173, 346
Morton, Bishop, 5, 18, 349
'Motives and Incentives to the Love of God' (Boyle), 284

NELSON, Robert, 80, 92, 128-9, 168, 205, 210, 312, 329
Newton, Sir Isaac, 39
Nicholson, Governor of Virginia, 222
Nicolson, Abp., 36, 85, 215, 329, 348

Nonconformists and Church, 342-8
Nonjurors, 12, 41, 354 and *passim*
—, Services of, 168, 204-6
Norris, John, of Bemerton, 255, 282-3
North, Dr. John, 105, 141
North, Hon. Roger, 141
'Notes of Catechism' (Marshall) 268
Notices in church, 203-4
Nottingham, 1st Earl of (Heneage), 64, 124-5
—, 2nd Earl of (Daniel), 125-6

OATES' Plot, 352
Offertory, The, 196
'Office of a Chaplain' (J. Collier), 300
'Officium Eucharisticum' (E. Lake), 268
Oley, Barnabas, 5, 37-8, 89, 276, 300, 302, 305
Orange, Mary, Princess of, 71, 80, 182, 198, 269, 319
—, William, Prince of, 81 n.
Organs in churches, 184, 187
'Origines Ecclesiasticæ' (Bingham), 306
'Origines Sacræ' (Stillingfleet), 306
Ormond, Duke of, 260

PAINTINGS in churches, 201
Pakington, Dorothy, Lady, 139, 263
Pamphlets of the period, 307-8
'Parable of the Pilgrim' (Patrick), 276
Parish churches, condition of, 160
— —, Restoration of, 161-3
Parish clerks, 193-4
Parker, Samuel, 344
Parochial libraries, 222-4
Patrick, Bp., 6, 47, 50, 52, 77-9, 167, 174, 192, 196, 222, 250-1, 337, 340
Paul's S., Cathedral of, 162-3
Pearson, Bp. 21, 321
Penance, 325
—, Money commutation for, 326, 328
Pepys, Samuel, 74, 133, 180, 185, 187, 188, 203, 256, 308, 320
Pews, 202-3

'Pietas Londinensis,' 168, 175, 210
'Pious Communicant rightly prepared' (S. Wesley), 270
Plague of London, 78, 339–40
Platonists, The Cambridge, 5, 49–53, 255, 283
Plaxton, Vicar of Woodside, Leeds, 101
Pluralists, 297, 300
Pocock, Ed., 5, 45–6, 306
Polyglott Bible, 5, 37
Poor Palatinates, 351
Poverty of the clergy, 303–5
'Practical Catechism' (Hammond), 265–6
'Practical Christianity' (R. Lucas), 278
'Practice of Piety, The' (Boyle), 284
'Practice of True Devotion, The' (R. Nelson), 285
Presbyterians (England), 342, 343
—, (Scotland), 354
'Preservative against Popery' (Gibson), 352
Prideaux, Dean Humphrey, 42, 87–8, 200, 219, 334
'Primitive Institution, or Seasonable Discourse of Catechising' (L. Addison), 267
'Private Thoughts' (Beveridge), 274–5
Protestants, Foreign, 349, 351
Psalmody, Church, 184–8
Psalms,—New and old versions, 185–8
Puller, Timothy, 49
Pulpit prayers, 178–81
Puritans and amusements, 311, 312
—, Devastation of, 181, 343
—, Prayers of, 334

QUEEN Anne's Bounty, 228–230
Quotations from learned languages in sermons, 234

'RABBLED MINISTERS' (Scotland), 353
Radcliffe, Dr., 97
Ranelagh, Lady, 141–2
Rationalists, 50
Rawlet of Newcastle, 48, 93
Readers, 192–3, 298

'Reason and Religion' (Norris), 283
Rebellion, State of Church during the, 3–6
Recreations, Clerical, 311–6
—, Sunday, 317–9
Reeves, William, 306
'Reflections upon the conduct of human life' (Norris), 283
'Reformation of Manners, Societies for the,' 213–6, 320, 329
Reformed Churches abroad, 348–351
'Religio Medici' (Sir T. Browne), 277–8
'Religious discourse in common conversation' (Norris), 283
'Religious Societies, The,' 168, 174, 207, 213, 216
Reresby, Sir John, 9, 345
Revocation of the Edict of Nantes, 350
Riding, The Clergy and, 313, 315
Ritual of the period, 197–9
Robinson, Bp. of Bristol, 310
Rochester, John Wilmot, Earl of, 32, 46, 69
—, Lawrence Hyde, Earl of, 127
Romanism, Dread of, 208
—, Relation of Church to, 351–3
Royal Society, 5, 321
Russell, Rachel, Lady, 103, 146–7
Rust, Bp. G., 52

SACHEVEREll, Dr., 215
Sacred Poetry, 289–295
— —, Addison's, 291
— —, Comber's, 293
— —, Jeremy Taylor's, 290
— —, Ken's, 289
— —, Patrick's, 290
— —, Rawlet's, 292
— —, S. Wesley's, 291
— —, S. Hopton's, &c. 294
— —, Lack of, 295
Sancroft, Archbishop, 6, 53–57, 167, 337, 340, 344, 350
Sanderson, Bishop, 5, 18, 113, 331, 332, 344
Sanderson, Mrs., 153
Savoy Conference, 346
Scotch Church (Episcopal), 353–4
Scott, John, 52, 168, 309, 312, 317
'Serious Proposal to Ladies' (M. Astell), 148, 286

INDEX

SERMONS

Sermons, Love of, 231
—, Lack of, 232
—, Length of, 233, 258-9
—, Learnedness of, 233
—, Old and new style of, 235, 257-8
—, High standard of, 256-7
—, Written and unwritten, 259
—, Boldness in rebuking vice, 337-8
Seven Bishops, The, 11, 337
Sharp, Archbishop of York, 14 n., 47, 62-5, 96, 134, 179, 195, 215, 248, 333, 337, 338, 346, 353
Sheldon, Archbishop, 19-20, 54, 339, 344, 347
Sherlock, Dean W., 104, 167, 176, 328
Sherlock of Winwick, 48, 164, 177, 187, 299
Shooting, Clergy and, 314
Shottesbrook, The group at, 131, 206
'Sick man visited, The' (Spinckes), 288
Sitting during singing in church, 187
Skinner, Bishop, 4, 6, 35
Smalridge, Bishop, 85, 254
Smith, John, (Platonist), 51, 250
Smith, Thomas, (Nonjuror), 151
Smythies, William, 102, 207, 209, 252
South, Robert, 40-1, 238-240, 321
Sparrow, Bishop, 200, 203, 317
S. P. C. K., 216-8
Spectator, The, 180, 187, 285
S. P. G., 218-222
Spinckes, Nathaniel, 103, 205
Sprat, Bishop, 260, 332
Stage, The, 301-2, 309, 315
St. John, Sir Walter, 137
Stanhope, Dean, 104, 280
Sterne, Archbishop, 35
Sternhold and Hopkins, 186, 187
Stillingfleet, Bishop, 5, 49, 62, 74-6, 176, 184, 213, 241-2, 308, 310, 313-6, 317, 324, 328, 347
Stratford, Bishop, 85
Strype, John, 104
Sunday, Church teaching on, 316-21
—, Parliament and, 320
Surplice, contentions about, 188-9
Swift, Dean, 91, 193, 215, 220, 303, 304, 308, 323, 324
Sylvius, Lady, 140-1

WEYMOUTH

Tanswell, William, 32 n., 33
Tate and Brady, 186, 295
'Tatler, The,' 145, 149, 298
Taylor, Bishop Jeremy, 4, 6, 31-5, 109, 152, 184, 187, 235-7, 316, 330-1
Tenison, Archbishop, 6, 60-2, 176, 180, 214, 219, 328
Test Act of 1673, 170-1, 352
Thomas, Bishop of Worcester, 87
Thoresby, Ralph, 92, 133-5, 145, 172, 177, 188, 256
Thorndike, Herbert, 36-7, 318
Tickets for intercession, 203
Tillotson, Archbishop, 39, 57-60, 209, 214, 245-6, 257, 340
Toleration Act, 14, 345
Towerson, Gabriel, 49, 104, 185
'Treatise of Repentance and Fasting' (Patrick), 275
Trelawney, Sir J., Bishop of Winchester, 84, 97, 166, 327
Trimnell, Bishop of Norwich, 321
Tuckney, Dr., 346
Turner, Bishop of Ely, 37, 83, 166, 173, 205, 327, 351
Turner, Sir E., 222

'Unbloody Sacrifice' (Johnson), 271
Unequal distribution of Church revenues, 308
University degrees, 307
'Unworthy Noncommunicant' (Smythies), 271
Usher, Archbishop, 18

Wake, Bishop, 86
Wall, William, 103
Walton, Bishop Brian, 5, 18
— Izaak, 71, 113
Ward, Bishop Seth, 3 n., 29-30, 310 313, 344, 347
Warwick, Mary, Countess of, 142-4
Waterland, Dr., 126
Wells, Dr., of Cottesbach, 104, 312
Welton, Dr., 206
Wesley, John, 212
—, Samuel, the elder, 94-6, 177, 195, 212, 246, 252, 259, 299, 306, 325
—, Samuel, the younger, 96
—, Susanna, 156-7
Weymouth, Viscount, 73, 122-3,

Wharton, Henry, 104, 192, 304, 308
Wheler, Sir George, 92
Whewell, Dr., 206, 331
Whichcote, Dr. B., 255
Whiston, William, 64
White, Bishop of Peterborough, 83
— Gilbert, 218
'Whole Duty of Man,' 139, 261-4, 334
Wilkins, Bishop, 35, 58
William and Mary, state of Church under, 11-14, 199
William III., 353 and *passim*
Williams, Bishop of Chichester, 221
Willis, Dean of Lincoln, 221

Willis, Dr. Thomas, 111-3, 174, 193
Wilson, Bishop T. (Sodor and Man), 86, 145, 179, 224, 299, 327
— Mrs. (Mary Patten), 154
Woodward, Josiah, 104, 210, 214
'Work of the Ministry represented to the clergy of Ely' (Patrick), 275
Worthington, Dr. John, 255
Wotton, Wm., 103
Wren, Sir Christopher, 121-2, 161, 163, 202
— Bishop Matthew, 6, 20-1, 190

York, Duke of (James II.), 170

www.ingramcontent.com/pod-product-compliance
Lightning Source LLC
Chambersburg PA
CBHW030348230426
43664CB00007BB/571